Franz Kline in Coal Country

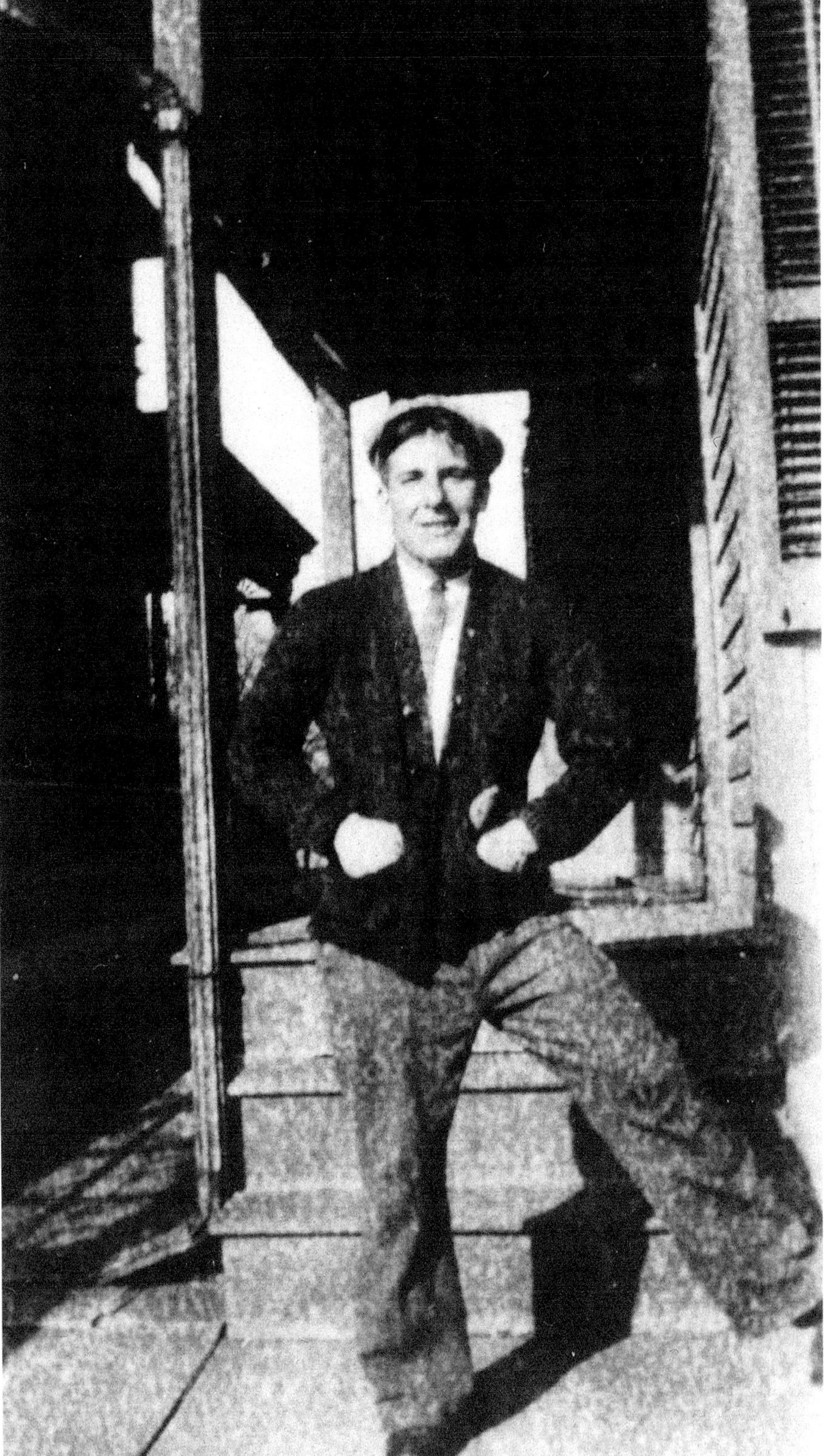

Franz Kline in Coal Country

REBECCA RABENOLD-FINSEL
AND JOEL FINSEL

AMERICA
THROUGH TIME®
ADDING COLOR TO AMERICAN HISTORY

Frontispiece:
Franz Kline, "the enchanter," at his home on South 9th Street, Lehighton, PA, in 1915. (*Harold Rabenold*)

I was sitting at a table in the dining room when Franz entered, carrying a bundle of papers. He was fifteen.

"What have you there?" I asked.

"My sketchbook," he replied.

"May I take a look?"

"Of course," he said, handing it to me.

I opened at random and saw a sketch of a hand resting on a flat surface, like fingers about to play piano keys. I remembered having seen a similar sketch in a museum. "Who did this?" I asked, expecting to hear a name like Leonardo da Vinci.

"I did," he said.

Somehow, I sensed I was looking at genius. But the complexity of living in that household erased the incident from my mind until years later. I never saw his sketchbook again.

Dr. Daniel Davies, former beau of Kline's sister, Louise
Personal correspondence

America Through Time is an imprint of Fonthill Media LLC
www.through-time.com
office@through-time.com

Published by Arcadia Publishing by arrangement with Fonthill Media LLC
For all general information, please contact Arcadia Publishing:
Telephone: 843-853-2070
Fax: 843-853-0044
E-mail: sales@arcadiapublishing.com
For customer service and orders:
Toll-Free 1-888-313-2665

www.arcadiapublishing.com

First published 2019

ISBN 978-1-63499-101-8

Typeset in 10pt on 13pt SabonStd
Printed and bound in England

Foreword

Rebecca Finsel and her son Joel present an in-depth picture of the little-known beginnings of a celebrated American artist with deeps roots in Northeastern Pennsylvania. They give us a portrait not only of Franz Kline in Coal Country, but also of the area itself, including the power of trains to unite rural hamlets with cities like Philadelphia and New York.

Beyond a compelling story (for Kline's life truly reads like a novel), this book contains a large collection of letters and rare works of art created during Kline's earliest years. The authors, with their close ties to the Lehighton area, began to seek out Franz's closest family and friends many years ago. The culmination of their research and insights into his early life and development—his athleticism, interests, cultural context, and accomplishments—is long overdue.

Kline became world-renowned as an "abstract expressionist." But the first important phase of his journey to artistic maturation began with traditional illustration and drafting. These early forms were utilized throughout his life, even as his later works became abstract. Ultimately, Kline's images became less recognizable yet perhaps more powerful, with more aggressive lines and figures, but the genesis of it all lay in coal country.

John Drury, President
Mauch Chunk Museum & Cultural Center

Preface

In the spring of 1986, I began to research Franz Kline for a newspaper article I was writing about his upcoming retrospective, *The Vital Gesture*. This major exhibition was scheduled to come to the Pennsylvania Academy of Fine Arts in Philadelphia after touring other parts of the country, including San Francisco and Cincinnati. At the time, I was writing for the local *Times News,* a daily newspaper in Lehighton, Pennsylvania; Kline's hometown and my own. The buzz about him that year was electric. Newspapers and magazines heralded an event that most fans considered long overdue. Never did I imagine that my article would evolve into decades of research—awakening a latent childhood interest in Kline that I had almost forgotten—and culminating over thirty years later in this book.

My connection with Kline began in the 1960s with the stories my aunt Gladys told around my grandmother's kitchen table. Although I did not know then that her tales had any historical value, I still sensed an importance to them. They certainly brought excitement to my young life.

Gladys, my father's sister, had been a friend of Kline's in high school. His family lived a couple of blocks away from ours. By the time I was ten years old, Gladys was married and came home regularly for Sunday dinner with her husband, Dr. Barney Stegura. At the dinner table, if the conversation turned to the arts, such as Masterpiece Theater or Maria Callas or something in that like, I knew my aunt would end up talking about her friend Franz. It was then that she had my complete attention. Stories about the famous artist who had grown up just down the street captivated me, and with them the adult voices got louder, back and forth across the table. Kline was a controversial subject in our town. Sometimes they spoke about his mother, Anne, or her husband, Amby, a railroader still living in the neighborhood. Their voices rose to a crescendo when they described the "good-looking" women Franz brought home from Greenwich Village, or how badly he needed a haircut, or how many holes he had in his shoes. Although I was just a girl, my dream was to become an artist in New York. I came to life when my father, an art teacher, brought home gifts from his classroom: colorful pastels, reeds for weaving baskets, or clay to mold and fire in his kiln. His instruction was our time together and because of this bond, art felt like not a hobby, but a birthright.

I found the stories of Kline's bohemian lifestyle exciting, connected as they seemed with my aunt's unique familiarity with him. She told us that Franz had stood out from the time he moved to town. He was a handsome heartbreaker newly released from an all-boys orphanage into a town of smitten young girls who would have done almost anything to have him. He was athletic, mannerly, and always drawing. Gladys was still enamored after three decades, and it speaks volumes to me that her grandson was later named Frantz.

Gladys was a close friend of Kline's sister, Louise, and the two girls spent many hours on the front porch of his family's Victorian home. Gladys said that Kline's mother was discriminating when it came to her children's friends. She was partial to athletes and intellectuals. As the former president of the debate team, Gladys recalled Mrs. Kline's prejudice with a faint whiff of pride.

As the Sunday dinner went on and the children were excused from the table, the adults often talked on over coffee. Despite their lowered voices, I still found ways to eavesdrop. They talked about Franz's wife, an English ballerina twice committed to a Long Island asylum, how she kept her schizophrenia hidden until after their marriage, like Mr. Rochester's ill-fated bride in Brontë's *Jane Eyre*. They talked about the mystery surrounding his father's suicide, and how so few locals appreciated Franz's abstract work. To me, his life sounded like a best-selling novel: born to wealth, sent to an orphanage, then love and heartbreak, destitution, and fame.

Discussions about his paintings were also interesting. Abstract Expressionism was controversial far beyond my grandmother's table. Much of America did not consider it "real art" at first, and neither did many of Franz's oldest friends. Looking back on it, my father was the only person I knew who did not criticize Kline's "switch" from figurative to abstract. In Lehighton, Kline's drawings and early paintings had long defined him, but the later abstracts (for which he would become internationally known) were an enigma many found disturbing.

Shortly after Kline died in 1962, Gladys's stories about him were replaced with a melancholy silence. My own memories of those conversations faded as I became a young woman, married, and had children of my own. I never moved to Greenwich Village to paint and write poetry. Instead, I bought my grandmother's house and focused on raising my family. When I read news releases about the retrospective, however, the stories all came rushing back. After pitching a story on Kline to my editor, I began to get anxious because there was so little information available on Kline's early years. Nothing in libraries or art history magazines. Then I realized that the stories were alive all around me, living in my neighbors' houses. I began to knock on doors. Months of research and writing became years and decades. The more I learned about Franz, the more I realized that most of the information I had gathered was not available anywhere else. I discovered firsthand how the scarcity of writing about his formative years created a gap in the overall understanding of his work. So I continued to set up interviews with his closest friends and acquaintances, logging hundreds of hours as I explored the many rabbit-holes of research that revealed themselves.

I also sought out members of Kline's family, including his sister, Louise, a retired English professor, who became a tremendous source of information and, later, a great mentor. When I mentioned my aunt Gladys to her, Louise opened up her life to me. She invited my family and me to her home three hours away in State College, Pennsylvania, where she kept a personal archive of her brother's photographs, works, and other paraphernalia (including mementos from his various studios). My favorites were a couple of antique silver teaspoons.

Around the same time, Louise told me that she was busy writing letters and making calls addressing what she considered to be "errors" and "inconsistencies" perpetuated about Franz over the years, some of which we have addressed for the first time in these pages. After realizing that Kline's own sister was unhappy about the way his legacy had been portrayed, I began to realize how much more there must be to his story.

A major breakthrough was the discovery of a generous man named Frederick Ryan, Jr., whose father had been one of Kline's closest friends. Ryan had collected a small cache of letters written by Franz to his dad. Among them was an unpublished essay, "Franz Kline as I Knew Him." These papers illuminated a lost chapter in Kline's development, a period spent at the Boston Art Students League after Boston University was forced to shut down its department during the Great Depression. The letters also shed light on Kline's time in London, his earliest years in New York, and the complexities of his marriage. These last, in addition to being important for an understanding of his personal history, are equally significant to art history as a whole, since two of his most studied paintings, *Elizabeth* and *Rocking Chair*, depict his wife in varying states of fragmentation. Mirroring the state of Elizabeth's mental illness marked Franz's own transition from figurative to abstract.

When Kline could no longer take care of his wife, he brought her "home" to stay with his mother (a nurse) in Lehighton, just a couple of blocks away from my grandmother's house—the setting for all those great Sunday stories—where so far five generations of my family have lived. Many evenings after my husband and children had gone to bed, I would stay up late to work on this manuscript. Deep in the night, I sometimes sensed my grandmother sitting at the kitchen table with a saucer of coffee, waiting for guests to arrive.

Rebecca Rabenold-Finsel
Lehighton, PA

Acknowledgments

We could not have completed this labor of love without the patient support of our spouses, Glenn Finsel and Jess James, as well as the encouragement of our parents, children, in-laws, teachers, siblings, and friends. We would especially like to recognize Joshua Finsel, our photographer extraordinaire, for traveling many miles to record (and many hours to edit) much of the work presented in this book.

We also owe a profound debt of gratitude to John Drury for believing in us early on. Special thanks also to Mrs. Geraldine Duffy and other Lehighton Memorial Librarians Becky Wanamaker, Bonnie Benner Vito, and Kathy Long; Legionnaires Carlos Teets and Tinker Brown; Rudy Bednar, Rufus Zogbaum, B. H. Friedman, David McKee, Rona Richter, Andrea Fisher, Sue Orr, Robert Manley, Dr. Mio Reynolds, John Jeremiah Sullivan, Dr. Robert Mattison, Robert Schweitzer, Dr. Stanley I. Grand, Daniel Finsel, Randolph Rabenold, Professor Howie Weiss, Ronald and Kim Rabenold, Richard and Lisa Rabenold, Dave and Susy James, Chris Potash, Dr. Robert Metzger, Edward Meneeley, Deborah Rabinsky, Litsa Tsitsera, Brad Kunkle, Brad Carney, Wayne Adams, David Rapp, G. B. Miller, Robert C. Smith, Lamont Ebbert, Gordon Ripkey, Barbara Loeffler, Lillian Rodberg, Anita Shapolsky, Carl Shafer, Jason Andrew, Frederick Ryan, Jr., E. Laurent, William and Joyce Schwab, Ruth and Russ Kresge, Brenda Harleman Dorshimer, Robert Mnuchin, Lisa Zemann, Hero Johnson, Charlotte Doyle, Dr. Gerald and Ellen Zinner, Maureen Ryan, Gloria Lippman, Kim Graver Steinberger, John Benscoter, Dr. Steven and Heidi Klein, Kenneth and Anna Seaboldt, and the entire wonderful Kline-Snyder family, especially Dr. Louise Kline-Kelly whose voice guided and encouraged us through the decades.

Lastly, we greatly appreciate the many people whose names appear as sources throughout. Without their contributions, this book would not exist.

Contents

1

Slate Cross: Franz was Born into Privilege in Wilkes-Barre, PA

In secret places where no other spied
I went without my sight
Without a light to guide except
the heart that lit me from inside.

St. John of the Cross
Dark Night of the Soul

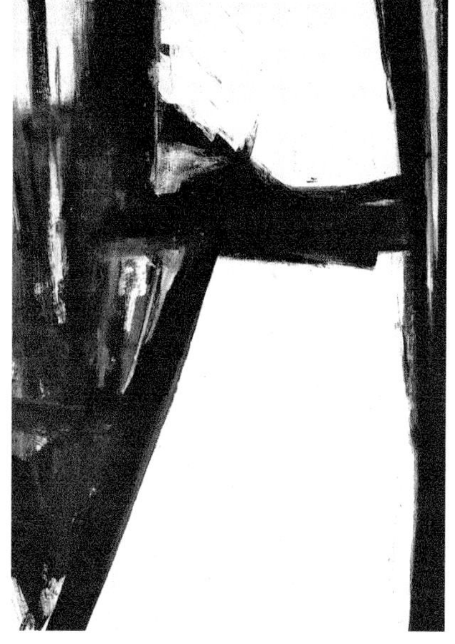

Slate Cross, 1961. Salvador Dali once told Franz that his work reminded him of St. John of the Cross, the Spanish mystic and poet of the night. (*Dallas Museum of Art © 2018 Franz Kline Estate/Artists Rights Society (ARS), New York*)

In 1910, at about the same time as the first commercial radio broadcasts and the introduction of the Ford Model T, Franz Kline was born in a small but rapidly growing coal-mining city a few hours west of Manhattan. Wilkes-Barre, Pennsylvania, was named in honor of John Wilkes and Isaac Barré, radical members of Parliament who had supported the American "Sons of Liberty" in the British House of Commons during the American Revolution. Men mined anthracite coal in Wilkes-Barre, six days a week, from sunup to sundown in mines as deep as 1,000 feet. Those lucky enough to escape the mines could plan their days around the chug, hiss, and roar of trains. These regimented sounds, interlaced with occasional ice-cream vendors' bells, composed the musical backdrop of Kline's earliest memories.

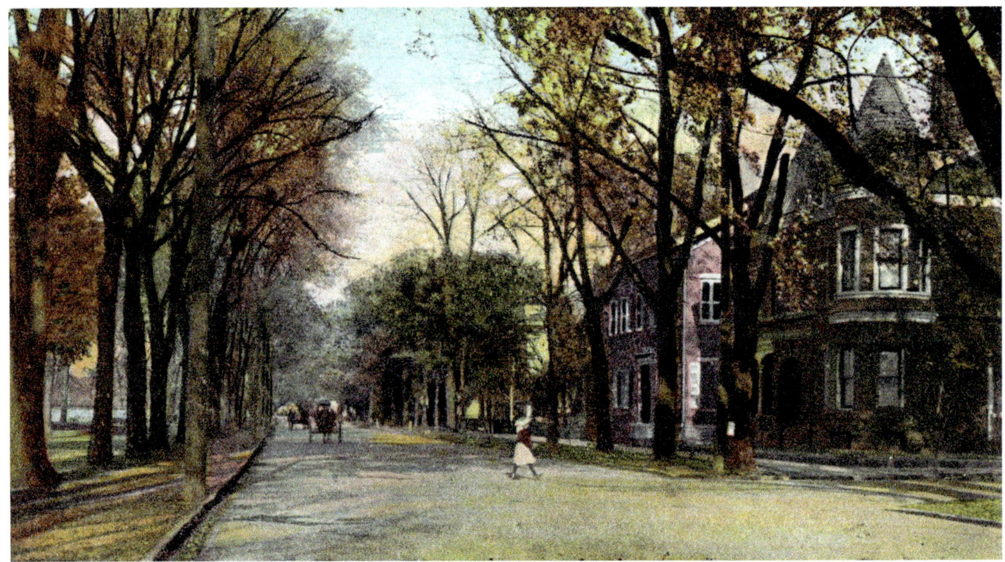

West River Street, *c.* 1910. The Kline family lived at No. 280 until 1917.

In those days, academies such as the prestigious Wyoming Seminary and the Wilkes-Barre Female Institute attracted the most privileged families in the area. But the city also had a less distinguished side, one where children often went hungry or without shoes, where "breaker boys" as young as five years old separated coal from rocks for 40 cents per day, dust penetrating their lungs.[1] While some Kline biographers imply a similarly bleak childhood for the artists, his sister, Louise, emphasized that the opposite was true. She and her three brothers had been born into a family of wealth and affection.

"When we were children in Wilkes-Barre," Louise said, "I remember sitting on our big front porch and watching the circus parades. And Mother, or Aunt Mary, tossing us nickels from the window upstairs so we could buy ice cream from the Hokey-Pokey Man. It was a very wonderful area. The Kline's were said to have money as big as cart wheels. We had wonderful childhoods and grew up and had normal lives. I should write this all down someday, you know, because others have Franz going from rags to riches."[2]

In late spring, flamboyant parades enticed families out of their homes to see the circus. Performers wearing bold colors led exotic animals, such as camels which could be seen carrying miniature dioramas of the Giza Pyramids or the Hall of Mirrors at Versailles. Elephants, roller-skating bears, and "tango dancing lions" also mesmerized the crowd.[3] There were snake charmers, and showgirls perched on swings waved the townsfolk on. Juggling clowns cajoled from the sidelines, various bizarre expressions painted on their faces. For the finale, a horse-drawn calliope steam piano.

Later on, as an adult, remembering the parades, Franz wrote to his wife: "I have always felt that I'm like a clown and that my life might work out like a tragedy, a clown's tragedy."[4]

Franz was drawn to clowns throughout his life. The Russian ballerina Vaslav Nijinsky (as the clown puppet Petrushka) became a recurring theme in his work, and his clown paintings are well known: *Red Clown Self Portrait* (1944), *Nijinsky as Petrouchka* (1948), and

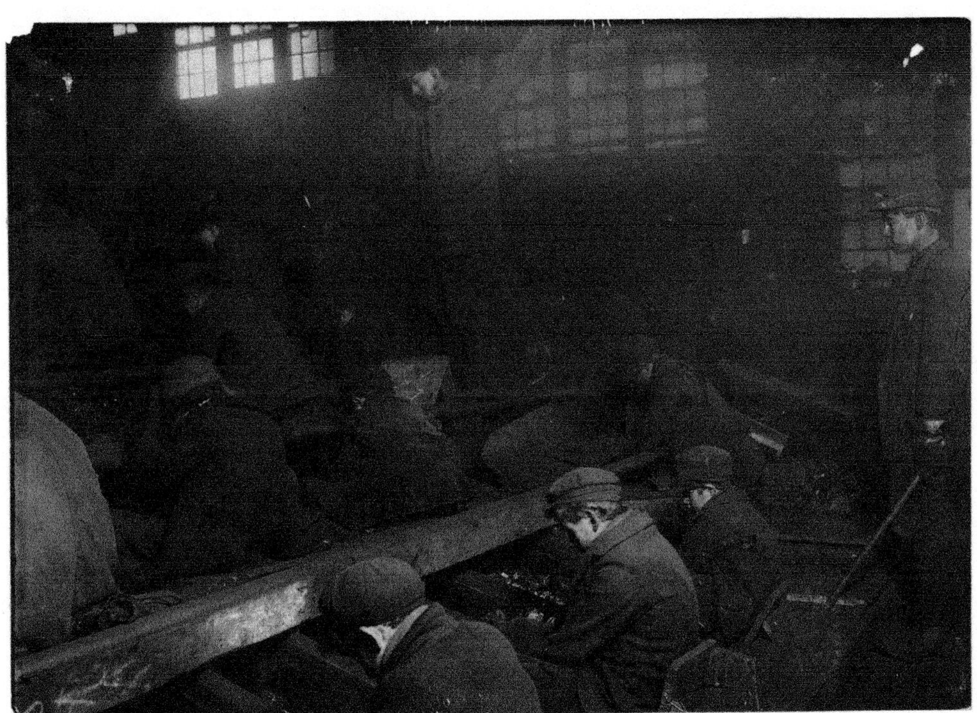

Above: Breaker boys as young as five work at a coal-breaker near Wilkes-Barre, PA. "The dust was so dense at times as to obscure the view." (*Lewis Hine, National Child Labor Committee Collection, January 1911, Library of Congress*)

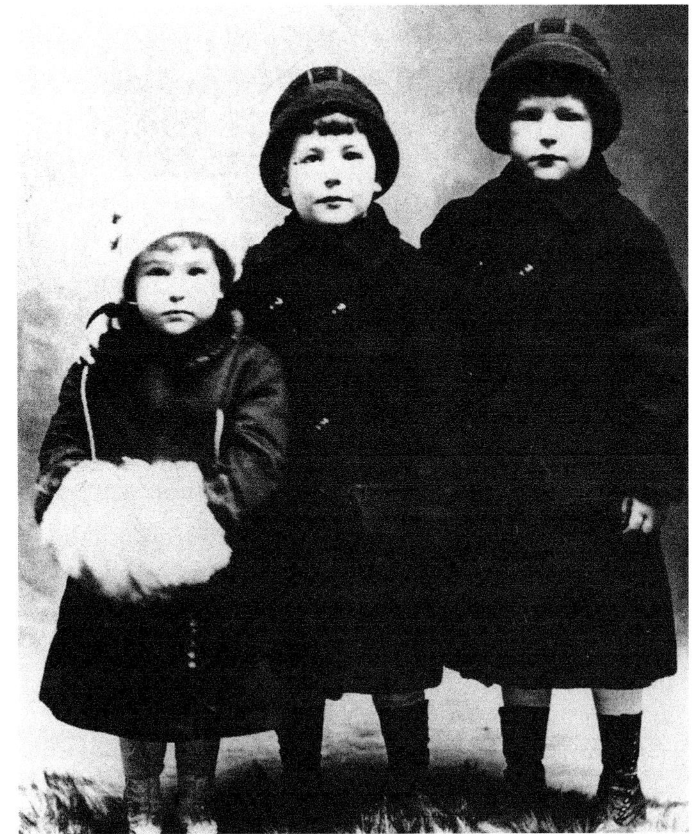

Right: The three oldest Kline children, Louise (left), Franz (center), and Frederick (right). "On many of our baby pictures," Lousie said, "Franz had his little arm around me and I'm hanging on to a button on his coat." (*Dr. Louise Kline-Kelly*)

Nijinsky (1950). Less is known about the clowns in the autograph books of Kline's friends and classmates from the late 1920s and early 1930s. Some of these early jesters appear on the decks of military ships wearing outlandish parodies of U.S. Navy sailor hats.

Kline's earliest known cartoon, *circa* 1925 and drawn with colored ink, depicts a buffoon playing the saxophone, possibly before the grandstand of the Lehighton fairgrounds. Below the figure is the word "*Mid-Nite*." Franz was fifteen. Florence Harleman Kresge, a former classmate who owned a similar sketch, said: "That was Franz's thing back then, anything to do with sailors, ships, and clowns."[5]

Another recurring theme in Kline's work were trains. In fact, later in life, he would always keep a small, iron Lehigh Valley train set and track in his many studios. In Wilkes-Barre, the cosmopolitan hub of the region, locomotives were a constant presence. Many different railroads, including the Lehigh Valley, the Pennsylvania Railroad, and the Central Railroad of New Jersey, passed through town hauling coal and other freight. Most also offered passenger service to New York or Philadelphia and many stations in-between. The thunderous engines and the crowds they drew explain Kline's early fascination with them. In his day, youngsters stared at trains with the same sense of awe and exhilaration as they do today at rockets launching into space.[6] As a young child, Franz's first drawing was a train made on a slate pavement with a rhubarb stick.[7]

Louise recalled reading about her brother falling in love with trains when he was in England and it made her "cross." She and her brothers grew up with trains. "We used to watch them come in all the time," she said. "Mother took us to the station to watch Aunt Sue board for New York by chair car. We all thought they were marvelous."[8]

Franz's father, Anthony Carlton, was one of the first generations of his family to be born in America in 1866, the year after President Lincoln was assassinated. Anthony's parents, Anthony, Sr. and Agatha (Gretel), established the first family residence and saloon at 163 S. Main Street, Wilkes-Barre. Of German-Catholic stock, Anthony Carlton was blond with blue eyes. Upon his mother's death in 1891, he and his six siblings inherited the family *biergarten* and built it into a "prosperous hotel" at the corner of South and South Main Streets.[9]

Anthony met Franz's mother, Anne Evita Rowe, at St. Stephen's Episcopal Church. Anne was fourteen years younger and spoke with a thick English accent. She had left the rolling sheep pastures of Cornwall for America alone in 1905. Her homeland, moors steeped in salty sea air, was a magical setting—formerly Camelot, the legendary home of King Arthur. In keeping with her fabled surroundings, Anne's childhood was filled with thatched cottages, prehistoric stone circles, and the ruins of medieval castles and abbeys. Whether she had been a peasant or led the life of privilege to which she often alluded—speaking of a wealthy grandfather left behind on a large estate—the south-west of England remained a strong influence on the tales she spun.

Anne was prim and petite. She had dark hair, brown eyes that required thick glasses, and maintained an aura of having attended fine finishing schools. Anne loved to tell stories and was known for transforming mundane circumstances into epic adventures. Her sojourn to America in 1895 may have actually been a boring trip across the sea, but her children listened with wonder as she recounted (down to the silverware) how she befriended the ship's purser and later dined with him at the captain's table. After arriving in America, Anne moved in with her brother, William, an insurance agent. One of her

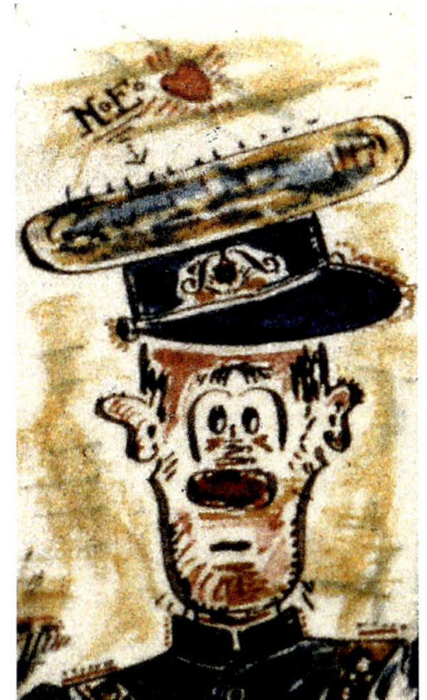

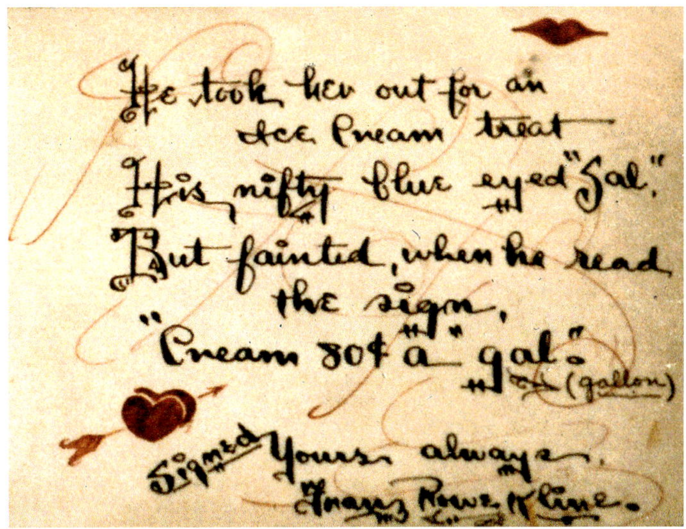

Untitled, Military Sketch, 1931. Humor was a key element in Kline's high school drawings, college less so. (*Mrs. Franz Wagner © 2018 Franz Kline Estate/Artists Rights Society (ARS), New York*)

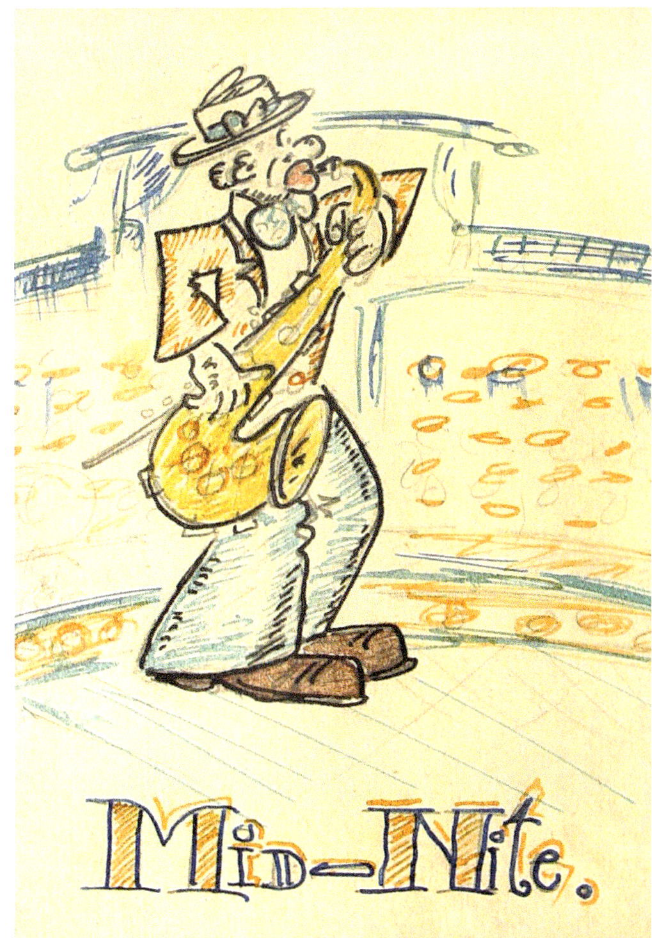

Mid-Nite, 1925, one of Kline's earliest drawings from a friend's autograph book. The clown-like figure plays a sax whilse the audience fades into abstract anonymity. (*Kathryne Oppold and Robert Warner © 2018 Franz Kline Estate/Artists Rights Society (ARS), New York*)

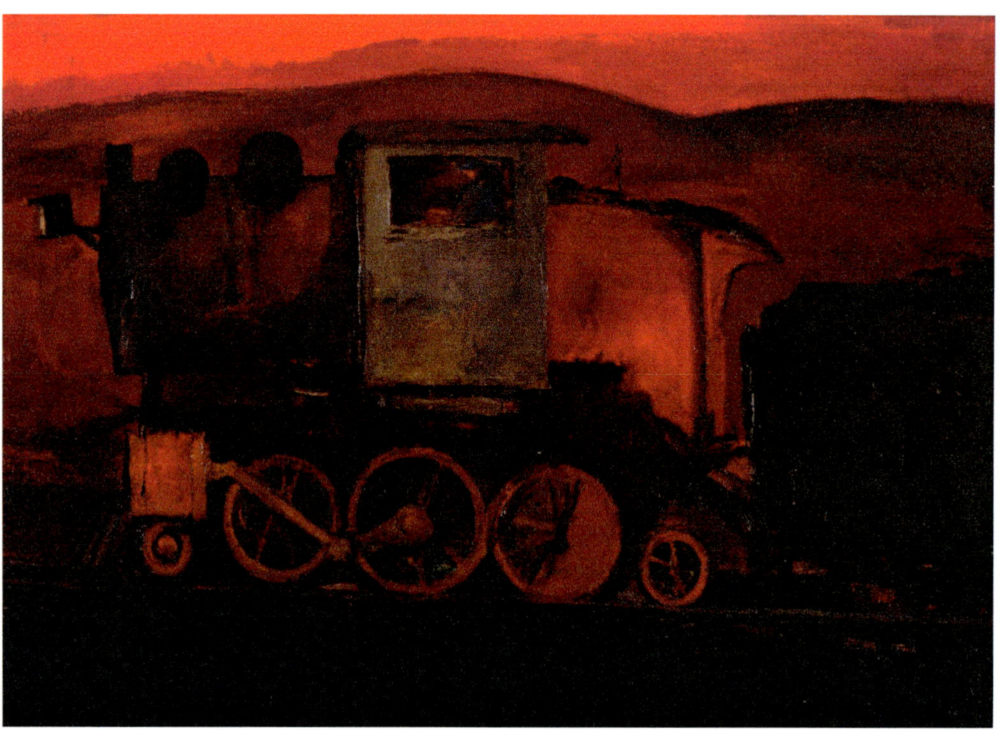

Chief (Train), 1942. (*Private Collection © 2018 Franz Kline Estate/Artists Rights Society (ARS), New York*)

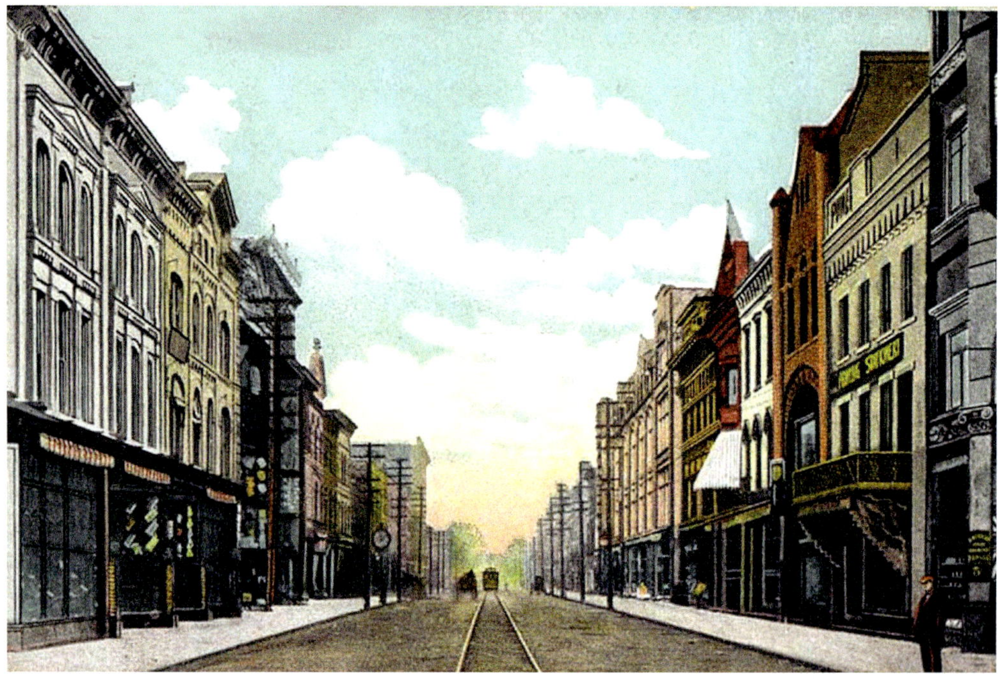

South and South Main Streets, *c.* 1915. An old copy of Boyd's Wilkes-Barre city directory includes the listing "Kline, Anthony Hotel, 320 S Main."

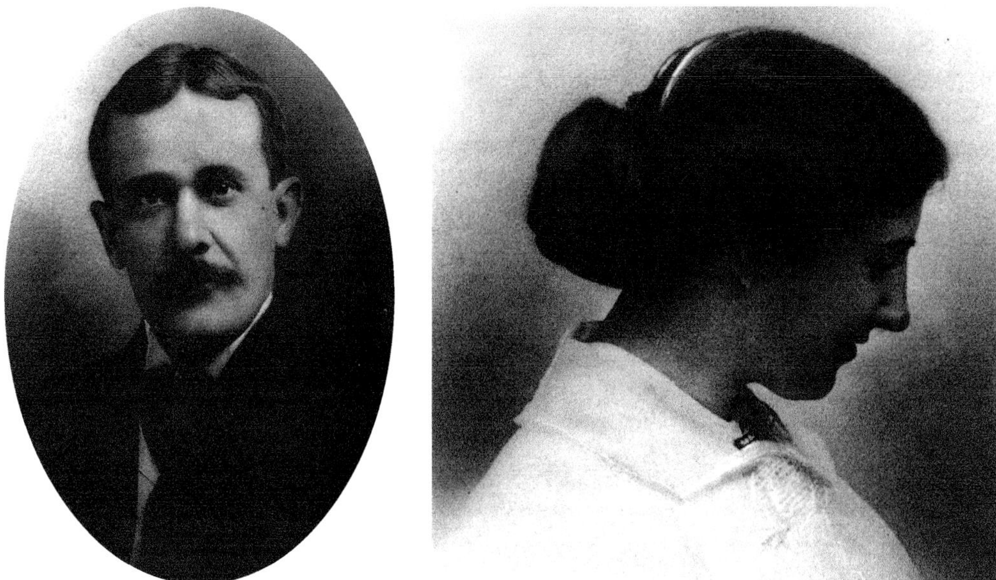

Above left: Anthony Carlton Kline, *c.* 1917, became prosperous in the hotel business and provided full-time employment for his siblings Mary, Frank, Louis, and Joseph. (*Dr. Louise Kline-Kelly*)

Above right: Anne Kline, *c.* 1915. "After the tragedy, she became our mother and our father. Franz once said, to me, 'You really have to watch Mother, she comes at you quick with all those questions.'" (*Dr. Louise Kline-Kelly*)

first friends was Susan Latimer, or, as she would become known to Anne's children, "Aunt Sue," Franz's godmother.

"Aunt Sue also went to St. Stephen's," Louise said, "and she got Mother a job at Isaac Long's, a fancy department store, where Sue did all the buying in New York. The manager gave mother a position making bows and was sort of looking after her. One day he called her into his office and said that she was too fine a girl for retailing, that even though she could probably sell the dust off the floor, that he thought she should enroll in nursing at the City Hospital, which she did, though never completed, because of Father."[10]

Anne was twenty-three when she married forty-two-year-old Anthony Carlton Kline on April 22, 1908. Reverend Henry Jones held the ceremony in the rectory of St. Stephen's. Anne and Anthony's first child, Frederick, was born the following year in 1909. Franz came on May 23, 1910. Louise in 1912, and Jacques, 1915. Each grew up to be well-educated, as was Anne's greatest wish, though the paths to Ithaca, Yale, and Heatherley would alter dramatically in a few short years.

All of Anne's children were born at home. The house was decorated with Hawkes crystal and English etchings, the master bedroom boasted an antique bed carved in Philadelphia by John Belter. Louise, who later became an English professor, was most fond of having, "Wonderful books: Dickens, Shakespeare, and Washington Irving. Franz loved the Headless Horseman. Mother knew Shakespeare by heart. I remember her reading Sir Thomas Malory's *Le Morte d'Arthur* to us at the kitchen table. When she got to the part about Sir Lancelot near the end, we all cried. We were surrounded with literature and paintings. One of my favorites was an engraving of Robespierre; another was a print by Rembrandt in a gorgeous walnut frame."[11]

Family friend Dr. Daniel Davies recalled his mother describing how she once saw Anne Kline in Riverside Park. Anne was pushing a baby carriage on a path along the Susquehanna River. "Nearby," he said, "two toddlers were running alongside. The grand carriage and their way of dress reflected signs of considerable wealth."[12]

All four Kline children were baptized in St. Stephen's, where the family maintained a private pew. Although born in May, Franz was not baptized until October as Franz Rowe Kline. In later years, he would often substitute Josef as his middle name, even on important documents and high school records.

Louise remembers her brother constantly sketching at church. "Did he do any drawing when we were young? Yes, of course he did. They weren't trained drawings, but a lot of our hymnals had his sketches of people in the choir. He was always drawing; not portraits particularly, but rather caricatures or cartoons."[13]

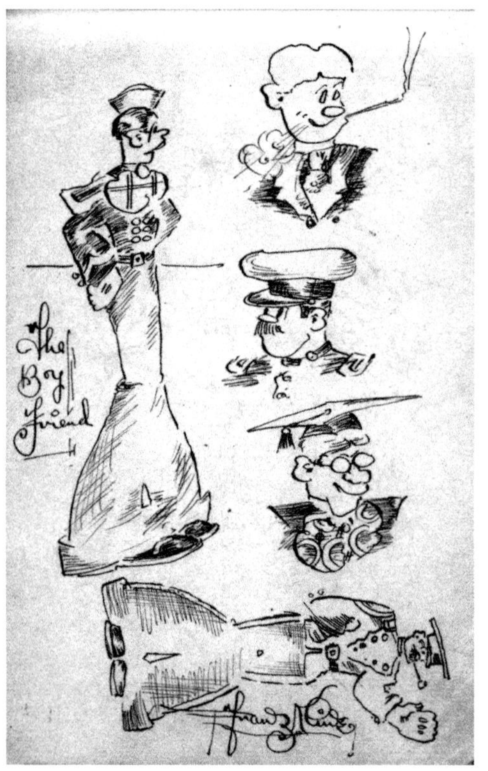

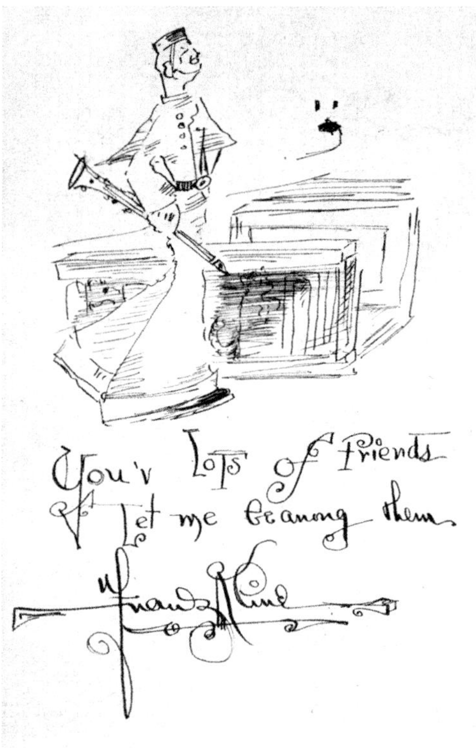

Above left: The Boyfriend, 1927. Franz was seventeen when he drew a sailor, a policeman, an officer, and a dandy in a friend's autograph book, but never indicated which was the boyfriend. (*Mr. and Mrs. Curtis Eberts © 2018 Franz Kline Estate/Artists Rights Society (ARS), New York*)

Above right: You've Lots of Friends, 1927. A pen and ink caricature found in the autograph book of a Lehighton high classmate. (*Mr. and Mrs. Curtis Eberts © 2018 Franz Kline Estate/Artists Rights Society (ARS), New York*)

While Anne heeded the traditions and ceremonies of the Episcopal Church, beneath her proper manners was a quick and irreverent wit. Her sense of humor was understated, intelligent, and, at times, lethal. Franz, who shared his mother's acumen, also developed quite the reputation as a storyteller. The Kline children appeared predestined to enjoy every comfort and advantage—cultural, educational, and social—until everything changed on August 21, 1917.

While many of the most able-bodied men had left home to battle the Germans and their allies in the Great War overseas, there was a different kind of war raging at home, one of temperance against drunkenness. To Anthony Kline, the threat of prohibition—in the form of various bills proposed in the legislature—was becoming a very real possibility in 1917, two years before the 18th Amendment passed in Congress banning the sale of alcohol in the United States, as it was already prohibited in Canada, Russia, and other parts of the world. In England, beer was intentionally watered down. Such concerns had been tumbling over in Anthony Kline's mind when he agreed to sell the family's real estate holdings, or the buyer might have used these arguments to sway him. It is also doubtful that Anne would have wanted her children to tend bar there or manage the hotel. Yet, when Anthony's sister, Mary, learned what he had done, she demanded that he buy it back. Not only would Mary, a housekeeper at the hotel, lose her home, but she and her brothers, Frank and Joseph, were bartenders there and would need to find new jobs. The cost of Anthony's impulsive move (i.e. the difference between what he received for the property and then spent almost immediately to buy it back), when adjusted for inflation a century later, was roughly $200,000. Too much to bear. Franz's father walked to the rear of the property with a pistol. A bad business deal, his brother Louis's unexpected death to pneumonia, and rumors of prohibition had been haunting him for months, deepening his depression. Remembering through a child's eyes, Louise recalls her mother breaking the news to her:

> Jack [Jacques] was born in 1915 and had no remembrance of our father at all, but Franz and I remembered father very well. How he walked us to Sunday School, and to the bake shop to choose a cake for our birthday parties. We had formal dinner parties and two servants then. Life was fine for mother who probably thought that she would never work another day in her life. We worshipped father and he worshipped her. I'll always remember him walking towards the house with flowers wrapped in green paper. And then he died.[14]

Franz was seven, the second oldest son, one year younger than Frederick, Louise was five, and Jacques only two. *The Wilkes-Barre Sunday Independent* printed this account:

> Business is business—probably this old excuse for legalized gain and worse will tend to soften the critic's attitude toward the real estate dealer whose trafficking in homes brought Anthony Kline ... to pay the two highest prices on record for the same property. First with his fortune and then with his life.... Anthony Kline—Tony to his family and friends—was the first to urge the sale of the family's holdings at the corner of South and South Main Streets. He became insistent finally and his brothers and sister agreed. Forty

> Thousand dollars was offered by Hyman Stakulsky, a real estate developer and the price was accepted as adequate. After a time, Tony was brought to understand the folly of the transaction. His sister in particular had become so attached to the old homestead that it seemed to be part and parcel of her being and she persuaded her brother to go back with the forty thousand dollars and return with the deed to the cherished property. There was where the real estate dealer showed himself a man of real business. The more a property is desired the more it is worth, and the market does not recognize any difference between sacred aspirations and pure commercial bidding.... Some say [Kline] lost $17,000 ... others put the fee of repurchase as high as $27,000. Whatever it was, it was more than Tony considered a fair bargain.... He brooded over the loss, and the melancholia that finally seized his mind drove him to suicide. Early last Tuesday morning he forgot his troubles by blotting them out with a bullet.[15]

Anthony's death certificate confirms the cause: a gunshot wound to the head. He was buried on August 24, 1917 in Hollenback Cemetery. There, among the trees and private mausoleums built of carved stone, the graves of more than 300 Civil War veterans, including the most recipients of the Medal of Honor, can be found on the gently sloping hills overlooking the Susquehanna River, the same body of water that Franz's tombstone faces today. Louise recalled that, perhaps for financial reasons, Anne ordered that no marker be placed on her husband's grave:

> There was a note on yellow paper from my mother to the cemetery board stating that the only marker was to be rhododendron bushes that were dug up from the yard on West River Street. The rhododendron was transplanted from our home with strict instructions that it should never be cut. Men had to come and lift it out with heavy cords when my brother Fred was buried. Years later, Franz and I gave our mother money for a tombstone, and she chose granite. She never really wanted a stone, for the rhododendron was to be enough.[16]

Following the shock of her husband's death, Anne was thrust into the role of supporting her four children. Fortunately, married life had not diminished her strong sense of self-reliance. Knowing that the majority of their remaining money was held in a trust for her children's education, she returned to nursing.

"Our mother developed into a strong woman from that experience," Louise said. "She did not take any nonsense. She remained a firm disciplinarian."[17]

Anne was accepted at St. Luke's Hospital School of Nursing in Bethlehem, Pennsylvania, 90-odd miles from her Wyoming Valley home. Her three oldest children were sent to a foundling home in Jonestown sponsored by the Episcopal Church. Franz's teacher there, Miss Powell, described him as "mischievous and often troublesome, though he responds to discipline."[18] Jacques, the youngest, remained with his uncle William's family.

Two years later, in March 1919, Franz entered Girard College in Philadelphia, a school for fatherless boys. "Our Episcopal minister advised my mother to have the older two boys take the entrance exam for Girard College," Louise said. "Of course, poor Fred had eyes like my mother and wore heavy glasses. Franz had no trouble and passed the exam.

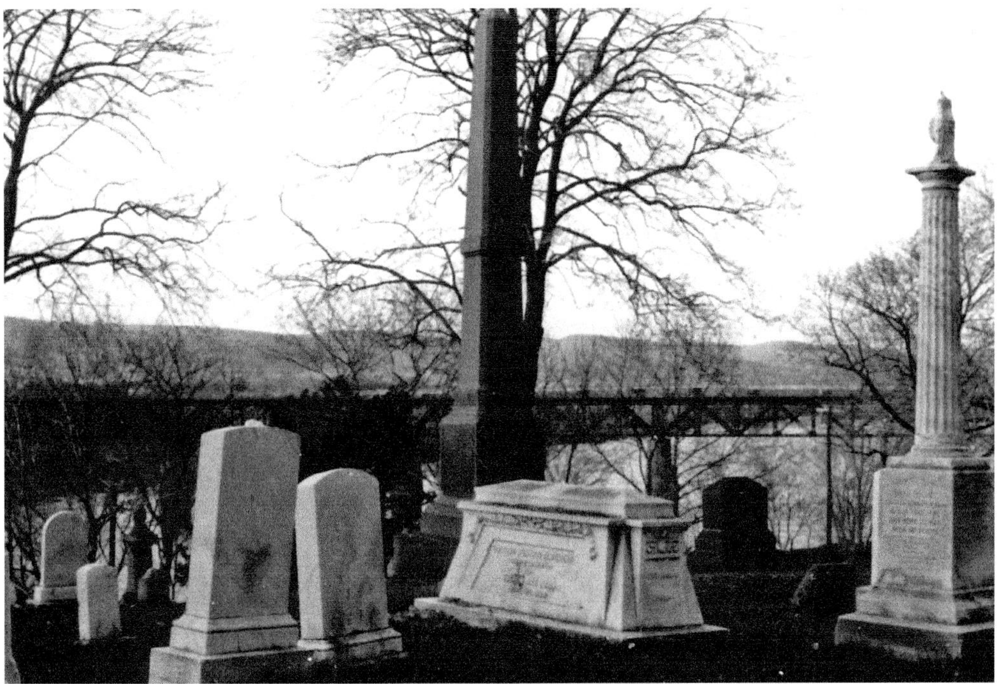

Hollenback Cemetery, Wilkes-Barre, PA, is the burial ground of Kline and family. (*Author's collection*)

So, there was Franz, all the way down in Philadelphia alone—well, it must have nearly killed him."[19]

Because nursing schools were residential at the time, they required students like Anne to secure help taking care of their children. Her choice of schools remained central to the locations of her sons and daughter, as St. Luke's in Bethlehem was approximately halfway between Philadelphia and Wilkes-Barre. She promised her children that she would bring the family back together as soon as possible.

"They were good to us at the Episcopal home," Louise said, "and those were pleasant years for Fred and me. They let us have a small flower garden."[20]

Franz was seven when his father died. Although he would retain some memories of Anthony Carlton and his boyhood in Wilkes-Barre, he rarely spoke of either. Never again would he listen to the familiar sounds of trains and bells with the same light-hearted innocence. By his ninth birthday, he was one of more than a thousand orphans living within the high stone walls of Girard College. His father's death was the first of the two great tragedies to bleed color from his life.

2

Corinthian: His Father's Suicide Scattered his Family

Instead of playing soccer or baseball, we gave up our only free time to paint and draw.

Robert Scheirer, Kline's classmate at Girard College
Personal correspondence

Corinthian II, 1961. *Corinthian I* was destroyed by fire in March 1961. (*The Museum of Fine Arts, Houston © 2018 Franz Kline Estate/Artists Rights Society (ARS), New York*)

The boy who grew up to become Stephen Girard—prominent Philadelphia mariner, banker, and philanthropist—was actually born with the slightly more exotic name of Étienne, and not in America at all, but rather in Bordeaux, France. Son of a sea captain, he lost the use of his right eye at the age of eight and had little formal education. In 1776, after establishing regular trade between New Orleans and Port au Prince, Haiti, Girard was driven into Philadelphia by the British fleet, married, and settled there as a merchant. After the Revolutionary War, he became a naturalized citizen. Fourteen years later, his wife, Mary, was institutionalized. Her diagnosis: lunacy.

When Caribbean refugees brought yellow fever to Philadelphia in 1793 and most of the wealthy fled (including President Washington), Girard remained to supervise the conversion of a mansion into a hospital.[1] He later personally helped care for the sick, tending to as many as fifteen patients a day. If anyone doubted his allegiance to the stars and stripes, the fact that he saved the U.S. from economic collapse during the War of 1812 by underwriting a majority of the new government's loans laid their questions to rest.[2]

At the height of his career, Girard was the wealthiest man in America. When he died in 1831, he bequeathed the majority of his fortune to charitable causes. He endowed a large portion of his estate in Philadelphia to found a boarding school for "poor male white orphan children."[3] He was particularly sympathetic to the sons of coal miners. In preparation, he asked his advisors to make inquiries abroad and examine what curriculum and administrative practices worked best in European institutions. In the end, he described his vision as "A permanent college with suitable outbuildings, sufficiently spacious for the residence and accommodation of at least three hundred scholars, and the requisite teachers ... as well as books and all things needful to carry into effect my general design."[4]

Girard went on to stipulate the school should avoid "needless ornament."[5] However, for recreation, he allotted for an artificial pool "for the bathing and amusement of pupils."[6] The entire 64-acre campus was to be surrounded with a wall. The wall, 10 feet high and 14 inches thick, was to be "capped with marble" and "guarded with irons on the top ... to prevent persons from getting over."[7] Entrances had dual gates, opening in opposite directions. An iron gate, "in the style of [Girard's] Banking house," opened inward.[8] Opening outward was a wooden one fortified with sheets of iron.

Liberties were restricted (the wall was not just a symbol), but the boys were well cared for: the infirmary employed full-time doctors and a cadre of nurses. Teachers were well paid, and one of the best surgeons in the city was perpetually on call. Here is a copy of the rigid schedule the boys were expected to follow:

6:30 a.m.	Wake to the sound of the chapel bell
7:00 a.m. to 7:30 a.m.	Breakfast
7:30 a.m. to 8:45 a.m.	Recreation or study time
8:45 a.m. to 9:00 a.m.	Interdenominational chapel service
9:00 a.m. to 12 p.m.	Academic classes
12:00 p.m. to 12:30 p.m.	Clean-up for dinner
12:30 p.m. to 1:00 p.m.	Dinner followed by chores
1:00 p.m. to 4:00 p.m.	Vocational classes
4:00 p.m. to 5:30 p.m.	Recreation time and drill/band practice
5:30 p.m. until 6:00 p.m.	Boys cleaned up for supper
6:00 p.m. to 6:30 p.m.	Supper
6:30 p.m. until 7 p.m.	Break
7:00 p.m. to 8:30 p.m.	Study time

Girard envisioned a refuge for disadvantaged boys, but he also understood that the road to self-sufficiency required discipline. Students were expected to mend their own clothing, sweep their dormitories, and make their beds. Meals were silent. Boys marched in groups, two by two, wherever they went. The shorter ones up front, taller in the back. Vocational instruction was assigned on the basis of aptitude for the development of job-training skills. But while technical courses dominated the curriculum, others included French, Spanish, drawing (until age twelve), writing, bookkeeping, chemistry, and others. As valuable as the education was, the boys did not earn a high school equivalency, but rather

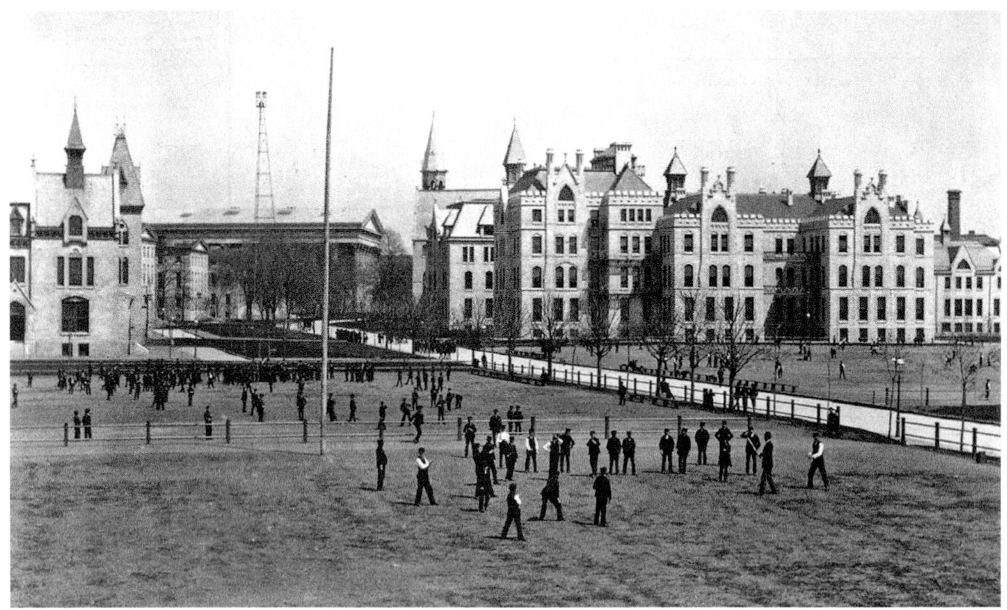

Girard College, 1920. The campus had a surreal quality. The students are dwarfed by the tall steeples and spires of their dormitories. Founders Hall has the front door of a giant, measuring 30 feet tall. (*Dr. Louise Kline-Kelly*)

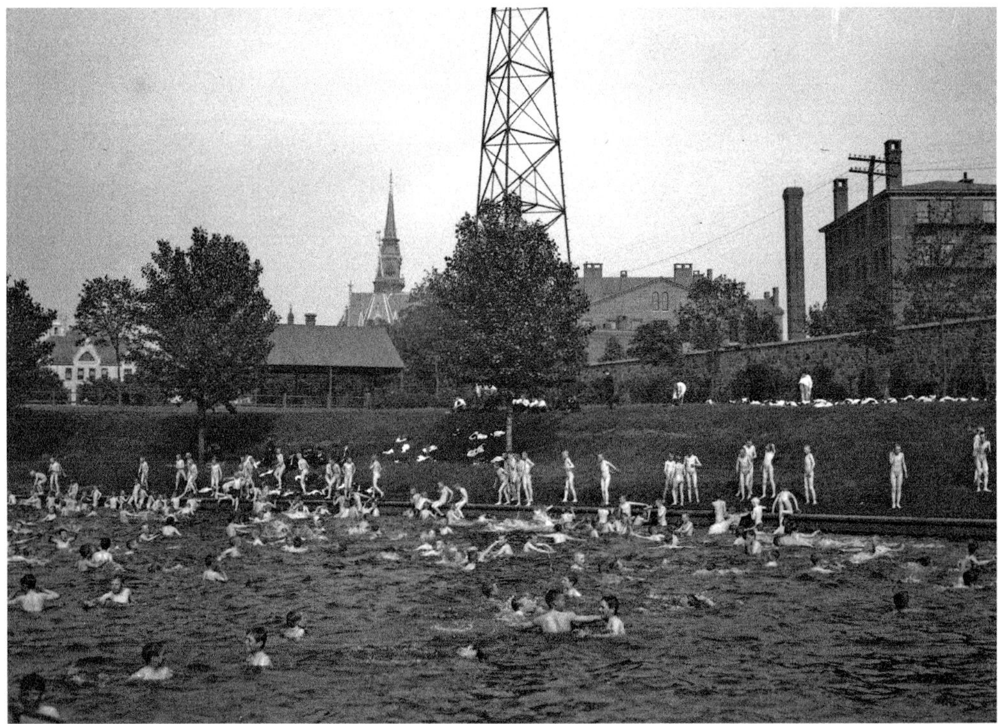

Girard Boys Swim, *c.* 1920. In the outdoor pool, shielded by the 10-foot wall, boys shed their school uniforms on the grass to swim *au naturel*. (*John Nolen Papers, #2903. Division of Rare and Manuscript Collections, Cornell University Library*)

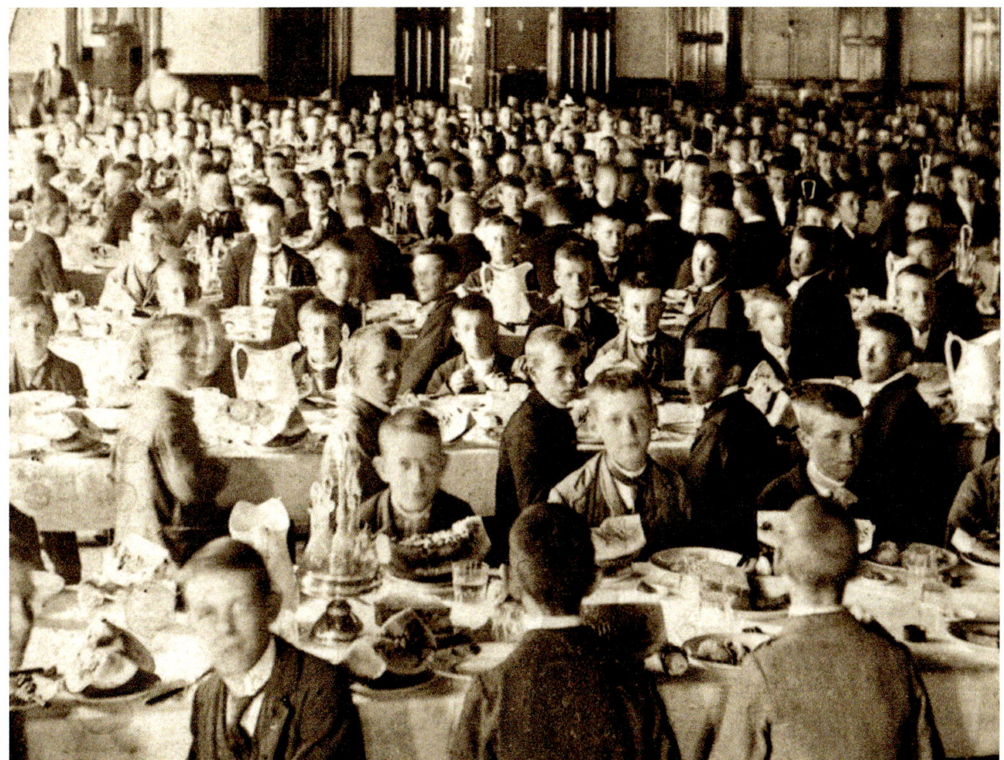

Girard College Dining Room, *c.* 1920. There were several dining rooms at Girard College, students marched to meals two by two, with taller boys in the back.

a sort of vocational certificate, not the prerequisite diploma most universities required for admission. By the time Franz's mother graduated from nursing school and began to reunite her family, this fact troubled her to the point of obsession.

When Mr. Wagstaff, the housefather of the church home in Jonestown, delivered Franz in late March 1919, Girard College housed more than 1,500 boys, five times the founder's original intent. The campus was like a cloistered medieval town. It was hard to get in and even more difficult at times to get out. Boys were screened for both physical health and intellectual ability, and the terms of admission were strict. Once in, all were to remain until graduation or their eighteenth birthday.

Robert H. Scheirer was a fellow student who remembered Franz there. They lived in different dormitories and spoke little to each other, but both boys were part of a small group of students invited to attend a special art class. Scheirer described Girard as a place where a new kid often felt lost and was likely teased, especially if he had an accent. "We were homesick and glad if we could get home at Christmas and Easter," he said, "yet many of us would later have tears in our eyes when we graduated."[9]

For most students, early evening consisted of free time to play games before dinner. But for a group of twelve outliers, it was dedicated to art. Scheirer described the group as "not particularly popular with the rest of the boys" and "at least a little odd."[10] Most kids preferred to play sports. The boys already sat in class for six hours a day, plus ninety minutes of study time, so anyone who gave up recreation for further study "was definitely different."

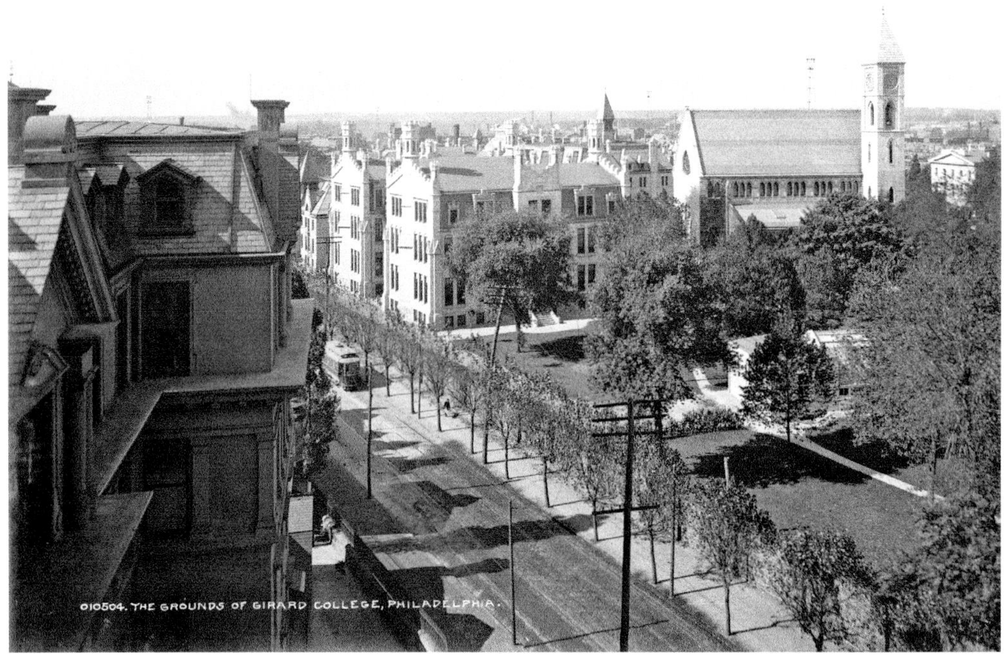

Aerial View of Girard College, 1898. "None can know without its experience the loneliness of a boy bereft of his father; as the boy separated from all he loved, entered upon his life in Girard College." Theodore DeBow. (*Detroit Publishing Co. Collection, Library of Congress 1901*)

The special art class met on the second floor of the main building, known as Founder's Hall, an imposing Greco-Corinthian structure resembling the Acropolis in Athens. Girard's remains are interred there behind a statue of him created by the French-Philadelphian sculptor Nicholas Gevelot in 1851. The classroom was large and full of natural light. The teacher, Miss Edith Bregy, was the daughter of a prominent judge and a graduate of the Philadelphia School of Design for Women in 1907. She studied under Charles Woodbury and her oil painting *Philadelphia Street* was displayed at the Pennsylvania Academy of Fine Arts. Her painting *Pride Roses* is housed at the Indianapolis Museum of Art. She began teaching at Girard in 1922, when Franz was twelve years old. Her first task was to seek out students with special gifts.

"Our teacher was an eccentric old maid," Scheirer said. "She seemed as though she was volunteering her time to work with us."[11]

One of Bregy's assignments was to draw "Animals and Their Friends."[12] An observer later wrote that after Bregy introduced the afternoon's subject "eagerly the pencils were put to paper and the work produced [was] worthy of praise." Bregy insisted on good drawing and encouraged her students toward realism, "certainly never anything abstract," recalled Scheirer.[13] Regarding his classmate, he added, "I do not remember Kline's works being outstandingly better than anyone else. I'm quite sure he did not win any of the annual prizes."[14]

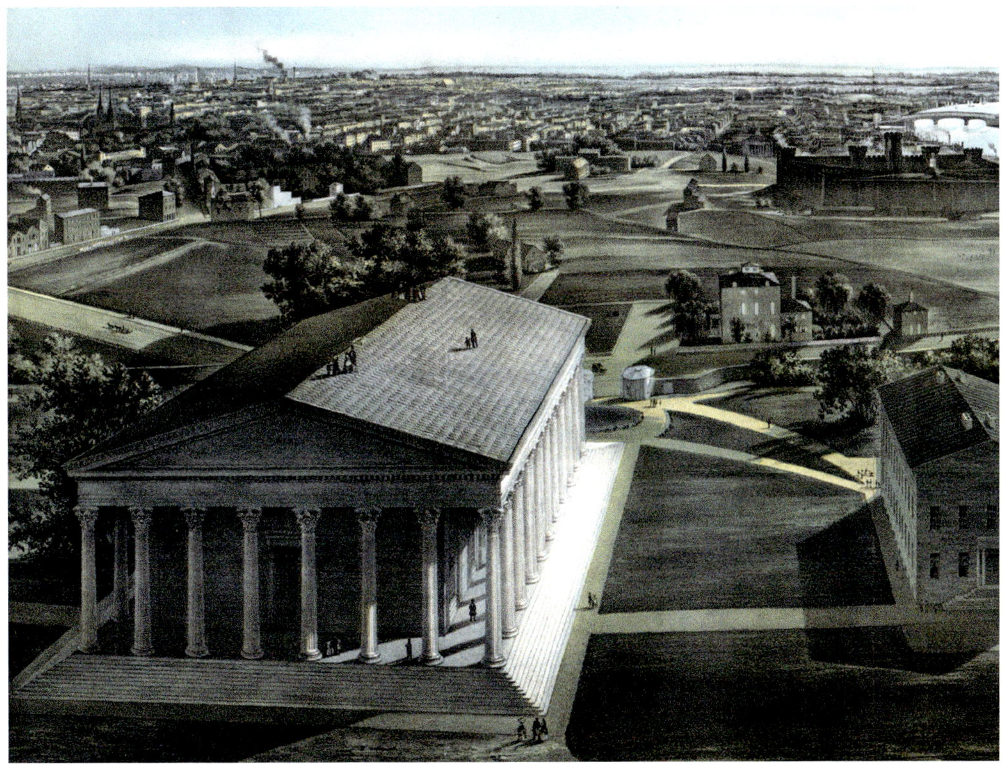

Above: Founders Hall at Girard College, Girard and Corinthian Avenues, Philadelphia, PA, 1850. (*Library of Congress*)

Right: Untitled, Clown, 1929. (*Kathryne Oppold and Robert Warner © 2018 Franz Kline Estate/ Artists Rights Society (ARS), New York*)

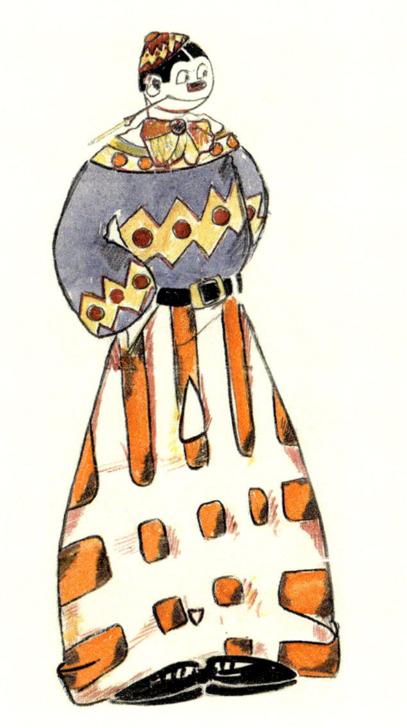

Although Franz may not have won any awards at Girard, his selection for the special art class was significant, and potentially therapeutic, as his years there in Philadelphia were not without trauma. Shortly after his arrival, he became a chronic sleepwalker.[15] He was eventually forced to tie his wrist to the bedpost to keep from wandering. Was his somnambulism a visible repercussion from the post-traumatic stress of his fractured family? For most Girard students, the unwavering structure of the school helped illumine a path through the darkness. We know very little about Kline's first years there, when he would have been most vulnerable. While his mother studied nursing at St. Luke's, Franz rarely saw his family. Boys with relatives living in Philadelphia could go home on weekends, but out-of-towners like Franz returned home only during summer vacation, if at all.

Franz remained behind the wall for six years, some of which his mother spent campaigning with letters to secure his release. "At Girard College, Franz was being trained with tools, and that horrified mother," Louise said. "She didn't want him in mechanical work, so she wrote countless letters to the headmaster to justify him coming home."[16] Before his mother graduated from nursing school and remarried in 1920, Franz spent the summer at Girard as well.

Scheirer remembered trying to visit Kline in Lehighton the summer after Franz reunited with his family there. Scheirer's cousin, Dot Harleman, lived a few blocks from Franz on Iron Street. One afternoon, he walked over to Kline's home and knocked unannounced. "A woman's voice rose from inside the dark house, asking, 'What do you want?' I spoke my name," Scheirer said, "and said that I attended Girard and asked to see Franz. 'He's not home,' she said, dismissing me. If it was Franz's mother, I did not see her. She remained in shadows."[17]

Thirty-seven years later, at the height of his artistic career, Kline painted a dynamic abstract called *Corinthian.* Could its inspiration have anything to do with memories of his time at Girard College on Corinthian Avenue? *Corinthian* was huge (80 × 120 inches), about the size of a small billboard. It was painted in a barn in East Hampton in the summer of 1957. With massive black strokes plowing through a surreal whitewashed background, the painting was exhibited in the Sidney Janis Gallery in New York. It was purchased by Nelson Rockefeller in June 1968 and hung in the Governor's Mansion in Albany for three years until a fire consumed it. When the Governor asked Franz to recreate it, he painted a similar piece, although not an exact replica, *Corinthian II.*

"Franz would never duplicate a painting," his sister said, "even when Rockefeller wanted an exact duplicate. [Franz] just couldn't bring himself to do it."[18]

Action painting was about the experience.

3

Ninth Street: After Nursing School, Kline's Mother Recollected her Children

We are ducks, who have hatched a wild swan.

Florence Nightingale
Eminent Victorians

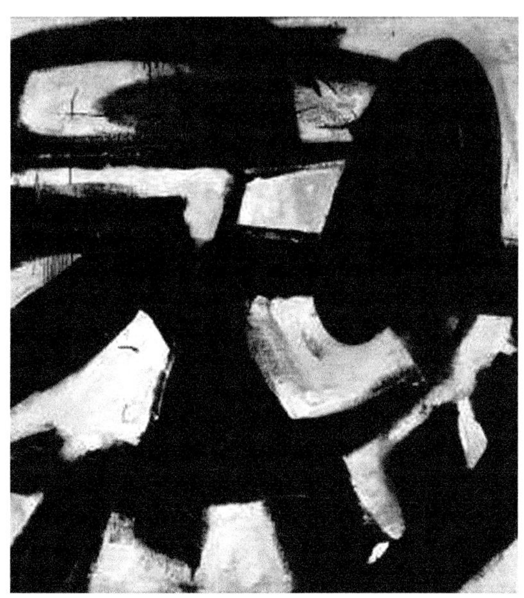

Ninth Street, 1951. (*Private Collection © 2018 Franz Kline Estate/Artists Rights Society (ARS), New York*)

Following her husband's suicide in 1917, a weaker woman may have allowed her circumstances to overcome her, but Anne Kline, with four young children to support, did not bow. When she learned that her husband had squandered their wealth, she called on the purchaser of the Kline family homestead and biergarten in Wilkes-Barre, Hyman Stakulsky, for his explanation.[1] When whatever he said only infuriated her more, she became irate in his office. Stakulsky reached for his telephone, desperate to have her removed. In the ensuing melee, he allegedly struck her with the receiver, knocking her to the ground. She saw a doctor for her injuries and filed a lawsuit for assault.[2]

Her husband's recklessness had altered everything. Suddenly alone and on the brink of poverty, Anne was forced to make a series of difficult decisions. With most of her remaining money held in trust for her children's educations, she retraced her steps to before ever setting eyes on Anthony Carlton, back to when she was still working at the department store with Aunt Sue, and the manager said that Anne would make a fine nurse.

She was accepted at two nursing schools: The Hospital of the Protestant Episcopal Church and St. Luke's. The first, in Philadelphia, would have been the closest to Franz at Girard College, but Anne chose St. Luke's, in Bethlehem, Pennsylvania—the most central to all her displaced children. In a letter saved by her daughter, Louise, Anne is depicted as a desirable candidate. The directress of the PE hospital, Miss Katharine Brown, wrote that she was "anxious to know" whether Anne still wished to enter the school, punctuating her query with, "Hoping for a reply."[3]

Once all of her children were safely placed, Anne moved to Bethlehem. St. Luke's was a Nightingale School, for the famous "Lady with the Lamp" Florence Nightingale, founder of modern nursing. In practical terms, this meant that the school was attached directly to a hospital. Students split time between lecture halls and wards, making rounds and caring for actual patients. Moreover, the principles Anne pledged are the same still in effect today. Specifically, that nursing should be seen as "an art and a science."[4] Nurses should be "sober."[5] They should spend their time caring for patients, "not cleaning."[6] Nurses should follow the physician's orders but also "use discretion."[7]

Fueled by an intense longing to reunite her family, Anne dedicated herself to her work. We, the authors, discovered three of her nursing-school notebooks for sale at the Lehighton library in 2012. Her handwriting in each is carefully composed, and the books are marked "very good" in multiple places in red ink by her instructors. Among symptoms and dosages are lines like "digitalis is derived from purple Foxglove leaves" and "immediately after birth, bathe the baby's eyes."[8] She cared for the sick—taking temperatures, applying cold compresses, and emptying bedpans—for two years. It forced her to set aside her own personal woes. When she finally graduated, she worked briefly at a boarding school in New Jersey, but left abruptly when an opportunity opened closer to home, back at St. Luke's, where one afternoon she met a fateful visitor named Ambrose Snyder.

Remembered for his easygoing smile, Ambrose was a tall and stocky supervisor with the Lehigh Valley Railroad. He recently lost his wife, Elva, followed by their infant son, to the horrible flu pandemic of 1918. There were so many deaths in Lehighton at that time that undertakers waited until nightfall to remove the deceased from homes. Ambrose lived with his remaining three children there, just under half the distance, roughly 67 miles, from St. Luke's Hospital to Anne's old home in Wilkes-Barre. According to his sister-in-law, Ida Snyder, Ambrose seemed so desperate for help at home that others offered to adopt his youngest daughter, Latour, but he refused to give her up.[9]

It seems too abrupt to simply say that Ambrose proposed, but it is true. He was visiting the hospital and was overcome with curiosity about the English nurse. When he learned that she was a widow, he may have felt that their paths had crossed for a reason. They needed each other. Neither one could move forward without a spouse, someone to help share the load. Anne stated plainly that such an arrangement would be solely for the benefit of the children. Her response reveals a lot about her situation, even though we will probably never know her exact words. In May 1920, three days before Franz's tenth birthday, Anne and Ambrose married as virtual strangers.

Anne R. Kline
St Lukes Hospital

37

of milk, a binder retards secretions,
while pumping and massage
encourage it.
After a mother has been in bed
six days she should be allowed to
sit up long enough to nurse the baby
Care of the new born
Immediately after delivery, the
baby eyes mouth and then the
whole face should be washed
with boracic solution, seeing
that all mucus is taken from
its nose and mouth. The best method
for doing this is to introduce a
catheter and aspirate. always
see that the baby gets a good breath
and cries loud, be sure there is no
mucus in the lungs
When the mucus gets into the
bronchial tubes and prevents their
functionating properly. this is known
as atelectasis
When the baby is born, the nurse
must be ready to receive it, and
place it on its right side, and wrap
in a warm blanket. The nurse
must see that a sterile ligature
is ready in case the doctor wants
to suture the cord. After the eyes

A page from Anne Kline's notebook with signature, 1919, from St. Luke's School of Nursing. (*Author's collection*)

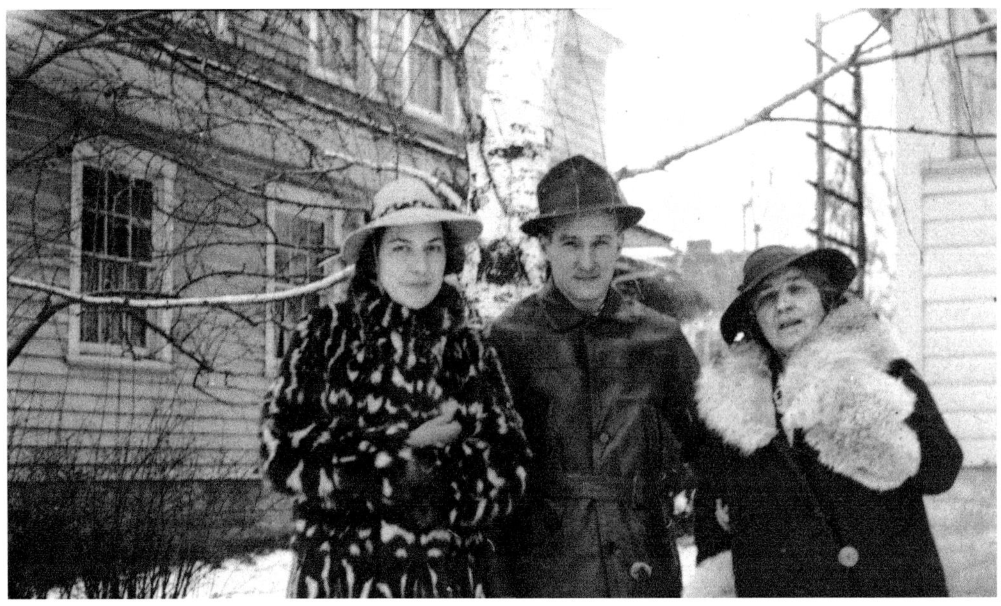

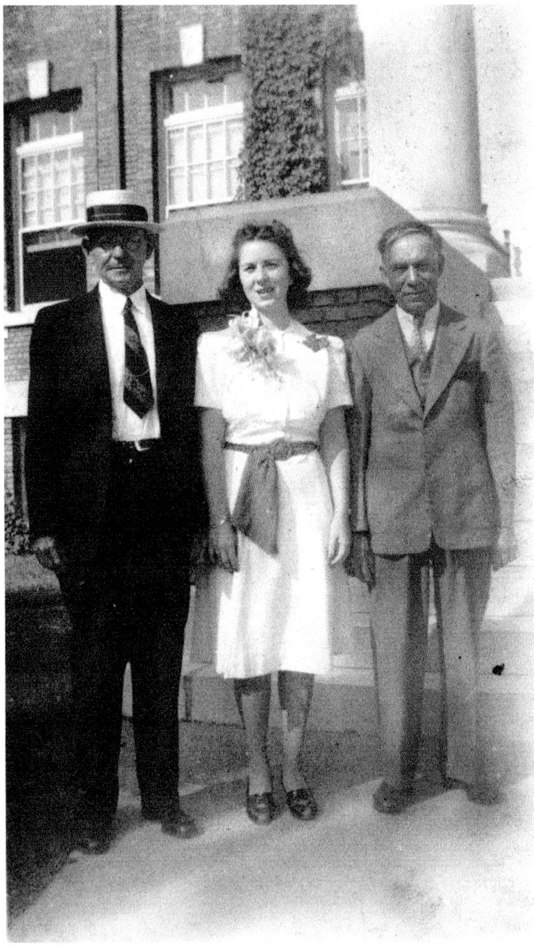

Above: Anne Snyder (far right) with children, Louise (left) and Jacques, 1935. Life was not easy for Anne in Lehighton, to a considerable degree she remained an outsider. (*Kim Graver Steinberger and family*)

Left: Ambrose Snyder (left) with daughter, La Tour, 1935. Ambrose had many eccentricities, he loved people-watching in New York when visiting Franz. (*Kim Graver Steinberger and family*)

Dr. Daniel Davies, a former beau of Louise, recalled the unorthodox situation. "Mr. and Mrs. Snyder made a pact," he said. "Ambrose supplied the home in Lehighton and his wages to support both families. It was strictly business and not a happy arrangement."[10]

Despite her mother's initial aversion to Ambrose, Louise described her stepfather as warm and attentive. She insisted that he was good to her mother, even though they rarely showed affection. "They were just too different," Louise said. Romance aside, the arrangement worked well in practical terms. At his core, Ambrose appeared content with a hot meal and well-kept home. He also seemed to enjoy having a woman around to tease with idle threats and practical jokes, like removing Anne's eyeglasses—without which she was nearly blind—from their usual places. Louise said her stepfather was good with children, protective over the girls, but also a bit boyishly sensitive: "One day Father was walking behind Franz and a friend when he overheard Franz say, 'oh, you know the old man' and it bothered Ambrose. I think he saw himself strictly as father, which meant worthy of a certain respect."

The oldest son of a large family, Ambrose often told stories about his boyhood working on the railroad. He excelled at math and often helped the children with their homework, even though he left school after eighth grade. Despite their best intentions, Anne and Ambrose's tempers often flared into arguments. Their neighbor Grace Ahner recalled one of their stormier moments: "On summer evenings, when the windows were open, you could hear Ambrose and Anne hollering all the way up the street about who would outlive the other."[11]

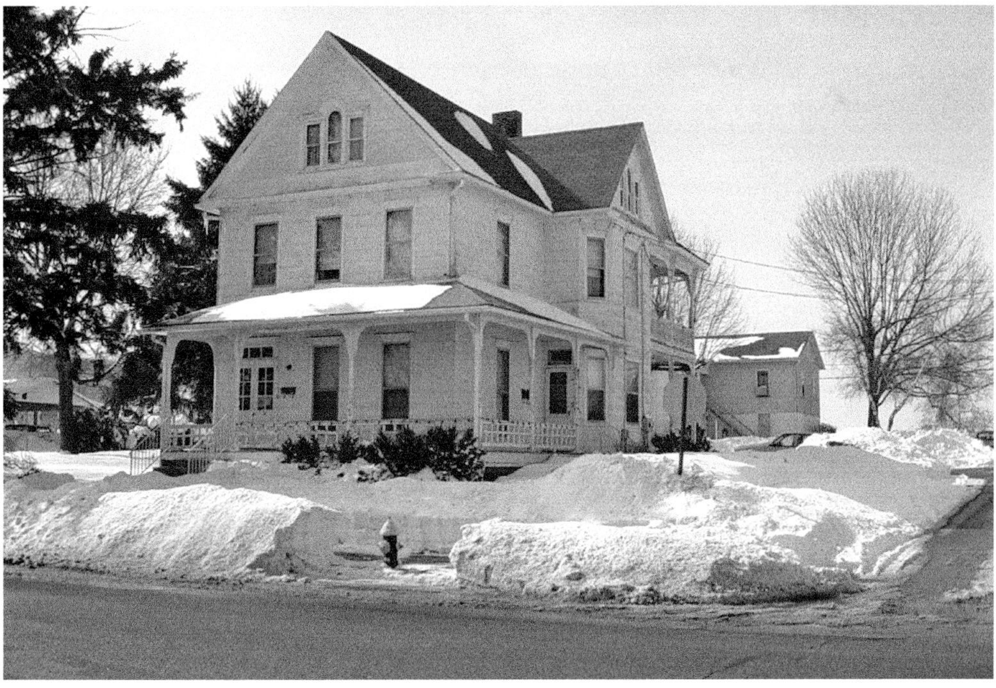

The Kline-Snyder home at 300 S. 9th Street. (*Joshua Finsel*)

While certain aspects of his new wife irritated Ambrose, he accepted the changes she introduced to their home. The white Victorian at 300 South 9th Street had a spacious front porch, upstairs balcony, and a barn/coach house at the far end of a yard filled with *philadelphus* (mock orange) and honeysuckle. The back of the property overlooked 50-plus acres of fairgrounds, meadow-like but for a few weeks out of the year when troupes of gypsies and carnies arrived to work at the county fair. There was a long row of yellow clapboard horse stables with green trim, and the empty stables were one of Franz's favorite spots for high school romance.

Prior to moving into her new house, Anne insisted on hiring a crew from the Isaac Long's Department Store in Wilkes-Barre to remodel the interior. The workers rented hotel rooms for two weeks, as Anne directed them in transforming her new home with paint, French wallpaper, and embossed leather wainscoting. Anne and Ambrose shared one of the larger bedrooms on the second floor but kept separate beds. Daniel Davies remembered the boys discovering Ambrose's pin-up magazines under his bed.[12] Anne's antique urns, silver, and other remnants from her former life in Wilkes-Barre made a beautiful home, the only one in town boasting a Chinese gong.

Ambrose quickly learned Anne's rigid standards. Despite their lovely home, there was often friction. It may have stemmed from the culture gap between the rough and hearty Pennsylvania "Dutchman" and the refined English lady, or simply a clash of strong personalities. When Ambrose thought he was right about something, he could be stubborn. Although Anne's life was nowhere near the same as it had been with Anthony, she refused to lower her standards. In Lehighton, she remained a perpetual outsider, a remarried European widow. She was not the submissive wife Ambrose may have expected. Her regal manner, which had brought respect and admiration in Wilkes-Barre, may have come across as cold in Lehighton. But Anne worked hard to keep her home elegant, as described by Grace Ahner, a friend of Maybert:

> Anne spoke with a thick accent. The young boys would snicker sometimes as she talked, but she couldn't see them because her glasses sometimes steamed up. All the serving dishes had matching lids, and she wheeled them in on a cart. We had pork and English potatoes, whole with parsley, and other vegetables. Everything was proper. Anne acted formal in her manners but dressed like a gypsy. After Franz and Fred finished eating, they had to ask to be excused. She replied with, "Alright, Franz, now you go weed the irises." And then she gave Fred some other chore, and he would get angry and flustered because he didn't like being told what to do. But Franz was gentle, and he said, "All right, Mother, I'll get it done." He was always kind to her and didn't want to show disrespect, but then again, when we went outside a little later, he was gone. He never said when he would get it done.[13]

Ambrose, like most Pennsylvania Germans, expressed himself in "Pennsylvania Dutch," which meant that his English was often interspersed with the old-country dialect of German peasants, a.k.a. Deutsche, specifically those from around the Rhine River. Franz, whose father had also been German, was fascinated with the local culture and language. Later, when he lived in Greenwich Village, he named his black cat Kitzker, *Pennsilfaanisch*

Deitsch for cat. The culture was full of characters for Franz to imitate, specifically the old-time farmers and railroaders. After a fashion, Anne enjoyed poking fun at them too.

Louise remembered one morning when Franz, home from Girard College, was painting the walls in the kitchen. While telling a story about a local farmer, Franz had just begun to imitate Ambrose when he knocked over the can, spilling green paint all over the floor. "And Mother," Louise said, "using her best Pennsylvania Dutch, told him, 'Get that cleaned up before Father wakes up, you *schlopp fus!*' She was a real comedienne."

Aside from helping Anne to expand her vocabulary and add layers to her sense of humor, Ambrose's extended family showed his new wife other Pennsylvania Dutch traditions, including new methods of preserving food. She and Ambrose's mother developed a strong friendship while making *schnitz*. In order to preserve apples from the garden, locals hung them on strings in their attics to dry. The dried apples could then be used throughout the year as snacks and when making pies or roasting pork. They also dried string beans for soups, a tradition that has survived. However, most people today use their ovens set at a low temperature instead of their attics. During Anne's day, putting up food for the winter was a tradition involving the whole family. Louise said that not even Franz, who still lived most of the year apart, was exempt.

"Each summer Mother had us string apple slices," Louise said. "She'd peel, and we'd string them and tell our jokes and stories and have a good time. I think Mother liked hearing about what was going on in our lives. When we finished them, she'd hang the strings in the attic and throw last year's away."[14]

Lehighton is located on the cusp of the Mahoning Valley surrounded by the Blue Ridge Mountains. In the eighteenth century, the town was the furthest point a white settler could go in Pennsylvania before leaving lands protected by Native American treaty. Ambrose was proud to show his new family the area, including the village of Packerton where he worked in the roundhouse, servicing trains. At a time when coal-fired steam engines symbolized conquest and power, having a railroad foreman for a father came with unique privileges. The first time Ambrose took Anne's children to the railyards, he asked them to wait at a spot at the top of a bank. Louise said she was never as scared in her life. A short while later Ambrose chugged up to them in a small Dinky engine and called out, "All aboard!" before taking them for a ride around the switch-yards. They finished their tour inside the roundhouse, a place of tremendous pride to Ambrose. It was the largest in the region, which put Lehighton in the center of railroad maintenance and construction of freight cars. He showed them how the turntable spun an engine around for its return trip.

The Kline children would not have seen many coal miners in Lehighton. Most of the entrances to the mines were located further up river in towns like Coaldale, Nesquehoning, and Summit Hill. The mountains and fields of Lehighton were verdant. People did not live aside huge piles of ash. Many of the homes were historic, not built hurriedly from scrap lumber during a boom. Lehighton was much older than the speculator's encampments that seeded mining towns. It was built on an old Moravian Brethren mission called *Gnadenhütten* or "huts of grace," and Benjamin Franklin once commanded troops there during the French and Indian War.[15]

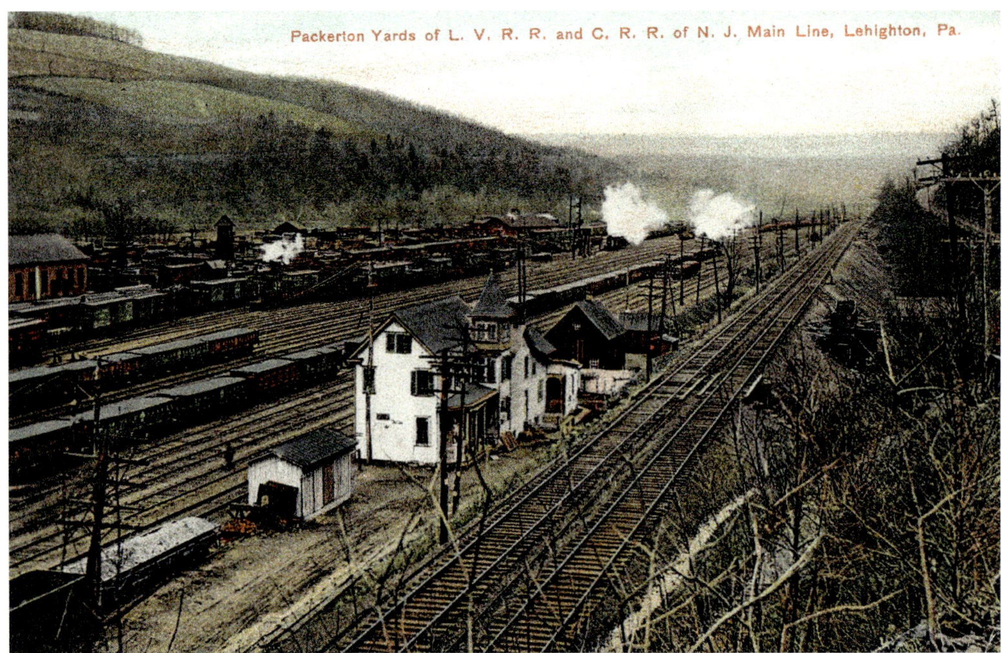

The Packerton Yards of the Lehigh Valley Railroad, *c.* 1915, the heart of the railroad industry in Carbon County and had the appearance of a village. The yards were situated on 60 acres, half were in the Lehighton borough.

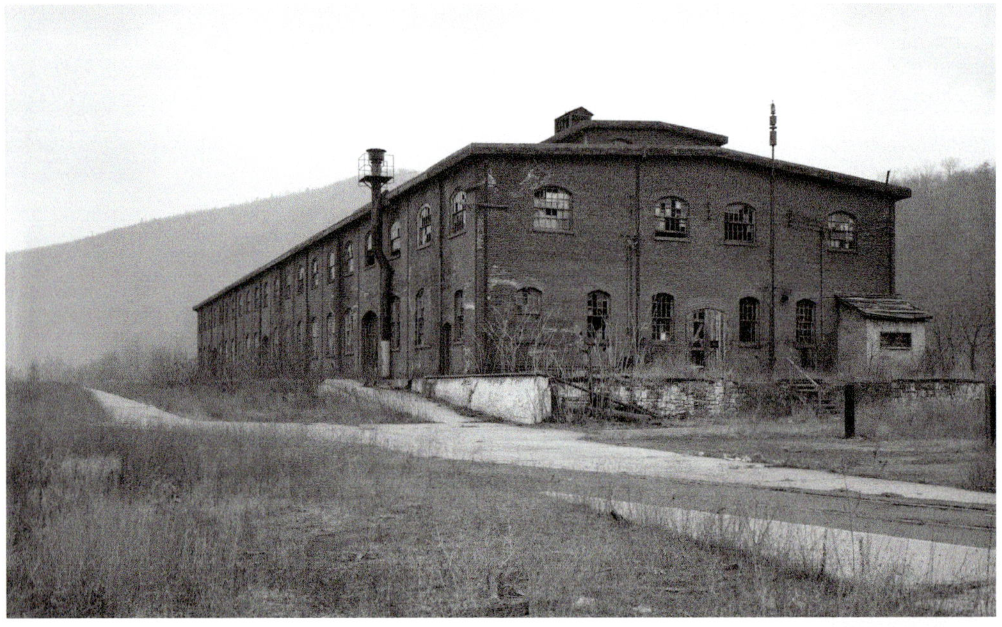

The last building standing at the Packerton Yards of the Lehigh Valley Railroad, Packerton, PA. Once part of an extensive complex of railroad freight car construction and repair shops. (*Historic American Buildings Survey/Historic American Landscapes Survey, Library of Congress Prints and Photographs Division*)

When Franz first came to Lehighton to see his family in 1920, the local economy was strong. Over a hundred million tons of "black diamonds" were mined each year just upriver. Powerful trains hauled the coal off to places like Bethlehem Steel, and almost all of them were serviced in Ambrose's roundhouse. The industry reached an apex just as Franz began to grow familiar with the town. In 1922, during his third summer away from Girard College, railroad workers in Lehighton participated in the nationally organized Railway Shopmen's Strike. On July 1, some 400,000 workers across the country walked out in response to deep wage cuts, but Ambrose did not join the strike, and because he continued to work, Franz's stepfather aroused the anger of the mob.[16]

In Lehighton, crowds gathered on vacant lots.[17] About 176 men from Ambrose's shop participated.[18] This left only about twenty-five experienced men, not nearly enough to train the stream of unskilled workers who rushed in to fill the vacancies. Those who crossed the picket line were called "canaries," "wharf rats," and "yellow jackets."[19] Sympathizers threw rotten eggs, tomatoes, and peaches at them as they came and left.[20] Others marched. About a month into it, strikers "held a big parade.... Music was furnished by a drum corps, and two American flags floated at the front."[21] *The Daily Times* described "one of the principal attractions" as an "effigy of a strike-breaker with a wooden leg ... gracefully draped by the neck from the cross-arm of a telegraph pole."[22]

Stones pounded the outside of the roundhouse for fifteen straight nights while Ambrose continued to work.[23] Company men mounted searchlights on the south side of the water

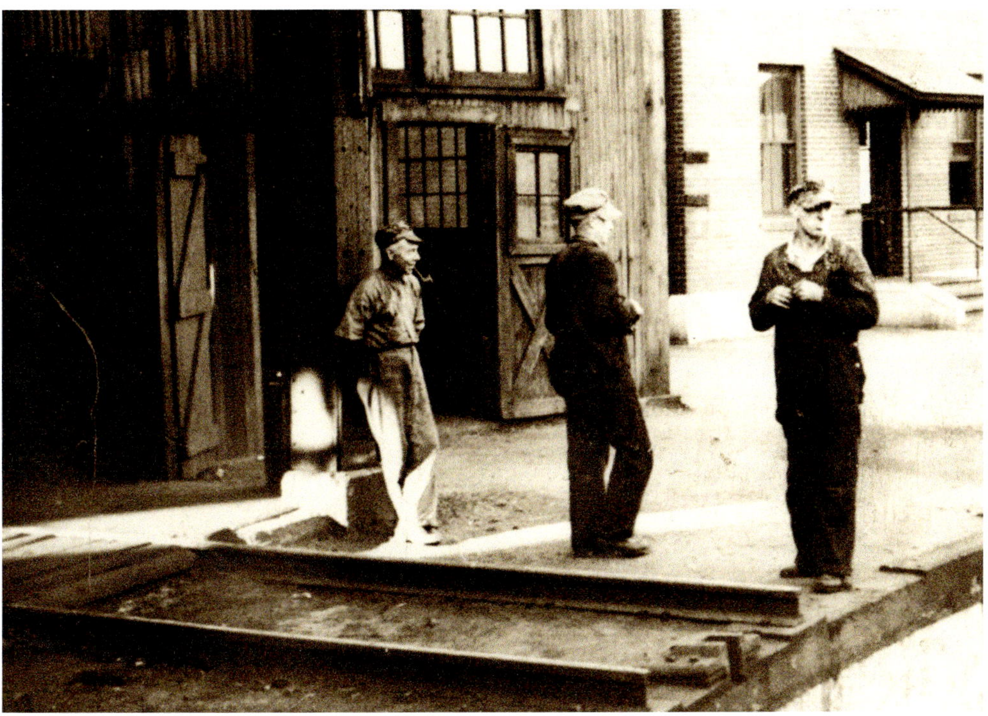

The Engine House at the Packerton Yards, 1939, from a Kline-Snyder family album, likely taken by Ambrose Snyder. (*Kim Graver Steinberger and family*)

tower facing the protesters one afternoon, but the lights were stoned the same night.[24] Workers required police escorts home. Edward Kimler arrived at home to see brown letters spelling out "scab" painted on his house.[25] Charles Smith had three shots fired after him.[26] Ambrose testified that strikers turned spotlights on him as he walked along the street.[27] The judge overseeing an injunction hearing in a "packed" courthouse called it a "cruel war."[28]

The violence went both ways. One striking shop worker, Edward McGinley, "a well-known and popular young man," was shot by the Chief of Police and abandoned to bleed out in the snow.[29] The shooting further inflamed the strikers and their sympathizers. Someone blew up the Beaver Run Dam, "one of the [railroad's] largest water power supplies." According to *The Wilkes-Barre Evening News*, September 7, 1922, "dynamite was used" and "water is pouring from the reservoir." A week later, a former railroad guard named Walter Klein took his own life. He worried so much over leaving his position that his mind became "unbalanced and he suicided with one of the cartridges used by him as a guard."[30]

Elisabeth Zogbaum, Kline's companion during his later years, said that Franz often told stories about one particular close call he experienced during the strike:

> When Franz and his family walked through the house they would duck down below the windows because strikers would throw rocks at the windows. One night, when Franz was in the bathroom, someone hurled a can through the window loaded with dynamite, thinking it was Ambrose's bedroom. Fortunately, the bomb didn't go off and no one was hurt. After this incident, his mother sent the children to sleep at various friends' and neighbors' homes for the next few nights.[31]

Five men were later arrested and charged with conspiracy. In addition to blowing up the dam, they confessed to throwing dynamite at the roundhouse and blowing up a store and several homes.[32] The strike would last deep into the fall and never quite be resolved to everyone's satisfaction.

Despite the social upheaval of the times, Ambrose did his best to make his new children feel at home. In contrast, his own kids—son, Arlington, and two daughters, Maybert and LaTour—did not always have an easy time with their stepmother. Harold Rabenold, a close friend of Franz, said Arlington complained regularly about how his new stepmother never seemed to approve of him. In return, Arlington was brutal to his father.[33] There were times when LaTour lived with relatives outside the home. Maybert, the oldest, became pregnant while unmarried and still in school. She and her stepmother would often squabble about the proper care of the baby, Janny, who became an "unexpected gift of joy."[34]

When not keeping house, Franz's mother often worked outside in the garden. It helped her relieve stress. "She'd sometimes prune her bushes for hours," neighbor Grace Ahner said, "but it never looked like she did a thing."[35] Anne's nocturnal strolls inspired a more mischievous pastime. She became known for combing the streets at night and stealing flowers from other people's yards. It made her neighbors mad, and she was caught a few times.

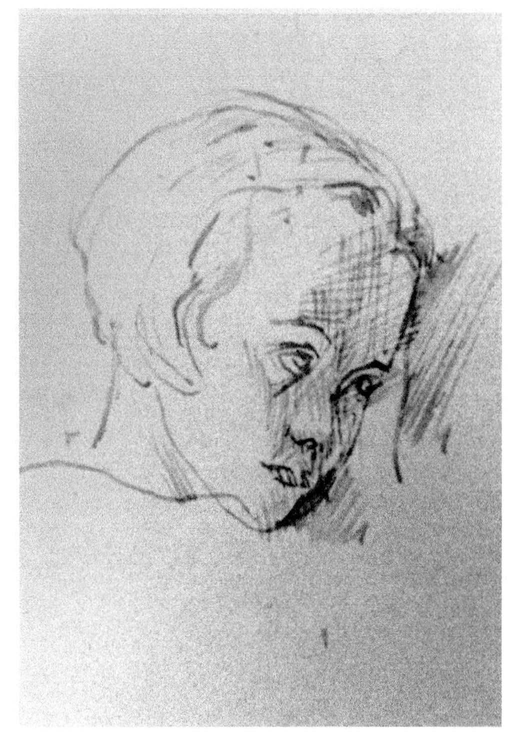

Right: Janny, c. 1935. View 1, "An unexpected gift of joy; like Phoenix rising, she bonded with Louise in a lifelong and deep sisterly love." Dr. Daniel Davies. (*Dr. Louise Kline-Kelly © 2018 Franz Kline Estate/Artists Rights Society (ARS), New York*)

Below left: Janny, View 2. (*Dr. Louise Kline-Kelly, © 2018 Franz Kline Estate/Artists Rights Society (ARS), New York*)

Below right: Janny, View 3. (*Dr. Louise Kline-Kelly © 2018 Franz Kline Estate/Artists Rights Society (ARS), New York*)

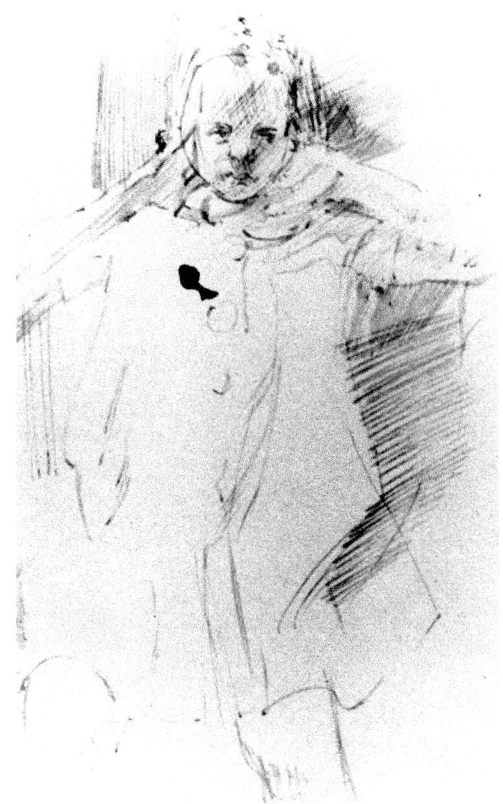

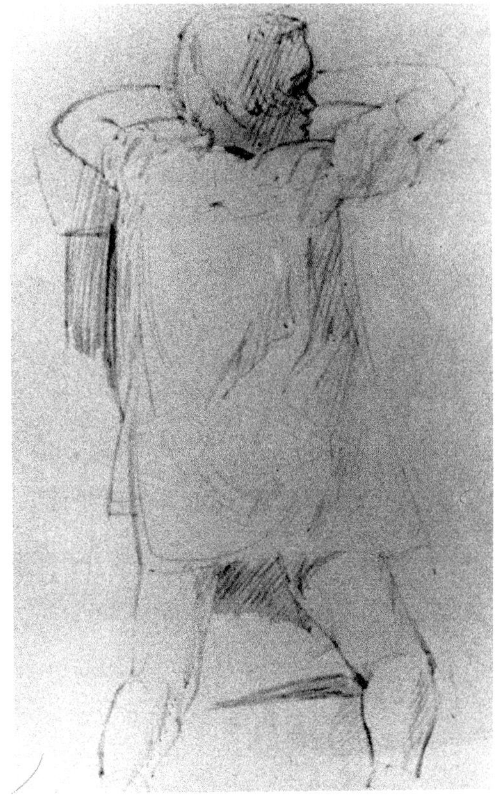

To his credit, Ambrose kept a well-manicured garden. Louise called it "beautiful." She remembered her parents cautioning her to stay away from his flower beds. "Mother loved her shrubbery," she said, "so Father used that as leverage. He would say, 'If I ever catch one of the children in my flower beds, I'll pull your mess out,' meaning her shrubs. But for all his threats, he only did it once."

Anne may have looked the part of upper-class gentry when she walked through town, but inside her home, she was, according to a family friend, an "original Bohemian."[36] While cooking over a hot stove, Anne wore a bandana over her hair and layers of ankle-length aprons and skirts. Marrying Ambrose may have renewed her sense of security, but it also doubled her workload. She now ran a house with up to seven children at any given time. That was a lot of cooking and laundry, and this time without hired help. Adding to her stress, the administration at Girard College repeatedly denied her requests to release Franz. Although her letter campaign did not succeed, her pleas had been apparently so well-written that the headmaster sometimes read them out loud to the students.

During Franz's first summer in Lehighton, his stepbrother introduced him to the other boys in the neighborhood. They called themselves the West End Gang, and Franz played baseball and other street games with them in a vacant lot nearby. One morning, waiting for the rest of the players before a game, Franz fell while climbing a fence and broke his right arm. Louise remembered seeing him in the kitchen, wincing with pain as he waited for the doctor. "It seemed as if a great tragedy had occurred," she said.

Anne insisted on getting the best doctor to set her son's arm, and Franz spent the rest of the summer with a cast. After the doctor returned to remove it, he realized that Franz's arm had healed crookedly.

"Mother was horrified," Louise said. "Dr. Trexler took him out behind the coach house and tried to pull his arm straight."

"It hurt so bad," Franz later told her, "that I slapped him in the face."[37]

"Imagine that young boy!" Louise said. "And that's so unusual for Franz—but if you were being tortured, you'd slap someone too!"

After the doctor's failed attempt, Anne devised her own solution. At the far western end of the fairgrounds was a place they called Ash's Castle. Locals called it Gypsy Hill because it was where the gypsies parked their wagons and set up camp when the county fair was held in town. It was deserted in July when she took Franz there. She told him to hang from a tree branch and allow the weight of his body to help straighten his arm. From that distance, he could scream as loud as he needed.

"That was her therapy," Louise said, "and slowly, the arm began to strengthen and straighten. It was the perfect arm, the one he used to paint."[38]

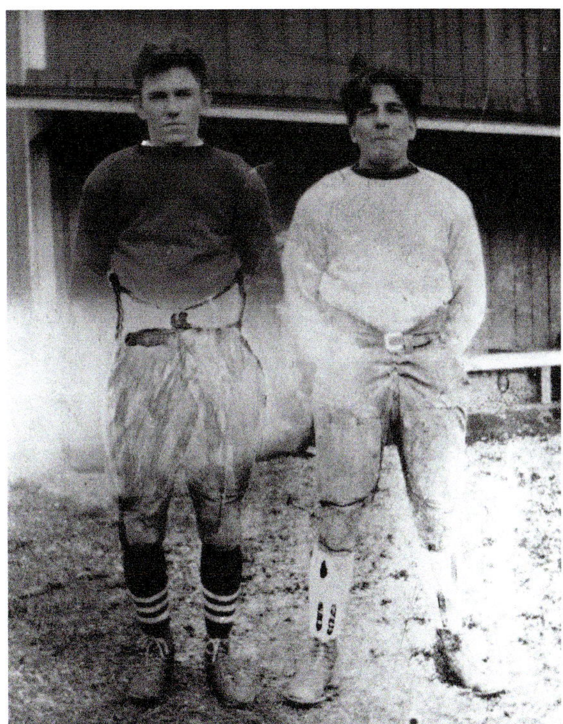

Franz Kline (right) and his step-brother Arlington at the Lehighton fairgrounds in 1927 after football practice. Franz attempted to fix this photo with a pen where it faded. (*Glen Claypool and family*)

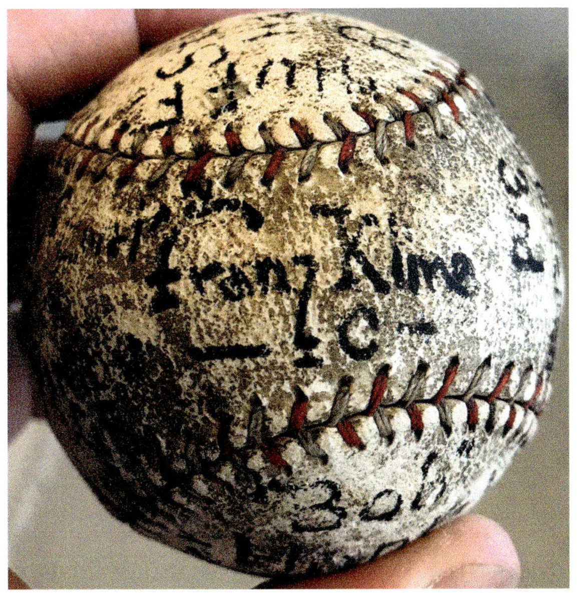

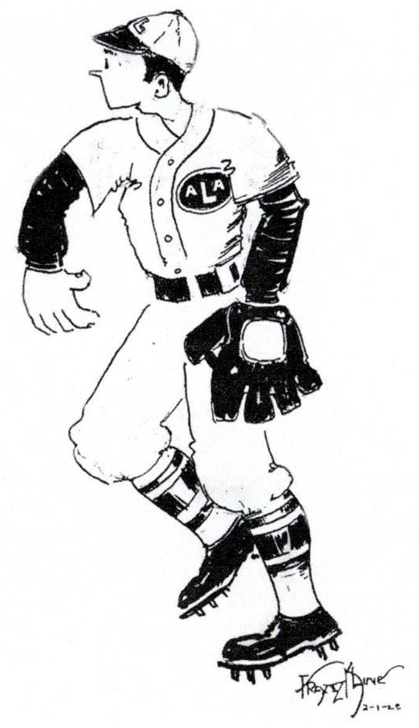

Above left: Game Ball, *c.* 1930, from a Lehighton Indians and Palmerton Blue Bombers baseball game. Lehighton lost the game, 7 to 6, in their sixteenth inning. Kline embellished the ball with the teams, score, and names of players. (*Dr. Gerald and Ellen Zinner © 2018 Franz Kline Estate/Artists Rights Society (ARS), New York*)

Above right: Untitled, Baseball Player, 1929. Kline "moved with an athlete's grace. We all knew the legend, back home in the Coal Country of Pennsylvania he'd played baseball and football." Pete Hamill, Piecework. (*Glen Claypool and family © 2018 Franz Kline Estate/Artists Rights Society (ARS), New York*)

4

Diamond: At his New School, Kline's Popularity Soared

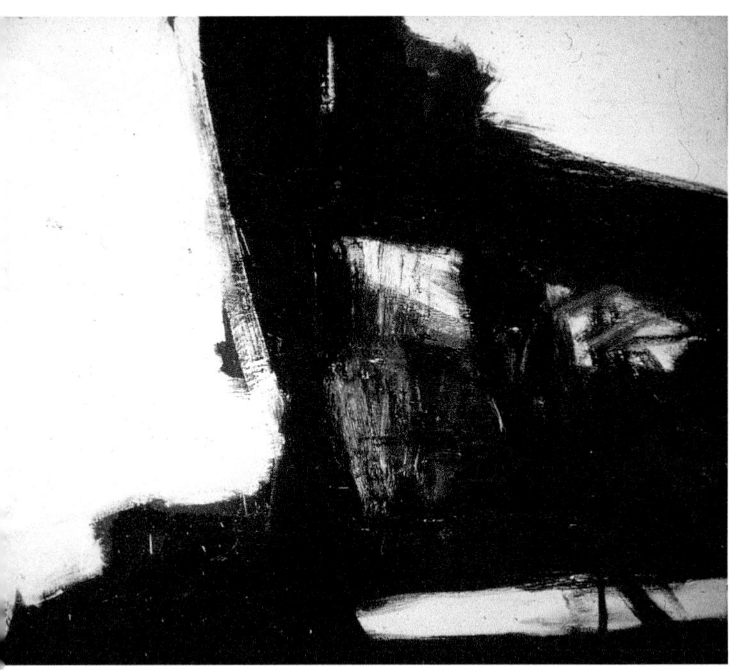

Anne Snyder ruled her roost like a Prussian General. With her iron will, she rode over everyone in the family, except Franz. With him, she turned into a cream puff. He was a superb con. During frequent times of conflict, Franz conveniently disappeared.

Dr. Daniel Davies
Personal correspondence

Diamond, 1960. (*Private Collection © 2018 Franz Kline Estate/Artists Rights Society (ARS), New York*)

Franz had just turned fifteen when he returned to coal country in 1925. His mother had been writing letters to Girard College's President, Cheesman Herrick, for almost five years by then, seeking out a loophole for her son's early release. She finally succeeded three years before Franz's eighteenth birthday. This was no small feat considering the institution's strict rules. Initially, no boy was accepted until their guardians had given, "by indenture, relinquishment, or otherwise power" to the "mayor, aldermen, and citizens of Philadelphia" who were directed to enforce "every proper restraint" to prevent relatives from "interfering with or withdrawing such orphans."[1]

But by Kline's time, there were hundreds of boys on a list waiting for an opening to live and study there. It was such a "privilege" that when every boy turned fifteen, their grades were up for review.[2] When Anne received word of Franz's struggling marks, she decided to use them to her advantage. She knew that one of the best ways to get him released was to secure work for him on a farm, which gave the administrators more reason to release him back to his family. "It was my highest ambition to have Franz graduate from Girard," Anne wrote in her final letter, "but since he has lost his chance, it is up to me to do the next best thing."[3]

Kline's official transcript lists his discharge due to "failure in scholarship."[4]

By the time he finally arrived in Lehighton to stay, Franz had little beyond his clothes. Accustomed to sharing close quarters, he set up his things in a room with three others: his brothers, Fred and Jacques, and their stepbrother, Arlington. Across the hall was Louise's room with Maybert and Latour.

Franz was already familiar with the town and many of its people from summer visits, and his mother took care to help smooth his transition by letting him stay up late, sip tea, and tell stories with friends. She was careful to give him time to shed any "militaristic influences."[5]

Franz began working for Small & Koch's Dairy, a few blocks from his home. His shift began before daybreak, retrieving the heavy metal 10-gallon cans of raw milk from the outer-lying farms and bringing them back in to town on a truck. In fact, his days as a milkman led to his first commercial assignment as a freelance artist when Small & Koch's competitor Fairyland Farms hired him to paint signs.

The signs advertising Fairyland Farms were painted in bold colors on white cardboard with original cartoon characters and freehand lettering. They include a strong man lifting a weight, a plump baby, and a boy on a tricycle. The signs were a hit and led to other commissions, including posters for the changing rooms at Graver's Swimming Pool. Besides collecting a small fee, Franz was given free admission to swim. Word reached business owners in surrounding areas. Even after relocating to Manhattan years later, Franz still returned for many years in September to paint signs for the "Great Lehighton Fair," and he sometimes stuck around to sketch caricatures of fair-goers for coins.

Franz had the run of the neighborhood all summer. One of his best friends was Claire Mosser, a boy who lived close enough to hear Anne and Ambrose bickering when their bedroom windows were open. "After Franz moved to 9th Street, there wasn't a day we weren't together," Mosser said. "Franz was quite something, like Clark Gable, with his hair all slicked back. He was a radical change from what we were used to. He took me to Girard College for Founder's Day and showed me the place where so many of his stories took place."[6]

Franz's playfulness and looks had strong appeal. He had "thick black hair" like his mother and was remembered for his rare combination of confidence, humility, and manners. He seemed to portray a higher level of sophistication than his new classmates, and rumors circulating about his father being a bootlegger murdered in Wilkes-Barre only added to his mystique.

After a while, Franz began to attract an entourage. He was not a large person, nor would he ever be, but it was said that when he entered a room, he filled it, just as later

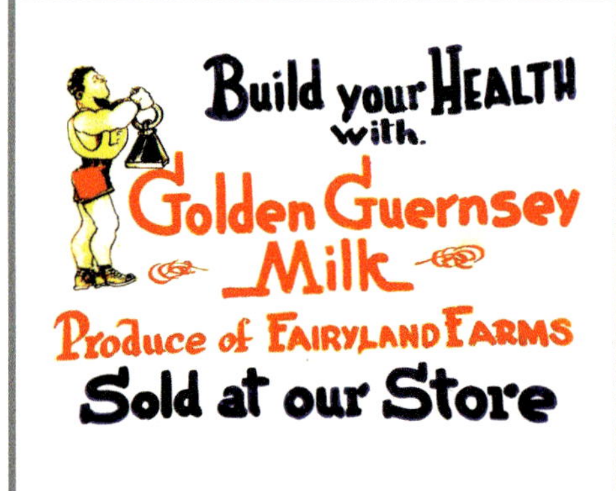

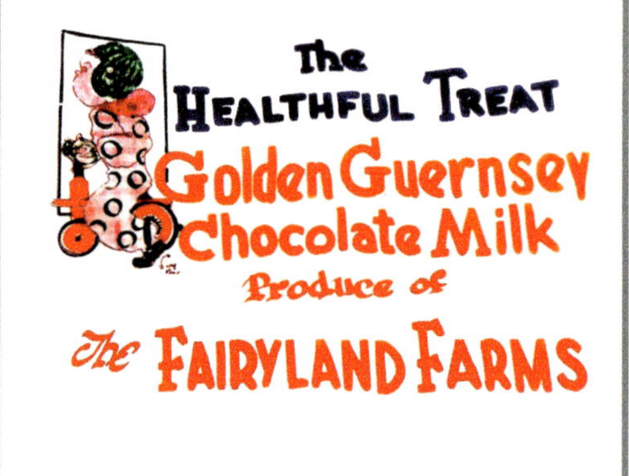

Above left: Build Your Health With Golden Guernsey, 1926. (*Winona Diehl Rifenbary © 2018 Franz Kline Estate/Artists Rights Society (ARS), New York*)

Above right: The Healthful Treat, 1926, proves Kline's artistic skills were well beyond his years, as well as his knack for salesmanship. (*Winona Diehl Rifenbary © 2018 Franz Kline Estate/Artists Rights Society (ARS), New York*)

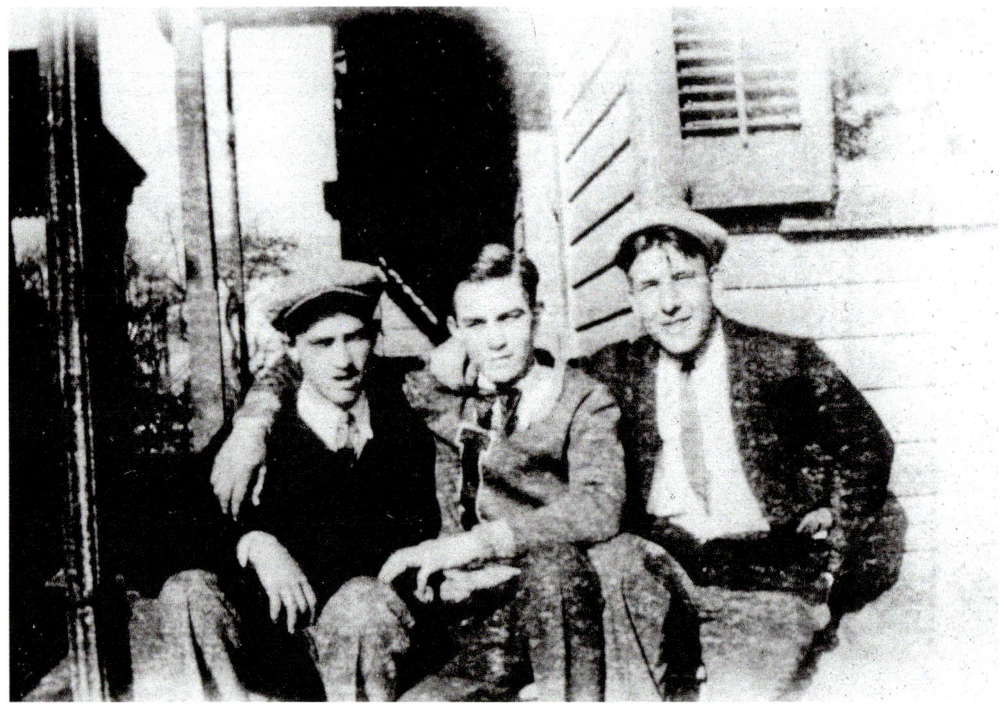

From right to left: Harold Rabenold, Claire Mosser, and Franz Kline in 1925 on 9th Street, Lehighton. (*Harold Rabenold*)

he could fill an entire canvas with a singular stroke.[7] His mother seemed to understand his destiny early on. He had too many gifts and experiences not to outpace mediocrity.

"Franz was of a dark complexion with olive skin and was quite good-looking and well-behaved,"[8] said Sue Hahn. Hahn's mother, a friend of Franz, said that he would sometimes come to her Sunday School class at her Presbyterian Church after his own. "He carried a sketchbook with him," she said, "and drew at random anything that caught his fancy."[9]

Franz resumed his place among the West End Gang, a group of youngsters who ran around the neighborhood between each other's yards. One can only imagine his first night of freedom: the glow of lightning bugs, the incessant chirp of crickets, and the golden dusk illuminating his mother's evening paper just below her line of sight as she pretended to read from her chair on the porch. Aside from basic rules, he was finally free to "Live in Lehighton and Prosper" as the town's welcome signs proclaimed. The slogan was fitting. Aside from embodying the optimistic attitude of the times, Lehighton did offer more opportunities than towns deeper into coal country. Along with neighboring Mauch Chunk (now called Jim Thorpe), they were hubs of local culture and activity.

Native Americans known as Leni Lenape or "original people" first inhabited the area. It became the sight of an early Moravian mission, Gnadenhütten, and at one time in the eighteenth century, Lehighton was the farthest point on the Pennsylvania frontier that a settler could legally stake a claim. It was the western border of a disputed treaty known as The Walking Purchase. The Moravians, funded by the Saxon Count Nicolaus Zinzendorf, sought to save the "heathens" by introducing them to the teachings of Jesus.[10] They established a camp on the banks of the Lehigh River in 1746. Nine years later, the Moravian settlement was a thriving forest enterprise with hundreds of Indian converts, until tragedy struck one winter evening and most of the Moravians were massacred. Survivors scattered into the forests. One Moravian who got away later told how she escaped by hiding inside a hollow tree aside the freezing river.[11] The Indian warriors felt cheated by the treaty.[12] To them, the Walking Purchase was a naked land grab. The men hired by the white lawyers to execute its terms—allowing for the whites to have as much land as a person could walk in a day and a half—were the fastest runners they could find.[13] To this day, traces of Native American heritage—arrowheads and other artifacts—are found in freshly plowed fields.

There was little danger of being massacred in Lehighton during Kline's day. Many townsfolk did not lock their doors. Some did not even own keys to their homes. When workers for the railroad were not on strike, it was an idyllic place where everyone knew most everything about everyone else. Worst case scenarios might be getting lost in the woods or venturing too close to the top of a slippery waterfall. Even the tramps who hopped trains and camped along the flat rocks by the river posed little perceivable threat as they wandered around seeking handouts. For an especially fine meal, one might exchange a hobo nickel.

In some ways, Franz's new home resembled his old one in Wilkes-Barre after his mother hired workers from Isaac Long's department store to renovate the house a second time, including new wallpaper. Louise remembered that she chose nursery rhyme characters of Jack and Jill tumbling down a hill for the girls' room.

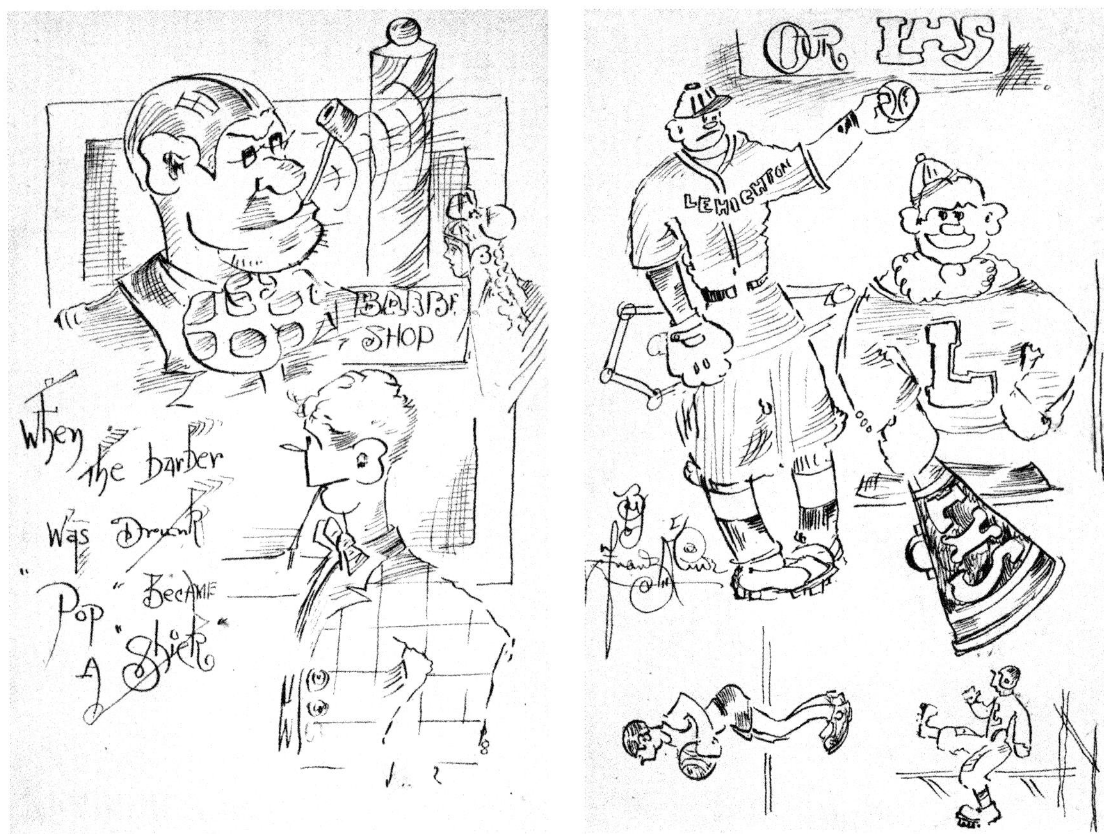

Above left: When the Barber was Drunk, Pop became a Sheik, 1928. Kline's astute drawing skills and wit in another Lehighton friend's autograph book. (*Mr. & Mrs. Curtis Eberts © 2018 Franz Kline Estate/Artists Rights Society (ARS), New York*)

Above right: Our LHS, 1928. A sports-themed autograph book sketch by Kline for a school friend. (*Mr. & Mrs. Curtis Eberts © 2018 Franz Kline Estate/Artists Rights Society (ARS), New York*)

The house had two staircases: one open in the front through double doors and a second in the back behind the kitchen. Downstairs included a large living room, dining room, and a music room offset by French doors. There, Anne added a colonial fireplace.

The back door led into the kitchen, small pantry, and laundry room. There were three porches, one in the front, back, and an upstairs balcony. Looking at the house from the side, Louise recalled Franz once telling her that all three porches figure prominently in his painting *C & O*.[14]

Kline's school records indicate that he enrolled in eighth grade in 1926. While most students his age were in tenth grade, he was placed two years behind them because his mother wanted to make sure that he received a solid academic footing. Unlike today's

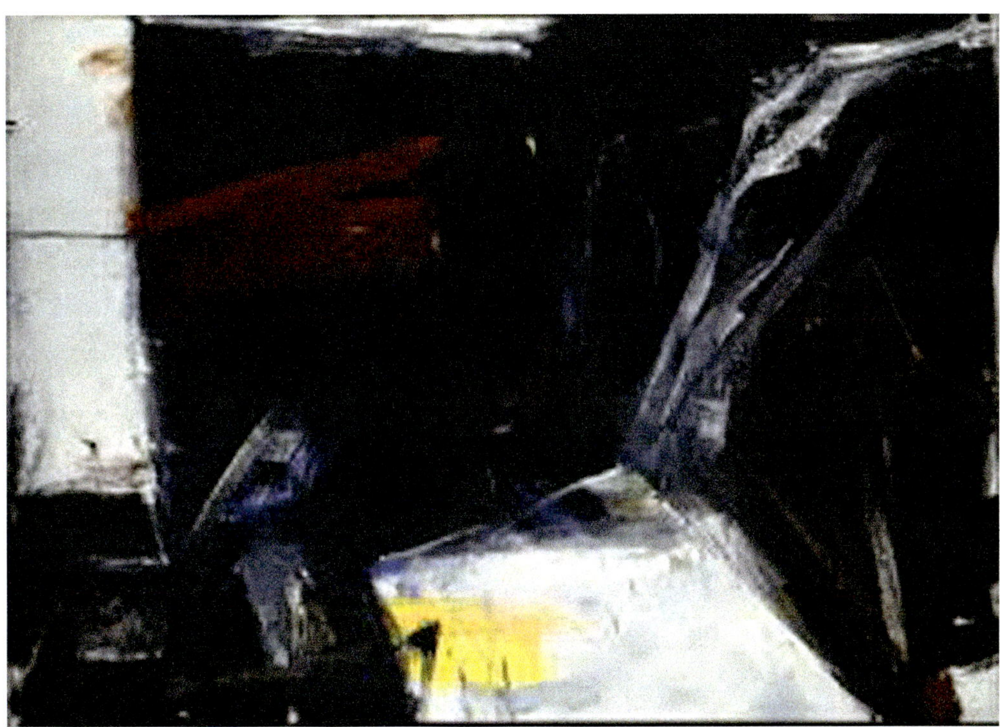

C & O, 1958. (*National Gallery of Art © 2018 Franz Kline Estate/Artists Rights Society (ARS), New York*)

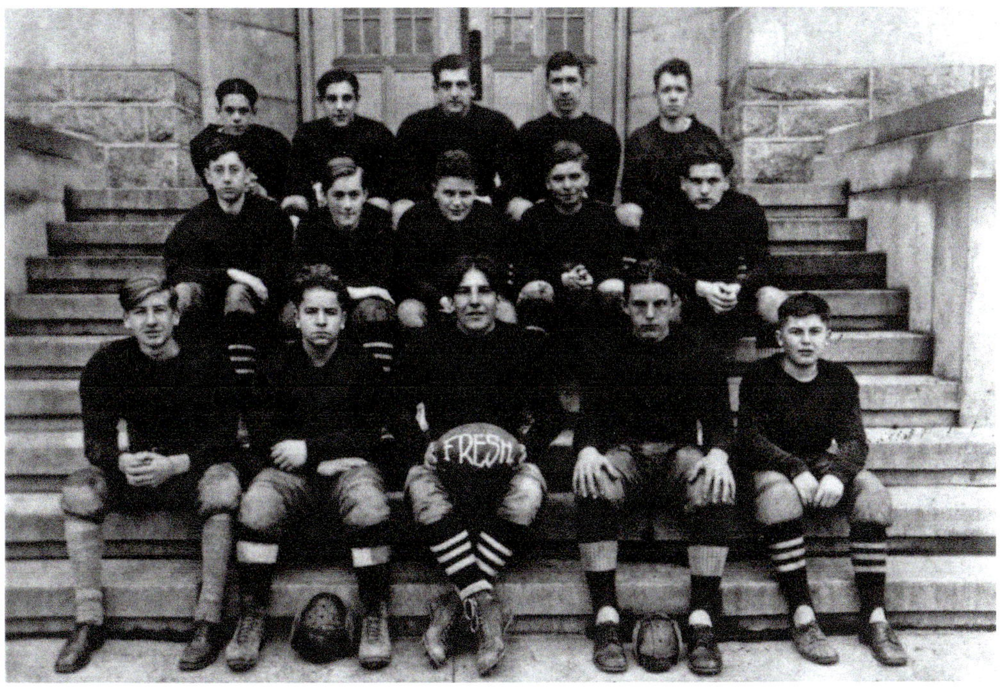

Lehighton High School Freshman Football Team, 1929. Kline is in the first row, center. Stanley Harleman sits to his left. Right behind Harleman is Claire Mosser. (*Mr. And Mrs. Gordon Hontz*)

rules, Kline's age did not interfere with his participation in sports. As his first year approached, Franz began football practice. It also intensified the ongoing adventure of pursuing girls, something he never experienced at the school for fatherless boys. He indulged in stylish clothes at every opportunity, and like most fifteen-year-olds, he did not want to share them with his brothers.

"The boys didn't have real nice clothes. Many times, the Kline brothers would fight over who would wear the nicer things," Grace Ahner, Kline's neighbor, said, continuing, "Once Franz was looking for a particular outfit to wear on a date and couldn't find it. Suspecting his brother had it, he tracked Jacques down at the park, grabbed him, and made him go into the alley and change right there, having brought some older clothes for him."[15]

On summer days, Franz and his friends tramped about the countryside, camping or splashing around in one of the many swimming holes. Sometimes Louise or Fred would tag along.

"Franz loved camping and going to the pool with my brothers. He could swim underwater for miles," Louise said. "I remember he always said to me, 'Put your legs apart and let me swim between them.' So many times I thought I was drowning because he always tipped me over."[16]

One popular hike was to the Bake Oven Knob, a mountain lookout with a view of both the Mahoning and Lehigh Valleys. The trail Kline took to get there was later absorbed into the Appalachian Trail. Another led to a place known as the Deer Pen, a kind of game preserve with a high fence. Children loved to watch the domesticated deer run around the rye fields inside as if on display at a zoo.

After crossing over the railroad trestle into Weissport, the boys sometimes hiked along the banks of the old canal. Newspaper columnist Samuel Wehr wrote: "It was easy to spend an entire morning and afternoon exploring the old boatyard filled with the half-sunken hulls of old coal barges, which were once pulled by mules from the switchback coal chute in Mauch Chunk."[17]

The station for the Lehigh Valley Railroad was on "the flats" below First Street. The Central New Jersey line station was up the hill, about a block away. A person could board for passenger service to Philadelphia or New York and from there the tracks were connected to destinations all over the country. To his family's good fortune, Ambrose's job allowed free passes for them to travel anywhere in Pennsylvania free of charge.

Second only to the mines, the railroad provided many jobs. Migrant laborers filled the boarding houses and hotels. "Even when the depression was going on around us," Randolph Rabenold, author Rebecca's father, said, "it didn't seem like Lehighton was as affected as other towns because of the railroad."

Between the tracks and the river was a baseball diamond called Riverside Park. The high school teams played and practiced there. Within sight of the field, the arrival and departure of trains was a daily part of life's social fabric. Many youngsters idolized the steam engines, in particular *Chief* and *The Black Diamond Express*. The magic of the latter was captured in two short films made by Thomas Edison. He had been seduced by the engine's awesome power decades earlier. Men wave white handkerchiefs to warn the hammer-wielding workers to step off the tracks as the locomotives approached. Because the film is silent, the

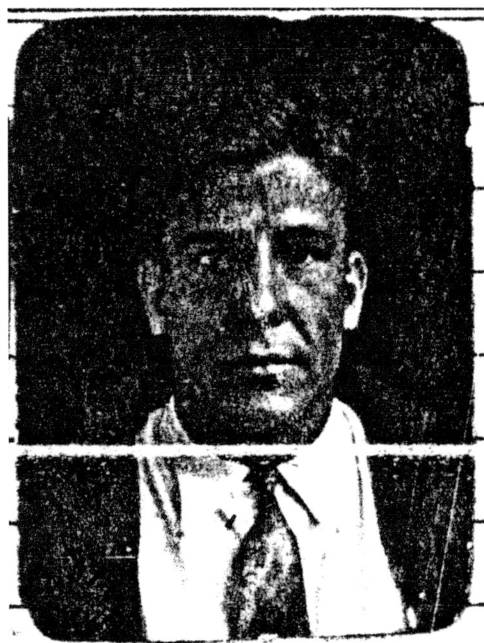

School photo of Franz Kline, 1929–1930, Lehighton High School.

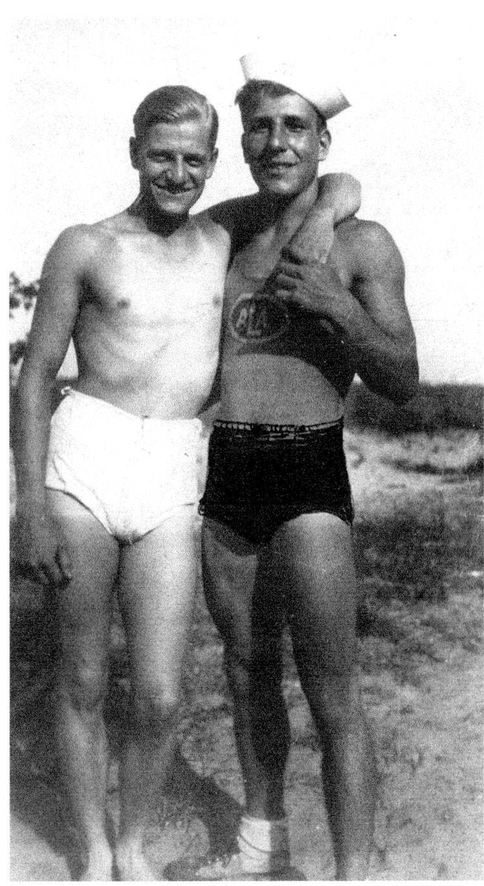

Classmate Harry Febich (left) with Franz Kline in 1929. (*Henry Bretney*)

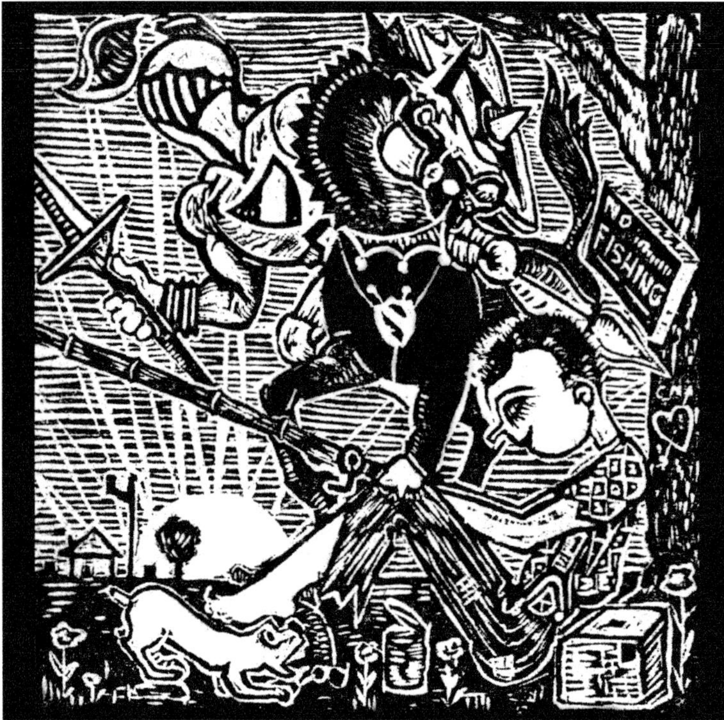

If I Were King, April 28, 1931, *The Leni Lenapian*. "Aspects are within us, and who seems most kingly is the King." Franz Kline's high school personality resonated with Thomas Hardy's words as his popularity soared.

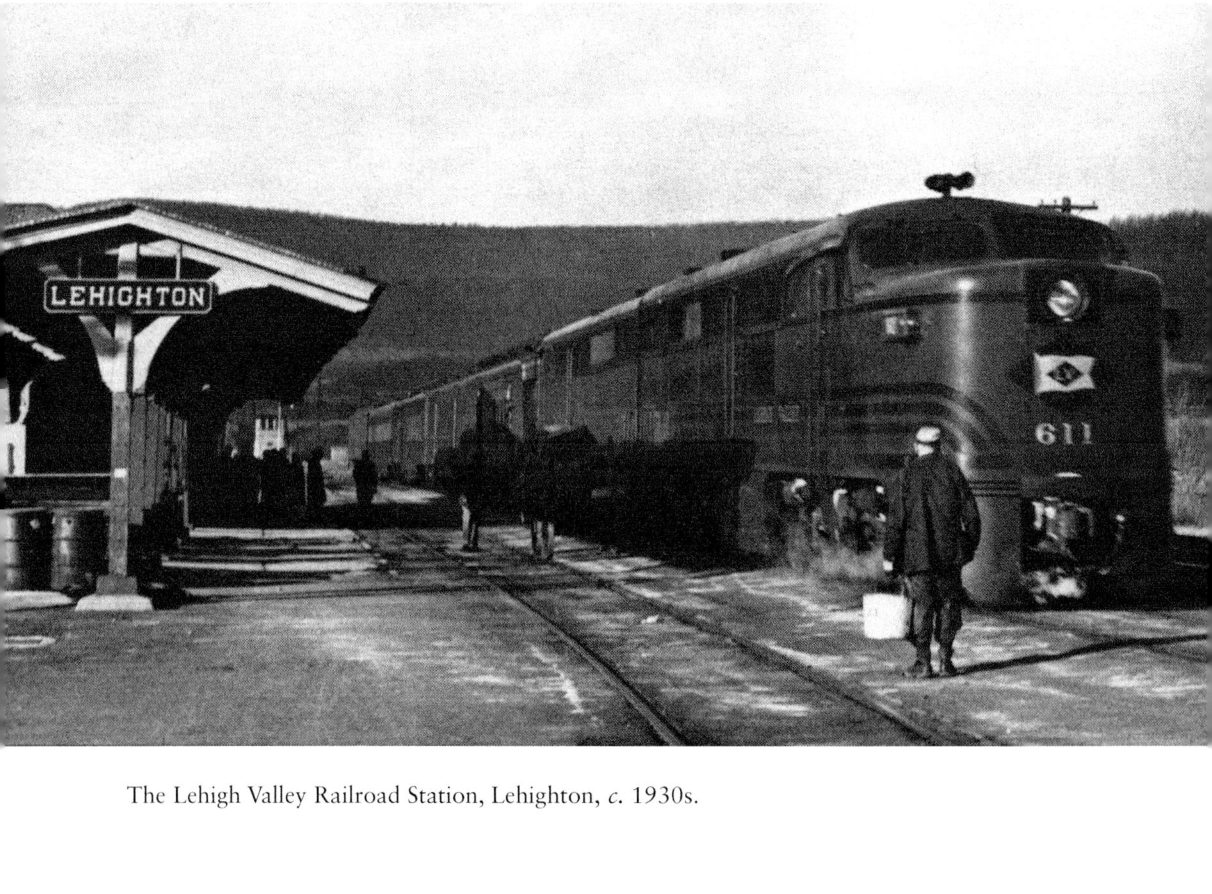

The Lehigh Valley Railroad Station, Lehighton, *c.* 1930s.

wail of its whistle is absent, but during Franz's youth, its high-pitched sound could be heard from miles around, and its signature black cloud could be seen hovering in the air long after it roared on. Awed by the power of trains, Franz often sat high on a bank above the tracks, sketching, the ground rumbling as the cars sped past.

A short walk from the stations led to a bustling downtown. First Street had become a stylish avenue with a variety of stores and other businesses, the place to socialize and catch up on news. The most popular hangout for high-schoolers was Pop Gillen's soda parlor. On South First Street, a jeweler advertised "inspection service" for railroad watches. There was Kennell's Bakery and Cohen's Department Store. Local merchants had everything most residents needed, but, if necessary, the city of Allentown was only 27 miles away, just under an hour by train.

"When Franz couldn't find a suit that would fit him for his Junior dance, Mother said, 'Alright, Franz, then go to Allentown.' And Franz came home with a dark green suit and he loved it," Louise said. "That color shocked everybody because everyone wore black and brown, *not green*! But he loved that suit and didn't care what anyone else thought. He marched to the beat of a different drummer."[18]

Many of the variety of businesses in Lehighton are depicted on Kline's mural of the area commissioned by the American Legion in 1945. Hotel Lehighton and the Carbon House are unmistakable. A trolley then traveled the length of town, its circuitous route ran past Obert Meat Packing, Krueger Shoe Repair, and a moving-picture house called The Lyric where one could watch a Will Rogers double-feature for 5 cents. The grassy hill where Franz played football with the "Park Ponies," a group of boys who practiced there during the off season, still exists as a park today.

During summer nights, Anne continued to give Franz free reign of her kitchen. If she had not let him bring his friends inside after dark, she knew they would only sit outside on the curb, talking, until she was forced to yell out, "if you don't come in, it will soon be morning."

From her bed upstairs, Louise often heard Franz and his friends in the kitchen, their muffled laughter punctuated by the whistle of the teapot as the rest of her family did their best to fall asleep. "They drank gallons of tea and used pounds of butter for cinnamon toast with the kettle going until 3 or 4 in the morning," Louise said. "When Mother got up, she would have to buy groceries again, because all the oranges, Shredded Wheat, and everything else would be gone."

During these late sessions, Franz amused his friends with stories while he sketched them. One of his football teammates, Gordon Hontz, remembered modeling for him. "During the evening we played a lot of pinochle, but if there was an odd number of players, Franz would take you into the other room and sketch you from the waist up," Hontz said. "It took about 10 minutes. Then, he'd throw the drawings aside and tell you to take them if you wanted."

During moments alone, Franz sometimes drew his own hands. "We had many tablets in our attic with his drawings of hands in them, marvelous hands. One summer, all he sketched with a pencil were hands holding things like keys," Louise said. "I also remember a drawing of a horse underneath an arc light. But mother threw all those tablets out when she cleaned the attic."

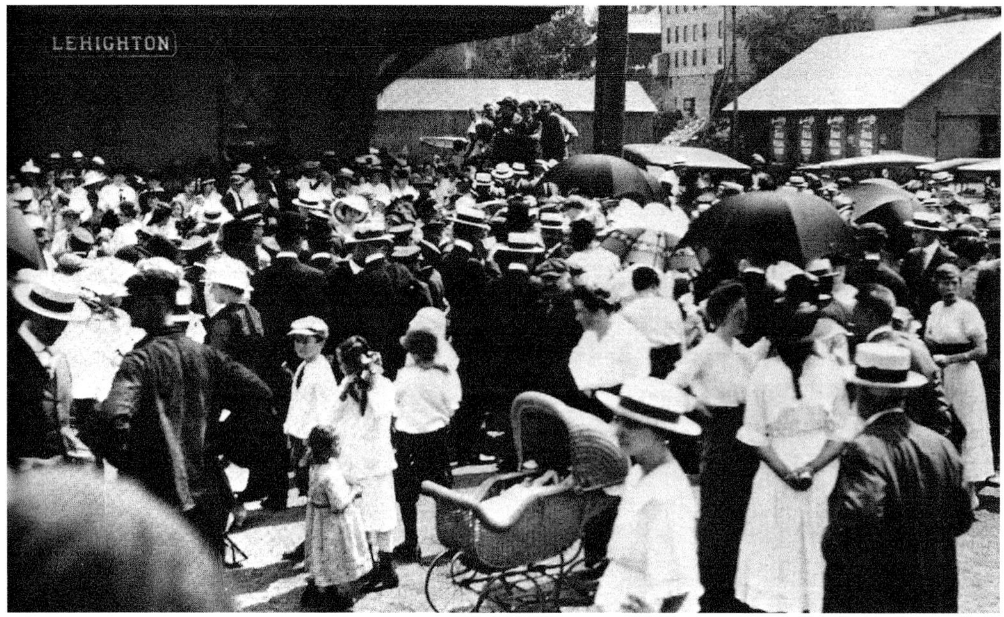

Arrivals and departures made for bustling crowds at the L.V.R.R. station, *c.* 1930s.

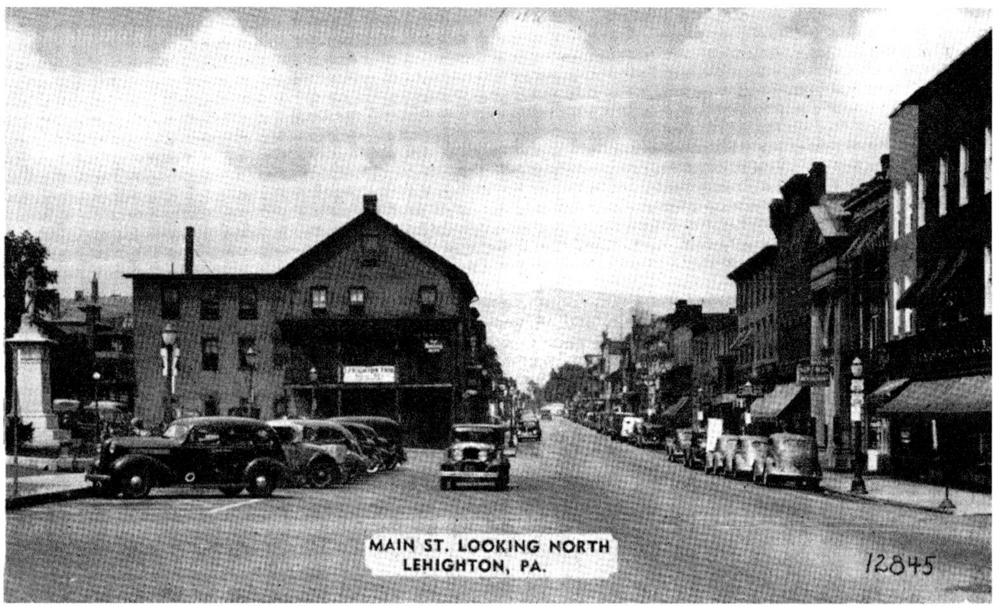

First Street in Lehighton in the 1920s.

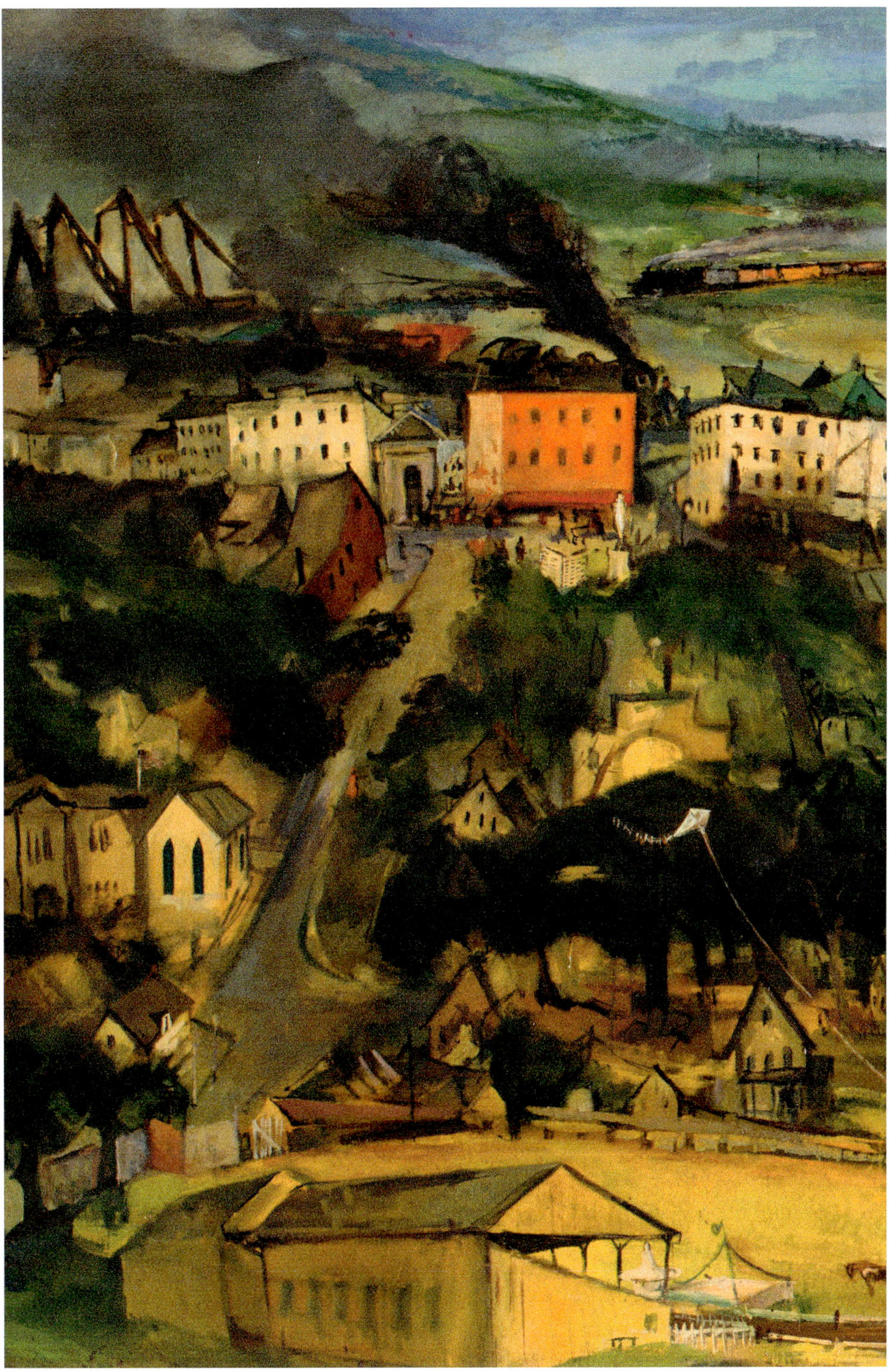

Detail, *Lehighton mural*, 1945, depicts the railroad trestle and two trains, *Black Diamond* and *Chief*. This also shows the Carbon House, Hotel Lehighton, the high school, bandshell in the park, and grandstand at the fairgrounds. (*Joshua Finsel/Lehighton Legion Post #314 © 2018 Franz Kline Estate/Artists Rights Society (ARS), New York*)

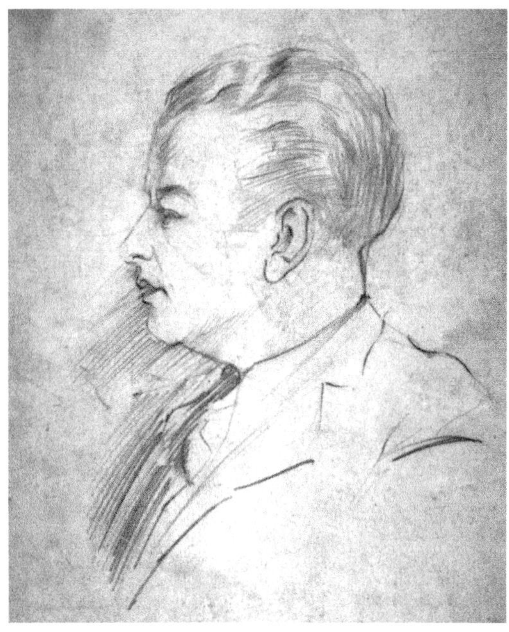

Stanley Harleman, sketch, *c.* 1930. From B.U., Kline wrote to a friend back home, "Dear Marie ... Stump is the nicest guy in town. The most clean-cut friend I have. Be his friend, will ya?" (*Mrs. Stanley Harleman and family © 2018 Franz Kline Estate/ Artists Rights Society (ARS), New York*)

At one point, Kline was inundated with requests to paint cartoon characters like Barney Google, Happy Hooligan, and Harold Teen on the back of other kids' rain-slickers. One young boy named Reds delivered newspapers to their house, and the Snyder-Kline home was near the end of his route. One day, he wore his little yellow rain slicker even though "there wasn't a cloud in the sky," remembered Louise. "Mother said, 'Don't bring him in here, it's suppertime, have him come back later.' But Franz said, 'No, Mother, I promised him. I'm going to paint it right now, he's come too far.' So Franz drew his favorite cartoon, Krazy Kat, and the boy was beaming from ear to ear."

Often absent from the dinner table was Ambrose, whose evening shift lasted from 3–11 p.m. On the evenings Franz ventured off to visit friends in the outlying areas, he often risked breaking curfew, since his mother's rule required everyone be home before their father. "He would walk many, many miles to visit a girl he was interested in," said Elisabeth Zogbaum, and some nights he would have to hustle to get home. [19]

"If Franz and Fred were not in before Ambrose got home from work, there would be all kinds of yelling going on," said Harold Rabenold.[20] Punishments were severe, but not all of Franz's late-night excursions brought retribution. At heart, Ambrose was a fair and honest man. He could be indulgent with Franz when what kept him out late was unavoidable, like this incident preserved in *The Leni Lenapian,* the Lehighton High School newspaper:

> The Lettermen of the Lehigh Valley Interscholastic League banquet was held at the Americus Hotel in Allentown. The Lettermen were entertained during the banquet by the Melody Girls Orchestra. Franz Kline, Granville Buck, and Stanley Harleman were unfortunate enough to be left behind in Allentown after the Lettermen's banquet last Monday. Franz, Bucky, and Stump had a nice time walking home from Allentown. They arrived in time to eat breakfast and get ready for school.[21]

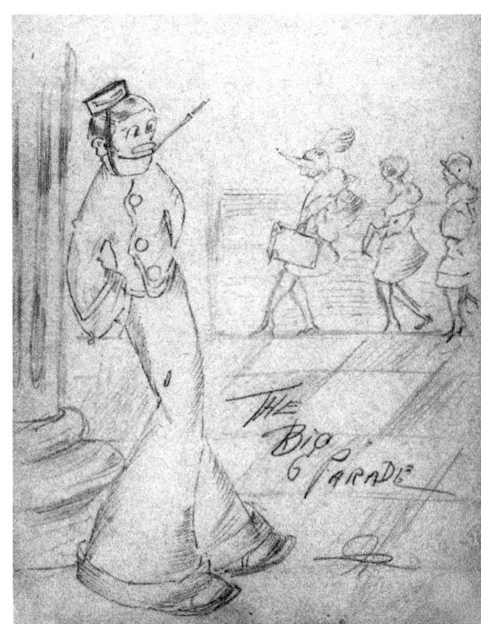

The Big Parade, 1930. A bellboy notices three stealthy women in the far distance of a classmate's autograph book. (*William Bittner © 2018 Franz Kline Estate/Artists Rights Society (ARS), New York*)

His mother knew Franz was popular with many of the "Dutch girls," as he referred to them in his letters, and Anne was not naïve when it came to the dangers of teenage sex. Her own stepdaughter's teen pregnancy was a steady reminder. To distract her son's libido, Anne encouraged Franz to go camping on weekends to avoid the girls.

"Marjorie Peters would park her car in front of our house and honk at all hours," Louise said. "So mother would have Franz pack and go to Lake Harmony or Delaware Gap with friends. But even while camping, he still found ways to create. He once painted an entire side of his tent with the head of an Indian, our school mascot."

With Franz in Lehighton, Anne's family was closer to being whole again. All of her children were back, on the college track, and relatively undamaged. In a letter Franz wrote to the President of Girard, he even praised its influence on his life:

> It surely enthuses me to hear you are really interested in me, knowing you have so many boys to care for. I wish I were still one of them, but I think mother did the right thing when she took me out of Girard's Tech School and placed me in High School up here. I often think of all Girard has done for me and of all the wonderful times I experienced while there. Although I am not a graduate of Girard, I surely enjoy my visits on Founder's Day. I haven't missed one yet.[22]

Gently ensconced in his room in Lehighton and ready to fall asleep, Franz listened to the train whistles fading away as they sped past the outskirts of town. The sheer power of the engines, the massive girders of their trestles, and the great tension of the bridges would all become leitmotivs in Kline's later works.

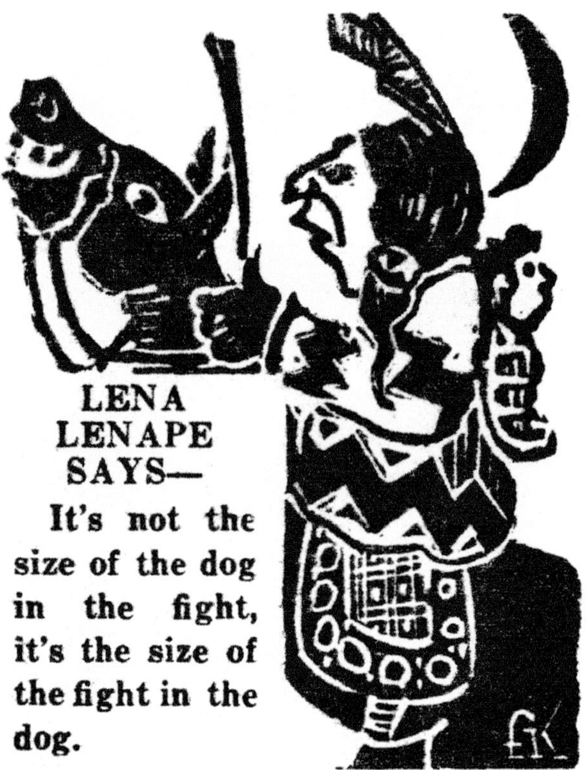

Left: Lena Lenape Says, 1930. A recurring *Leni* cartoon. The Native American imparted his wisdom, such as "It's not the size of the dog in the fight, it's the size of the fight in the dog," to L.A.H.S. students. (*© 2018 Franz Kline Estate/ Artists Rights Society (ARS), New York*)

Below: Lehighton–Weissport Bridge, *c.* 1920s, connects the two towns divided by the Lehigh River. "Steel girders riveted together fascinated Franz," remembered Dr. Harold Frendt. He and Kline worked together one summer for the L.V.R.R.

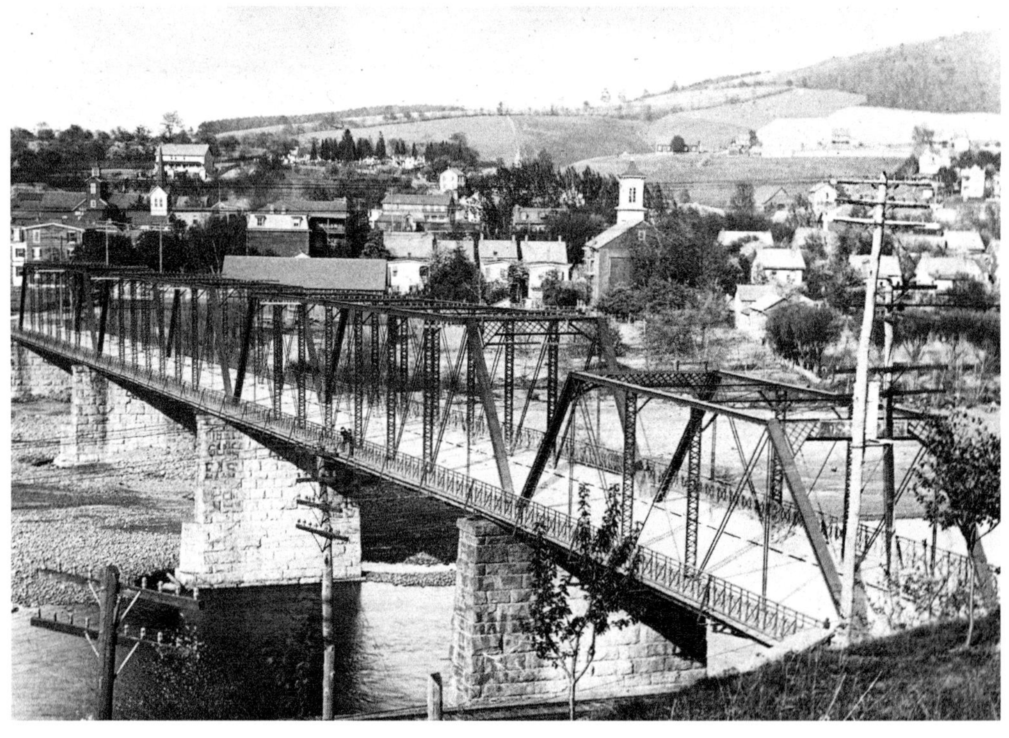

5

Mahoning: Franz Learned How to Hustle his Art Early On

[Kline's] signature looks like a train. Sense of power, motion, identity and emotion; mountains and valleys of Pennsylvania and childhood.

Fielding Dawson
An Emotional Memoir of Franz Kline

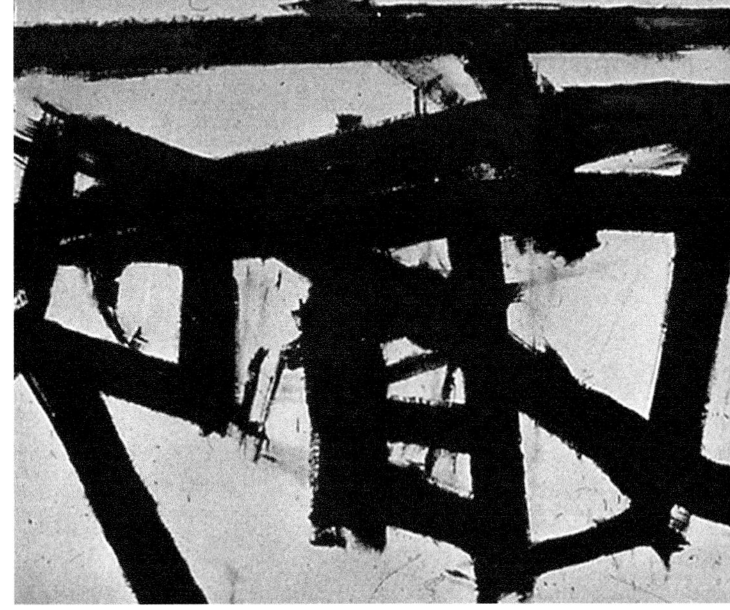

Mahoning, 1956. (*Whitney Museum of American Art © 2018 Franz Kline Estate/Artists Rights Society (ARS), New York*)

In 1956, Kline painted *Mahoning*, a piece that the Whitney Museum calls "a monumental armature."[1] If it contained a kind of ammunition for him, a resonance, a tension worth encapsulating in subtle layers of paint, it is worth noting that Franz created it decades after leaving the land for which it is named, although he often returned to its sanctuary.

Over 175 years earlier, when the first white missionaries arrived at the bend in the river later known as Lehighton, they encountered Native Americans from the Leni Lenape tribe who referred to the area as such. It meant "the place of salt licks," a spot where animals came to sip nutrients from the earth.[2] It was excellent hunting ground, and because the mineral deposits were often near spring water, Mahoning also came to mean "flowing stream."[3]

When Kline arrived to live in Lehighton permanently in 1925, both descriptions of Mahoning remained apt. Franz spent some of the most vital and fluid years of his life swimming in the same rivers and streams, camping in adjacent forests, and immersing himself in their natural restorative powers, and he never forgot the area, nor, while telling jokes to his friends in New York, did he ever seem to stop talking about it. Fielding Dawson, one of Kline's students at Black Mountain College who followed his teacher to Manhattan from North Carolina, mentions this fact in his *An Emotional Memoir of Franz Kline*. Others have echoed it too, including Grace Hartigan and Elaine de Kooning. Something inside Franz always seemed to long for the green, rolling hills of home.[4]

Beyond the natural beauty of the area, Kline's nostalgia also stemmed from the people he encountered there. As he continued to saturate himself in Lehighton life, his popularity soared among the locals. According to his sister, Louise, the attention was not something her brother ever sought, nor completely understood. Kline's companion later in life, Elisabeth Zogbaum, confirmed how easily he adapted to fame. "He was treated like a celebrity in Lehighton because of his athletic, storytelling, and artistic abilities," she said. "Always the center of attention, he never tried to be ... he suffered fools gladly."[5]

Lehighton High School was located on Third Street, about seven blocks away from Kline's home. The imposing stone structure stood on the former site of a frontier school made of logs. Neighboring on the south was the First Presbyterian Church, and to the north, a boarding house for teachers. The Kline children walked to school along Mahoning Street, a wide boulevard with stately brick and stucco houses, one of the main thoroughfares through town. It took about twenty minutes, depending on if it rained or snowed. Once in a while, someone like teacher "Callie" Niehoff would offer them a ride in his yellow convertible. The school, built in 1918, only seven years before Franz attended, remains an imposing stone structure. The words "Boys" and "Girls" are chiseled above gender-segregated entrances. Teachers walked up a flight of granite stairs to a pair of massive oak doors, and to anyone watching from outside, they appeared to be walking straight into the castle's mouth.

"When the Klines came to Lehighton in the early 1920s," classmate Alvirda Arner said, "a lot of teachers treated them differently, especially Franz, because they were different, entirely different."[6]

After entering inside, a student had two choices: stairs leading up or down. The stairs leading down led to the Industrial Arts and Home Economics classrooms, as well as the gym and locker rooms. The male and female halls met on either side of a cavernous gymnasium surrounded by concrete bleachers.

The stairs leading up, taking the first exit, and walking the length of the locker-lined hall led to Miss Hazel Stauffer's Art Room. Miss Stauffer, Kline's art teacher in Lehighton, was staunch and serious. Her lessons catered toward handicrafts, painting and drawing, and students decorated flower pots and bottles and made masks. They also experimented with oil paints, charcoal, and pen and ink. Franz excelled enough for Miss Stauffer to single him, and one other classmate, Joe Strohl, out. She encouraged Kline and Strohl to enter a contest sponsored by the Bayer Paint Store. Strohl, a well-regarded Lehighton artist in his own right, later wrote:

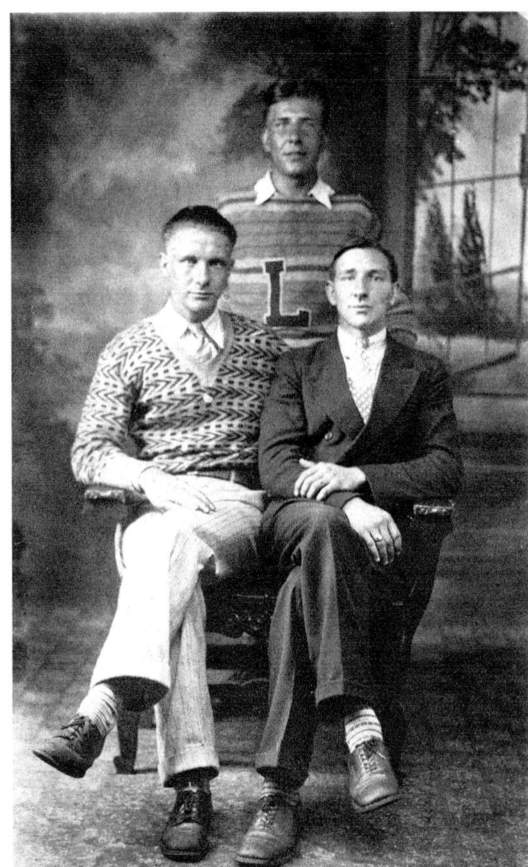

Right: Franz Kline (rear) wearing his letterman's sweater, with Portz and Henry Bretney, a photograph from Citizen's Military Training Camp, 1929. (*Henry Bretney*)

Below: Mahoning Street, Looking West, Lehighton, 1920s. A main street for walking or motoring to school, church, or shopping downtown.

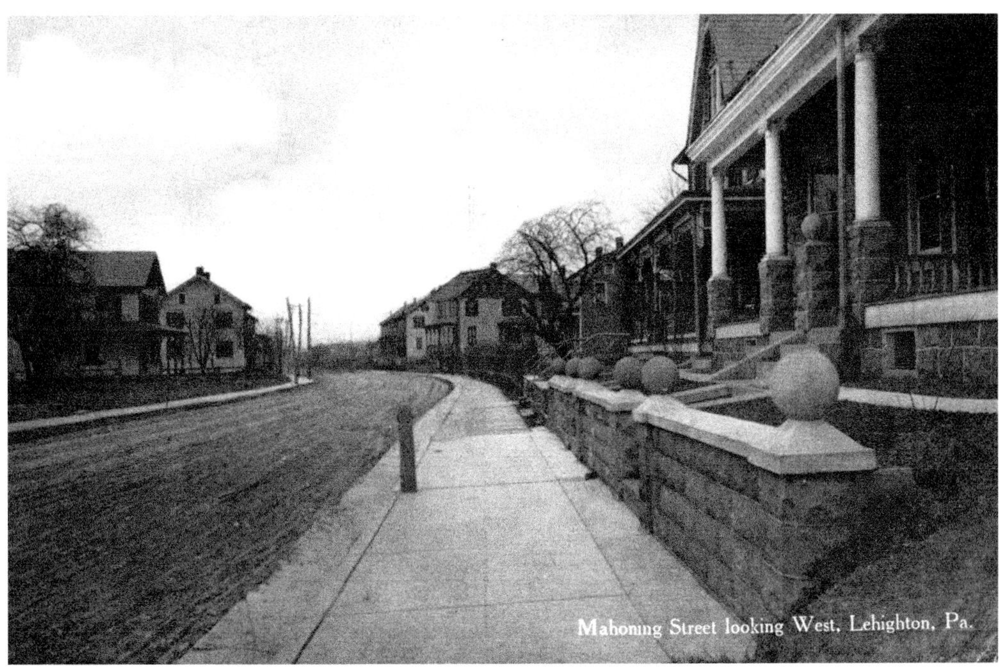

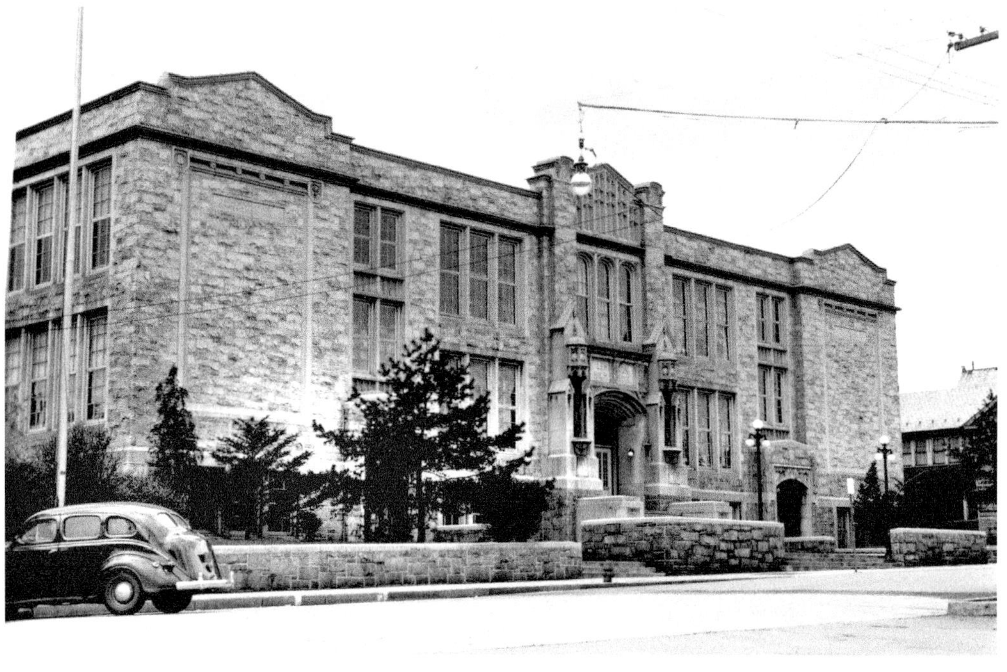

Above: Lehighton High School, *c.* 1930s.

Left: Lehighton High School Library Bookplate, 1931, "A cartoon, drawn by Franz Kline '31, a student at the Boston Art School, will be placed in the fronts of books belonging to the high school library as a mark of identification. The Indian design on this cartoon represents the wealth of Indian lore found in the region around Lehighton." *The Leni Lenapian*. (© *2018 Franz Kline Estate/Artists Rights Society (ARS), New York*)

> Both Franz and myself entered the art contest, and we both won a Devoe watercolor paint-set. Franz's painting was of an Indian with a canoe on his back crossing a stream. He painted a lot at that time, mostly signs for pocket money, including some for the used-car dealers in town. Years later, when he was living in New York, Franz would still come back to the Lehighton Fair to make money, and I talked with him there. He was a happy man, happy in what he was doing.[7]

His second year, in ninth grade, Franz's schedule included "Manual Training" or Industrial Arts, a.k.a. Shop. There in the all-male class in the bowels of the school, amid the drafting tables and heavy machinery used to shape metal and wood, Franz began to cultivate an easy relationship with his teacher, Fred "Pop" Henderson.

Pop's Shop, a favorite of many boys, would become a kind of refuge for Kline. Mr. Henderson was generous with his time, and he often helped make props for school plays, special events, or exhibitions. The school newspaper, *The Leni Lenapian,* often praised his help painting or sewing costumes. His classroom, despite being in the basement, had a row of long windows on one side allowing in plenty of natural light. Kline fashioned many things in shop that he later gave away as gifts, including a pair of Art Deco bookends. Like his teacher, Franz helped construct props, sometimes staying late after school to finish up. For one classmate, Alvirda Arner, he made "a two-foot high smoking stand on which he painted a Joe College cartoon."[8] Originally conceived by illustrator John Held, Jr., the Joe College character's signature round head and square nose adorned covers of *Life* magazine at the time. Using a jigsaw, Franz cut around Held's signature shape, and later painted on the character's face.

Louise, his sister, described another prop, a long plywood razor that her brother fashioned for a play he wrote and starred in called *Barber Q* about a barbershop quartet.[9]

"Franz was so talented," Arner said, "that other boys tried to imitate his style even then."

Outside of shop class, Kline contributed illustrations to *Junior Whispers*, the junior high newspaper. The staff photograph shows him towering over the other students in his grade.

Junior Whispers gave Franz's work its first real exposure. Written by students and faculty, the paper was full of stories and reports, including a list of the Honor Roll. It had a joke editor, often hosted contests, and included a section called "Historical Happenings." Kline's first cover, appearing in March 1926, features a shamrock-bedecked minstrel playing a cello. This, his earliest known published picture, shows definite refinement in the shading, detail, and cross-hatching. Even his signature in the lower-right corner is intricate, displaying an affinity for line drawing. He was sixteen. The original master is lost, but at least one print remains.

Kline's earliest evolution as an artist can also be traced through the autograph-book cartoons and drawings he made for classmates, many of which are similar in theme and design. His compulsion to draw manifested in hundreds of notes, letters, and sketches on everything from scraps of paper to program covers, the latter created as favors for teachers. In this regard, Franz had a habit of transforming simple projects into small masterpieces, and, fortunately for us, he left a wide trail among his friends and classmates.

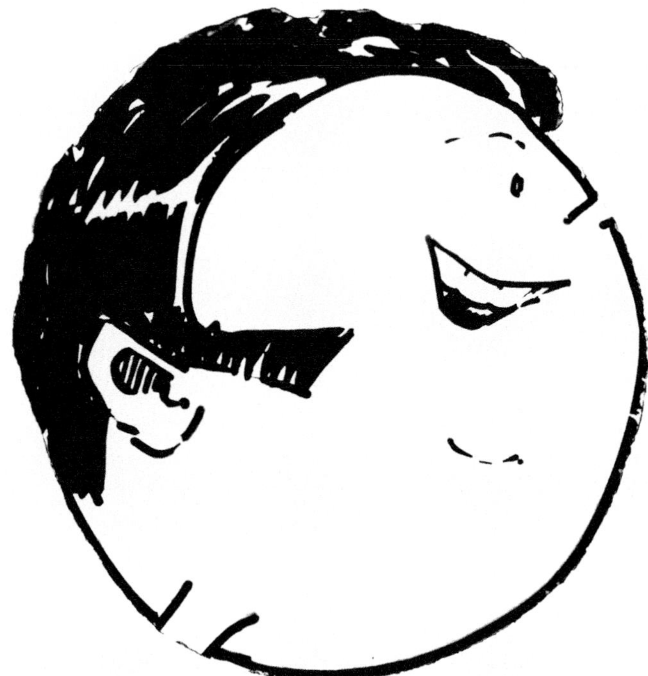

Left: Joe College, 1930. Joe Held Jr.'s popular Jazz Age creation was a favorite of Kline's. (*Mrs. Stanley Harleman and family © 2018 Franz Kline Estate/Artists Rights Society (ARS), New York*)

Below: Barber Q, 1931, *Gachtin Bambil*. A detailed cartoon from Kline's 1931 Yearbook Calendar. (© *2018 Franz Kline Estate/Artists Rights Society (ARS), New York*)

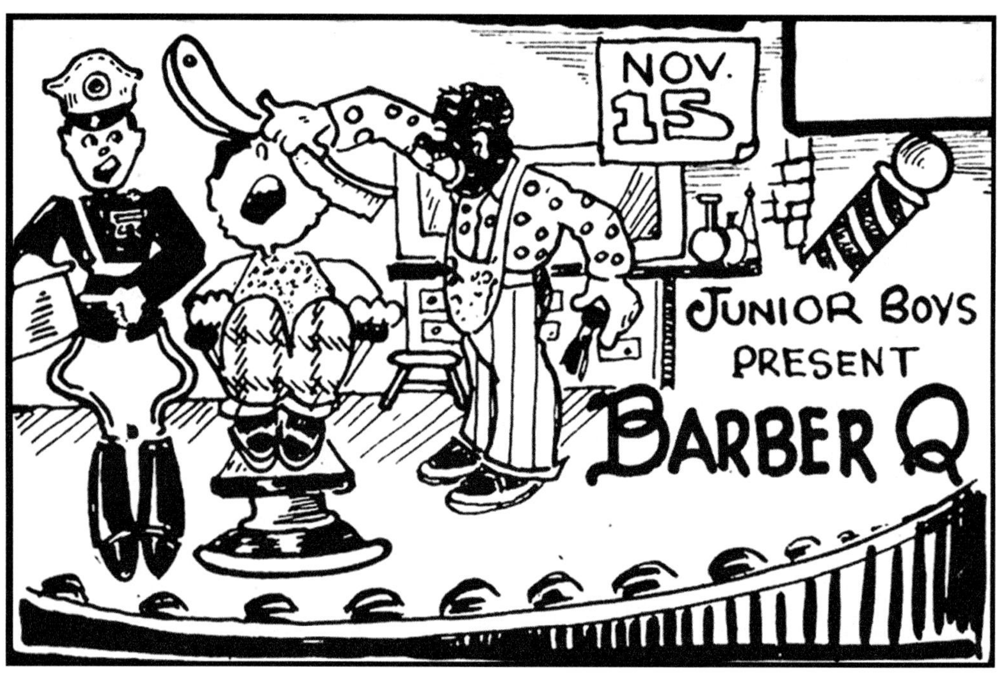

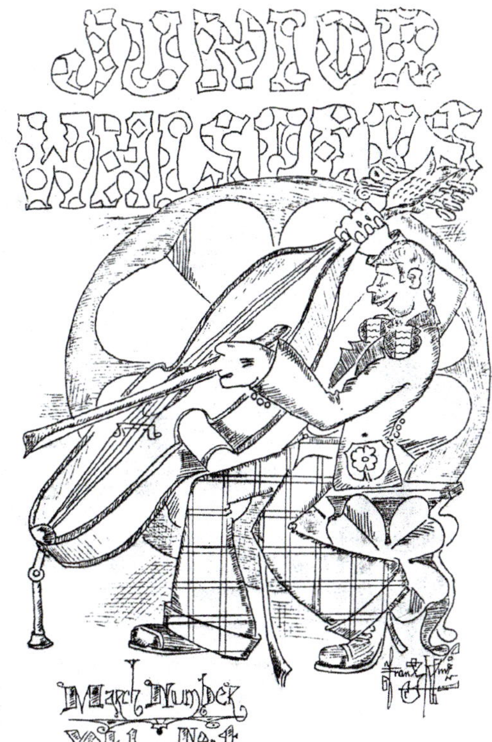

Above right: Junior Whispers, 1926. Kline's first newspaper cover as a junior high school student. (*Kathryne Oppold and Robert Warner © 2018 Franz Kline Estate/Artists Rights Society (ARS), New York*)

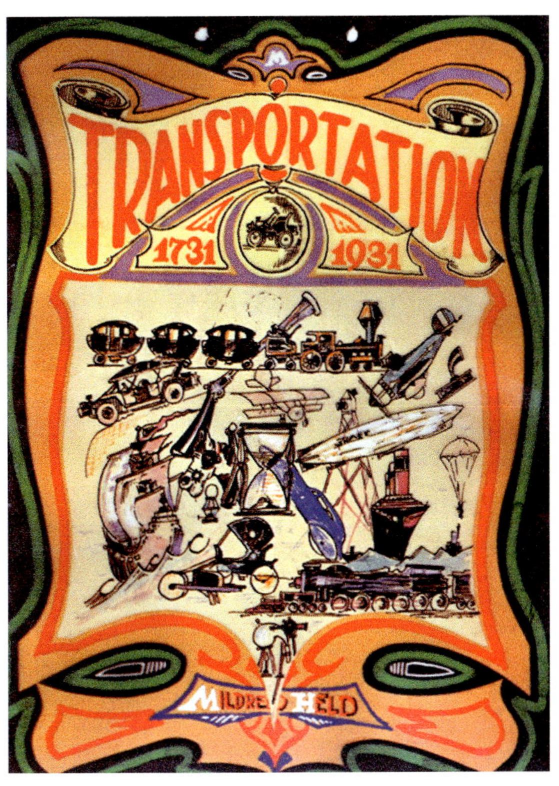

Below right: Transportation, 1929. A cover Kline drew for classmate Mildred Held's report depicting modes of travel from a rickshaw to a dirigible. (*Mildred Held © 2018 Franz Kline Estate/Artists Rights Society (ARS), New York*)

Classmate Mildred Held remembered a Roman shield Franz made for her out of cardboard for the gym team exhibition in 1929. The escutcheon resembled the Seal of the President of the United States. "Kline made different shields for every member of the team," she said, "each with its own unique design."[10] Kline also designed an elaborate Art Deco cover for a report Held wrote about transportation. Intricately designed with many small details, Kline's colored ink depicts various modes of transportation from stagecoaches and early trains to airships and automobiles.

Deeper insights into Kline's adolescent personality can be obtained by reading his letters. Many are included in Chapter 12, but one, written to Alvirda Arner, or as Franz called her "Virdy," is presented below.

"Franz had charisma," Arner said. "He was a fellow you could just sit and talk to, genuinely nice, reserved yet had the gift of being able to hold a conversation with anyone and a great sense of humor. We'd go to parties together. Franz's first love was art; in school he was always drawing. Some, I noticed, in the Junior yearbook have his girlfriend's initials hidden in them."[11]

Franz's letters to Virdy were written with an elaborate hand, full of embellishments. Note that some of the words are misspelled and have been intentionally left in their original form:

> Dear Virdy:
> I received your note and swell designs. (It won't be long now.) Why didn't you tell me you could draw, paint, design and I guess everything else Michael Angelo could do?

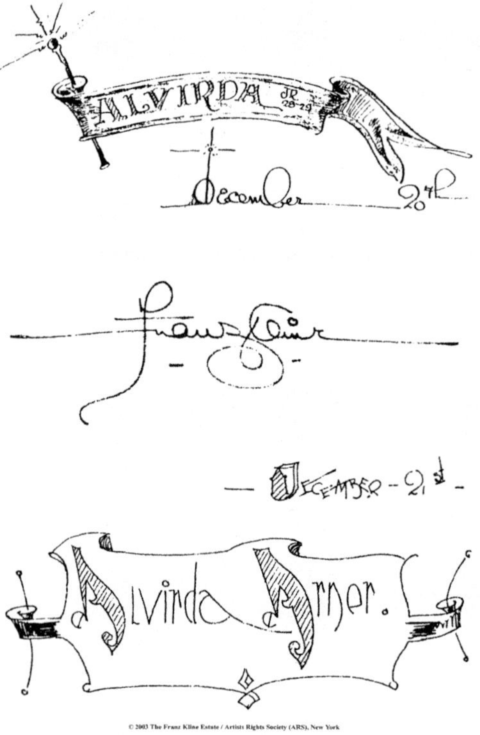

Alvirda Arner's name flourished beneath Kline's pen. He had a gift for transforming simple projects into small masterpieces. (*Alvirda K. Arner Ginder © 2018 Franz Kline Estate/Artists Rights Society (ARS), New York*)

> Enclosed you will find a sample of my inferior designing (sometime I'll hunt up some good ones here at home and send them to you.)
> I suppose you, too, treasure a collection of art. Mine consists mainly of cartoons of which I am fondest. I look forward to a career as a cartoonist, as you do a designer. But I guess I'll never amount to anything. How did you get a hold of my pictures? Where were the pictures taken? I'm sure they weren't taken in a football suit (Isn't that what Mr. Stofflet wants?) Explain that picture mystery in your answer.
> Just send all the work you want me to do cause when it's for you—to me it's a pleasure.
> Hoping you will answer soon.
> I remain with love—your Franz

Franz's letters to Virdy offer intimate snapshots into his teenage years, years when his football and baseball heroics were well-documented in the high school newspaper. When Coach Lewis Ginder instructed his players to "choose as captain a man who was a real leader and one to whom all the players will listen," his team chose Franz.[12] Not only was Kline a football star, he was also a good hitter and all-star catcher on the baseball team. Here is how *The Leni Lenapian* showcased him on September 9, 1930: "This lad is five feet six inches of bone and muscle. No fat helps constitute his avoirdupois. His hair is a dark brown, which compares with his eyes. His swiftness and ability are ably demonstrated."[13]

Franz's athleticism attracted recruiters from the armed forces, and as a result, he and some friends signed up to attend Citizens Military Training Camp twice. The first summer was at Fortress Monroe in Virginia. There, Franz drew cartoons for *The Salvo*, the camp's annual publication.[14] His second summer military camp experience was at Fort Meade in Maryland. But two summers were enough. Kline may have suffered fools, but he did not like would-be officers getting in his face. His classmate Henry Bretney said:

> [Classmate] Thomas Balliet recruited Franz, myself, and some other guys to sign up. Balliet was our drill master and very determined on making his squad the best. But Franz had just one thing on his mind, a vacation. So Balliet got rough on him. But Franz made it up to him later. Lucky for Franz, he could really play and won the position of catcher on the camp's championship baseball team. He had a quick humor and became popular with the officers. He could talk to anyone about anything.[15]

Teammate Carl Langkamer remembered playing football with Franz. "Our jerseys were maroon and white, and always torn," he said. "Most of us had to take our jerseys home for our mothers to mend after every game. We all had shoes with cleats, but Franz kicked barefoot. He could kick the ball from one end of the field to the other and punt 55 yards."[16]

On the same fields, known as "the flats," the boys also played baseball, and since it was near the train platforms, players often felt the ground shake beneath them as steam-engines thundered in and out of the nearby stations (there were two). After exchanging passengers or other cargo, the trains chugged on, vibrating the ground beneath the players' legs at the same time wood struck leather at home base and fielders chased after the ball.

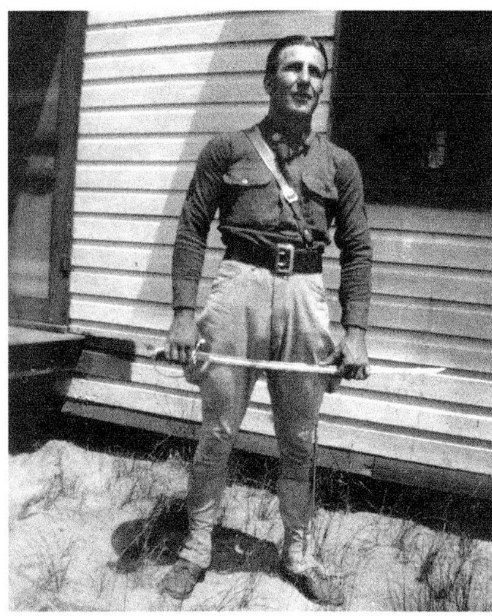

Left: Franz Kline, Citizen's Military Training Camp, Fortress Monroe, Virginia, 1929. (*Edith Smith*)

Below: *Lo Pal*, September 27, 1932, *The Leni Lenapian*. (© *2018 Franz Kline Estate/Artists Rights Society (ARS), New York*)

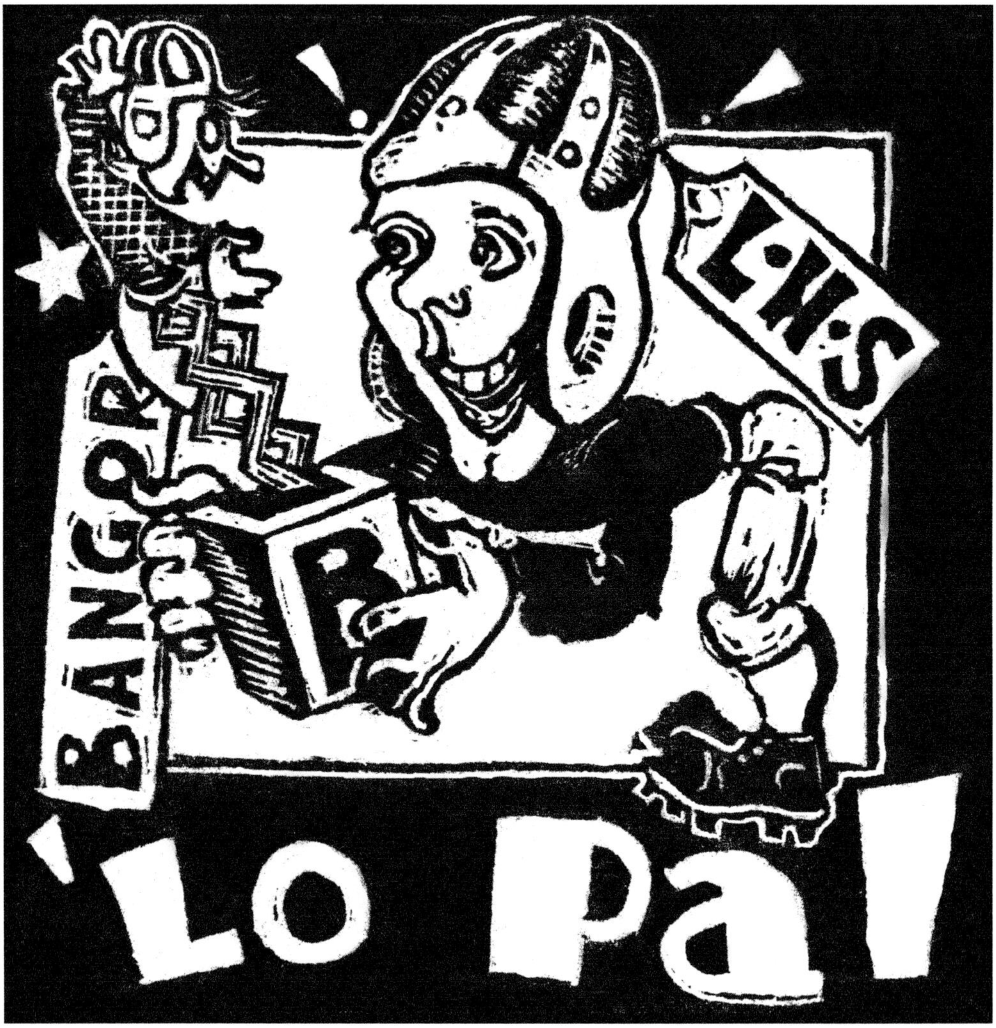

Franz was nearly arrested one night after a football game in 1929. Players from the opposing team, Mauch Chunk, began teasing his brother Fred about being "too pretty to play." Fred was wearing an eyepatch from another injury, and some players from the other team took it as an opportunity to tease him until "Franz clobbered the fellow." Louise said, "The police were going to put him in jail overnight, but he managed to talk his way out of it."[17]

Brave antics like this secured Franz's vote as "most popular" in the Class of 1931. He was also President of his homeroom, President of the Art Club, and cast for various roles in class plays. During his senior year, he played the role of the politician in *To the Ladies*, under the direction of his English teacher, Miss Mathilda A. Roedel, a woman who tutored him regularly and would play a major role in his life.

"I first knew Franz as a senior in the Lehighton High School class of 1931.... He played basketball, baseball, and football, excelling in the last and sustaining a permanent knee injury. He [Franz] had a minor role in the senior class play, which I was coaching," Roedel wrote, "a part requiring a long banquet speech. Just minutes before his entrance, he asked whether he could deliver it with a foreign accent. Although I did not know what to expect, I consented. He used a heavy, guttural German accent, and it was hilarious."[18]

A year earlier, as a junior, Franz created an autobiographical cartoon for his junior yearbook in which a boy in the first frame remarks, "Did you see those new teachers? '(Beautiful)'" Another responded, "Oh! How I love my school."[19]

Roedel paid her way through college as an usher for the Metropolitan Opera House in Philadelphia. In Lehighton, she was a cultural breath of fresh air. Born in November 1908, she was less than two years older than Kline. She was also single. Franz called her "Mars" and their relationship evolved into an elongated affair, the details of which are revealed in the following chapter.

During the time he was wooing teachers with cartoons, Kline enjoyed extensive coverage in the school newspaper. On December 18, 1929, *The Leni Lenapian* reported: "The maroon's only noticeable gain was made by Franz Kline after intercepting a forward pass. On this play the Captain was hurt and had to leave the game."[20]

On September 9, 1930, *The Leni* reported: "Did you know that Franz Kline has been out for football six years and has played on the Varsity team for four years? He is training for football at Weir Lake"[21]

Then, on October 28, 1930, again from *The Leni*: "Several senior boys visited Franz Kline at St. Luke's Hospital, Bethlehem.... Franz is convalescing rapidly from a recent operation due to an old basketball injury, which again developed in football practice. He expects to return home next week....[22] Did you know that Franz Kline is starting his fourth successive year as President of his home room?"

The Leni was printed in editions of 500 by the same press as the town's *Evening Leader*. Franz's cartoons and linoleum block prints were often highlights. As art editor, he supplied cartoons by using special tools to chisel into linoleum blocks. His work was so accomplished that the Pennsylvania Scholastic Press Association awarded Kline a Silver Award for outstanding work in 1930, specifically noting the following prints: "Patrick Wears the Green," "Easter," "Book Week," and "Circulation." The headline in *The Leni*

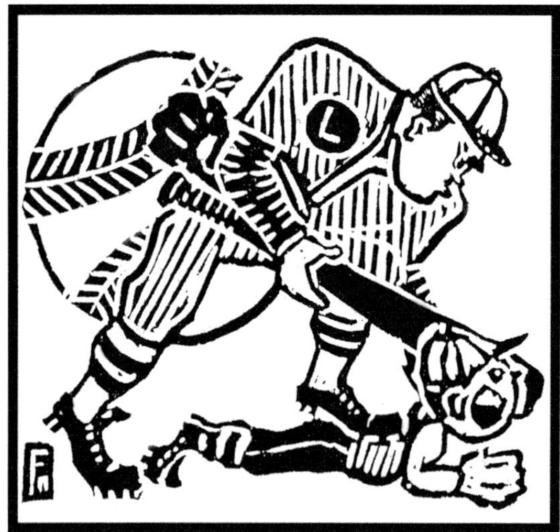

Left: Who's Next, May 6, 1930. *The Leni Lenapian*, linoleum block cut. (© *2018 Franz Kline Estate/Artists Rights Society (ARS), New York*)

Below: Franz Kline, middle row front, and fellow Lehighton Indians wearing white jerseys over maroon uniforms for a football scrimmage. (*Mr. and Mrs. Gordon Hontz*)

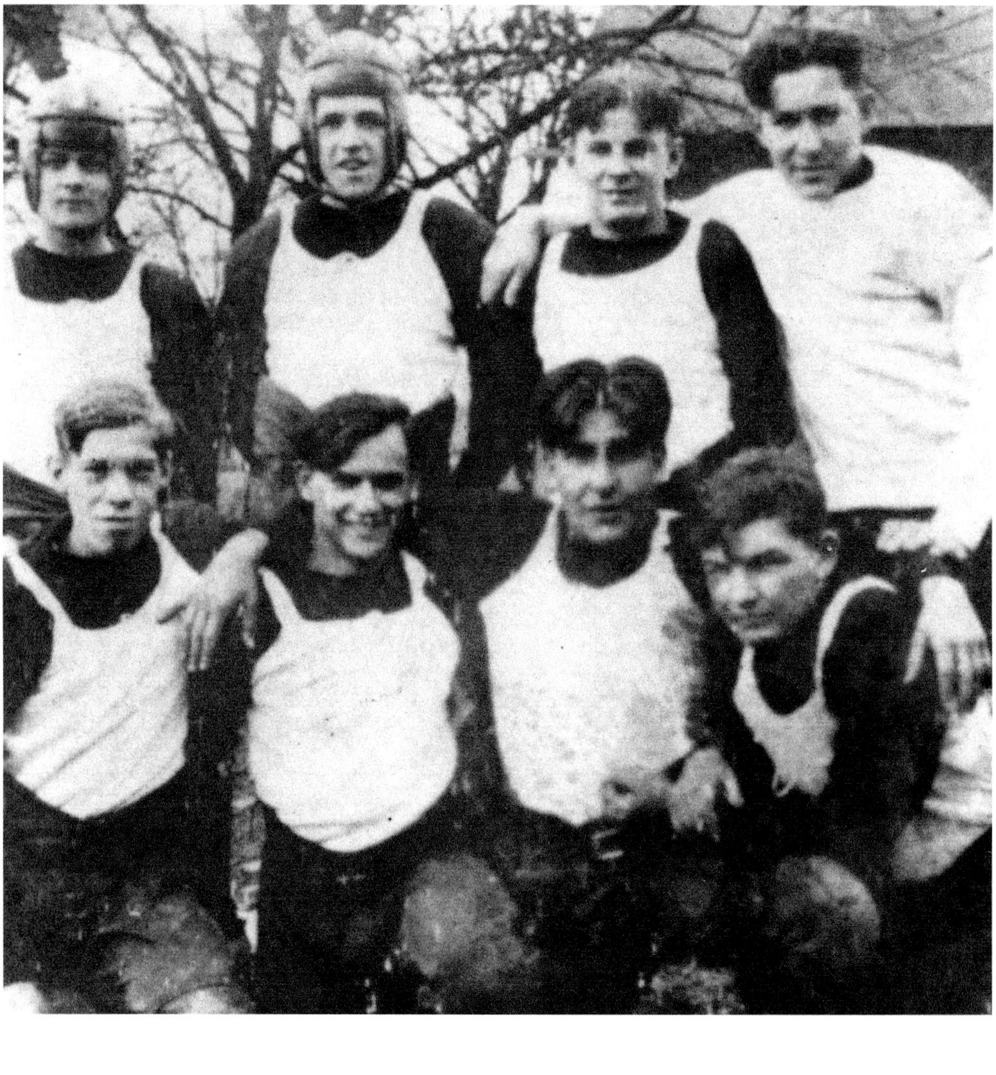

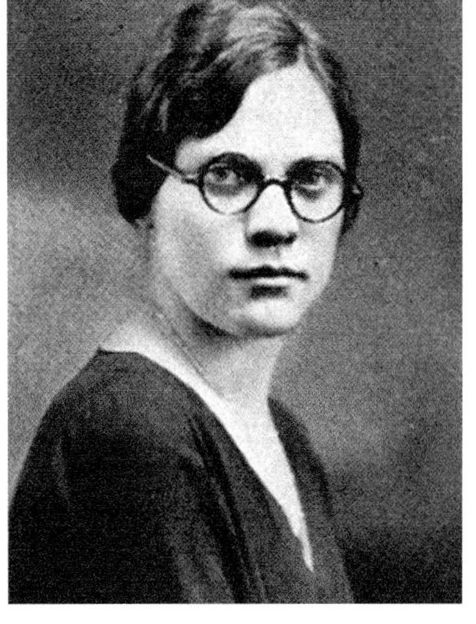

Right: Mathilda A. Roedel, Kline's High School English teacher and tutor.

Below: *We Love Our Teachers* (first day of school), *Gachtin Bambil*, 1931 calendar. The cartoon reflects the joy of new female teachers, including Miss. Roedel. (© *2018 Franz Kline Estate/Artists Rights Society (ARS), New York*)

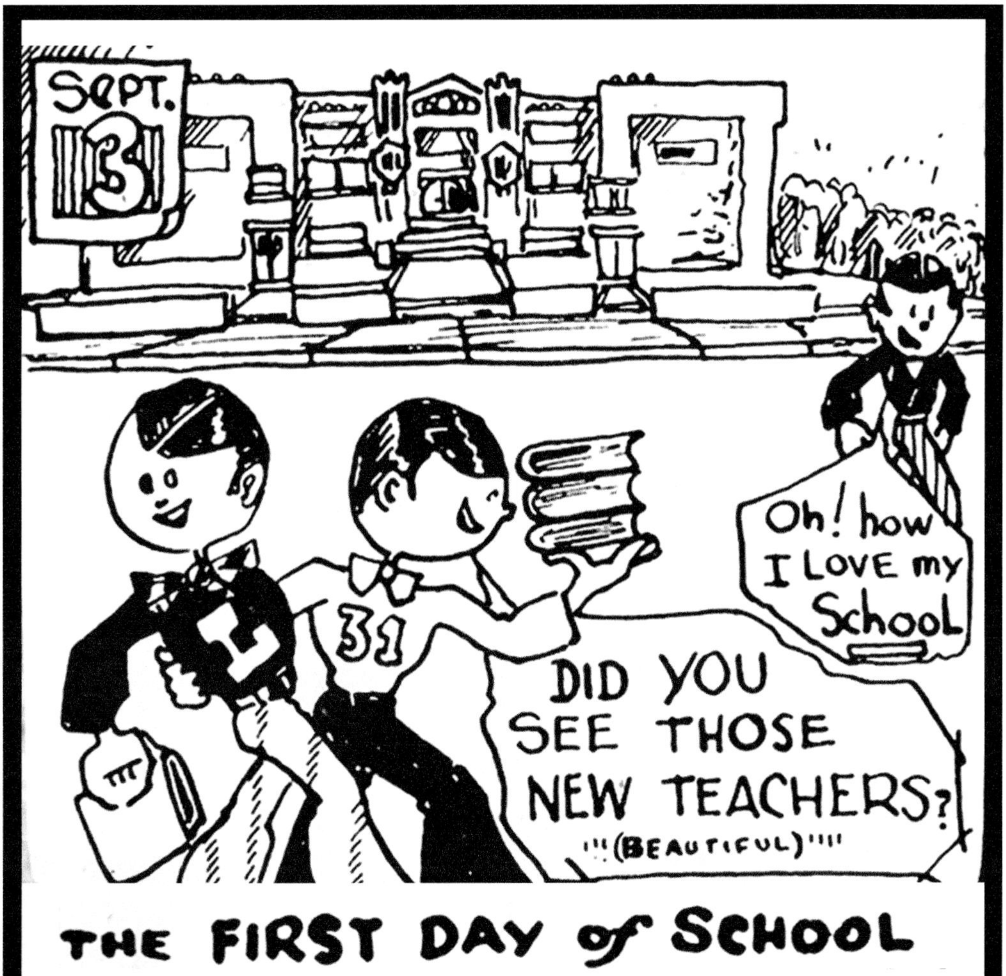

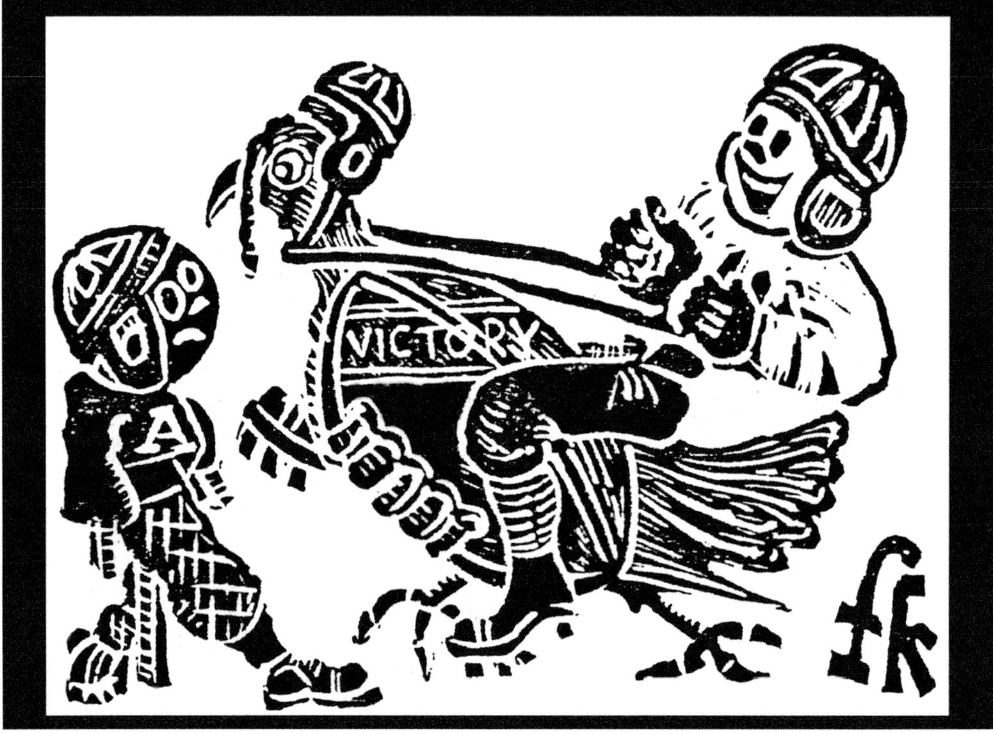

Above: Feed the Turkey, November 25, 1930, *The Leni Lenapian*, linoleum block print. (*© 2018 Franz Kline Estate/Artists Rights Society (ARS), New York*)

Below: Come On Gang, September 23, 1930, *The Leni Lenapian*, linoleum block print. (*© 2018 Franz Kline Estate/Artists Rights Society (ARS), New York*)

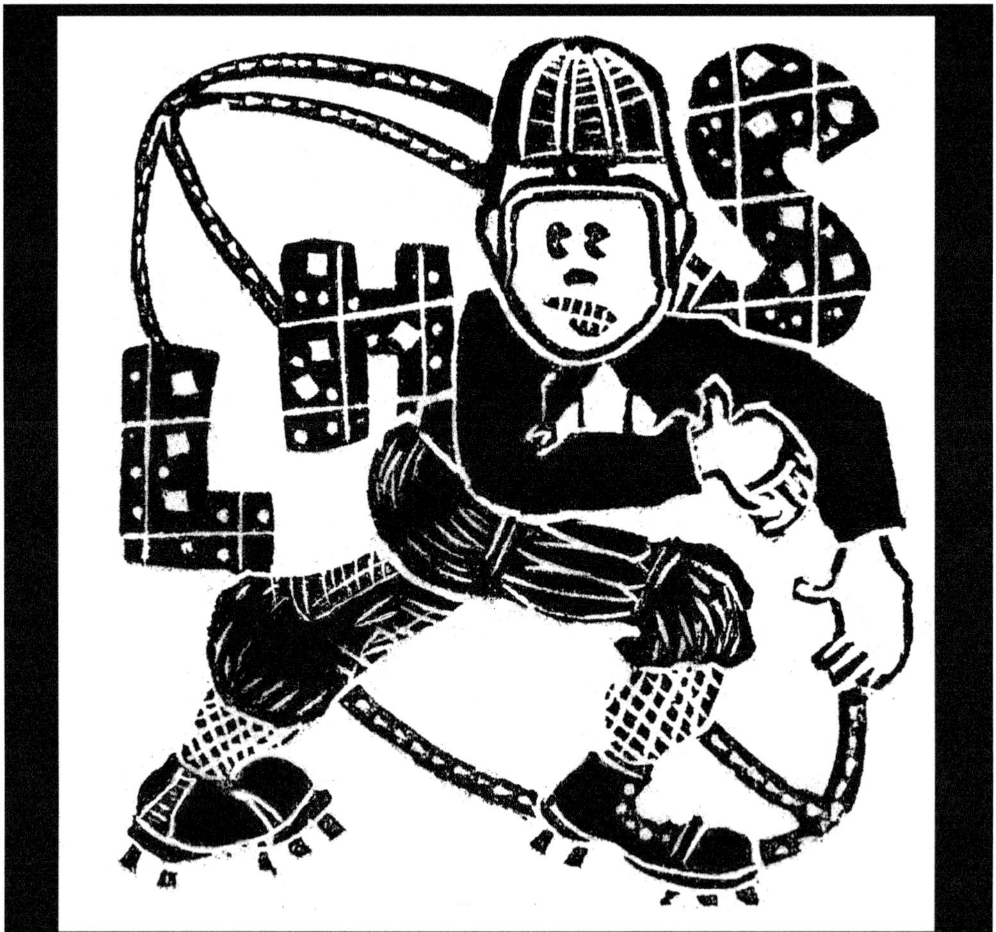

Lenapian read: "Silver Awards for *Leni*—for assistant editors, writers and for artist, Franz Kline."

The exposure expanded his audience across the state through a newspaper exchange program, and many students and educators took notice. One comment from the Jermyn High School newspaper staff read: "*The Leni Lenapian* is a well-balanced paper ... we especially enjoyed the last cartoon. Congratulations, Mr. Kline!"[23]

The Leni also recorded Kline's defeats. Lamenting Kline's career-ending football injury, the writer reported: "... the star quarterback of the LHS football team for the last three seasons ... will be lost to our team." Until the beginning of his senior year, most of Kline's sports injuries only benched him temporarily, but that changed during a preseason football scrimmage. The defensive line converged on his bullish charge. The Captain ducked his head and leapt, but instead of landing on the padding of the other players, his knee smashed hard on the ground. He was abruptly sidelined for the rest of the season. In only the second week of his senior year, his athletic career was over. He limped the three-blocks back with his teammates to the locker room. Stanley "Stump" Harleman later drove him the rest of the way home.

Few students had their own cars, but Stump drove a 1929 Chevy. He also had an airplane housed in a hangar on the other side of the fairgrounds behind Kline's house, which, for most of the year, remained "a large open pasture divided by a fence."[24] Stump's plane was red with an open-cockpit and he often took friends up for rides. Louise said, "I can still see him sitting in the plane like a statue."

Harleman once flew Mars Roedel all the way to Camden, New Jersey, for Christmas break. In her memoir, she wrote:

> Over my heavy coat I wore one of his flying suits. Onlookers said the seat of the uniform dragged to the ground when I stepped onto the wing. I was outfitted with a helmet and a large silk handkerchief to cover my face. I was crammed down into the cockpit together with a long parcel containing a Mickey Mouse rug for my two small nephews. No pin could have been thrust in.... We had agreed that when we arrived at Allentown, he would kick the backboard ... and if for any reason I wanted us to land, I was to kick back. I didn't. It was glorious.[25]

Stump's plane gave his friends, including Franz, a bird's-eye view of the area, the kind of vantage point that inspires a person to look beyond their immediate barriers. Benched from the field, Kline channeled his energy into creating many funny and expressive drawings.

Kline became a kind of chronicler of the times, even highlighting the past achievements of teachers in one series of cartoons. His comics in the *Gachtin Bambil* yearbooks are exceptional. Each little chamber encapsulates some aspect of the school year, resplendent with the artist's personal charm. Accompanying one about the Debate Club, Franz joked: "Resolved, that you talk too much!"

We know of at least two murals that Kline painted around this time, though he likely created more. Most were made in secret because his mother did not always approve. "When Franz returned from a job in a barroom he would hide his paints under the large

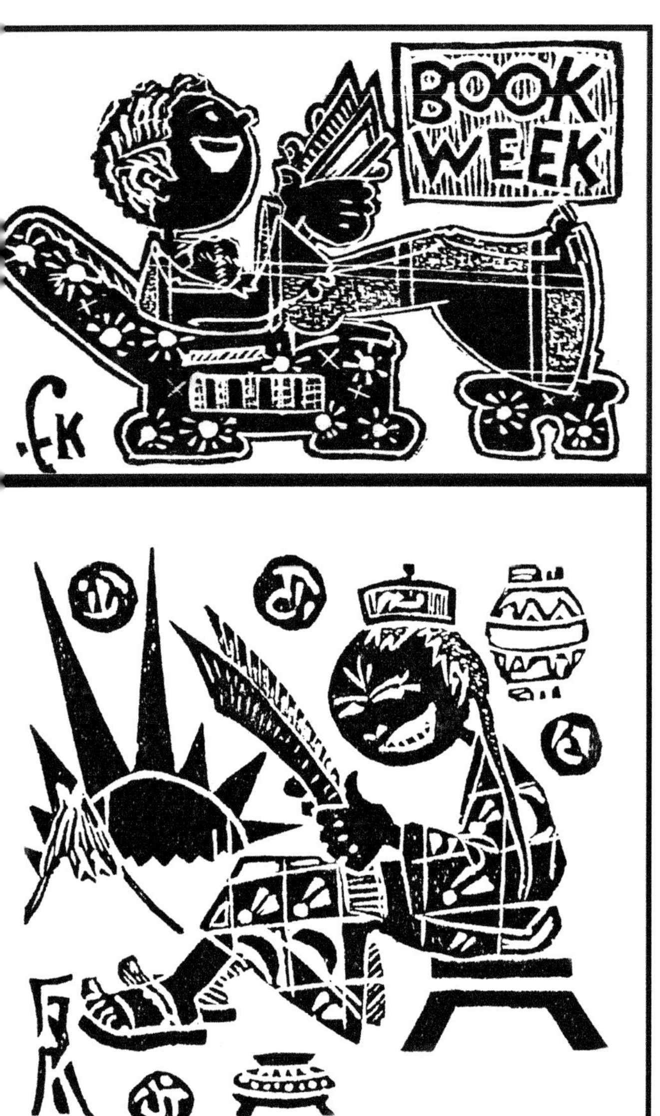

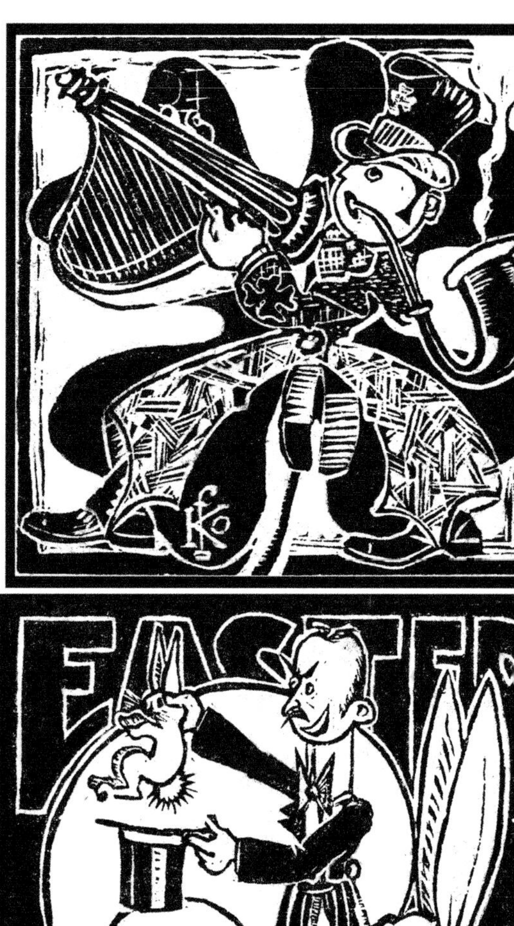

Above left: Book Week and Circulation, 1931, *The Leni Lenapian*, linoleum block prints and recipients of the Silver Award. (*© 2018 Franz Kline Estate/Artists Rights Society (ARS), New York*)

Above right: St. Patrick Wears the Green (top) and *Easter*, 1931, *The Leni Lenapian*, linoleum block prints and recipients of the Silver Award. (*© 2018 Franz Kline Estate/Artists Rights Society (ARS), New York*)

Opposite above: Juniors Wreck Seniors, 1931. *Gachtin Bambil* yearbook from the calendar page. (*© 2018 Franz Kline Estate/Artists Rights Society (ARS), New York*)

Opposite below: Detail, *Lehighton mural*, 1945. Airport hangar established by Martin Jensen in 1928 at the Lehighton Fairgrounds with Stanley Harleman's red plane in the sky. (*Joshua Finsel/ Lehighton Legion #314 © 2018 Franz Kline Estate/Artists Rights Society (ARS), New York*)

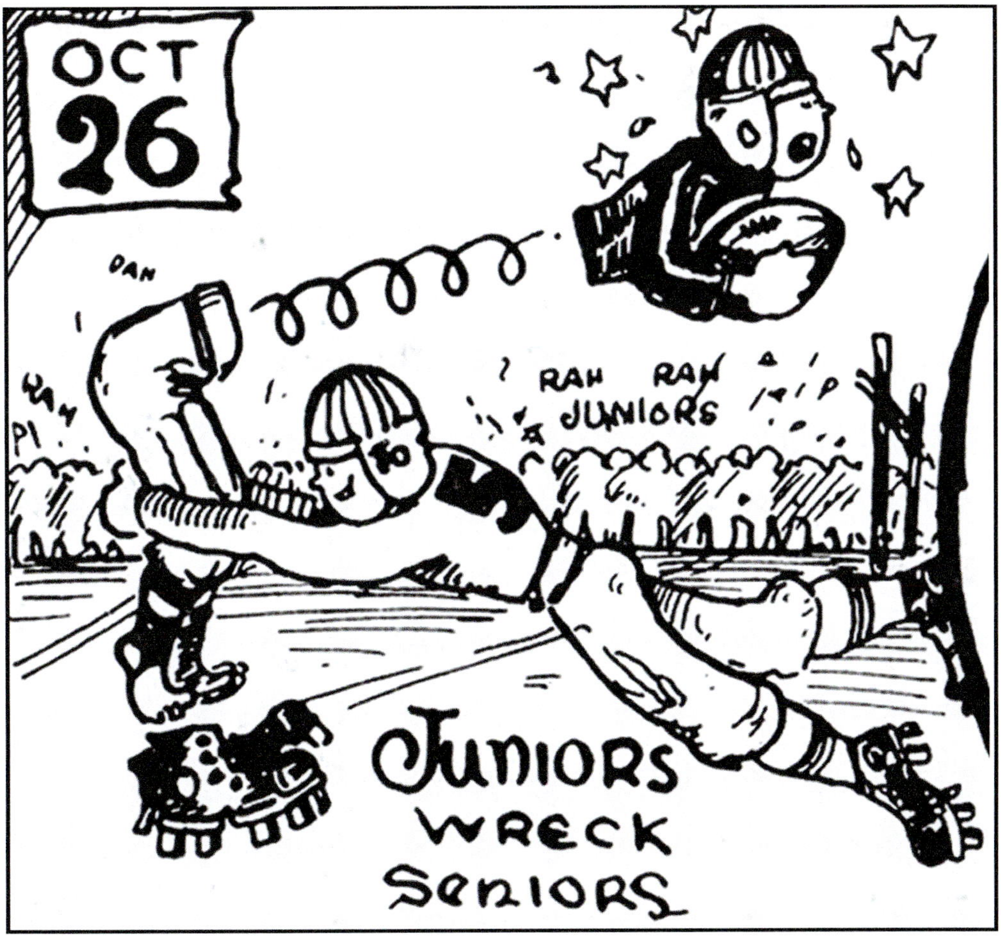

OCT 26
RAH RAH JUNIORS
JUNIORS WRECK SENIORS

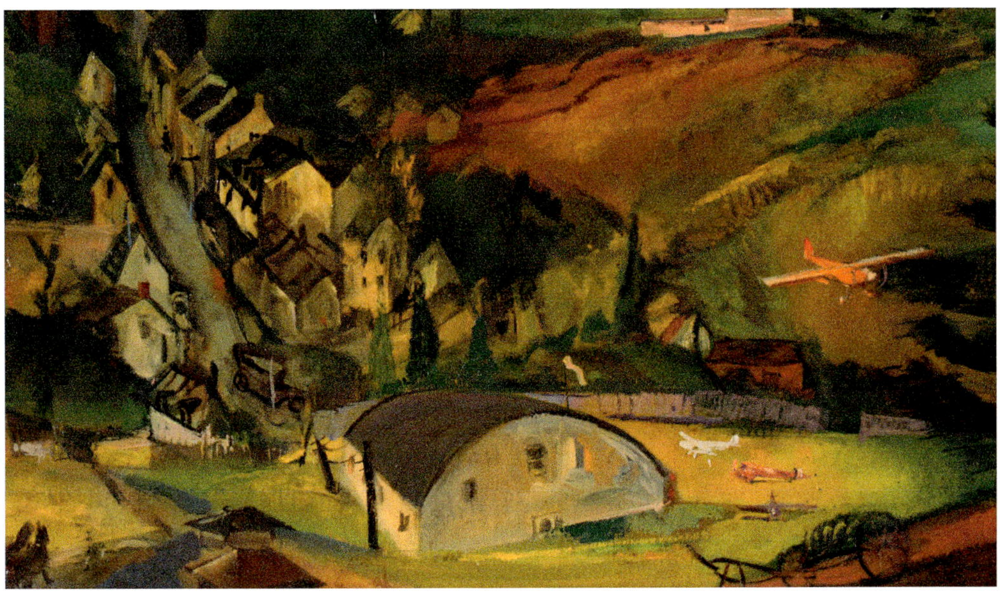

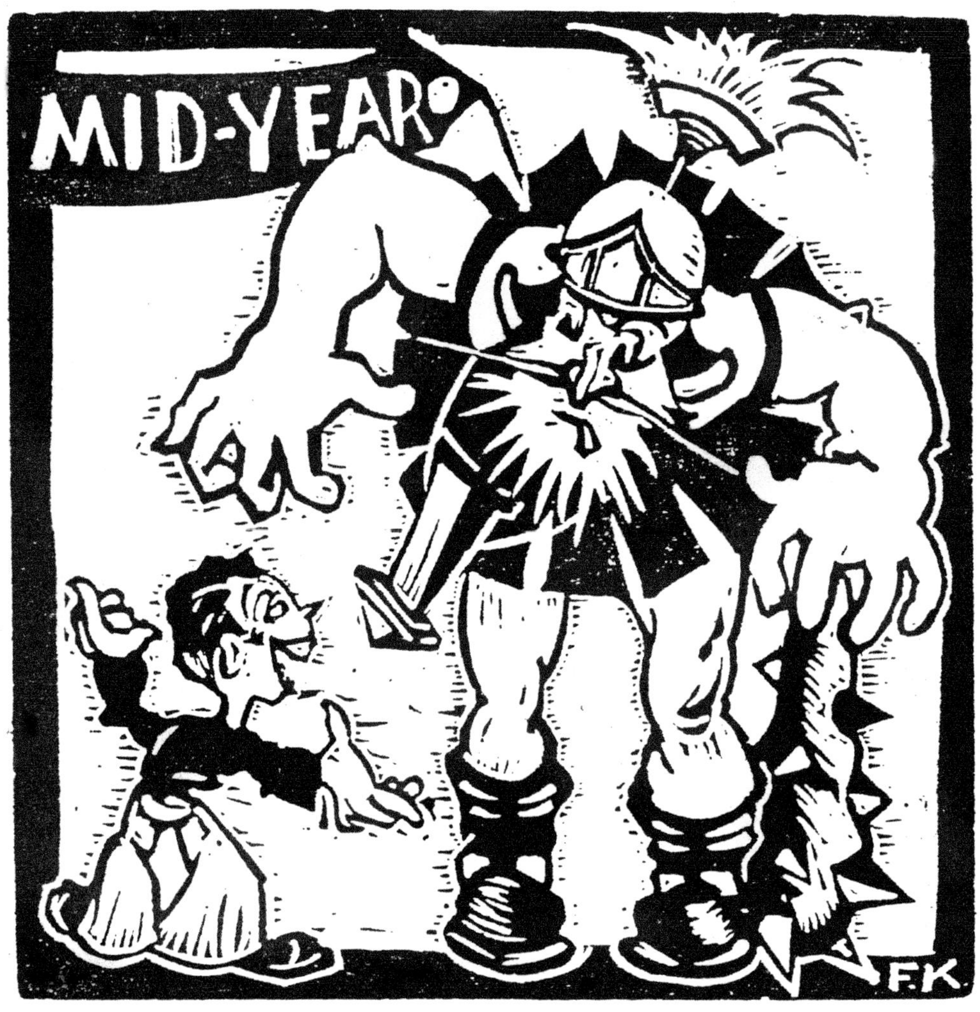

Mid-Year—Viking You Can't Scare Me, January 17, 1933, *The Leni Lenapian*. (*© 2018 Franz Kline Estate/Artists Rights Society (ARS), New York*)

rhododendron bushes near the front porch steps," Elisabeth Zogbaum said. "His mother considered sign painting beneath him."[26]

One of the murals remains a mystery. Commissioned in a bar in neighboring Palmerton, this work was reportedly his largest effort while in high school and took several weeks to complete. The logistics meant hitch-hiking 8 miles back and forth for several nights.

No one knows for sure today where the mural might be. Many have speculated that it was painted over, and the amount of reliable information dwindles with each passing year. Together with the former Director of the Sordoni Gallery at Wilkes University, Dr. Stanley Grand, we spent hours scraping paint from the walls of a former church and VFW Post (now a warehouse) but came up empty. It is possible that the tavern owner did not like Kline's work because, according to Harold Rabenold, the proprietor refused to pay what was owed. "So Franz got a bunch of us guys together," Rabenold said,

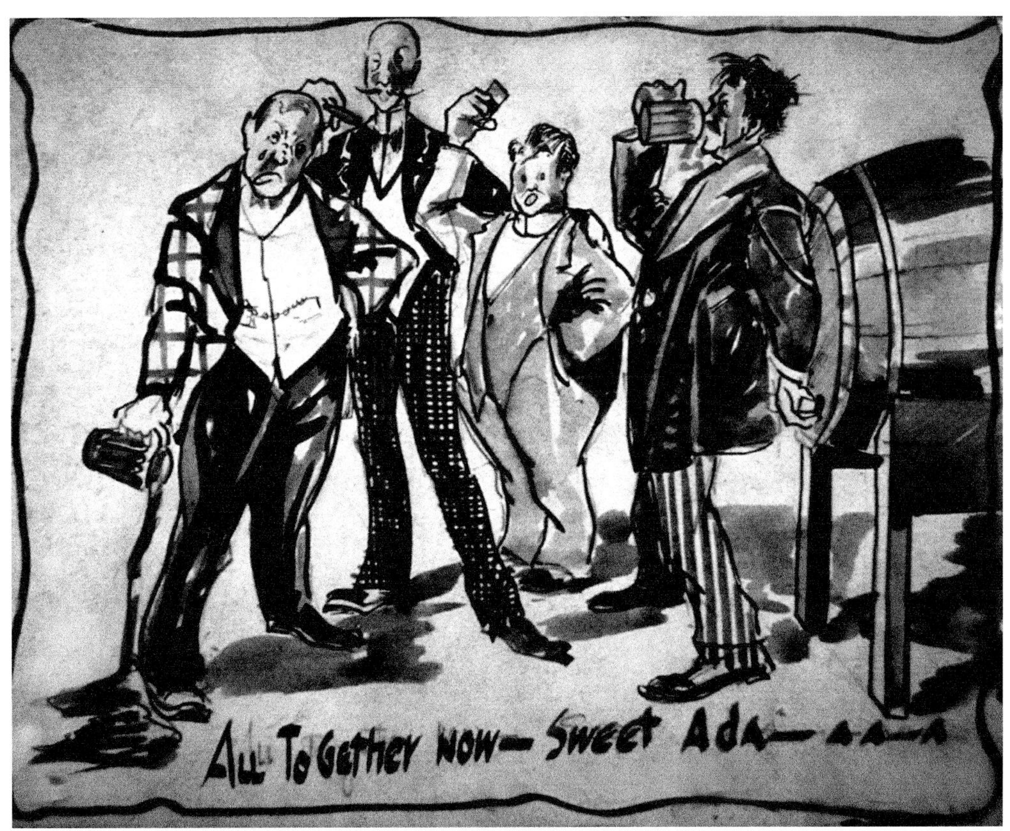

All Together Now, 1931, an ink drawing on cardboard with two familiar figures. Nearest the keg is Kline. Center, with arm held high, is Stanley Harleman. (*Mrs. Stanley Harleman and family © 2018 Franz Kline Estate/Artists Rights Society (ARS), New York*)

"including me and we went down and drank five dollars' worth and then we all walked out."[27]

Another mural painted while Kline was in school featured a group of musicians on the wall behind the band platform of Graver's Skating Rink. The figures demonstrate Kline's debonair style. There is a drummer gripping a fly swatter, a minstrel with a megaphone, and balloons and musical notes float above a trombone and saxophone. A tradition arose that the musicians were caricatures of the rink's full-time band, Eddie Lentz and the Wee Georgians. It is likely that Franz based the six musicians on a variety of acts that played there, including Bud Henry and his Alpine Syncopators, Nat Heiligman and His Orchestra, the Nichols Orchestra, and The Lehightonians.

Before the skating rink was demolished, the owners, Larry and Charlene Graver, carefully cut the figures out of the wall with a saber saw. The rescued mural was brought out in pieces. The year of creation is debatable, but our information indicates that it was probably between 1930 and 1931. Although there were originally six musicians, only five survived intact: a trombonist, a tuba player, a drummer, the bandleader, and singer—each measuring roughly 33 × 33 inches. The sixth, playing a saxophone, could not be saved.

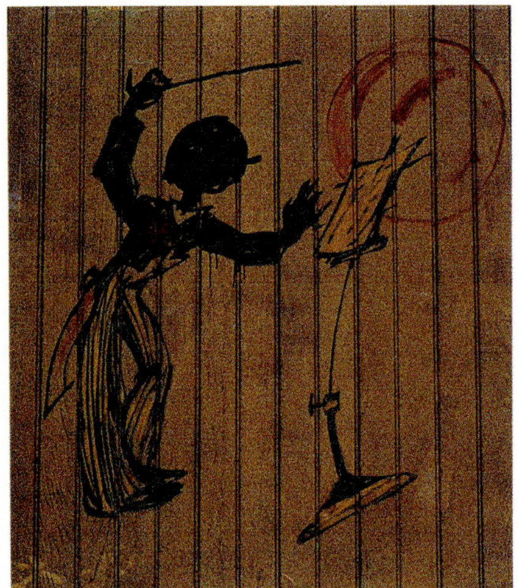

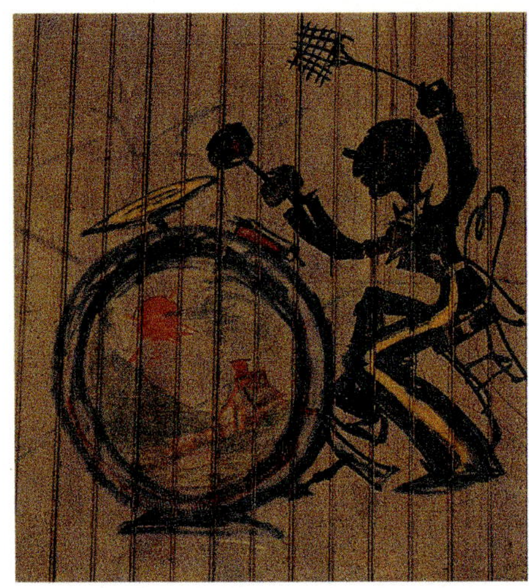

Franz Kline: *The Lost Murals*

Above: "Kline was an aware young man who was familiar with the popular culture of the time on which the Jazz Murals were based," Robert P. Metzger, curator, *Franz Kline: The Jazz Murals*. (*Charlene and Larry Graver © 2018 Franz Kline Estate/Artists Rights Society (ARS), New York*)

Below: Dr. Louise Kline-Kelly (center-right) at Bucknell University's opening of *Franz Kline: The Jazz Murals*, 1989, curated by Dr. Robert Metzger. (*Author's collection*)

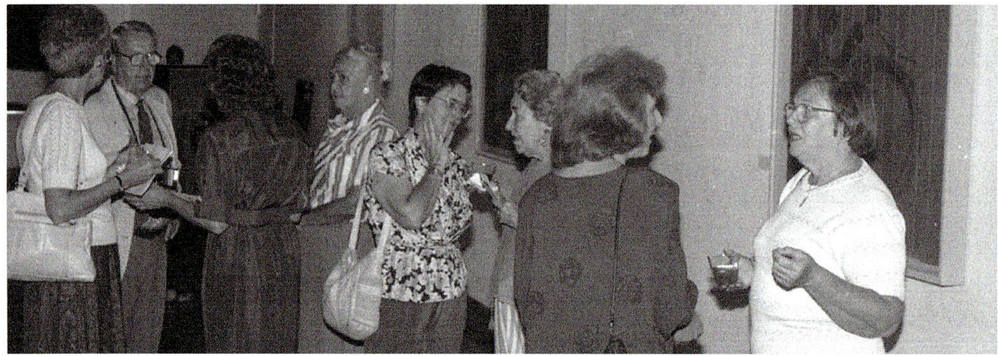

The musicians were first exhibited as "The Jazz Murals" at Bucknell University in 1986. The band members are a good example of Kline's progression from the primitive cartoons of his early teens to the more refined characters of his later Lehighton years. They were painted on yellow pine tongue-and-groove boards and contain some of the same gestural qualities found in his later abstracts. All are sweeping, large, and full of movement.

6

Mars Black and White: A Scandalous Affair

Yes, I knew Franz Kline—quite well … in his memorial exhibition at the Sidney Janis Gallery in 1963, my sister and I found a painting that bore my name as its title. In the catalog, Elaine de Kooning speaks of a series of paintings bearing my name and hints that a private connotation had another implication for the public. I like to think of myself as being in that category.

Mathilda A. Roedel
Third and Last

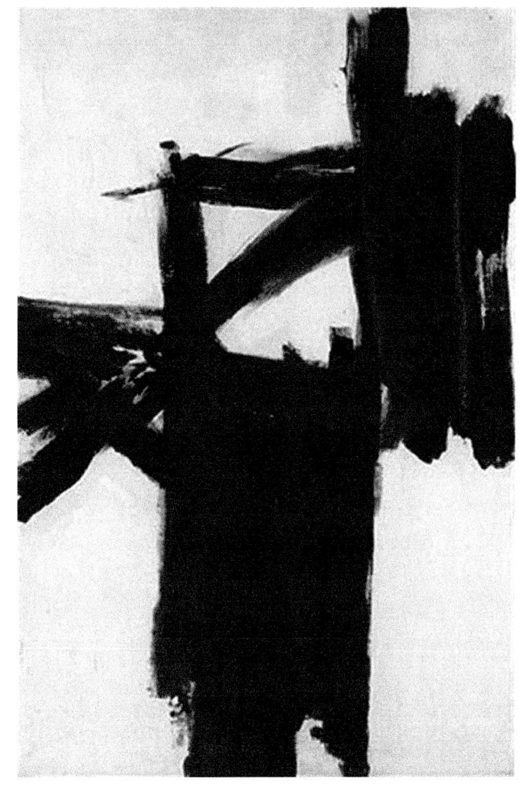

Mars Black and White, 1959. (*Private collection © 2018 Franz Kline Estate / Artists Rights Society (ARS), New York*)

One afternoon, in front of Pop Gillen's soda parlor in the fall of 1929, a young girl named Edith Smith sat on the steps outside the store watching Franz perform for her.

"He was doing his best to impress me," Smith said. "And he was quite an actor, but then suddenly his mother came out of a store with a pair of arctics. When she saw us talking, she took a long look at him, another at me, and threw the rubber boots around his neck. 'Come along, Captain,' his mother said. She always called him that. Then she turned to me, 'And now you, young lassie, go home and wash your mother's dishes.'"[1]

Kline's mother had exceptionally high standards for her children. Like many parents, she strove to provide a better future for them. Having sacrificed so much—including the sanctity of her bedchamber—to reunite them, Anne did everything possible to ensure for their success, even if it meant shielding Franz from girls.

"Gosh, Virdy," Kline wrote to one high school sweetheart, "I'm sorry you thought I intended to visit you at your home! Cause Gee! kid I know my mother wouldn't allow it any more than I think your mother would."

"You stayed away from his mother," Edie Smith said. "My mother idolized Franz, and he would visit her when he came home from New York, but Anne did her best to keep me at bay."[2]

Kline's neighbor, Grace Ahner, had a similar impression. "His mother disapproved of every high school girl that showed an interest in Franz," she said. "She only went for the educated."[3] Louise noticed it too. "Mother wanted to know all about a girl's family lineage," she said. "She always said that if you can't travel in good company, travel alone." Whatever the root of Anne's mindset against local girls, her attitude shifted with the arrival of Mars.

Mathilda Alberta Roedel joined the Lehighton High School faculty in 1930 as an "instructress" of Senior and Sophomore English. She was the youngest of four children born to John, a cigar-maker, and Anne Seip, in Philadelphia, both first-generation Americans of German descent. She loved Shakespeare and graduated from Temple University. In her memoir, she wrote about working as an usher at the Metropolitan Opera. There, seated on a pile of programs stacked against a marble pillar, "opera glasses glued to my face," she saw her first opera, *Gianni Schicchi*.[4] She was mesmerized. At the end of the performance, a passing candy vendor noticed the tears streaming down her face.

Her first teaching position was in Lehighton, located about 80 miles north of her home. It was a railroad town in coal country with a population of about 5,000 souls. Philadelphia, by comparison, had over 1.5 million at the time. Mars let an apartment on Third Street near the school. There she devoted her time to preparing lessons and corresponding with pen pals, particularly her French friend Odette. In the classroom, she liked to get her students up out of their seats to act out scenes from the classics. She gave musical readings, helped produce plays, chaperoned school functions, and even helped track down a snake that escaped Mr. Kresge's science class.

Ruth Ritter Baum, a former colleague, described Roedel as "exceedingly cultured in a way that made it hard to know her, a kind of a loner who was not terribly anxious to go out socially. She was reserved, your typical old-maid type. But she was artsy and coached plays. She was erudite with a very narrow field of interest."[5]

Physically, Mars was a paradox. Remembered as both attractive and matronly, she rarely wore any makeup or the latest fashions. Of average height, she was curvaceous

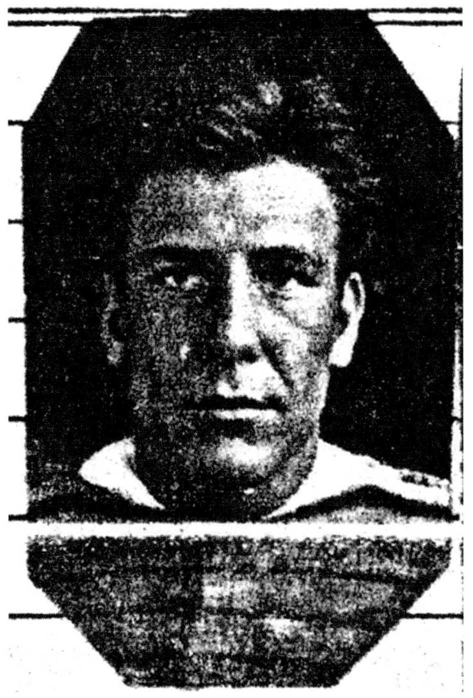

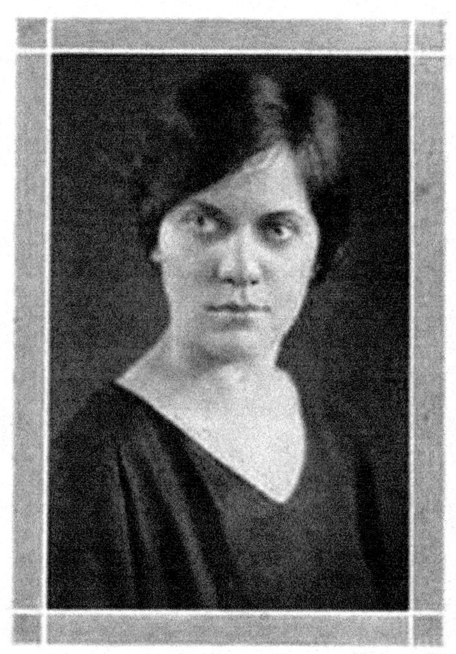

Above left: Sophomore school photo, Lehighton High School, 1928.

Above right: Mathilda Roedel, Temple University Yearbook, *c.* 1929.

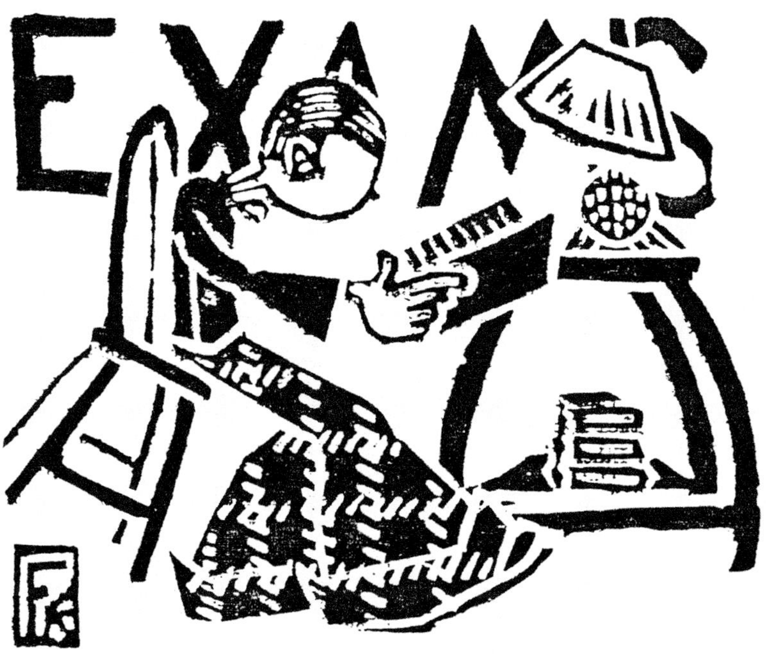

Oilin' Up for Exams, January 23, 1930, *The Leni Lenapian.* (*© 2018 Franz Kline Estate/Artists Rights Society (ARS), New York*)

enough to draw a second glance, depending on what she was wearing, a trait that she either remained naïvely unaware or hid well behind her horn-rimmed eyeglasses.

Franz entered her classroom as a nineteen-year-old junior. Having both lived in Philadelphia, they developed a bond. Perhaps Kline thought he could charm her into an A. His grades in English had been all Cs and Bs up to that point. He impressed her with his wit. He was, she wrote, a "clever mimic and excellent storyteller," despite seemingly always drawing in class when he should have been taking notes.[6] After his mother and Mars began to correspond, his teacher was invited to dinner and eventually won a place in Anne's inner circle. "From the pictures on the walls to the rugs on the floors, the Kline home had a certain atmosphere of elegance," Roedel wrote. "I spent a great deal of time there."[7]

One of Kline's football teammates, Ralph Beisel, said that when he would go to Franz's home, "Roedel would be the one pouring tea."[8] It is not clear when Franz entered into a sexual relationship with Mars. Rumors circulated almost from the start. "Miss Roedel always knew where Franz would be, and she would often walk after him in the halls to his classes and try to be where he was," classmate Lavona Edgar said. "She didn't know that he had another girlfriend."[9]

Louise suspected that her mother's alliance with Mars was centered on her hope of cementing a relationship between them. "Mars would come to our house for supper many nights," Louise said, "and when it came time for her to leave, Mother would say, 'It's getting dark, you can't go home now.' So Mars would sleep at our house on the roll-out bed even on a school night. But sometimes she would say that she forgot her toothbrush or something silly like that, and then designate Franz to walk her home."

Mars remained discreet about their relationship until after Kline graduated. Commencement took place on Friday June 5, 1931. Although he was still harboring the dream of being a cartoonist (and several teachers encouraged him to study commercial art), Franz set his sight on Boston University, despite being "ill-suited scholastically."[10] In a haze of parties and odd jobs, the summer passed quickly for Franz, and there was an awareness of Mars solidifying herself as a fixture of his family, even beginning to relate to him as a steady beau.

That same summer, Franz took a part-time railroad job with his football teammate Harold Frendt. The boys were assigned sections of track to maintain, which meant tamping dirt and gravel around replacement ties. While making their rounds, the boys often paused at the trestle to sit and roll their own cigarettes. Frendt believed that there was something significant about the vantage point that resonated with Kline's later abstracts. "Those great big black angular steel girders riveted together fascinated Franz," he said fifty years later. "I'm sure they had something to do with how he painted."[11]

In addition to painting signs, Franz began "calling" for The Lehightonians, a local band with their own Sunday radio show. Franz hitched the 2 miles to Moyer's Hotel twice a week to lead the dance. Melvin Moyer, a band member whose father owned the hotel, said that Kline's "great baritone" was really good at "mixing it up with jokes and impersonations."[12] Kline also collected the money, usually 10 cents, from the taxi dancers in a cup as they spun around the floor. At the end of the night, he and the other entertainment split the take.

"Tillie Roedel came to the dances too," Moyer said, "chasing Franz of course."[13] After graduation, Mars no longer took pains to conceal their relationship. But Franz was not as forthcoming, nor was he comfortable with all of Roedel's not-so-subtle hints.

"Mars told me that she would marry Franz," Louise said. "She wanted him very much. Franz gave me away when I got married, and Tillie designated herself as my Maid of Honor. She told me, 'When Franz and I marry, I would like to have two little boys.'"

Roedel did not realize Franz considered their relationship as more of a casual affair. Tension ripened near the end of the summer as he prepared to leave, and the rumors intensified.

Daniel Davies drove Franz to Boston on his way to Harvard in a 1928 Ford Model A. Davies said that on the trip, Franz was quiet and not his usual effusive self. "His primary mission, as engineered by his mother as soon as he graduated from high school, was to get him out of town. She feared, not without some justification, that he might impregnate one of the more than willing local young girls who gave 'my Franz,' as she referred to him, a come-on look.... I had lots of time to chat and to get better acquainted during that time-consuming drive ... but my strong recollection is that I knew no more about Franz at the end of the drive than I did before."[14]

Later, in a letter, Dr. Davies clarified that the girl who "became pregnant" was "a teacher in Lehighton ... who got a crush on Franz."[15] Roedel resumed teaching in the fall but only after she first "enjoyed an ocean trip to Europe," missing the first two weeks of school.[16] Could she have been recovering from more than a broken heart?

The Kline family's official stance, according to Louise, remained, "There was no child."

Kline entered Boston University in the fall of 1931. While many of his high school teachers felt that he was not suited for college, perhaps Mars's private tutoring gave him an edge. In September, during his first semester at Boston, Franz found time to design tickets to support the hometown baseball team. *The Leni Lenapian* reported: "Quite a bit of favorable comment has been heard upon the novel ticket designed by Franz Kline. As Kline states, 'the new design is worth the price of the cardboard alone.'"[17]

Four months later, in January 1932, Kline made *The Leni* again with an announcement about being "elected Secretary of the Art School" of Boston University.[18] Franz continued to write letters to his friends and family, as well as contribute cartoons and linoleum block prints to *The Leni* during his freshman year away from home.

Only a few drawings from Kline's Boston years have surfaced, along with a handful of old letters to friends. The letters reveal an exuberance and an enthusiastic view of the world. In addition to writing his high school friends, he sent witty, chatty letters to Anne. "When Franz was in college, he'd cut those illustrated ads out of the newspaper for Lucky Strike cigarettes," Louise said, "and send them home to mother after writing on them, 'Say, doesn't that look like our Louise with the red dress on?'"

The following two letters, written in fall of 1931, give a glimpse of his first semester at Boston University, right down to the green artist's smock that he was forced to wear. All misspelled words remain as Kline composed them. The first is a two-page letter with illustrations featuring Duke Ellington and Clara Bow, as well as other assorted characters. The second letter he illustrated with a small cartoon of Paul Revere. Additional letters are located in Chapter 12:

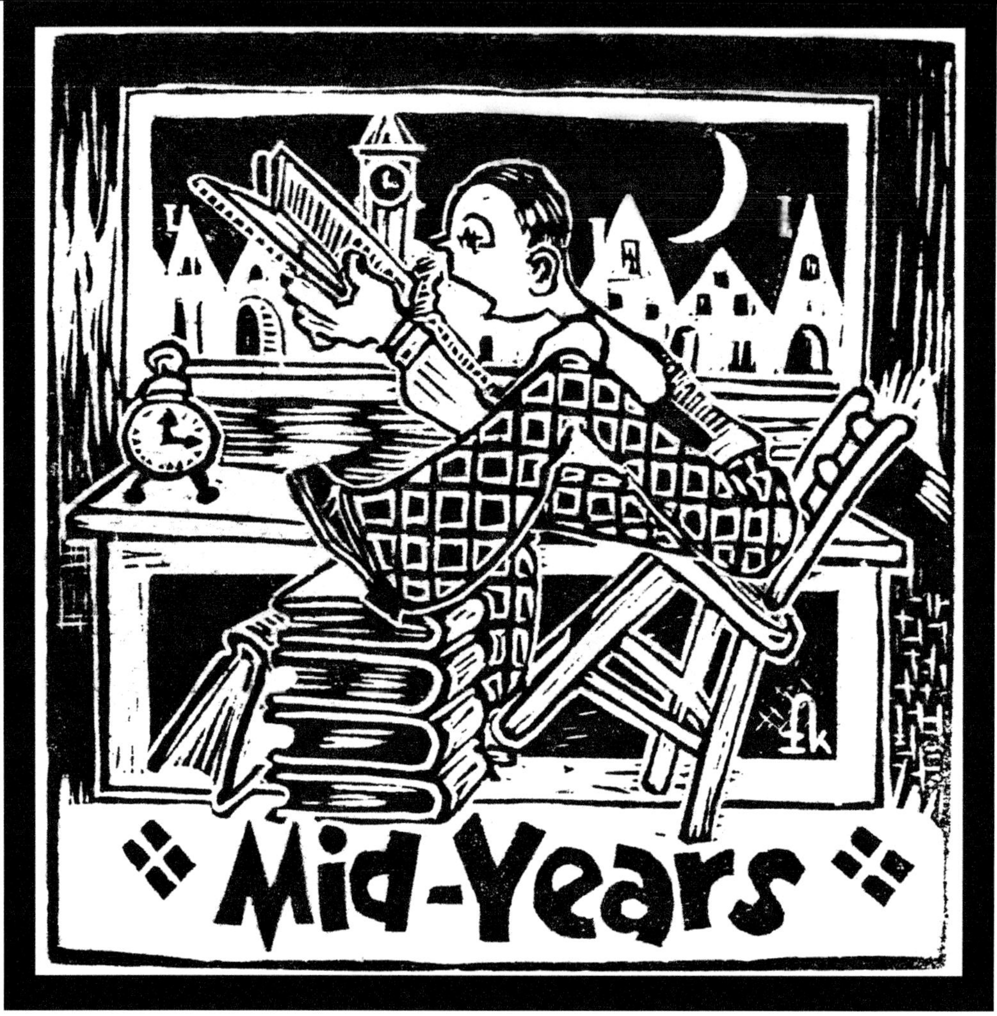

Above: Mid-Years (Yawn), January 20, 1931, *The Leni Lenapian*. Kline's printmaking background affected not only his development as an artist, but his move to the abstract. (*© 2018 Franz Kline Estate/Artists Rights Society (ARS), New York*)

Below: Anne Snyder and Mathilda Roedel, 1931. Mars became a regular part of the Kline-Snyder family. (*Patsy Gernerd Aldrich and family © 2018 Franz Kline Estate/Artists Rights Society (ARS), New York*)

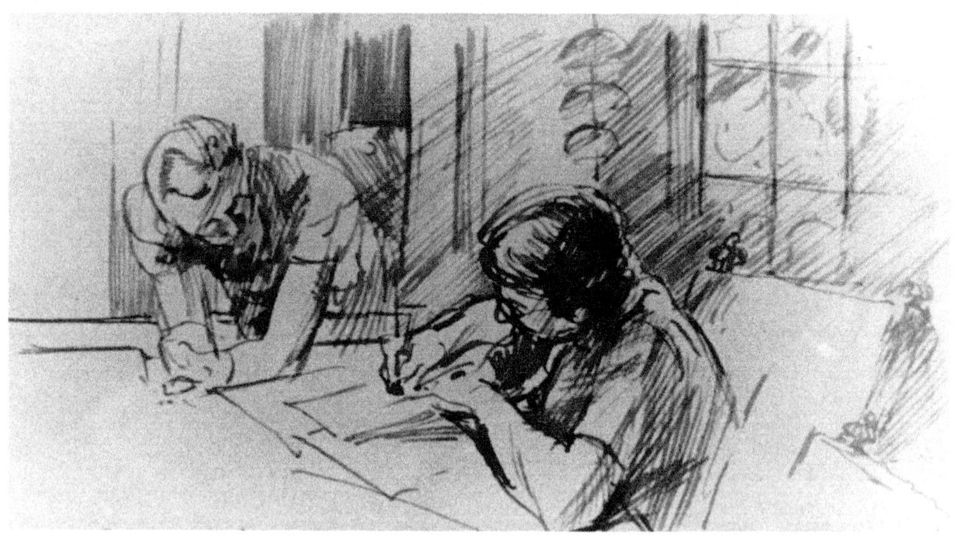

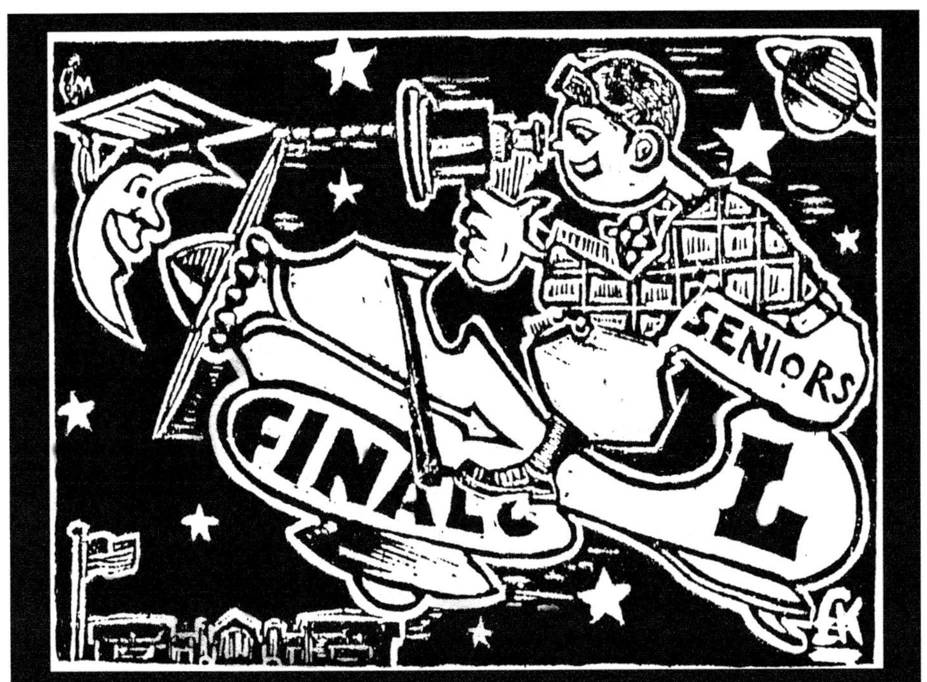

Above: Reach for the Moon, Finals, May 12, 1931, *The Leni Lenapian*. (*© 2018 Franz Kline Estate/Artists Rights Society (ARS), New York*)

Below: School Daze, June 2, 1931, *The Leni Lenapian*, Kline's last linoleum block cartoon for *The Leni* before graduation. (*© 2018 Franz Kline Estate/Artists Rights Society (ARS), New York*)

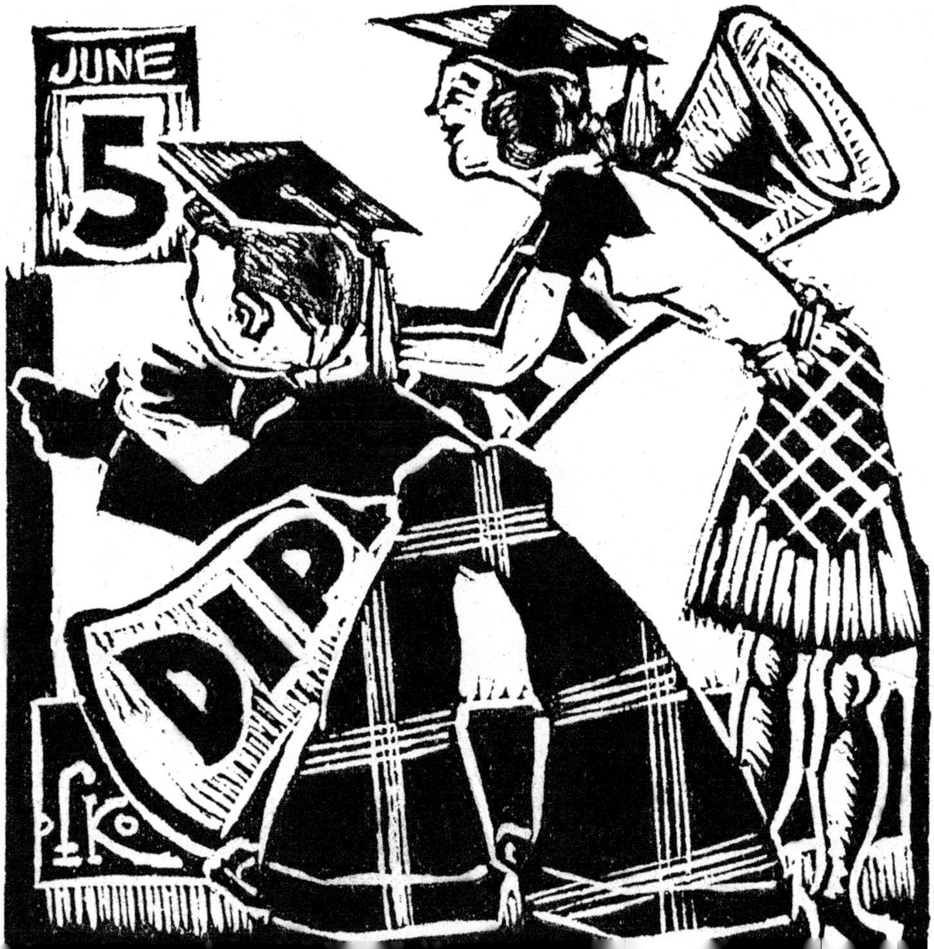

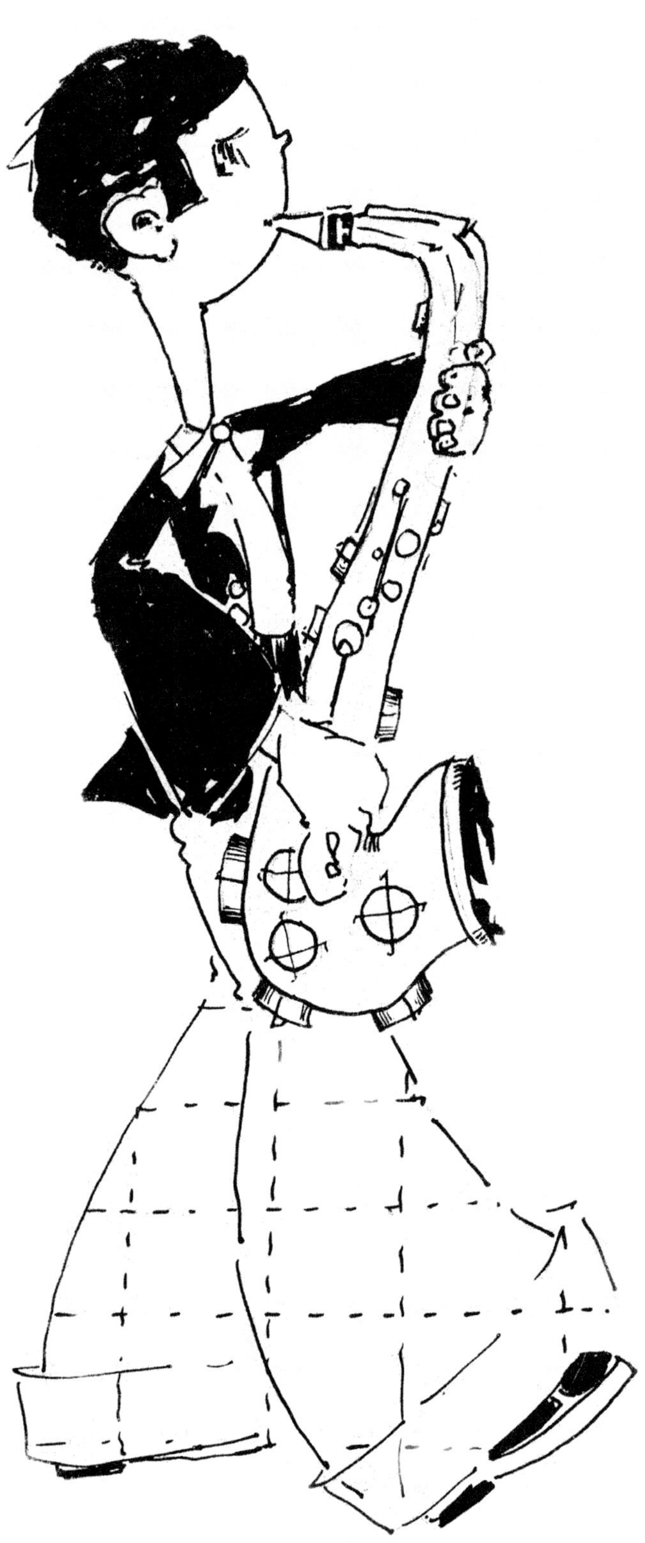

Untitled Saxophone Player, 1928. "The great parties took place at our house," Louise said. "We had an Edison and Victor radio and Mother stood around making sure everyone would dance. There was to be no billing and cooing in the corners." (*Glen Claypool and family © 2018 Franz Kline Estate/ Artists Rights Society (ARS), New York*)

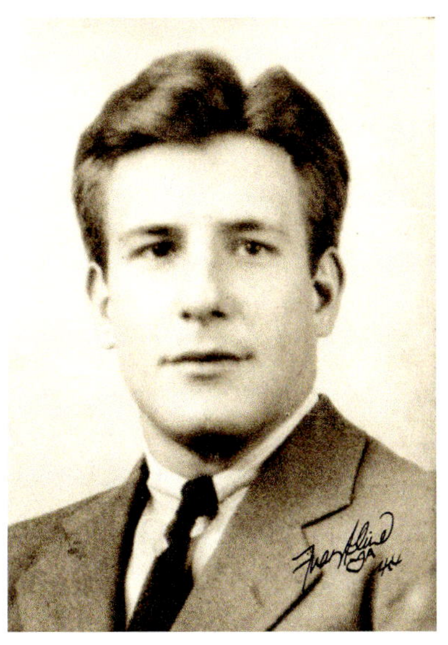

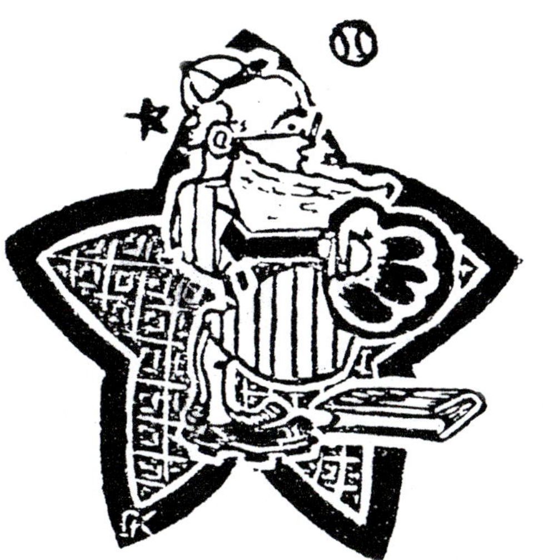

Above left: Franz Kline in 1935. (*Paolo Pelosini*)

Above right: Tickets, March 31, 1931, *The Leni Lenapian*, advertisement, Kline said, "Buy your Faculty Varsity Game Ticket today, the new design is worth the price of the cardboard alone." (© *2018 Franz Kline Estate/Artists Rights Society (ARS), New York*)

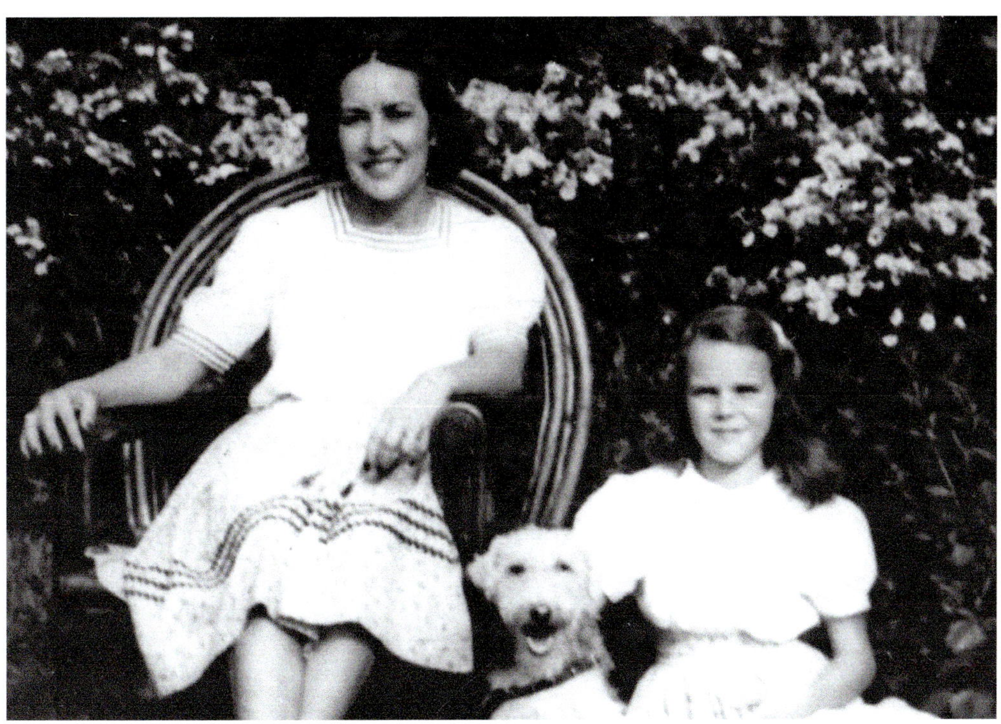

Photo of Louise (left) and Janny, Lehighton, 1940. (*Kim Graver Steinberger and family*)

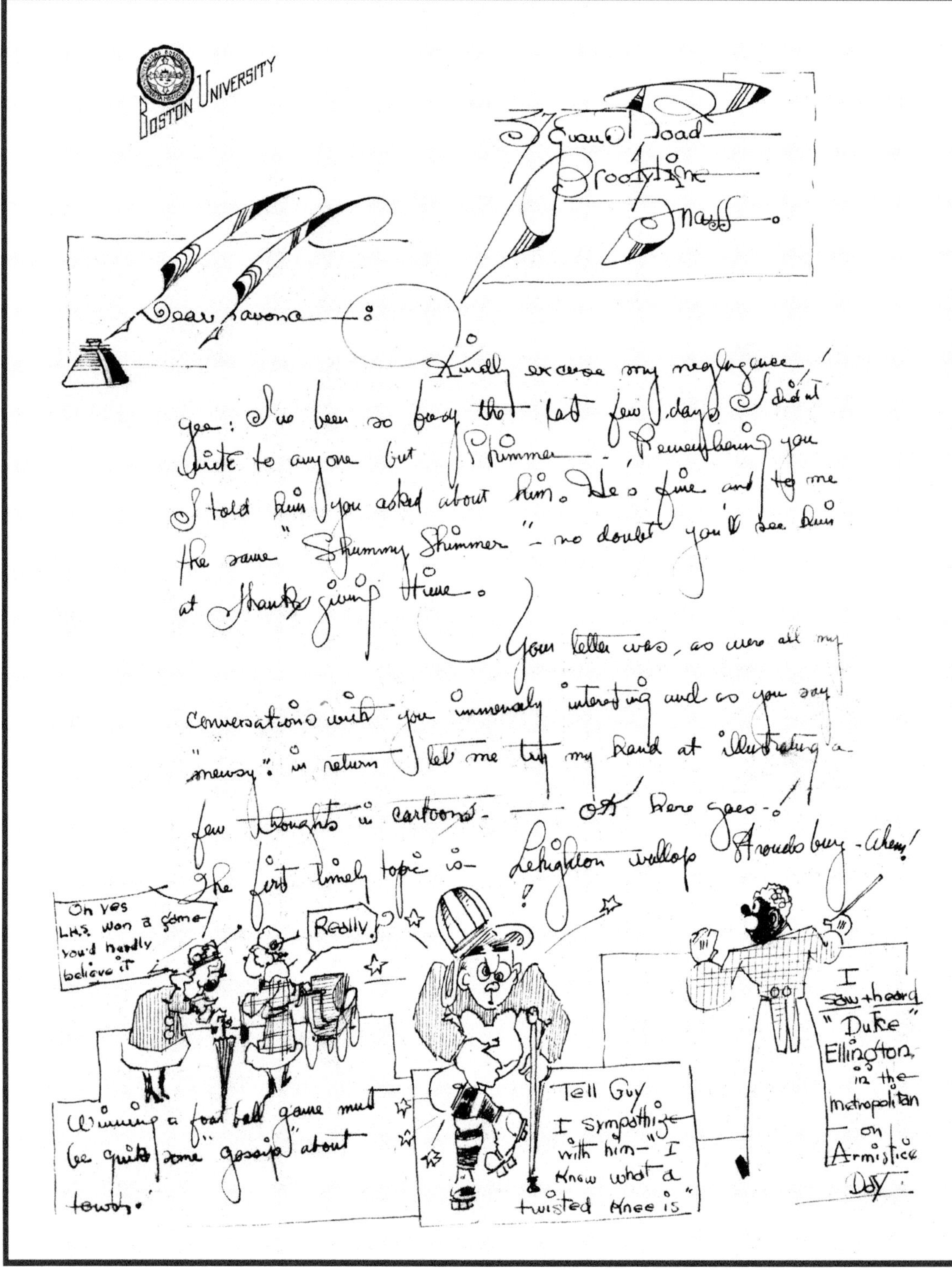

Boston University

37 Evans Road
Brookline
Mass.

Dear Lavona:

Kindly excuse my negligence, yes: I've been so busy the last few days I didn't write to anyone but Shimmer. Remembering you I told him you asked about him. He's fine and to me the same "Shummy Shimmer" — no doubt you'll see him at Thanksgiving time.

Your letter was, as were all my conversations with you immensely interesting and as you say "newsy": in return let me try my hand at illustrating a few thoughts in cartoons — off here goes! The first timely topic is — Lehighton wallops Stroudsburg — ahem!

Oh yes L.H.S. won a game — you'd hardly believe it

Really

Winning a foot ball game must be quite some "gossip" about town.

Tell Guy I sympathize with him — "I know what a twisted knee is"

I saw + heard "Duke" Ellington in the metropolitan on Armistice Day.

Illustrated Letter, 1931, from Franz Kline to Lavona Edgar, "Let me try my hand at illustrating a few thoughts." (*Mr. and Mrs. Curtis Eberts © 2018 Franz Kline Estate/Artists Rights Society (ARS), New York*)

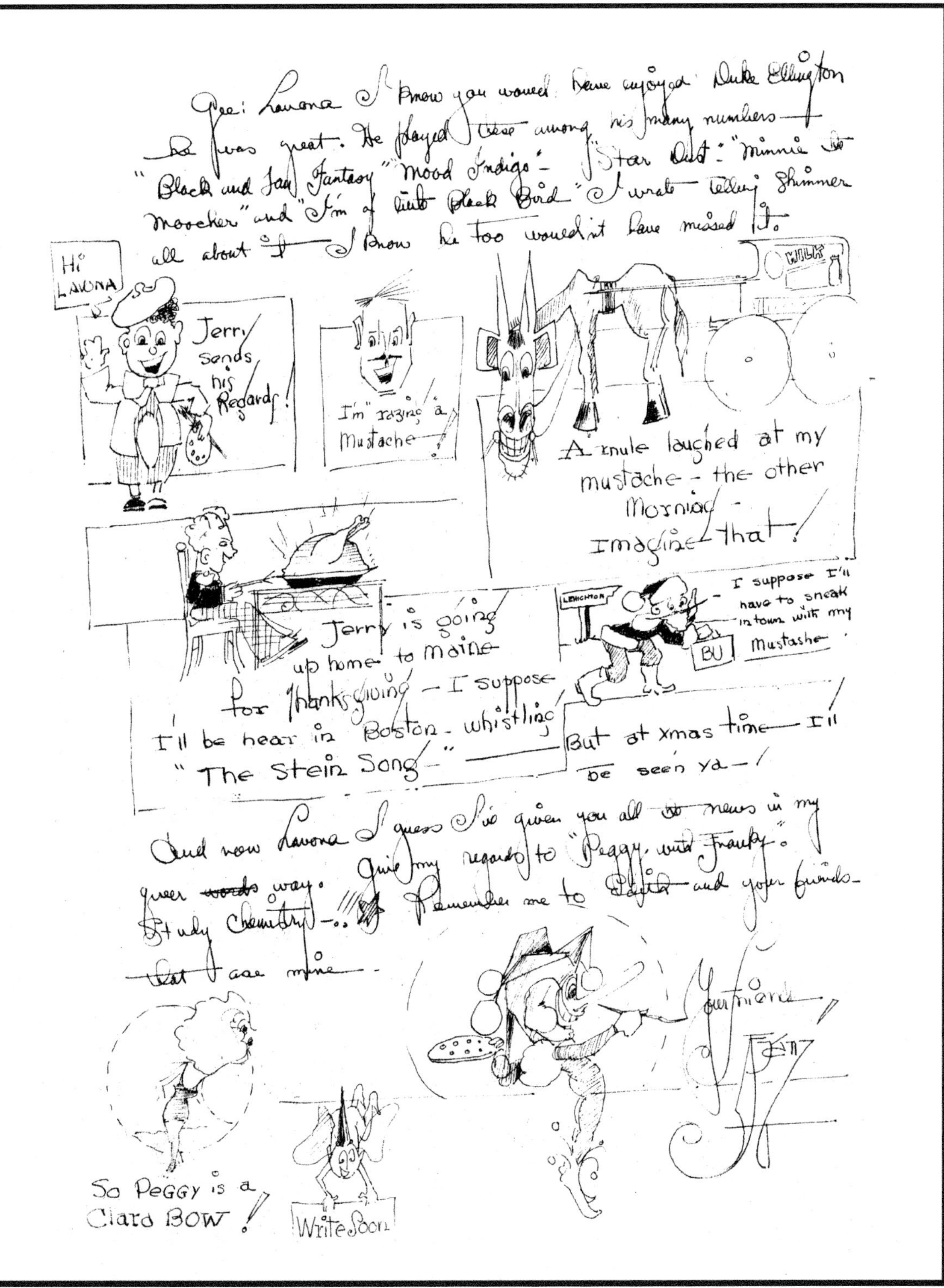

Gee: Lavona I know you would have enjoyed Duke Ellington he was great. He played these among his many numbers — "Black and Tan Fantasy" "Mood Indigo" — "Star Dust" — "Minnie the Moocher" and "I'm a little Black Bird" I wrote telling Skimmer all about it I know he too wouldn't have missed it.

Hi LAVONA

Jerry sends his Regards!

I'm raizing a Mustache!

MILK

A mule laughed at my mustache - the other Morning - Imagine that!

LEIGHTON

I suppose I'll have to sneak in town with my Mustashe

BU

Jerry is going up home to Maine for Thanksgiving — I suppose I'll be hear in Boston - whistling "The Stein Song" — But at Xmas time I'll be seen ya —

And now Lavona I guess I've given you all the news in my queer way. Give my regards to "Peggy" with "Franky". Remember me to [illegible] and your friends — Study Chemistry — .. that are mine —

Your friend Franz

So Peggy is a Clara BOW!

Write Soon

Illustrated Letter, November 1931, page 2, from Franz Kline to Lavona Edgar. (*Mr. and Mrs. Curtis Eberts © 2018 Franz Kline Estate/Artists Rights Society (ARS), New York*)

Lehighton, PA

November 1931

Dear Lavona:

Kindly excuse my negligence! Gee: I've been so busy the last few days I didn't write to anyone but "Shimmer," remembering you I told him you asked about him. He's fine and to me the same "Shimmy Shimmer"—no doubt you'll see him at Thanksgiving time.

Your letter was, as were all my conversations with you immensely interesting and as you say, "newsy." In return let me try my hand at illustrating a few thoughts in cartoons—ok, here goes! The first timely topic is—Lehighton walloping Stroudsburg—ahem! Oh yes, LHS won a game—you'd hardly believe it. Really? Winning a football game must be quite some "gossip" about town. Tell Guy I sympathize with him—I know what a twisted knee is.

I saw & heard Duke Ellington in the Metropolitan on Armistice Day. Gee! Lavona I know you would have enjoyed Duke Ellington, he was great. He played these among his many numbers—"Black and Tan Fantasy," "Mood Indigo," "Star Dust," "Minnie the Moocher," and "I'm a little Black Bird." I wrote telling "Shimmer all" about it. I know he too wouldn't have missed it.

Hi Lavona—Jerry sends his regards! I'm razing a mustache! A mule laughed at my mustache—the other morning—imagine that. Jerry is going up home to Maine for Thanksgiving—I suppose I'll be here in Boston—whistling "The Stein Song," I suppose I'll have to sneak in town with my mustache. But at Xmas time—I'll be see'n ya—!

And now Lavona I guess I've given you all the news in my queer way. Give my regards to "Peggy with Franky." Study chemistry !!! Remember me to Edith and your friends that are mine.

So Peggy is a Clara Bow!

Write soon.

Your friend
Franz

37 Evans Road
Brookline, Mass. Nov. 3, 1931
Dear Marie,

I just received a letter from Margaret, naturally her lovely sister Marie, whom I neglected writing to last summer, came to my mind. So in order to prevent criticism such as I experienced upon my arrival from Virginia, I'll just pack these four slabs of wood with all the news and gossip I can think of. Beginning with what I think to you would be of most interest I will tell you of my roommate—Ready—Ok—His name is Jerry, he's a native of Maine, yes a true, very true (Mainiac)—he even snores the "Stein Song" in his sleep—curly hair, blue eyes, and the Palmolive skin you love to touch. He is in my class at the colorful new "Alma Mammy"—B.U. An artist of unusual ability and a lover of lovely little "Dutch girls"!! His address is the same as mine, and he loves to write letters—Now listen Marie, I don't mind your writing to him but answer mine first!!! The second point of interest is—ready? Picture me in a green smock! Yes, green, we freshman are forced to wear them, even out to lunch! The BU studio is just packed with beautiful ambitious wimmen who love their smocks but Jerry & I just wear them as a joke. In them, I can't tell whether I'm a "budding" artist or a "Bloomin' fool. However I love the work and I'm making out wonderfully. Who wouldn't amongst a pack of Boston's fair young feminine sex? The only one in my class from Pennsylvania is a girl from Pittsburgh—so the only thing we have in common are coal dirt and a good sense of Pennsylvania humor. We're both quite a novelty up here with our "foreign slang."

Well Marie how does it feel to be a junior? No doubt your all set to have that yearbook picture taken, look pretty as you are Marie—now watch the birdie—smile—now there, that'll do. I'll look for the results in the '32 yearbook.

Stump tells me you ignore him—stuck up—Here's news—Stump has two rabbits and he named one Franz Josef. Bless his angel heart. Now I'm a bunny! Marie I want you to realize Stump is the nicest guy in town. The most clean-cut friend I have. I can't understand you're not at least recognizing him. Please do Marie—I'm serious. Stump's had lots of tough luck and he needs friends—like, you, Marie. Edith may act as if she never knew him but don't you, Marie, your too different. Be his friend, will ya?

How's the piano and violin com'in along? I can picture you now, pick'n away in Jacky Yenser's symphonic orchestra.

By the way, Marie what's happened to Lehighton's football team. Will they win a game this season? I suppose they'll call off the alumni game! Did L.H.S. hold their usual Hallow'een parade? No doubt the juniors capped first prize. We had a masquerade ball at the BU studio and I went as Paul Revere. With my little wooden horse I had the time of my life! Hoping to hear from you soon.

Let me remain your friend,
Franz

Kline's letters portray his energy, popularity, and sense of humor. While he still did not know if he was a "budding artist or a bloomin' fool," he loved the work and was "making out wonderfully." He and the only girl in his class from Pennsylvania were "quite a novelty" with their "coal dirt" and "foreign slang." He felt good about where he was going, and he remained a hero to many underclassmen in Lehighton, just as, years later, *ArtNews* would describe him as "one of the heroes of the New York School."[19]

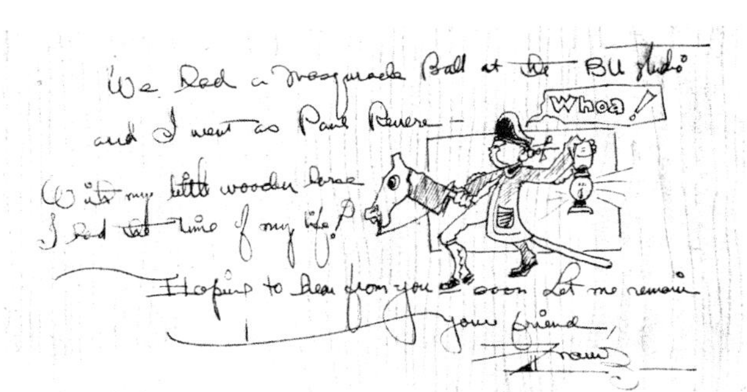

Paul Revere, October 1931. (*Marie Walck © 2018 Franz Kline Estate/Artists Rights Society (ARS), New York*)

7

Intersection: Franz left Pennsylvania to Study in Boston

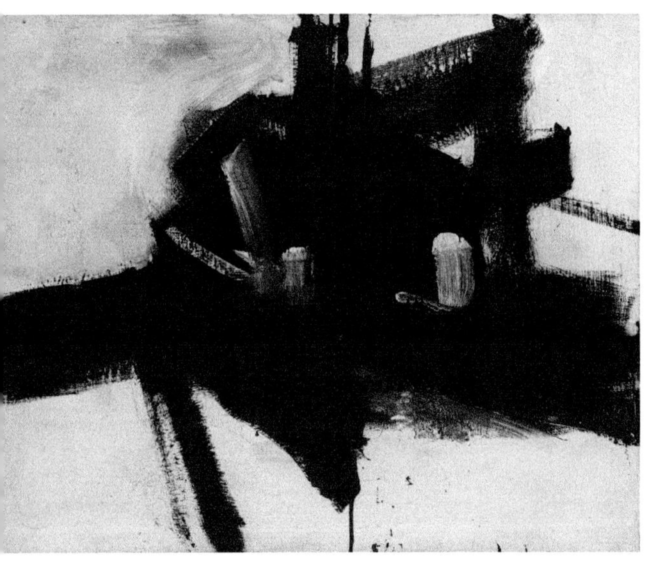

Surprising as it may seem, in view of his later world fame as an abstractionist, his contempt for abstract art was at that time bitter and undisguised.

Frederick Ryan
"Franz Kline As I Knew Him"

Intersection, 1955. (*Private Collection © 2018 Franz Kline Estate/Artists Rights Society (ARS), New York*)

One of the few surviving items from the young artist's years in Boston is a Christmas card Franz sent to Stanley Harleman in 1931, Kline's first winter away from P.A. The card contains a self-portrait inside of Franz wearing the university's signature green smock.

Kline was close to the entire Harleman family, having once even lived in their home for a few weeks when members of his own family had been quarantined with scarlet fever. Stanley's father died during that time, and Franz, who, of course, had already lost his father, offered comfort, strengthening their brotherly bond. Stanley's sister, Florence, referred to Franz as "her brother's best friend."[1] She remembered Kline as "very polite, sensitive, soft spoken, and always right there to help."

Franz returned to Lehighton in the spring of 1932 while school was still in session. Lorraine Rabenold, who wrote as "The Spider" in her column for *The Leni*, described

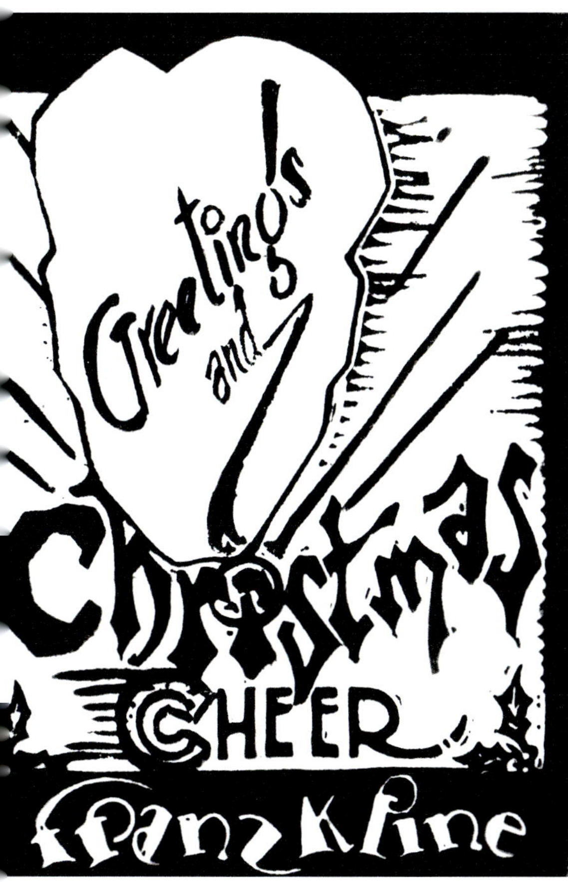

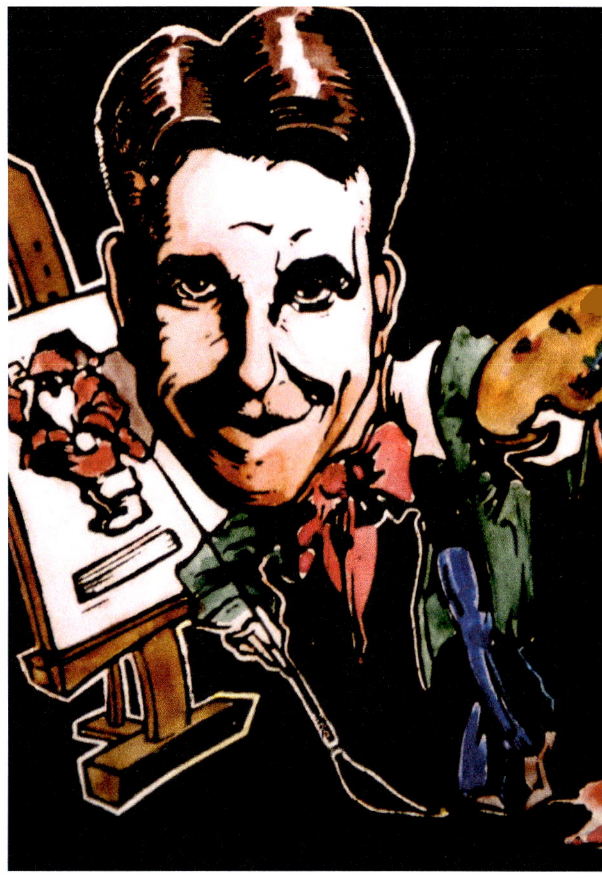

Above left: Self Portrait Christmas Card, Boston, 1931. "Wishing my old pal Stump and the whole family a Merry Christmas. Picture me in a green smock! Yes, green, we freshman are forced to wear them, even to lunch." (*Mrs. Stanley Harleman and family © 2018 Franz Kline Estate/Artists Rights Society (ARS), New York*)

Above right: Page 2, Self Portrait Christmas Card, Franz Kline 1931. As a freshman, Kline made enough of an impression to be elected secretary of the art school. (*Mrs. Stanley Harleman and family © 2018 Franz Kline Estate/Artists Rights Society (ARS), New York*)

his visit. "And listen to this ye chivalrous knights," she wrote, "Franz Kline and Claire Mosser of days gone by were attempting to push several brooms through the seats and desks as well as over the floors last week."[2]

Shortly after returning to coal country, Franz learned that Boston University was closing its art department. The *Globe* reported that it was due to "a lack of endowment."[3] Left adrift the same year that the stock market reached the lowest depths of the Great Depression, many students, including Kline, matriculated to the newly formed Boston Arts Students League. It became a kind of haven for the displaced. Classes were held in the large basement beneath Fenway Studios on Ipswich Street. Here, Kline met Frederick Ryan, a classically trained oil painter who recently returned to Massachusetts after studying at the École des Beaux-Arts in Paris.

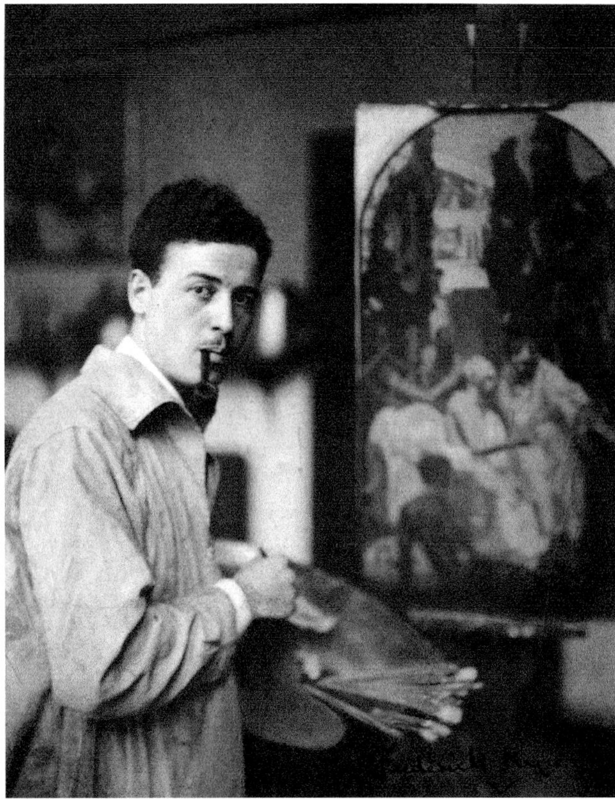

Frederick Ryan, 1929, in his Parisian studio while studying at the École des Beaux Arts. (*Frederick Ryan, Jr.*)

The Boston Art Students League was formed by two former B.U. instructors, Frank Durkee and Arthur Argue. Durkee, "a superb figure draughtsman," had been trained by George Bridgman at the original Art Students League in New York.[4] Bridgeman had produced the series of anatomy and figure-drawing books once considered to be the "art student's bible."[5] He could also count Dean Cornwell and Norman Rockwell as students.[6] From this long tradition, Durkee patterned his vision for Boston's own Art Students League, intending to build from a nucleus of pupils from B.U. who wanted to continue under his instruction. Argue became registrar and general manager; Durkee, chief instructor.

Frederick Ryan described the art market in New England as practically "nil," so he decided to bide his time and dedicate his efforts to further study. As the Great Depression wore on, commercial illustration appeared to be the artists' salvation. Looking back, Ryan wrote that among the students in Boston in 1932, "A passion to master the secrets of fine figure drawing governed the school like a religion."[7] In fact, several instructors, including John Crosman and Richard Andrew, who had been a pupil of Jean-Paul Laurens in France, were so "impressed by our zeal" that they "donated their services as part-time instructors."[8]

Crosman, a renowned pen-and-ink illustrator, worked upstairs in Fenway Studios. The four-story brick structure was built specifically to help artists after fire consumed many of their homes and work in 1904. Each of the forty-six studios has northward-facing light and 12-foot windows. After B.U. closed its Art Department, Fenway seemed the logical

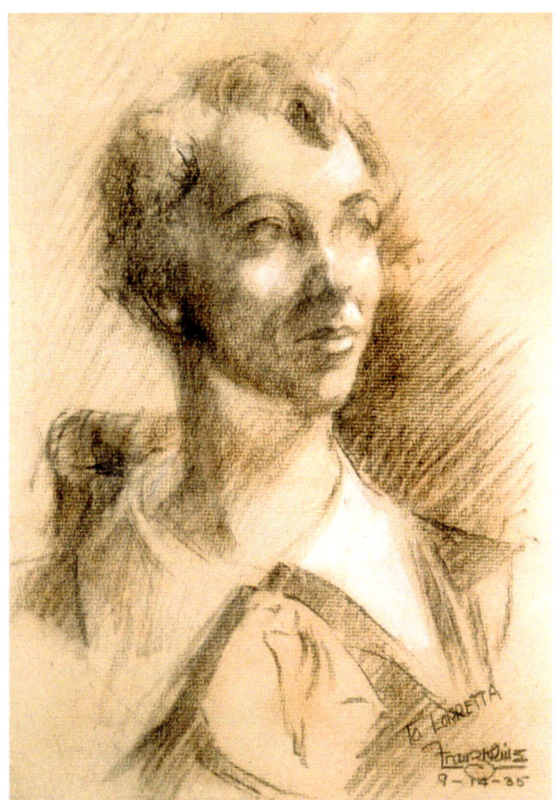

Loretta Gernerd, 1935. "Within minutes and without preparation, he had sketched my mother," recalled Patsy Gernerd Aldrich. (*Patsy Gernerd Aldrich and family © 2018 Franz Kline Estate/ Artists Rights Society (ARS), New York*)

place to regroup. But pen-and-ink was a difficult medium, according to Ryan, and he and Kline were Crosman's only students.

Part of Crosman's instruction involved lending out-of-print volumes of drawing catalogs for them to copy. These included works by Edwin Austin Abbey, as well as some of Crosman's own. Ryan wrote that he and Franz would "rummage" through public libraries to find prints of "the imaginative drawings of Joseph Clement Coll."[9] According to an unpublished, handwritten essay sent to us by Frederick Ryan's son:

> [Kline was at that time] 22 years-old, short in stature and muscular in build with a breezy devil-may-care manner and a rollicking sense of humor.[10] Franz drew with a great deal of facility and slickness if not always with accuracy. One day I heard Mr. Durkee tell him: "You have an awful lot of facility, but if you don't look out it's going to ruin you!"[11]

Franz's goal at the time was "to draw easily a 'smart' type of female figure that would make him a successful and money-making illustrator."[12] His male subjects "ran more to character studies, including figures created out of his head resembling Dickens and the actor W. C. Fields, which appeared over and over again."

For extra cash, Kline continued seeking out commercial jobs. One involved returning to Pennsylvania in 1933 to paint "decorations" inside the Palace Club, a new cabaret in Palmerton, a town neighboring Lehighton. According to *The Morning Call*, Kline's

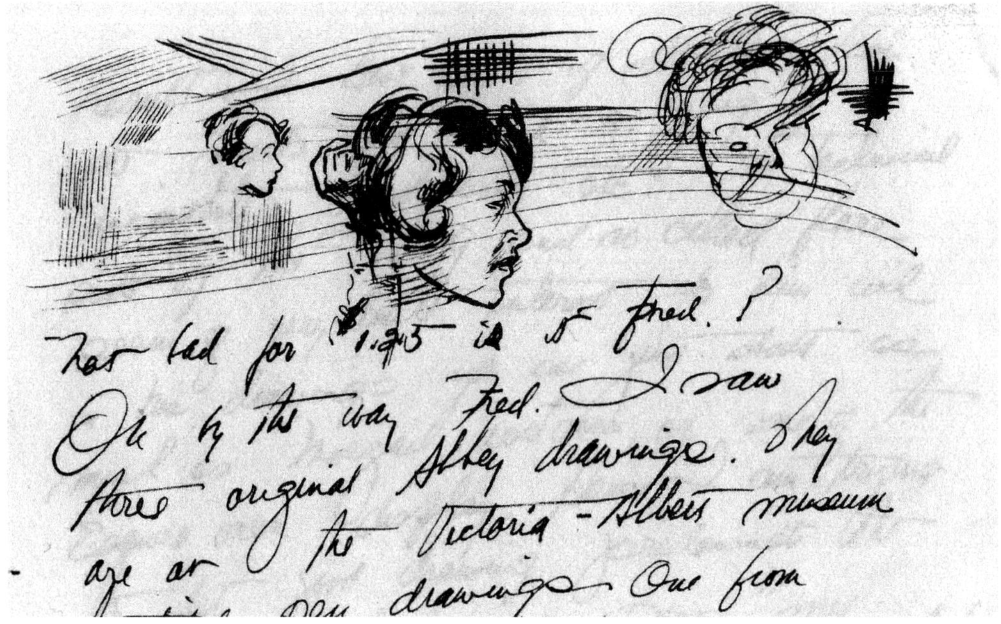
Oh by the way Fred. I saw
three original Abbey drawings. They
are at the Victoria-Albert museum
drawings. One from

"Wish you were here or I were there." Franz Kline to Frederick Ryan, from London, January 21, 1940. (*Frederick Ryan Jr. © 2018 Franz Kline Estate/Artists Rights Society (ARS), New York*)

"modernistic" work inside the cabaret at 2nd and Lehigh Streets made the establishment "one of the most unusual entertainment spots in Carbon County."[13]

Back in Boston, Franz secured another gig and asked Ryan to help him apply gold leaf to a doctor's office window. "I had never handled gold leaf," Ryan wrote, "and then I discovered that Franz hadn't either, [yet] he had accepted the job anyway."[14] The doctor, a plastic surgeon, told the boys stories as they worked. One tale revolved around a tough-looking character who came in for a consultation on behalf of a "friend" who wanted his face changed to become unrecognizable. "The doctor was certain that he was the gangster John Dillinger," Ryan wrote, "and turned him down."[15]

Franz and Frederick Ryan "bluffed their way through the job" with "fantastically adroit clumsiness" like the Marx Brothers. Luckily, the window was five stories above Boston Commons, high enough that "no one could detect [their] bungling incompetence." Throughout the caper, Franz wore an "air of confidence and knowing that was a masterpiece of showmanship. He was a natural born raconteur."[16]

Their studies in those days consisted of drawing nudes for three hours each morning with charcoal. Aside from breaks, the models maintained the same pose for the duration. After lunch, the artists switched to pencils, and the models changed poses every twenty minutes. As far as Frederick Ryan could tell, Kline showed "little interest at all in avant-garde art."[17] Instead, Franz, "preferred drawing on a small and even tiny scale; and his influences and idols were for the most part illustrators of the recent past who are practically unknown to present day art students."[18] He was specifically impressed by the "pearly tones" of Edwin Austin Abbey, who "virtually painted with a pen."[19]

Through a hometown connection, Charles Gernerd, Kline was introduced to John Richard Flanagan, a popular pulp artist and idol of Kline's.[20] Flanagan drew all manner of people scenes from couples kissing to strangers glaring at each other in everything from Rudyard Kipling short stories in *Cosmopolitan* to Fu Manchu's daughter in *Collier's*. Kline looked up to him, and Flanagan seemed to notice something special enough about Franz to gift the young artist with a sketch.

Returning to Boston, Kline regaled Ryan with "whatever hints ... he could glean."[21] But for all of Kline's early influences, the one he was most passionate about was Phil May. In the evenings after class, he and Ryan often went to exhibitions or rummaged around for used books and back-issues of *Studio International*. Because they were also neighbors living just a few doors apart, they "burned a great deal of midnight oil struggling," often sketching each other, before submitting the drawings for Mr. Crosman's criticism.[22] Franz first discovered Phil May while browsing in a used bookstore, and there was immediately something about the Englishman's work, the way it straddled the line between Victorian and Modern, the classic with the new, that became for Kline "a lifelong passion."[23]

Crosman's own technique involved first photographing models to preserve the lighting of the scene. Often there were times when he asked his students to stand in, resulting in "recognizable likenesses" of Kline and Ryan appearing as fictional characters in *Ladies' Home Journal*, *Collier's*, and *McCall's*.[24] The pair considered this "a real lark," as well as also a kind of initiation into the field.[25]

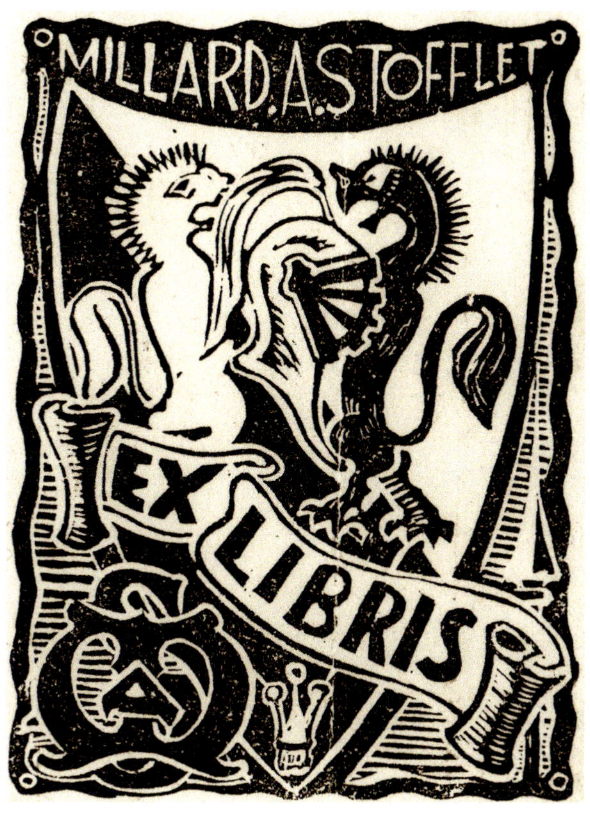

Millard Stofflet, Ex Libras, 1931. Bookplate made for Kline's French teacher, Mr. Millard Stofflet, who warned Franz about his failing grades and "tom foolery." (*Mr. Millard A. Stofflet © 2018 Franz Kline Estate/Artists Rights Society (ARS), New York*)

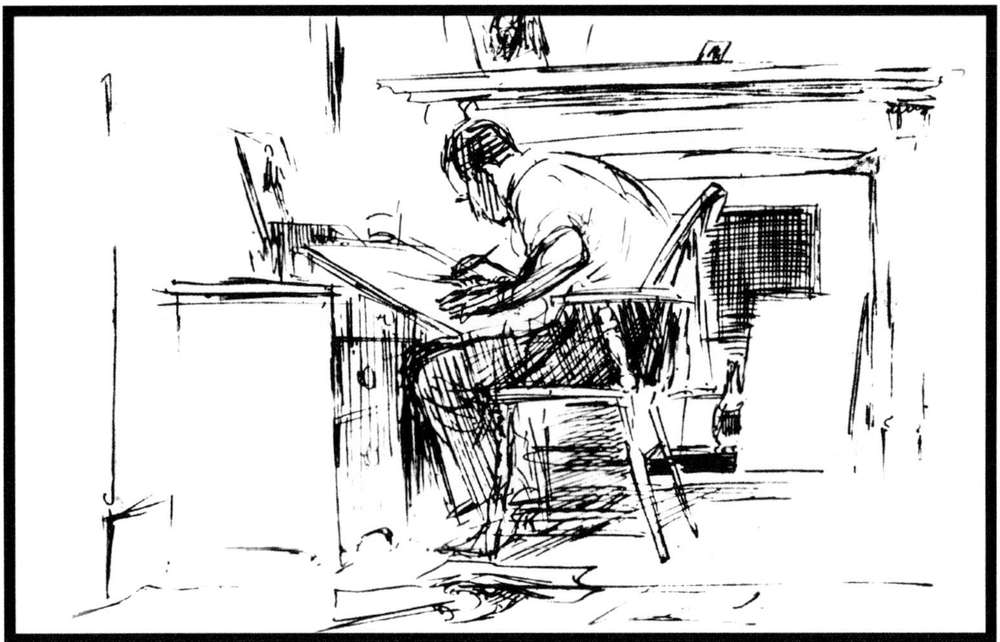

Untitled Self Portrait, c. 1944. A self portrait of Kline working in his mother's music room. (*Patsy Gernerd Aldrich and family © 2018 Franz Kline Estate/Artists Rights Society (ARS), New York*)

One of Kline's favorite models at the time was fellow art student Martha Kinney. Ryan introduced her to Franz at a party. Shortly thereafter, Kinney, "a slim, pretty, and long-legged girl," and Kline rarely separated.[26] She became his "constant date and favorite model for a period of years" to the point that her "proportions and characteristics dominated all his drawings of women."[27] In return, Kinney introduced Ryan to the woman who later became his wife, Beatrice Benoit.

The four spent much of 1934 together until, once again, their school was forced to close. Frank Durkee's health had deteriorated (he had been gassed during the war), and in 1935, no one had been willing to take up his mantle.[28] Times were uncertain. *The Boston Globe* sought out artists to create posters for their annual Emergency Campaign to benefit the hospitals, and Kline's drawing was chosen. It shows parents at the foot of their child's hospital bed, with a nurse standing by. Kline's sister, Louise, kept a framed copy of it on the wall in her home, and *The Globe* reprinted portions of it, soliciting aid.

Apart from the Great Depression, a Dust Bowl devoured the American plains. The mood of the times was heavy. Across the ocean, an Austrian-born German Chancellor named Hitler began a secret campaign of rearmament, a blatant middle-finger extended to the Treaty of Versailles.

At the same time, it appeared to Kline and Ryan that their roles in society remained increasingly vital. In 1935, the year the Boston Art Students League disbanded, Walt Disney released his first short color film of Mickey Mouse, *The Band Concert*. New frontiers were materializing everywhere. For Kline, his new direction meant Europe, to the homeland of Phil May and his mother, to study abroad in London at The Heatherley School of Fine Art.

8

The Dancer: Studying in London, Franz Met his Future Wife

From an art standpoint, I found Franz's works contain a lot of tragedy.

Louise Kline Kelly
Personal correspondence

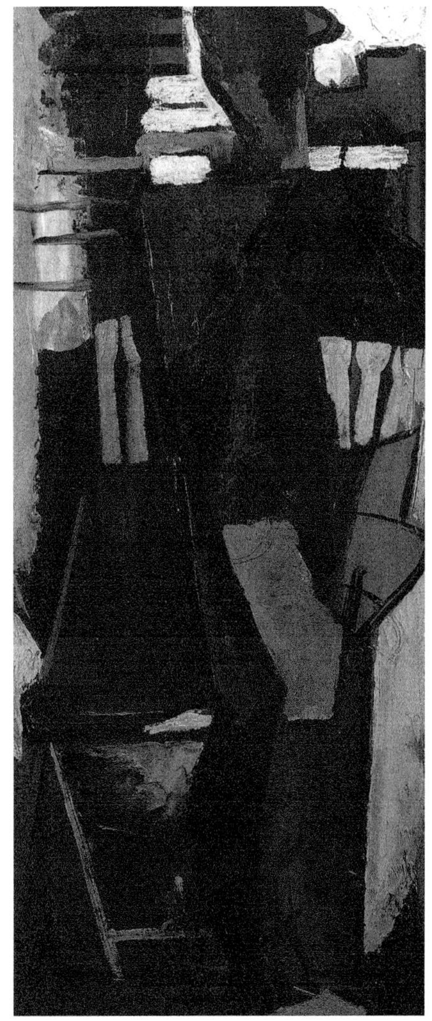

The Dancer, 1940. (*Private Collection © 2018 Franz Kline Estate/Artists Rights Society (ARS), New York*)

Franz left New York for London on Saturday, October 5, 1935 on board the S.S. *Europa*, a diesel-powered motor ship.[1] The day before leaving, he visited the Metropolitan Museum of Art with his sister. Louise was on a break from Skidmore College and had joined him in Manhattan. She remembered walking through the museum with him, taking in the collections. Realizing that a piece that he most wanted to see was not on display, Franz charmed an attendant into taking them to where it was stored. Louise followed him into the depths of the building. The museum worker led them along a corridor to a small room. Inside, among other works, was the first actual ink on naked paper by Phil May's own hand that young Kline had ever seen. "The expression on Franz's face," Louise said, "was as if he'd just been shown a small glimpse of his future."[2]

May, like Kline, had also lost his father while young. He had been nine, two years older than Franz when his own father had died. As a teen, May slept on park benches and lived among the destitute, before finally landing work designing theater posters, costumes, and cartoons. Throughout his short life (he died in 1903 from tuberculosis, aged thirty-nine), May's ability to pair "a vigorous economy of line" with a sympathetic wit helped catalyze the shift from classic Victorian drawings to modern cartoons.[3] He also chose subjects that other artists tended to ignore like guttersnipe (homeless kids) and costermongers (street vendors).

Franz bought at least one postcard on the way out of the museum. Before boarding his ship, he dashed off a note on the back to the Gernerd twins, stating: "Dear Chas. & Geo: Here he is, Remember him? Best Regards, Franz." As the small picture of May wound its way back to coal country, Franz set off across the Atlantic. A small entourage, including Mars Roedel and Elizabeth Sherer, the high school librarian whose bust of Ben Franklin Franz once painted a mustache, waved handkerchiefs and whistled as Franz performed from the deck until his ship faded out of sight.

Franz chose to study abroad after the Boston Arts Students League dissolved. He had never been to Europe before, but stories of his mother's homeland had always fascinated him. On board the ship, Kline met another traveler around his own age named Frank Hahn, who would later become his roommate.[4] Kline's life in London is richly described in his letters to Frederick Ryan, many decorated with small drawings, as well as various strokes and scribbles to demonstrate results with a particular pen. Many describe how much he enjoyed his new surroundings, wandering around and drawing newsboys and quacks, draft horses pulling carts, and raucous pubs. He later gifted a page from his sketchbook to Frederick Ryan, one depicting the interior of Kline's studio.

Ryan wrote that, in London, Kline's "taste for subtle and refined line drawings did not wane, but if anything, it was intensified." In Kline's own words, postmarked January 21, 1936:

> Well Freddie it's no use going on how much I like London. You can imagine it all. From every standpoint it's great. Subject matter of all types and the home and working grounds of all our illustrator masters, Whistler, Abbey, May etc. And if Sargeant, Whistler and Abbey liked it enough to work here I certainly would be a Jerry Milliken if I wouldn't.[5]

Kline mentioned a visit from Mars Roedel, who spent a week with him before flying to Paris.

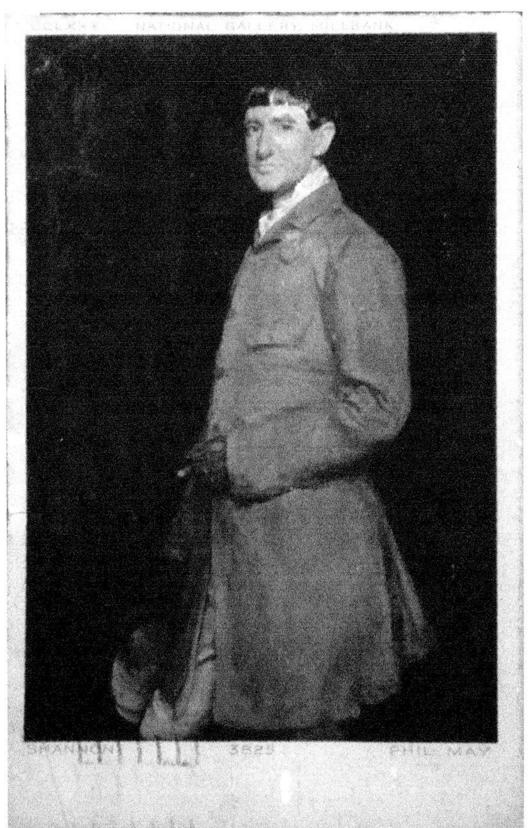

Right: Phil May postcard with note to Charles and George Gernerd, October 1935. (*Patsy Gernerd Aldrich and family © 2018 Franz Kline Estate/Artists Rights Society (ARS), New York*)

Above right: Phil May postcard (back) with message. (*Patsy Gernerd Aldrich and family © 2018 Franz Kline Estate/Artists Rights Society (ARS), New York*)

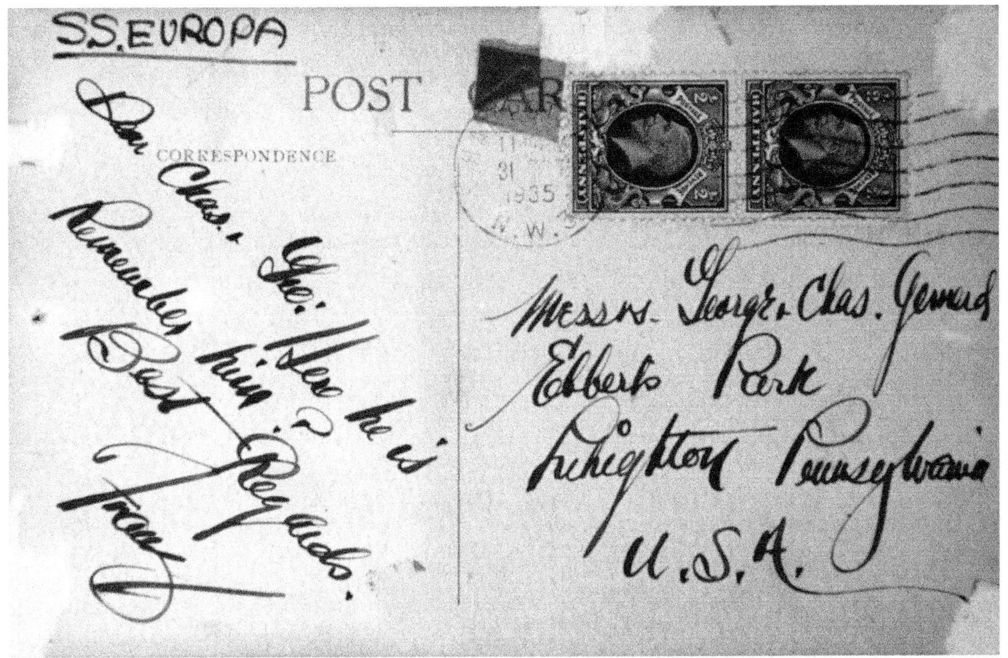

SS. EUROPA

POST CARD

CORRESPONDENCE

Dear Chas. + Geo: Here he is
Remember him?
Best Regards.
Franz

Messrs. George + Chas. Gernerd
Elberts Park
Lehighton Pennsylvania
U.S.A.

> I took it upon myself to show her what I knew of London from the Abbey to St. Paul's, to the museums and May's originals. Anyhow she bought three original pencil studies of Sir Henry Irving for £5 and gave them to me. Beautiful studies, they are valued at £20. So I have still to get over the excitement and enjoyment of it all. One of them is reproduced in James Thorpe's book on Phil May. By now I have ten books on him, some first editions, so you see I still have old Phil in the blood.[6]

Kline later wrote to tell Frederick Ryan that four of his studies had been selected by *The Artist* magazine for a piece about future artists. "I think 15 were chosen, and four of them were mine. I haven't yet found out when they will be published but shall let you know."[7] The magazine would publish two, a nude and a portrait of Martha Kinney.[8] Kline signed off with, "Wish you were here or I were there. We could have a nickel hamburger and a coffee. Good luck and many strong lines."[9]

Mars Roedel was not the only woman who stayed with Franz abroad. Martha Kinney also crossed the ocean to live with him for a while. She was his muse in Boston. All of the girls he drew at the time took on her "proportions." Kinney, whom Kline called "Nutsy," was so enamored with him that during a visit to Allentown she had "Franz J. Kline" tattooed on her chest.[10] She traveled alone on the M.V. *Britannic*, but even after a week at sea, she was delayed further due to fog. "The voyage was deadly," Kinney wrote, "I'm terribly anxious to get there because Franz has a darling place picked out to live ... 28 Queensborough Terrace."[11]

We are unsure what exactly caused Kinney to abandon Kline's bohemian dream abroad, but she eventually succumbed to her parents' pleas to come home. The cold, wet weather might have had something to do with it—and hunger. Perhaps they pulled the plug on her allowance. Kline's only lines describing her there say Kinney was "propped up in bed eating candy and reading," and, "for her there's no place like the USA until she gets there."[12] Kinney, whose parents repeatedly told her that Kline would not amount to anything, returned home in 1936, just before Christmas. Whether or not a certain model from Frederic Whiting's illustration class had anything to do with Kinney's decision to leave remains unclear.

Dark, young, and beautiful, Elizabeth Vincent Parsons was a life drawing model who struck Franz so intensely that he later asked her to pose for him privately. Older than Kline by a few years and divorced, Elizabeth was the daughter of a colonel. She had a brief career as ballerina and was once presented at Court.[13] While English, she was quite different from Franz's mother. Although similarly refined, Elizabeth had no illusions of ever playing house. Kline somehow charmed her enough to pose for him even after she realized he had little money to pay for her time, except to take her out for her first Coke.

In a letter home to Ralph Beisel in Lehighton, Kline wrote: "London is swell; I'm wild about all this picturesque quaintness. School with Mr. Spurrier, though quite different from my Boston studies, is ideal. I know you are faring well Chicken both in classes and on the gridiron, wish I could see you in action"[14]

By the time Kline entered Steven Spurrier's class at Heatherley, the elder was in the process of transitioning out of a career in magazine illustration into a painter of high repute. Born of a silversmith in London, Spurrier apprenticed under his father while also

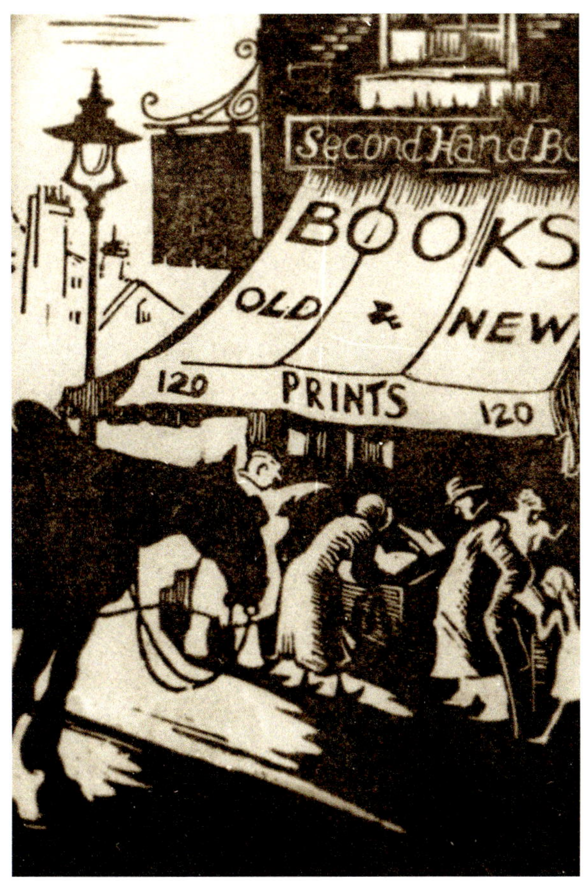

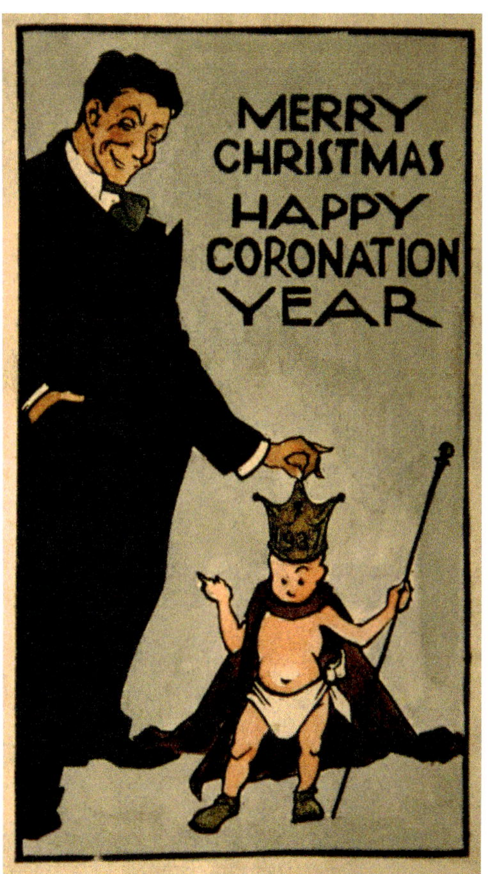

Above left: London Bookshop, c. 1937, lithograph. (*Dr. Louise Kline-Kelly © 2018 Franz Kline Estate/ Artists Rights Society (ARS), New York*)

Above right: Merry Christmas—Happy Coronation Year, 1937. In England, Kline made income from Christmas card commissions such as this card from the Queen's Coronation year. (*Mrs. Stanley Harleman and family © 2018 Franz Kline Estate/Artists Rights Society (ARS), New York*)

Right: Just About There—Cheerio, Christmas 1938. (*Mrs. Stanley Harleman and family © 2018 Franz Kline Estate/Artists Rights Society (ARS), New York*)

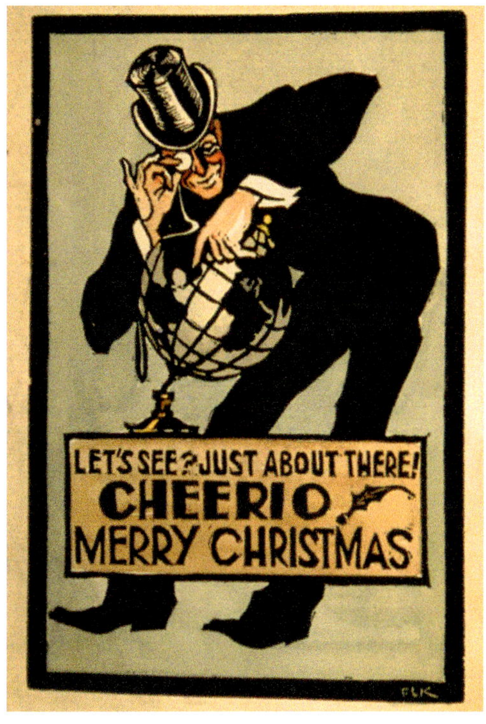

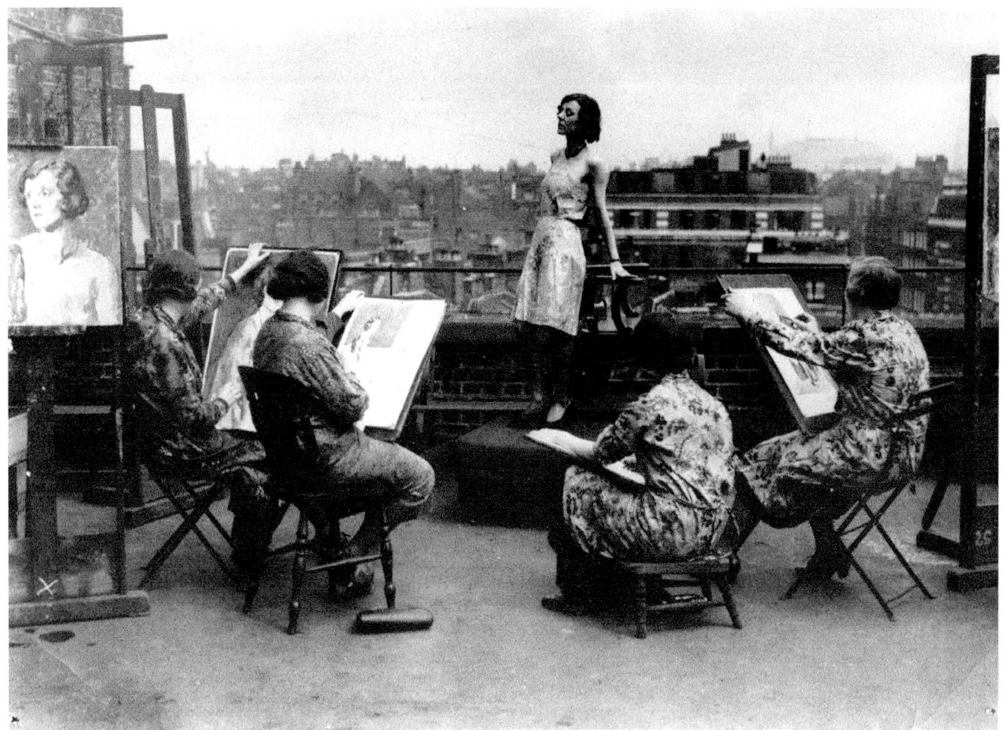

A life drawing class at The Heatherley School of Fine Arts in London, 1935. (*The Thomas Heatherley Educational Trust*)

taking night classes at Heatherley. By the time he had turned twenty-two, Spurrier gave up working with silver to dedicate his time to drawing. He later contributed to *Radio Times* and *Illustrated London News* among others. During the First World War, he worked with British Admiralty designing and painting "dazzle camouflage" on warships. Rather than try to blend an object into its environment to conceal it, dazzle camouflage—or, as it became better known, "razzle dazzle"—attempted to confuse the enemy by painting geometric shapes and contrasting colors on the sides of warships.[15] No two designs were alike. To fool the enemy's read on the correct position, dazzle lines interrupted and intersected at random. Sometime after the war, Spurrier returned to Heatherley. But this time to teach. While there, colleagues described him as a man who "disports himself in a manner more charming than serious."[16]

When Kline entered his classroom, Spurrier encouraged the young artist to develop a more fluid style, to "let good drawing predominate the technical smartness" of his work.[17] Not an easy lesson. One assignment included drawing a series of animals over and over until his students learned how to capture the particular differences between a rabbit and a hare. Spurrier encouraged his students to loosen up, to back away from technicality in favor of something closer to what was considered art.

Outside the classroom, the depression in America had crossed the Atlantic into England. Crowds of unemployed people stood outside workhouses. Parliament abandoned the gold standard. An early advocate of free trade, Britain initiated protectionist tariffs to encourage

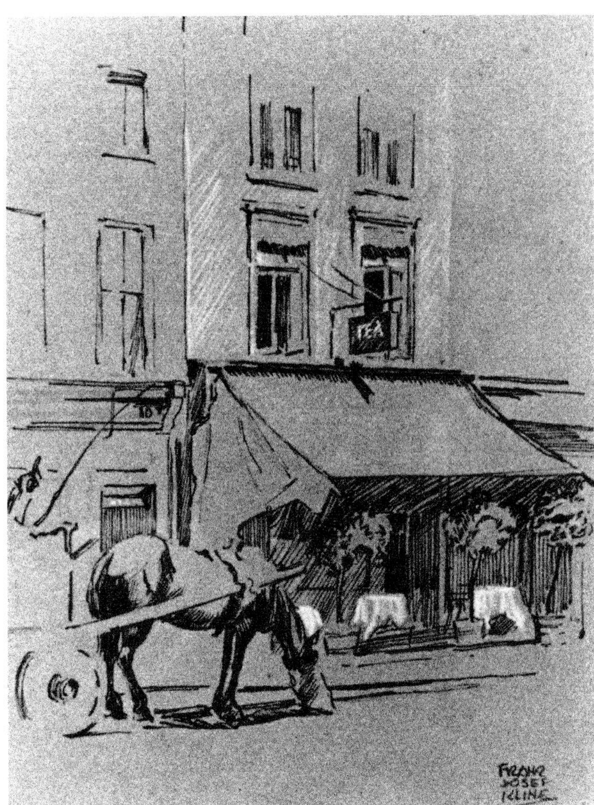

A London Cafe, 1937. "London was the answer to all the good ideas in taste and Princess Margaret was his idea of when a girl was really beautiful," Robert Rauschenberg said, December 1965. (*Dr. Louise Kline-Kelly © 2018 Franz Kline Estate/Artists Rights Society (ARS), New York*)

people to buy and sell locally. As the traditional odd jobs Kline depended on for pocket money dried up, he came to rely on his education trust to also pay for food. He and Hahn were evicted from the flat at 29 Belsize Crescent for not paying rent. While Kline was evicted a total of five times in London, Hahn left shortly after moving into their second, a basement apartment on Westbourne Grove, for a job in Singapore.[18]

Mars Roedel, always the devoted friend, continued to send gifts. After her visit in 1936, she wrote, "It was very pleasant being met at Waterloo Station and having Franz as an escort for the next six days."[19] At the time, Franz had a small white puppy named Michael. His diggings were "a large, barren room with a small fireplace that appeared to be inadequate for winter warmth."[20] She mentioned browsing in a bookseller's shop one afternoon where Franz found a pile of drawings by Phil May. "One he especially liked was the rear of an old cab, with the portly figure of the cabby exuding humor," she wrote.[21] Roedel later returned to the shop to purchase and have it delivered to Kline after her departure. She learned some time later that he had sold it, "ostensibly to buy food."[22]

Franz remained in London for two years, and, as usual, he stood out. In the London column of *The Daily Sketch*, a columnist known as Mr. Gossip (Patrick Balfour, Earl of Kinross) singled him out:

> London is not nearly as empty as some people imagine. There are, for example, artists of many nationalities who find August in London attractive. I met Franz Josef Kline, the

> American artist, who is over in England on his first visit. He is 26, dark and an athlete, has been an officer in the U.S. Army, football captain at the Lehighton High School and a boxer. His mother is English—from Cornwall—and his father is of German extraction. Some of his biggest and most amusing pictures now adorn a Kensington restaurant. One I liked was a big one, eight feet by seven of Mexicans playing and cheating at cards in a Mexican inn. One man on the floor is handing up the ace to his pal at the table. Kline does every type of work—oils, watercolors and etchings. He seldom has a sitter, preferring to work from imagination after a scene has been impressed on his mind. He likes London types. The other day he was sketching a coal cart and driver when the driver stopped, saying: "Don't hurry mate, me and my horse will stay still for five minutes." He painted his first picture when he was four with the juice from a plate of stewed rhubarb.[23]

This kind of exposure helped Kline land enough work to stay above water. "In London," Elisabeth Zogbaum said, "Franz became quite adept at illustrations for a while until Henry Patrick Raleigh warned him to stop or risk losing affection for his art."[24]

As Kline's two-year term neared its end, he applied for British citizenship. He was enamored with Elizabeth and London and thought that his mother's dual citizenship might help his case. He worked briefly at Selfridges Department store. However, when he learned he would not be allowed to continue working for eight years, he had no choice but to return home. Three months before his twenty-eighth birthday, on February 12, 1938, Kline boarded the S.S. *Manhattan* in Southampton. He arrived in New York five days later, his destination appearing incorrectly on the ship's manifest as "300 S. 9th Street, Whigton, Pennsylvania."[25] What do we make of this clerical error? If anything, it lets us hear fragments of Boston, London, and Pennsylvania coal country accents intermingle. It gives us a sense of his enthusiasm, or lack thereof, about returning home. Home to Ambrose and his mother, his younger sister and brothers. Home to a neighborhood of eager friends. Home to Mars.

All accounts indicate that Kline was restless when he finally arrived. In her memoir, Roedel described him as noticeably withdrawn and unhappy, like he was just marking time. She wrote about the various activities his family devised to keep him occupied, including the construction of a life-size snow woman:

> We scooped up piles of snow and offered plenty of advice while he sculpted her. She was really quite handsome, a pioneer woman, rising proudly from a broad base, her molded face upturned. Someone brought a frilly hat from the house. It was sad later to see her disintegrate the same way our chances of keeping [Franz] around melted before us.[26]

Franz's mother expected him to settle down, possibly even marry Roedel. Louise recalled part of the dinner conversation that evening, "Mother asked, 'Now, Franz, why don't you go to the high school and apply for the position teaching art?' Nobody thought you could earn much of a living with art, but she never discouraged him. So he said, 'Oh, I don't want to teach. Mother, I want to create. I'm going to New York.' And he did."[27]

Franz never intended to stay home for long. Roedel helped him land a job in Buffalo, New York, as a window decorator. Her sister lived there. Many artists later cut their

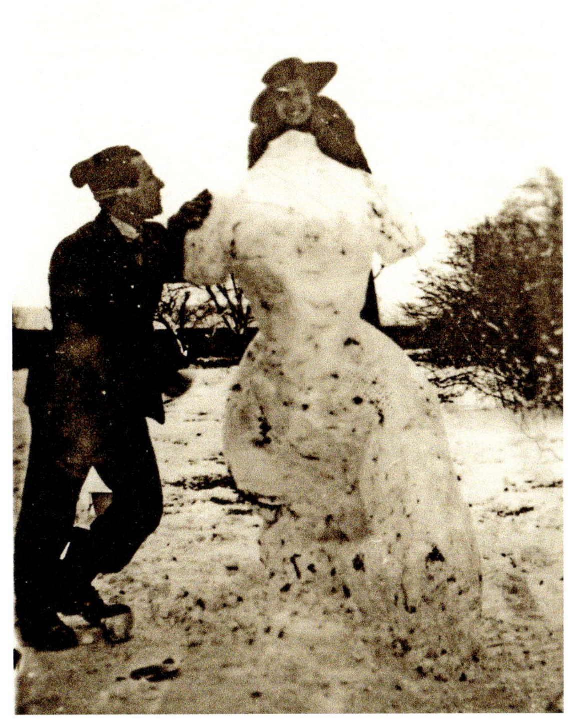

Franz (left), newly arrived from England, and longing for New York, February 1938. Kline "marks time" with Louise building a snow woman in their mother's yard in Lehighton. (*Kim Graver Steinberger and family*)

teeth designing window displays for department stores, including Andy Warhol and Robert Rauschenberg. Mars helped Franz get his start at the Oppenheim Collins shop as an art designer and layout man. Buffalo, as the western terminus of the Erie Canal, was booming. Its population was second in the state. Franz took the job, and Mars sought him out on weekends. She later confided to Louise about the time he returned from work to find her wearing nothing but "his bathrobe."[28]

But Kline did not remain in Buffalo long. Imagining what his future there might look like—creating displays and illustrations to sell hats and shoes—he decided to move again, this time to Greenwich Village. Once Franz received word that Frank Hahn, his old roommate in London, was willing to put him up until found his own place, Franz moved on. Roedel later wrote:

> Franz became affiliated with the 8th Street Gallery in the Village, from whose owner he procured a few pupils and, it being the Christmas preparation season, a few commissions for cards, chiefly linoleum block prints and etchings. He came back to Pennsylvania for his sister's wedding with enough coins in his pocket to provide either a shoeshine or a haircut. We opted for the shoeshine. He had just paid a dental bill with a picture. Before he left again for the city, from my slender salary I pressed upon him some wherewithal to fend off starvation.
>
> I had been spending my weekends in the city and realized that he had to have some place as a base. One cannot hang in space. Frank Hahn was getting married and giving up his large apartment. So we visited the office of Mr. Albert Strunsky, guardian angel

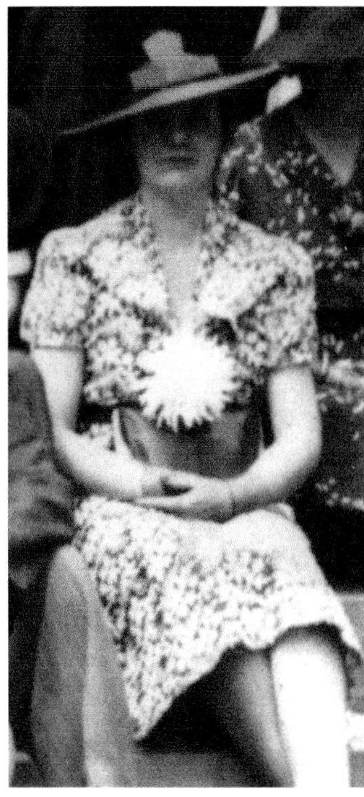

Mathilda "Mars" Roedel at Jacques Kline's graduation from Lafayette College. (*Kim Graver Steinberger and family*)

> of impecunious artists, who owned most of the studio apartments in the vicinity of Washington Square. We found a small one on MacDougal Street that would suffice for a while. I paid the rent through the next month.[29]

Mars Roedel wrote those lines in the midst of great personal sorrow, as Kline's heart ultimately belonged to another. On November 16, 1938, Elizabeth Parsons arrived on Ellis Island, having crossed the ocean on the same ship Franz had taken nine months earlier, the S.S. *Manhattan*. Her ship's manifest does not list her occupation, only that she was born in London, and was thirty-one years old. Most interesting, perhaps, is that she is the only passenger to have the letters S.I. next to her name. This suggests something out of the ordinary about her enough to warrant a "special inquiry," as if she had spent some portion of the voyage in the infirmary, or something else.

Elizabeth Vincent Parsons wed Franz Rowe "Josef" Kline the following month, December 1938, in Greenwich Village. Claire Mosser was his best man. His wife, Loretta, was the bride's attendant, and the two couples remained close friends for many years. The Mosser's often visited with gifts of clothing and other sundries.

"Elizabeth always seemed normal to us," Mosser said. "Her lifestyle had nothing to do with her problems. She knew what she was getting into when she came here, the poverty. She and Franz were our best friends even though we didn't see them but every couple of months."[30]

Franz broke the news to Roedel in a letter.

"Then he married the other woman, newly arrived from England," she wrote. "The first words in his letter to me were 'I must go on with her.' I couldn't accept it and dropped out of living for two long years."[31]

9

New York: From Struggle to Celebrity

It seems so odd to be that Abstract Expressionist referred to. Of course I've been here now for the past twenty years. Here in the Village all that time wondering what painting is—wanting to paint, influenced like we all are by other painters and friends like us who follow the muse.

Franz Kline
Letter to Frederick Ryan, December 14, 1958

New York, c. 1948. (*© 2018 Franz Kline Estate/ Artists Rights Society (ARS), New York*)

On December 5, 1938, Franz Kline married Elizabeth Parsons in Greenwich Village. On the same day, Mars Roedel resigned from teaching in Lehighton due to "ill health."[1]

After Kline's unexpected wedding to Elizabeth, his former teacher lived on in a state of shock. Roedel wrote, "So was I once a sitter on benches. The days of that first winter of my soul's rehabilitation were spent chiefly on a bench in the square. I watched the passing throng but did not see."[2] She began taking voice lessons and sang "Ich Liebe Du" ("I love you") under the window of the Kline's cold-water flat.[3] "Wherever Franz moved," Louise said, "Mars followed as closely as she could get."[4]

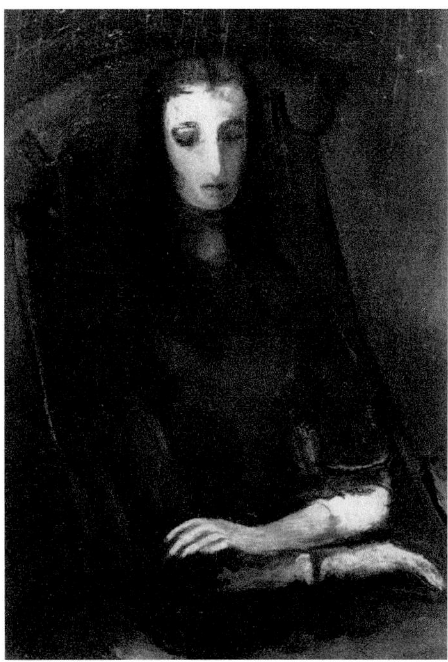

Elizabeth, 1946. Col. Stanley Backman gave Franz and Elizabeth a pair of turquoise vases as a wedding gift. They also gave Elizabeth "a strand of imperial jade," but she thought it too pale for her brunette complexion. (*Private Collection © 2018 Franz Kline Estate/Artists Rights Society (ARS), New York*)

Roedel left Lehighton for a flat on Hudson Street in New York and would later move many times to stay within blocks of Franz. "Miss Roedel was involved in a terrible scandal," friend Patsy Gernerd said. "She used to go to Franz's flat on weekends before his marriage. Things like that were unheard of in those days."[5] Whispers swirled in their wake.

One of Franz's jokes at the time was about how a bohemian was "someone who could live where animals would die."[6] Horribly, this happened once while he was dog-sitting.[7] He returned to his studio to find the animal had perished beside a half-eaten bar of soap. He described his living conditions during the winter as "hell ... mainly because we have had to heat all our hot water in a tea kettle on an electric stove."[8] Elizabeth was often ill. The couple burned newspapers for heat, wore layers of sweaters, and, at times, went hungry. With his breath visible, he painted, listening to the radio. Much of the news was about the war: Nazis, Kamikaze pilots, how long before Paris fell? Would London be next? Then the radio switched back to jazz.

He still could not help but run into Mars every day. Wherever Franz went, Mars orbited around. His wife also noticed this too and later wrote, "Roedel encouraged him in his ambitions to become an artist, but otherwise was later an obstructive influence in his life."[9] Claire Mosser called Mars "the bane of Kline's existence."[10]

Many of Franz's friends from Lehighton came to visit him in New York. Following their trips, they often talked about his harsh living conditions. About Kline's attic apartment in Greenwich Village, Charles Gernerd said, "It had very little furniture, and I was scared just getting up into the place."[11]

When Gernerd told Henry Bretney about Kline's situation, Bretney mailed Franz money for food. Ever gracious, Kline thanked his friend by sending Bretney an oil painting called

The Green Fishing Boat. The work is 16 × 20 inches and painted predominantly in green and ochre. It hung in Bretney's living room for over fifty years. "In the 1940's Franz looked like one of those old bums you'd see in New York," Bretney's wife, Dot, said, "his hair was wild, and he wore a long overcoat. He didn't have much money, but he always asked us to take him to some antique shops. We must have gone in every one from Gilbert to Allentown."

One of Kline's best friends, Stanley Harleman, was "very upset" after his first visit to New York. Stanley's wife, Melba, said that her husband was "horrified" to find how badly "Franz needed a haircut, how his clothing was tattered, and he needed food. It was probably more shocking to Stanley because Franz had been the high school football hero and most popular guy with the ladies."[12]

Franz often returned to Pennsylvania in late September for the Great Lehighton Fair, the biggest social event of the year, a large carnival spread out on the grounds behind his parents' backyard. Replete with livestock auctions, horse racing, a Ferris wheel, cotton candy stands, fortune tellers, hootchy-kootchy shows, goat races, dunk tanks, and games of chance, the fair allowed Kline time to catch up with friends and make money painting signs and drawing caricatures. But, because Elizabeth did not travel well, Kline's visits home were often short-lived, usually lasting only a couple of days. Anne and others kept Elizabeth company while Franz hustled between jobs and visits with friends.

Classmate Lavona Edgar remembered walking along at the fair and being startled by someone touching her arm from behind. "Franz had a beard and long hair and dressed odd. He never mentioned New York when he came home. He always asked about people. What's this one doing? What's that one doing?"[13]

Kline often returned to New York with holiday card commissions: one such design showing the interior of his studio with him and Elizabeth and their printing press in the background. Kline pieced together an income by painting murals, portraits, commercial decorations, and an inventory of "small oils" to sell at the next outdoor show.[14]

Hopeful that his wife would soon return to health, Franz described her condition in a letter:

> Elizabeth has been the one to suffer mainly—lack of baths etc. discomfort and ill health being a result ... [she] hasn't been really well since the beginning of the new year.... She's had several cases of Flu and colds—and I'm sure that getting out of New York for the summer would be the best thing for us both.

Kline talked to friends about pursuing illustration full time, yet he ultimately heeded Professor Raleigh's warning about the risk of losing affection for his work. While Franz certainly was not in a place to turn down any jobs, his persistent tracking of the muse—or what he referred to as "the dream"—did eventually lead to its own rewards.[15]

"Franz entered the Washington Square Outdoor Art Show in 1939 and took a prize, a trifling amount that could be considered the faintest indication that here was talent," Mars Roedel wrote. "At another outdoor show, as I wandered about looking for his exhibit, I came upon a rather small oil of the head of a tramp. There was no mistaking the eyes. It was a self-portrait."[16]

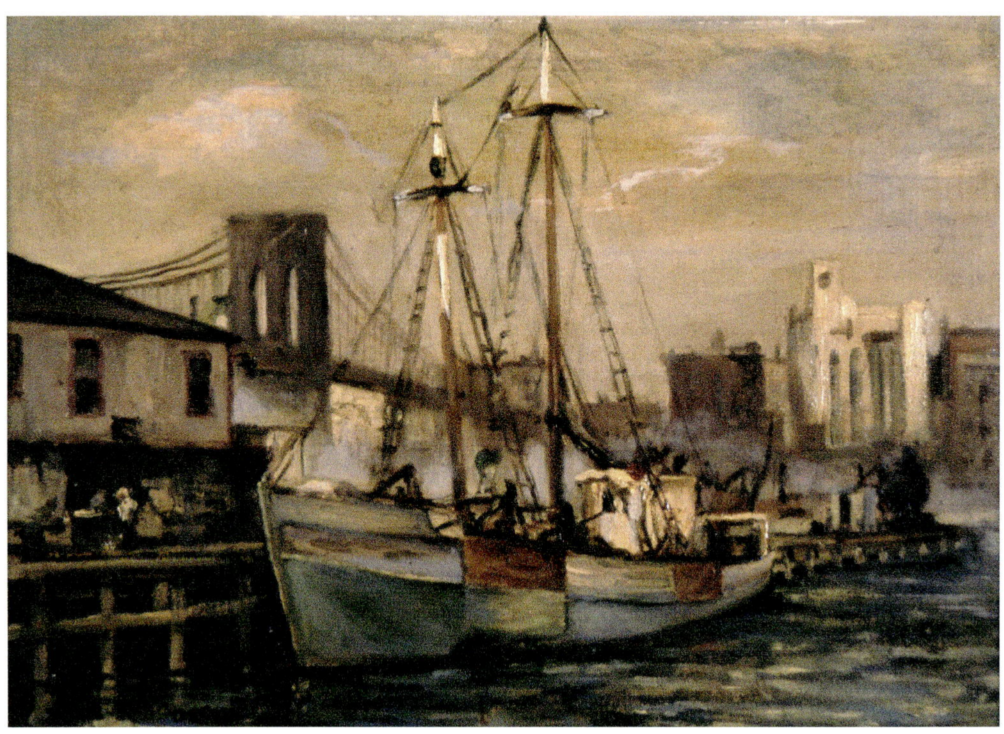

Green Fishing Boat at the Fulton Fish Market, 1942. (*Henry Bretney © 2018 Franz Kline Estate/ Artists Rights Society (ARS), New York*)

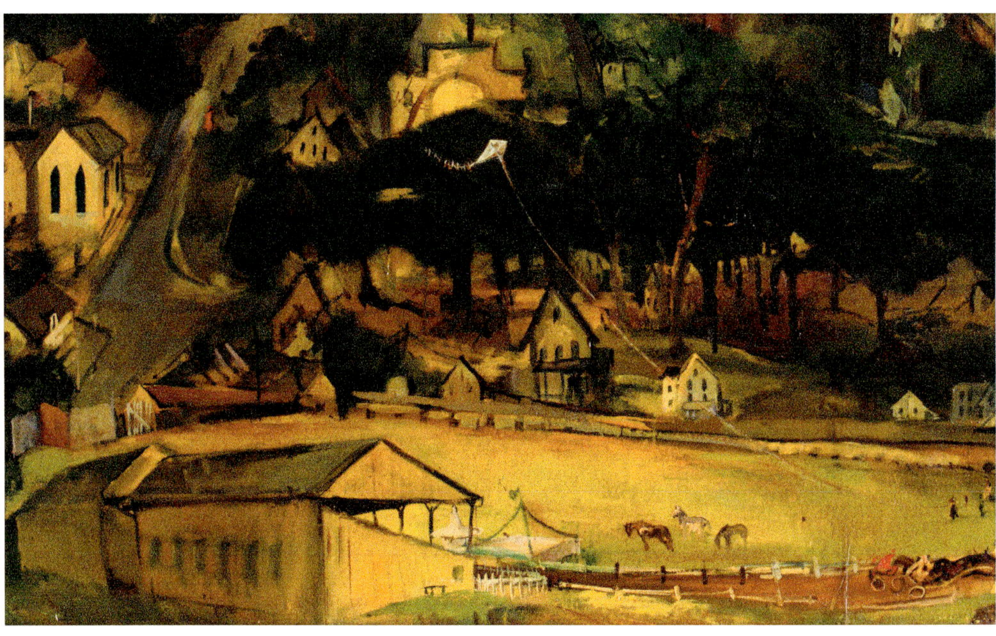

Detail, *Lehighton mural*, 1945. The grandstand at the fairgrounds with the race track and children flying kites on the infield. (*Joshua Finsel/American Legion Post 314 © 2018 Franz Kline Estate/ Artists Rights Society (ARS), New York*)

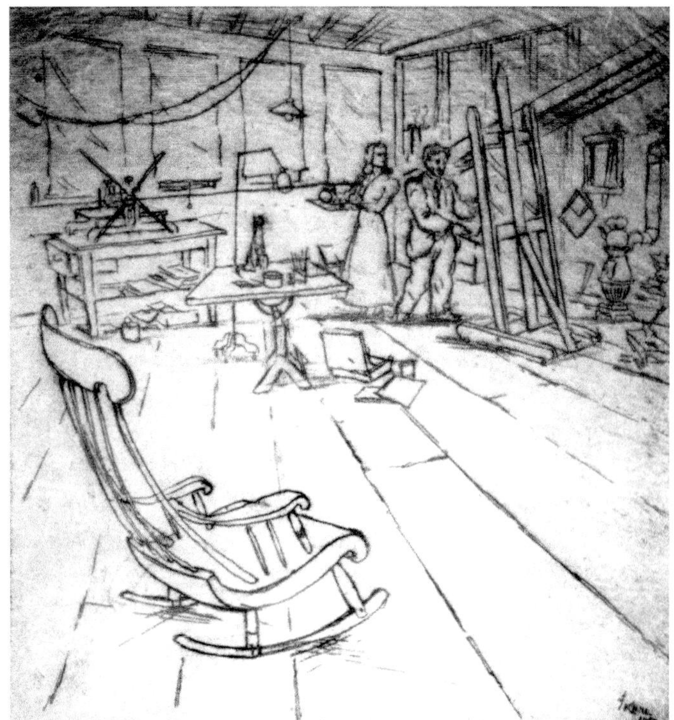

Studio Interior, 1942. This Christmas card depicts Franz and Elizabeth in their loft complete with printing press and his familiar rocking chair. (*Mrs. Stanley Harleman and family © 2018 Franz Kline Estate/Artists Rights Society (ARS), New York*)

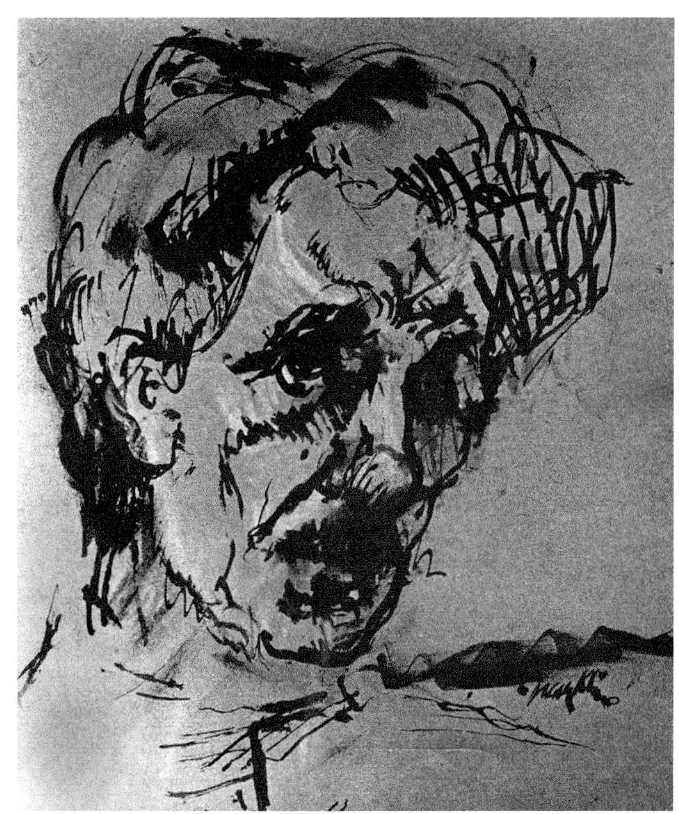

Untitled Self Portrait, *c.* 1941. "I came upon a rather small oil.... There was no mistaking the eyes. It was a self-portrait," said Mathilda Roedel. (*Paolo Pelosini © 2018 Franz Kline Estate/Artists Rights Society (ARS), New York*)

The Washington Square Show was in its fifteenth year and had grown to include the "fronts and sides of buildings and iron and wooden fences extending in a broken panorama from Eighth and MacDougal Streets to the south side of the square, branching off into Thompson and Sullivan Streets, and extending even into West Broadway."[17] A total of 290 artists took part. Others were turned away for lack of space. Participating for the first time, Franz won fourth place in etchings and prints.[18] Mrs. Franklin D. Roosevelt was scheduled to award the prizes, but she was forced to cancel. A city assemblyman filled in. Sales "popped at the very start of the exhibit ... each artist serving as a salesman for his own creations."[19]

The following June, Kline wrote about selling two works during another outdoor show: an oil for $15, and a sketch for $2. A few other people had placed orders, but he had doubts about whether they would come through with payment. "All the sales were bad," he wrote.[20] "However, I did get the first prize award—in black and white—a pen sketch which will hang in the Whitney Modern Museum in the coming week and then join a traveling show to important eastern cities."

To supplement his income, Kline left New York for several weeks in 1940 to work in a doll factory in Massachusetts. The workshop, known as The Small World, manufactured "Minikins," which were miniature rubber mannequins with bendable arms and legs dressed in stylish, colorful outfits. They were the brainchild of Frederick Ryan's wife, Beatrice, and sold nationally in stores like FAO Schwarz. Frederick advanced Franz the bus fare between New York and Massachusetts. Frederick and Beatrice had just moved the business from Boston to an eighteenth-century farmhouse with a barn and 5 acres near Hopkinton, MA. Today, the town is best known as the start of the Boston Marathon. Kline traveled there twice to work on up-fitting the buildings and, later, constructing dolls, specifically buffing the seam flashing.

In a barrage of letters exchanged before his departure, Kline wrote to Fred and Beatrice that Elizabeth was "anxiously looking forward to seeing the New England part of the world." In another, he asked if Elizabeth could bring her cat.[21] Despite descriptions of Elizabeth's ill health, Franz remained upbeat. "I've been working on those Dutch water colors—and am still waiting for payment from the dealer," Kline wrote. "If & when it comes totaling about $30 we'll be able to give the landlady half and pack off.... You see, Fred, it is necessary to pay up a few bills and at least a month's rent in advance before we can go and be assured that our things are safe."[22] But then Elizabeth finally backed off. On June 23, 1940, Kline wrote: "The light and gas have been changed—in our name and now Elizabeth can have the convenience of hot water and baths—enabling her to get back to normal in readiness to join us. Sooah! Fred I will leave this weekend.... Elizabeth will stay on here and John [Erin] will probably use the studio in my absence as a hang out and company for Elizabeth."[23]

Aside from the money, Franz's work visits to Hopkinton gave him time to catch up with Ryan, his friend from the Boston Arts Students League. They drew and painted together like old times and went to country auctions in search of old picture frames. Of the many long conversations shared with Kline, Ryan later wrote:

> In spite of his past intense interest in illustration, [Kline] somehow didn't seem to fit into the New York illustration field at all. He was always essentially a sketcher never seeming

> to correct or finish anything to the standard that success as an illustrator in New York demanded or would have required. Also the fine line type of illustrations of the past in which he had steeped himself was no longer in demand and new and different full-color techniques and mediums reigned supreme.... Surprising as it may seem, in view of his later world fame as an abstractionist, his contempt for abstract art was at that time bitter and undisguised and on one occasion he said, "In order to be a success in art today one has to do something so utterly absurd that nobody can ignore it!" Whether or not his later huge, overpowering black and white abstracts, produced with house-painters' brushes, were done with tongue-in-cheek to pull the legs of critics, the reader will have to judge for himself.[24]

Upon Kline's return to New York, he wrote: "Keep the buffers going." Though struggling financially, Kline rarely allowed empty pockets to hold him back socially. There were often parties, openings, and other happenings in the city. When not in his studio, he hung around places where word of employment could be found, and in many cases, this meant public houses or pubs. Perhaps the most famous nexus for artists at this time was the Cedar Street Tavern. Irving Sandler described it as "no different in appearance from thousands of other lower-middle-class American taverns, except that there were English sporting prints on the walls, but no other art ... and its lack of television discouraged neighborhood folk from coming in."[25] Robert Motherwell held weekly salons at his studio nearby, and the scene often migrated to the Cedar afterwards. Legends persist about Jackson Pollock ripping the men's room door from its hinges and Jack Kerouac urinating in an ashtray.

We know some details about Kline's interactions at the Cedar from his friend Claire Mosser, whom Franz introduced to Jackson Pollock there. "Pollock was a big guy," Mosser said, "but with not much to say."[26] Kline then took Mosser on a tour of bars he helped decorate, including the Minetta Tavern with "caricatures of people on the walls, which Franz did to pay off bar tabs."[27] Then to the "new cocktail lounge at El Chico, New York's famed Spanish night club" to see Kline's "bull-fighting scenes."[28]

Pollock, whose fame only seemed to bring about a more tortured existence, held Kline in high esteem. According to *The Party's Over Now*, Pollock "adored Franz" because he could talk to him despite Pollock's aversion to conversation.[29] Words often made Pollock uncomfortable, as did people in general. In a letter to his brothers, he wrote, "People have always frightened and bored me."[30] Franz, however, appeared to be an exception. Here is a scene featuring their interaction inside the Cedar Street Tavern, as recounted by one of Kline's students:

> I was sitting at the bar having a beer, and I heard John, the bartender, murmur, "Oh, No."
>
> In the small square window of the red front door, I saw a part of Jackson's face; one brightly anxious eye was peering in. John walked down the duckboards towards the end of the bar near the door, and stopped, put his left fist on his hip, and extended his right index finger at the small window. He shook his head. The eye looked hurt. John was tight-lipped. I was laughing.
>
> The eye disappeared.

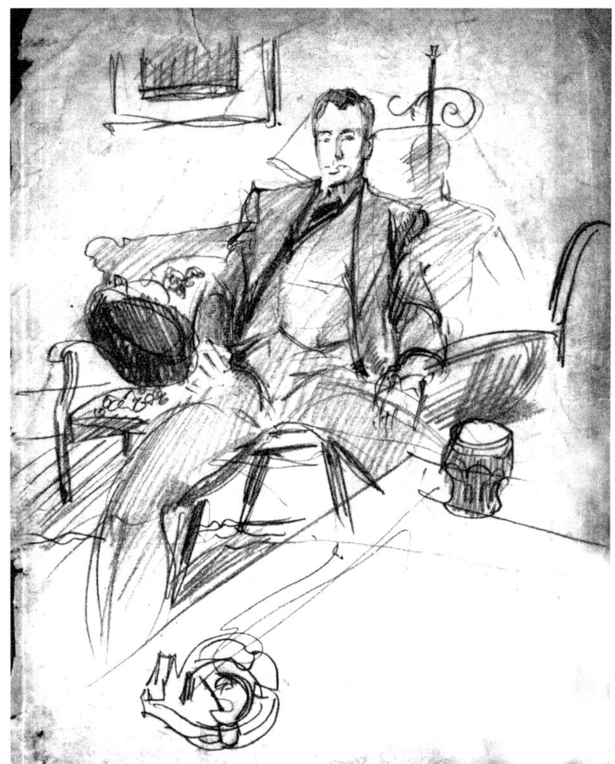

Left: Jacques Kline, *c.* 1938. A sketch of Kline's brother Jacques in Lehighton. (*Elizabeth Bayer and Atty. Margaret Chaplinsky © 2018 Franz Kline Estate/Artists Rights Society (ARS), New York*)

Below: Franz Kline, Gladys Backman, unidentified guest, and set designer Cleon Throckmorton at El Chico's Night Club on Grove Street in New York, June 1945. (*Ian Hornak Foundation, Eric Ian Hornak Spoutz, Rosemary Hornak and Natasha Hornak Spoutz*)

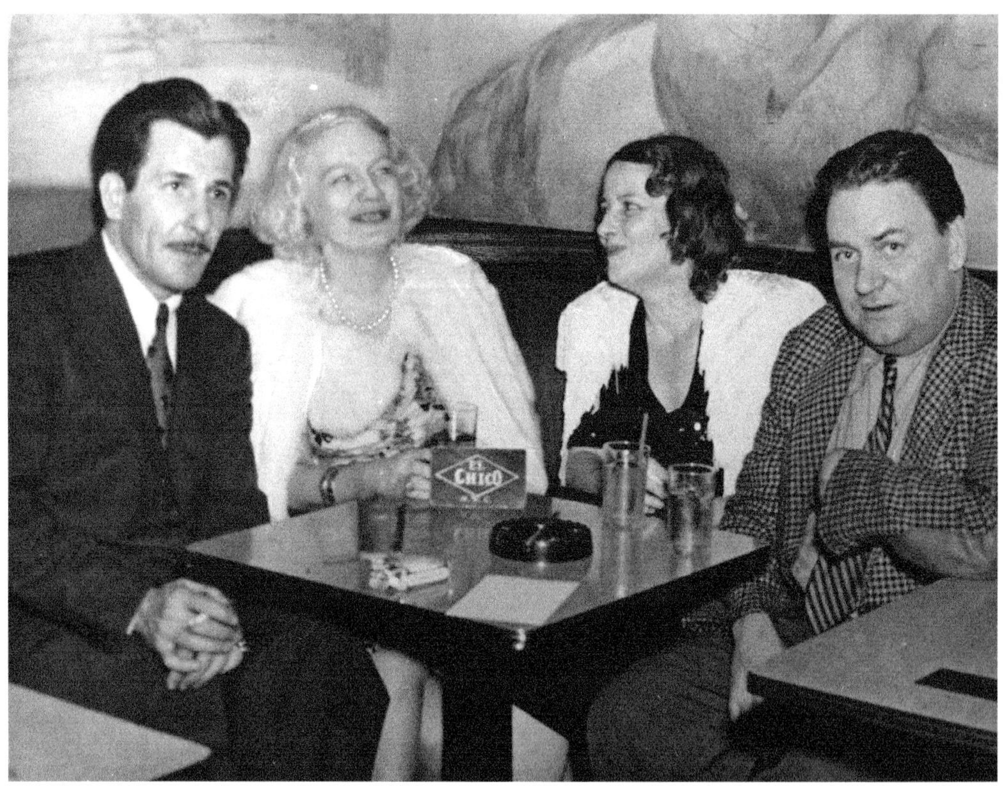

John muttered out of the corner of his mouth and he is a man who can mutter out of the corner of his mouth, "He'll be back."

We watched the square window.

Jackson's eye peeped in.

"NO," John yelled. "YOU'RE 86 JACKSON!"

The eye was sad and puzzled. Me 86?

The eye got angry. Jackson's face slid across the window; then his whole face was framed by it; mask of an angry smile.

"NO," John shouted, shaking his head. "Beat it!"

Jackson's eyes became bright, and he smiled affectionately. John shook his head.

"Whaddya gonna do? I can't say no to the son of a bitch."

He sighed. "All right!" he cried, and pointed to the window, wagging his finger, "But you've got to be GOOD!"

The door opened and Jackson loped in and they faced each other over the corner of the bar. Jackson had a happy friendly smile. John jabbed a finger in his face.

"Remember—one drink and you're finished." John leaned forward. "Do you get that? No cussin', no messin' with the girls—"

Jackson said, darkly, "Scotch."

With the drink in his hand Jackson left John angrily wiping the bar; and as I was the only one at the bar that Jackson vaguely recognized, he made his way toward me, looking intently at me. You never knew. When he got to the empty stool beside me he put his hand on it and a little stooping gave me his flickering friendly Rumpelstiltskin smile, "Okay if I sit here?"

I stammered sure Jackson sure, and in my apprehension rather compulsively arranged a pack of matches exactly in the center on top of a new pack of cigarettes. Jackson watched me, and glanced down at my neat arrangement, and then at me, then at the cigarettes; then at me. He gravely shook his head. Wrong. He crushed my smokes and matches in his left hand.

He gazed back where people sat at tables, eating supper. Many of them were watching him. It was the right beginning for another eight-cylinder Monday night. They had come from the Bronx, from Queens, from New Jersey and from the upper East Side to eat at the Cedar and wait until Jackson finished his fifty minutes with his analyst, and came down to the bar to play.

Jackson walked by each table glaring down at them. They trembled. Pity the poor fellow that brought his date in for supper, for Jackson was happy to see her. He immediately sat beside the fellow, glared nastily at him and then gave his full crude nonsensical attention to the girl while the fellow said—something—timidly—"Say, now just a minute—" Jackson turned to him, and looking at the poor guy with a naughty smile, swept the cream pitcher, salt, pepper, parmesan cheese, silverware, bread butter, napkins, placemats, and drinks on the floor, while the waiters screamed, John shouted, Jackson leaned toward the guy with an expression as if to say, how do you like that?

We all got a little of it. But Franz was the real one who gave it back, and then some. One time Franz and Nancy were sitting at the bar, talking, unaware Jackson was behind them, staring at Franz. Jackson grabbed Franz by the hair and threw him backwards off the barstool onto the floor. Franz got up, straightened himself, glanced at Jackson, and said, "Okay Jackson, cut it out."

Jackson had backed away, slightly stooped, head thrust forward, eyes bright. He was so happy he glittered. After Franz had sat down Jackson did it again.

"Jackson!" Nancy cried.

But when Franz got up the third time, he wheeled, grabbed Jackson, slammed him up against the wall and let Jackson have it in the gut with a hard left-right combination. Jackson was much taller, and so surprised, and happy—he laughed in his pain and bent over, as Franz told me, whispered, "Not so hard" ... Jackson whipped off Franz's hat, crushed it, and tossed it up, out of reach on the shelf which overhung the bar. Franz was angry and laughing; Jackson was happy. One night shortly thereafter, Jackson reappeared at the bar with a brand new bowler hat on, and when he reached Franz, he glared at him, took off the bowler, crushed it, and tossed it up on the shelf.... Jackson and cars, and Franz and painting and women—the two men loved each other, sense of energy, and violence clear up from childhood. Franz's trains. I think so.[31]

In times of despair, nearly penniless, the mood of the times weighing heavily on him; Kline turned to the camaraderie of friends and alcohol to fuel his work, seeking solace in creation. From the titles of his paintings—*Mahoning*; *Palmerton, Pa*; *Lehigh River, Winter*; *Scranton*; *Lehigh V Span*; *Hazelton*; *Bethlehem*; *Delaware Gap*; and a great many others—the impact of Pennsylvania on his work becomes plain. According to Dr. Robert Mattison, "People who knew [Kline] said that he would talk endlessly about coal country and what it was like, the mines and the miners, and talk about the names of the cities. So many of his paintings are named after coal areas. The titles are almost a type of code for the feelings that are behind those paintings."[32]

Decades earlier, Elaine de Kooning had captured this same particularity of Kline in *ArtNews*:

Some artists hide. Others—Michelangelo, Cellini, Delacroix, Van Gogh, and Dostoyevsky—expose themselves, keep journals, write sonnets. And some, like Franz Kline, talk. For these, nothing they have ever done or thought or said is irrelevant. Everything helps. For Franz Kline, 'talk' was an activity, which he always kept going around his art. He was never silent or secret. Everything he said, the wisecracks, the miscellaneous bits of lore, the hilarious reminiscences, all were pertinent to his creation and our understanding.

His anecdotes, told in half sentences and unfinished gestures, expressed the inexpressible. His jokes, for which with a helpfully contagious laugh—he was his own best audience–were inimitable. His stories half-told half-acted, communicated beyond mere words. There were always, one felt, a deep message that somehow, a moment later couldn't be interpreted. But it didn't really matter.... Anecdotes were Franz Kline's shoptalk. Literature, religion, philosophy, art theory were subjects to be avoided (too vague, too ponderous). He was in love with the actual and the specific; the time it took Cunningham to run a mile in the Melrose track meet, why they took Jim Thorpe's medals away from him after he won the Decathlon, how many fights Phil Scott lost before he retired a rich man, how Ronald Coleman mounted a horse in old French Foreign Legion films, and why Lautrec wanted to draw like Degas who wanted to draw like Ingress...[33]

Mark Rothko felt similarly about talking about his work, saying that such explanations tended to induce "paralysis of the mind and imagination."[34] Pollock also did not like to talk about art in public, and, in fact, actively lobbied against others doing so. Early one morning before Franz was awake, Jackson showed up at Kline's studio pounding hard on the door. The day before, Franz had been on a panel at the Museum of Modern Art with Josef Albers. Keeping up his pact with Pollock, Franz sat on stage but did not talk. The moderator, Sam Hunter, spoke for him. It must have been an odd scene, with Kline sitting there silently the whole time, except during the question and answer period. Albers had a hard time hearing the questions from the back of the audience and asked Franz for help. Kline repeated the question for Albers, only that, but Jackson still "barged in" the next morning and growled, "I heard you were talking yesterday."[35]

This paradox between Kline's talkative nature, his clowning around and "drolly expressive unfinished sentences," and his refusal to talk specifics about his own work assumes a kind of Falstaffian archetype, the holy fool, the mythological usurper, the person most dangerous to tyranny because his comedic heart could never be controlled.[36] Kline had a kind of magic about him, one that inspired Robert Motherwell to call him "an enchanter."[37]

"When women came to the booth," wrote Pete Hamill, "[Kline] always tried to rise and bow in greeting, like a *boulevardier* ... when he rose to go to the john, he moved with an athlete's grace, giving off the same muscular aura that emanated from the paintings ... he had a word and a smile for everybody."[38]

Frank O'Hara said: "Franz did not tame his work, but he thus tamed the role which he suspected so correctly society would, if allowed, impose upon him as it had on the unsuspecting Pollock."[39]

At times a grand conversationalist "holding court" in Greenwich Village bars, Kline seemed suited to life in the city, yet he never completely let go of small-town Pennsylvania.[40] Fellow coal country artist Edward Meneeley said that when he first met Kline in the Cedar Tavern and realized that they had both been born in Wilkes-Barre, the conversation quickly transformed into a kind of private language. Sipping pints of Stegmaier beer, they tossed around local idioms, words like "hunyok" and Native American place names like "Tamaqua," "Kittatinny," or "Mauch Chunk" as the rest of the confused crowd sunk back.

"We'd say to him, 'Franz, where's it at?' as if he knew a sacred truth," Meneeley said. "Then Franz would wave his arm high and say, 'It's not up here.' Then he'd wave his arm low and say, 'It's not down here.' Smiling slyly, he would then wave his arm around in the middle, 'It's right about here.'"[41]

Many nights, after fellowship at the Cedar, Kline returned to his studio to work, often into the early morning. Switching from beer to English tea, Kline directed his vision inward, stripping off the figurative forms of life, "arriving at abstraction," in the words of Irving Sandler, "by simplifying and enlarging the contours of his figural images."[42]

"Sometimes I make preliminary drawings, other times I paint directly, start a painting and then paint it out so that it becomes another painting or nothing at all," Kline said.[43]

"If a painting doesn't work, throw it out. In other words, these are painting experiences. I don't decide in advance that I'm going to paint a definite experience, but in the act of painting, it becomes a genuine experience for me."

One of his first significant public recognitions in New York happened in 1943 when the National Academy of Design awarded Kline the S. J. Wallace Truman Prize for *Palmerton, Pa.* The $300 check was a godsend. Biographer Harry Gaugh described the winning painting as "a composite of images, not of yesterday or the day before and not sketched on the last trip home, but aged in memories. The painting's mood is a reverie, a daydream not of the problematic future but the generous past."[44]

Louise remembers her brother sending the prize receipt home with a letter. "Franz said, 'You know, mother, it's an abstract.'[45] Well, you wouldn't call it an abstract today, but yes, it's the way he recalled our darling little station where we took the train to go everywhere," Louise said.[46] "I can see across the tracks where the poor people lived. When we were growing up, Mother had us put all our old books on a coaster wagon and take them down to those children to enjoy. I always considered *Palmerton, Pa.* one of my favorite paintings because it showed the Mauch Chunk trestle and where we would get off of the Central to go to the Lehigh Valley station and watch the Black Diamond come and go. It's not all located in Palmerton *per se* but he put it all in the painting, you see."

The same year, 1943, Franz helped organize and jury awards of The Village Art Center's first exhibition on Barrow Street. A reporter covering the event for *The New York Times* wrote that although much of the work on display was "villagy, Washington Square outdoorish, Society of Independence-esque," some of the paintings "are far more accomplished," mentioning Kline by name.[47]

But for all his hard-won reputational success, Kline still fell behind on bills. His commissioned murals and odd jobs—once working as a filing clerk on Governor's Island, another time helping Cleon Throckmorton with theater sets—were irregular.[48] Less than a decade later, in 1950, Weldon Kees described the artists' struggle with poverty that he saw around him in New York as "either heroic, mad or compulsive.... One is continually astounded that art persists at all in the face of so much indifference, failure and isolation."[49]

A year after winning the National Academy of Design's Truman prize for *Palmerton, Pa*, Kline won the same award again in 1944 with *Lehigh River, Winter.* For some reason, the prize was only $250 this time, fifty dollars less than the year before. One hometown paper reported that "the picture was inspired by [the artist's] many trips with his father, the late Anthony C. Kline, up and down the Lehigh River."[50]

Louise described Franz returning home with the prize: "He had received one of those lovely medals in a velvet box. He came in and said, 'Louise, take the medal up and show it to Mother.' I said, 'No, you take it up and tell her about it.'"[51]

Louise went first to check on her. Anne had recently come home from the hospital and Louise helped powder her face and fix her hair. "She was like a queen sitting there when Franz came in, but still very frail," Louise said. "'Well mother, here's the medal I won,' he said, and her gorgeous big black eyes looked up and she smiled and said, 'Well, Franz, you always win the medals—don't you.' I thought he'd collapse on the floor with laughter.

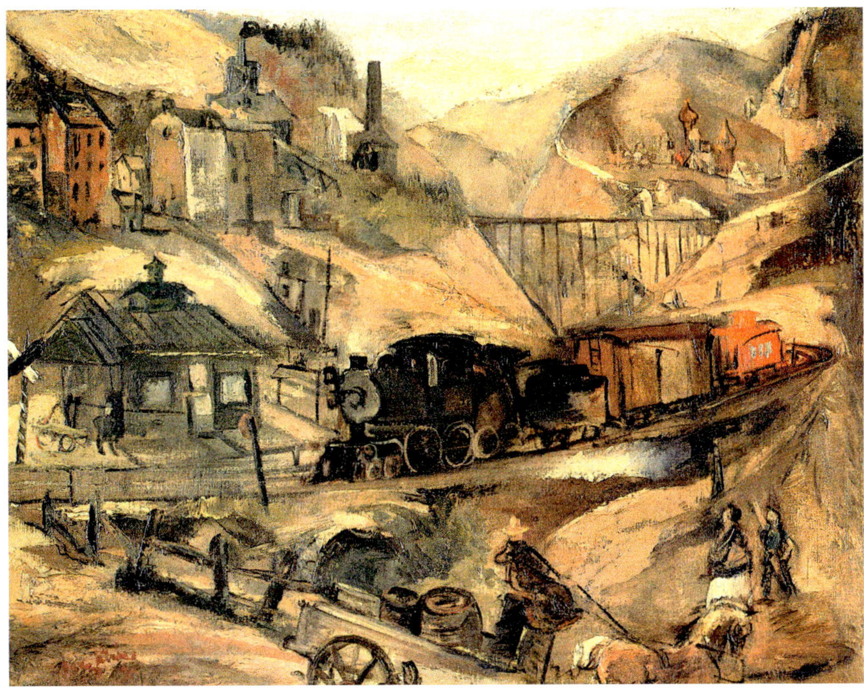

Palmerton, PA, 1943, on permanent display at the Smithsonian Museum. (*Smithsonian American Art Museum © 2018 Franz Kline Estate/Artists Rights Society (ARS), New York*)

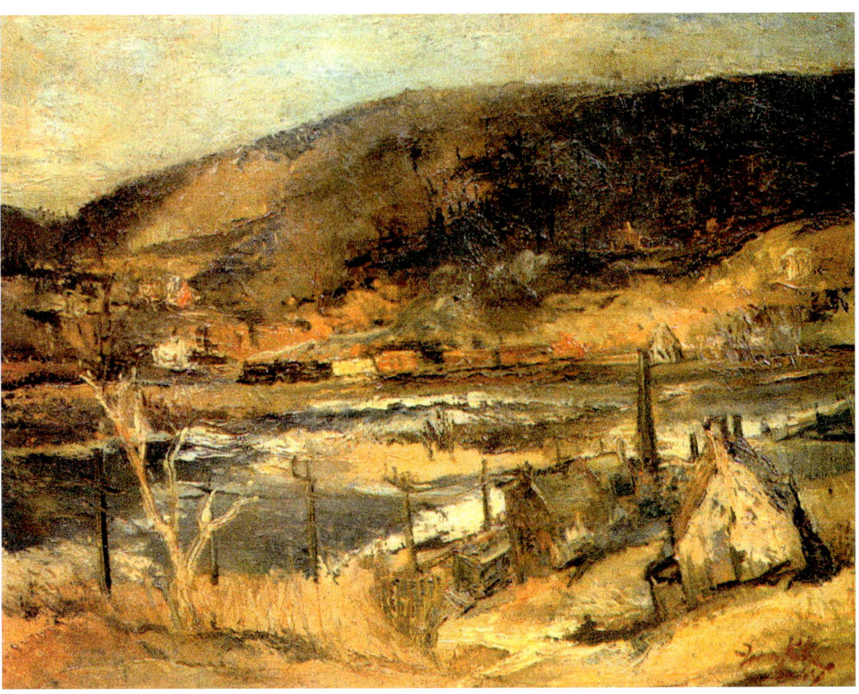

Lehigh River, Winter, winner of the S. J. Wallace-Truman prize in 1944. (*Private Collection © 2018 Franz Kline Estate/Artists Rights Society (ARS), New York*)

In other words, she meant, 'When are you going to start making money?' And he shook his head and laughed and said to me on the side, 'Mother is something, isn't she? She's pretty alert.'"[52]

Both award-winning works, *Lehigh River, Winter* and *Palmerton, Pa*, exemplify the importance that coal country played in Kline's creative process. The town of Palmerton is 8 miles down the Lehigh River from Lehighton. These and later titles, like *Thorpe* and *Harleman*, suggest a reservoir of youthful memories and feelings, ones that may have required the catalytic power of New York to elevate to a higher plane.

Not always able to afford the train, but depending on his visits home to receive monetary support, Kline often hitched a ride to Lehighton with a truck driver named Kenny Lobien:

> "We always stopped at the Dixie Diner in Hillside, New Jersey," Lobien said. "On Fridays Franz never had money, but when he went home his mother gave him some and the first thing he would do was go and buy art supplies. His place was only partially furnished; he said that furniture 'would be too distracting.'
>
> "For the longest time he had a big canvas on the wall and I teased him, 'What do you use that one for, Franz, to clean your brushes?' He said he could sit at that painting for days and maybe add one stroke and that he had been working on it for four months. There was also a painting of a caboose and I told him I'd love to buy it. He said he had a showing that week and that if he did not sell it he would give it to me."[53]

Kline's hand-to-mouth existence was a drastic contrast to the lifestyle of most of his Lehighton friends. Buying a home, settling down, and receiving a regular paycheck like his old football buddies was the conventional thing to do. But Kline broke with conformity for his art. Many thought he was irresponsible; fewer others, something like heroic. Nevertheless, he remained an enigmatic staple of conversation.

Unbelievably, his mother appeared to be oblivious to the magnitude of Franz's poverty. She may have been in denial. She was proud of her children and loved to boast about them on her daily rounds through town to the Episcopal Church and along First Street, stopping in various stores before heading home.

"She always wore wide-brimmed hats and usually picked flowers on her way, dandelions or violets, and she would bring in articles about her children and things," print shop owner Grace Rhoads explained.[54]

Under the assumption that her weekly allowance to Franz went to buy "extras," Anne had no idea that her son was so poor that he used phonebook pages for drawing paper. Perhaps he remained secretive about his actual plight because his mother had disapproved of his marriage to Elizabeth from the start.

"Franz told me that once when his mother came to visit him in the village," Elisabeth Zogbaum said, "she knocked on the door. When Elizabeth answered, Anne brushed by her, treating her as if she was a servant girl, and announcing that she had found the ideal girl for Franz to marry even though he was already married."[55]

Louise remembered many controversial visits with her mother in New York:

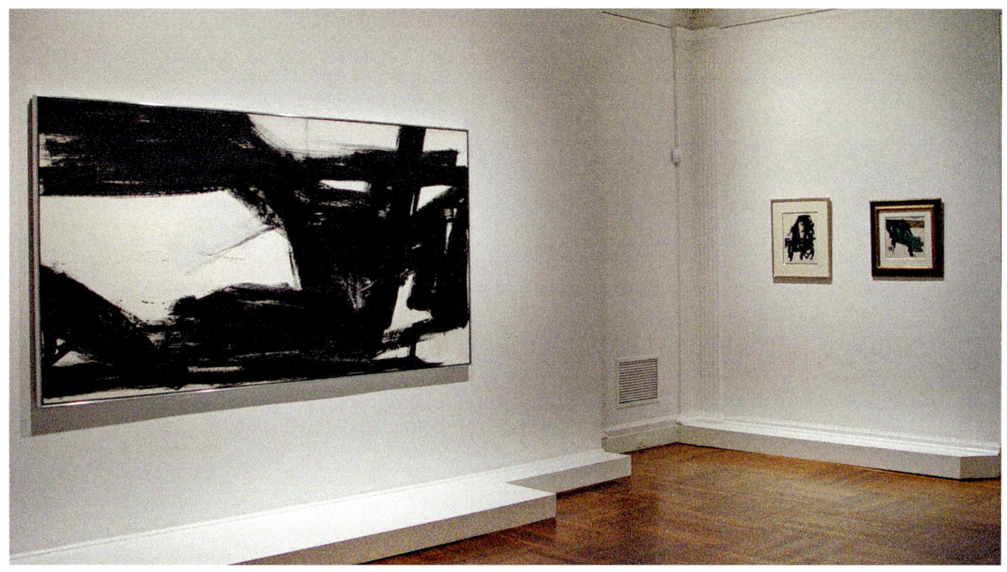

Above: Harleman, 1960. (*Robert Mnuchin Gallery © 2018 Franz Kline Estate/Artists Rights Society (ARS), New York*)

Below: Untitled Christmas Card, Star of Bethlehem/Washington Square, *c.* 1940. At the bottom left of the image, Kline placed palm trees and a full moon, while on the right sphere is Washington Square and the Empire State Building. (*Paolo Pelosini © 2018 Franz Kline Estate/Artists Rights Society (ARS), New York*)

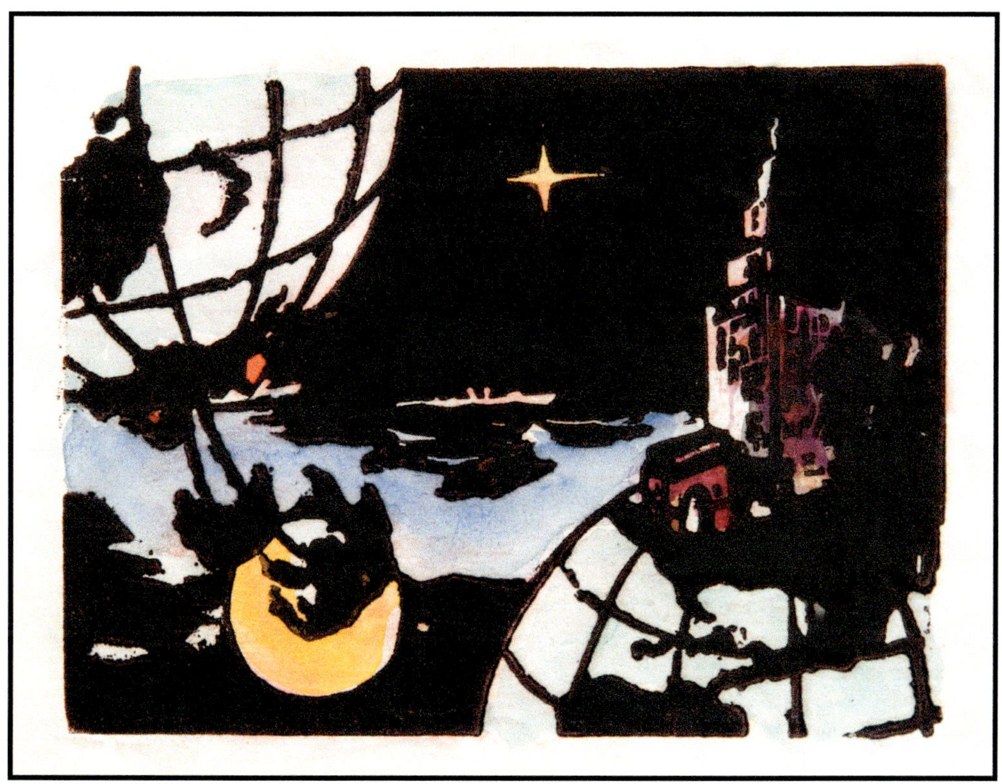

> When we visited Franz in the Village, Mother was appalled at his surroundings. This wasn't how he was raised, you see. I remember we went to see him and Elizabeth on MacDougal Street and when we got there, there was Elizabeth doing nothing and my mother looked at her and said, "Don't you have a broom to sweep this place?" It all stemmed from when Elizabeth was still in England and Mother would see the great big letters she sent to Franz asking for money, to pay her dentist, or this or that. Mother considered Elizabeth a woman who was looking for a man to support her. She and Franz were obviously good acquaintances in London, but how she got him to marry her, I don't know.

For many years, Kline's family remained unaware of Elizabeth's mental condition. Franz was just beginning to discover the depths of it himself. As his career showed signs of increasing notoriety, his relationship with his wife continued to deteriorate. Elizabeth's frequent infirmities included spells of paranoia. At times she insisted that there were Nazis on the roof. Finally, at a loss, he brought her to Lehighton, hoping his mother, a nurse, would know what to do. Louise said:

> Oh, you're never really cured. Yes, Elizabeth had schizophrenia, but it didn't mean that she was a mental maniac; nor a mumbling fool. They were hardly married before she started getting ill. It certainly made life miserable for both. When Franz got in touch with his mother-in-law in England, he found that Elizabeth had a history of schizophrenia that had persisted since early childhood and kept it hidden.[56]

As the years progressed, Elizabeth's madness became harder to conceal. She struggled with reclusive tendencies and hallucinations, and Franz's excuses for her behavior eventually

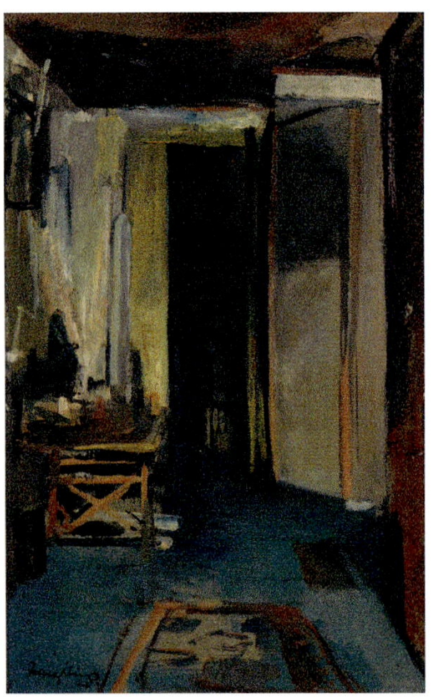

Studio with Cat, c. 1945. (*Doyle Auctioneers & Appraisers © 2018 Franz Kline Estate/Artists Rights Society (ARS), New York*)

wore thin. Kline's letters to Frederick Ryan reveal how hard he worked to give his muse a happy life despite an illness Franz would never understand. The letters substantiate the rumors going around the tight-knit community of artists about how Franz tried to placate his wife by combing her hair for hours. He'd only stop, they'd say, to fetch the kettle to add hot water to her bath, or to climb out on the roof in order to reassure her that no foreign army was invading New York.

There was room for Elizabeth in Lehighton by the mid-1940s, as most of Anne and Ambrose's children had married and moved on. While under Anne's care, Elizabeth often stayed in bed all day, getting up only at night. Louise described her sister-in-law as "retired from life" and "suffering from delusions of grandeur."[57] Louise had to coax Elizabeth from the house. "I got her as far as father's flower garden and she said, 'I know Franz plays the violin.' And when I said, 'Oh, no, he's never played the violin in his life,' she said, 'Oh, yes, he gives big concerts at night, but I don't know where.'"

Others, including Claire Mosser, remembered Kline's wife differently. "Elizabeth was a classic beauty, a pale-looking Meryl Streep type. I didn't think she was odd," he said. "We just thought maybe her being away from home had something to do with her sickness."[58]

Franz coped with his wife's mental illness by pressing on with his work, and with each shard of recognition came a bit of income. But even with increased patronage, he was often in need of a quick coin and continued painting portraits. He vowed to give them up altogether as soon as he could afford it, preferring his own brand of reality, not "Arrow collar ads," as he described them. Louise remembered a particular dinner that shed light on her brother's inner conflict.

When Elizabeth was unavailable for social calls, Franz invited Louise to join him for dinner with Colonel Stanley Backman and his wife, Gladys. Col. Backman had served under General MacArthur in World War II and his wife asked Franz to paint a portrait of her husband similar to one he had done in the Philippines. "After saying goodbye to the Backmans," Louise said, "we were walking on Fifth Avenue and Franz said, 'Now you see why I don't want to do portraiture, people just want a white-collar ad. I want to paint the character of the man, the sloping eyes and lines of the face.'"[59]

Kline's two big breaks economically came when businessman I. David Orr and physician Dr. Theodore J. Edlich, Jr., became interested in his work. Kline met Orr while selling his work on the street. Impressed with Kline's style, Orr became an important patron in his life and later renovated part of his home to create space for Franz to work whenever he wanted to get out of the city. This chance encounter was the beginning of a close friendship and over 100 commissioned paintings. Dr. Edlich made a professional call on Franz's studio at 146 MacDougal Street in 1939. Charmed by the artist and impressed by his passion, Dr. Edlich also became Kline's loyal patron and friend.

Works painted around World War II were primarily the rural and industrial landscapes of his boyhood, or local scenes of New York. Examples include *Pennsylvania Street Scene (Pennsylvania Mining Town)*, *Fulton Fish Market, Washington Square,* or *Street Scene Greenwich Village*. After the war, as photographs became more common, Franz chose to delve deeper. By the mid-1940s, he began focusing on lines and planes rather than subject, model, or even color. Coincidentally, at the time of his wife's mental deterioration, Kline's work also began to fragmentize.

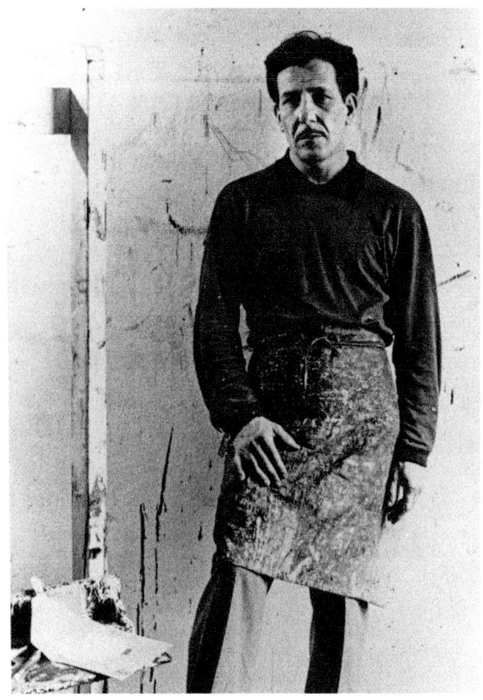

Franz Kline, *c.* 1960, New York studio scene. (*Walter Auerbach, photographer, Rudi Blesh papers, 1909-1983. Archives of American Art, Smithsonian Institution*)

In *The Vital Gesture*, Harry Gaugh explained that Kline's move to abstraction was not an instantaneous, total conversion, but a gradual process. Kline began by generalizing his subject's appearance, which becomes evident in preliminary studies for *Elizabeth*. Beginning with specific details, Kline broke down traditional forms into flat planes, then later discarded form altogether until he was left with only a few basic lines retaining more of the idea of the subject than the actual image. First, imagine an immaculate sandcastle, complete with armed sentry, chiseled parapets, and a long balustrade. Next, envision the same scene hours later when only a wind-swept mystery of its former glory remained. A similar erosion of detail is evident in Kline's early move toward abstraction. This can be best seen in the paintings of his wife. In *The Dancer* (1946), only a few figurative semblances remain, such as a leg and slipper. Such recognizable forms lend credence to the hypothesis that Kline's shift did not occur as an epiphany.

Had some part of Kline's subconscious compelled him to portray his wife this way, fading away right before his eyes, just as the figurative forms dissolved on his canvases? His sister said that Franz appeared to be at a loss about his wife's condition. When he asked Elizabeth if she would like to visit her family in England, she said no. When he contacted her parents, they assured him that she was safer with him in New York. With the help of Col. Backman, in 1946, Franz admitted Elizabeth to Central Islip State Hospital where she stayed for six months.[60] After she was released, however, her symptoms returned, and Franz took her back to Lehighton. By then, Ambrose had transformed the house at 300 Ninth Street into two apartments. Elizabeth was given a bedroom on the first floor, and her meals were brought in on a tray. She would lock herself in the bathroom some nights for hours after everyone else had gone to bed, making it impossible for anyone else to use it. The daughter of the friends who lived upstairs, Patsy Gernerd, remembered Elizabeth as someone she only ever saw in her nightclothes, yet was "beautiful, intellectual, and regal" who would "sleep all day only to get up to bathe and brush her hair for hours. She was slight, with dark hair, and rarely spoke."[61]

Kline painted many pictures of his wife, and two in particular are significant: *The Dancer* (1946), which he considered his "first abstract," and *Dancer at Islip*, painted three years later in 1949, which depicts a gray body confined within a cage-like barrier of heavy black strokes. In the time between the two works were made, Elizabeth was re-institutionalized at Central Islip in 1948.[62] Later the same year, Kline began experimenting with projecting his drawings using a strong source of light.

Willem de Kooning had a Bell-Opticon projector in his studio, which he had been using to enlarge some of his own drawings, and he invited Kline to experiment with the technique. Kline began by projecting his drawing of a rocking chair and was fascinated by the way the light distorted the image in a way that allowed for a more intimate glimpse of its essence. This, along with his wife's fragmented personality, catalyzed Kline's shift from representational work.

While most biographies are quick to mention the impact of the Bell-Opticon experiments on Kline's shift into abstraction, it was artist Karen Warshal's master's thesis that contained a groundbreaking insight. Warshal, on a tip from a librarian in Lehighton, knocked on author Rebecca Finsel's door in 1989. (Back then, co-author Joel, her middle son, was only eleven.) Warshal later wrote of their conversation that "it made me feel as if I were exploring each phase of [Kline's] work with a new insight."[63] Particularly, she said, there was something about the way Louise had described Elizabeth as a "real lady" who always "wore a dressing gown." This inspired Warshal to examine every drawing or painting that Kline painted of his wife in chronological order. Elizabeth from early days, "with person and dressing gown intact," to later with "her facial personality and the

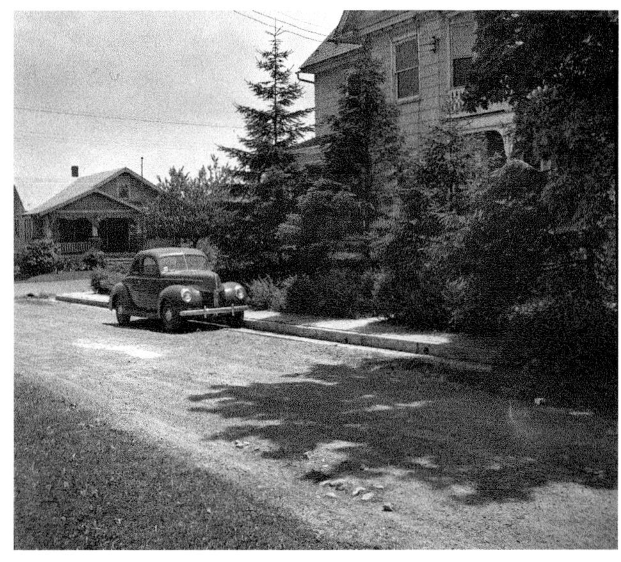

Kline's boyhood home in Lehighton became a shelter for his wife, Elizabeth, in the early 1940s when her illness became too much for Franz to bear on his own. (*Kim Graver Steinberger and family*)

dressing gown deteriorated." Warshal concluded: "It was as if not only her personality but her whole persona was coming apart."[64]

Was Elizabeth's mental illness the true turning point behind Kline's dramatic shift from painting recognizable figures and objects into something unrecognizable?

> He began to work on sheets of newspaper with a three-inch housepainter's brush and black enamel. The size of the newspaper, almost immediately, was unbearably confining. Then came the six- or eight-inch brushes, the six- or eight-foot canvasses, the five gallons cans of paint and the big, black images with the bulk and the force and the momentum of the old-fashioned engines that used to roar through the town where he was born.[65]

By the end of the 1940s, Kline had developed his signature style: large black-and-white canvases assaulted with thick slashes of paint. Dealers were quick to mention how closer investigation revealed that what might appear to be spontaneous attacks were often meticulously planned. This was demonstrated by sketches on discarded newspaper and pages torn from the telephone directory, some of which hang in museums today. But to many viewers, Kline's canvases suggest the opposite, that his method was not rational, but rather instinctive and impulsive. A random moment, a gesture caught in time like an insect stuck in amber. Some of the images in Kline's paintings have the sense that they are finished, as if one more stroke would be too many. Others appear as if they shouldn't end at the frame, but are rather interrupted by it, as if the line could continue beyond the canvas into a vast and unimagined world. The thrust often appears to be lateral, but it is usually also vertical, carrying the eye above the frame.

Could a child really paint just as well? Scientific evidence indicates otherwise. In one peer-reviewed study published in *Psychological Science*, researchers took the question further and asked whether people could "distinguish abstract expressionist paintings from highly similar paintings by children, chimps, monkeys, and elephants?"[66] To find what people really think, researchers showed students paired images: one by an abstract expressionist and one by an animal or child. Participants were then asked which they liked better. The first set of pairs were presented without labels of "child" or "artist," but in later rounds labels (sometimes intentionally incorrect) were added. In the end, a majority of people preferred professional paintings, "even when the labels were reversed." The results of their experiments led the scientists to believe that most people "see the mind behind the art."

Art has the power to hypnotize. Irving Sandler, the art historian Frank O'Hara famously called the "balayeur" or sweeper up after artists, said that the reason he became an art critic was because of a chance encounter with one of Kline's paintings.[67] Sandler wrote of the day when, as a history student at Columbia University, he was walking through the Museum of Modern Art and became "dumbstruck" by a particular black and white picture. The label read *Chief*. "It was the first work of art I really saw, and it changed my life ... it began my life-in-art ... like releasing the floodgates of seeing."[68]

Kline painted *Chief* in 1950, the same year I. David Orr helped him land a job teaching art for the summer at a resort in upstate New York. While Franz was away, a gallery owner named Charles Egan visited his studio and later offered Kline his first solo show. Opening on October

16, 1950, the exhibition consisted of eleven large abstracts.[69] Perhaps Egan's own family's roots in coal country drew him to Kline's work, along with the fact that Kline's timing was perfect. According to Dr. Robert Mattison, at that time "black-and-white painting was in the air."[70]

The following year, in 1951, Kline was invited into a group show at the Sidney Janis Gallery called *American Vanguard Art*. He was one of twenty, including Albers, de Kooning, Gorky Gottlieb, Guston, Motherwell, Pollock, and Tomlin, an All-Star team of American artists.

Kline traveled to North Carolina the following summer to teach at Black Mountain College. He wrote to Jack Tworkov about a dog named Tommy following him around, and his classes inspired at least one student, Fielding Dawson, to follow him back to New York. By the mid-1950s, Franz began showing with Sidney Janis, a dealer who commanded higher prices than any he had ever worked with before. Kline's career peaked in 1958 as a participant in The Museum of Modern Art's ground-breaking exhibition "The New American Painting," which opened in New York and later toured Europe, elevating abstract-expressionism to the level of jazz. By 1959, after his second show with Janis, Kline purchased a Jaguar and second home at No. 15 Cottage Street in Provincetown, Massachusetts.

Among his more ardent supporters was Adlai Stevenson, U.S. Ambassador to the United Nations.[71] In 1952, during Stevenson's unsuccessful bid for the presidency, Kline painted 'Vote for Adlai' posters. Kline was later offered exhibitions at the Museum of Modern Art, the Tate Modern, and the Venice Biennale.

As far as motif in his paintings, one might see images of Kline's youth: anthracite-driven trains cutting through snow-covered hills and valleys, or the New York City of his manhood: sooty bridges, rusty girders, the framework of demolished skyscrapers. However, Kline might object to such a reading.

"I'm not painting bridge constructions, skyscrapers or laundry tickets ... I don't paint a given object—a figure or table," he said, "I paint an organization that becomes a painting. If you look at an abstraction, you can imagine that it's a head, a bridge, almost anything—but it's not these things that get me started."[72]

Kline later elaborated: "You don't paint the way someone, by observing your life, thinks you have to paint. You paint the way you have to in order to give. That's life itself, and someone will look and say it is a product of knowing, but it has nothing to do with

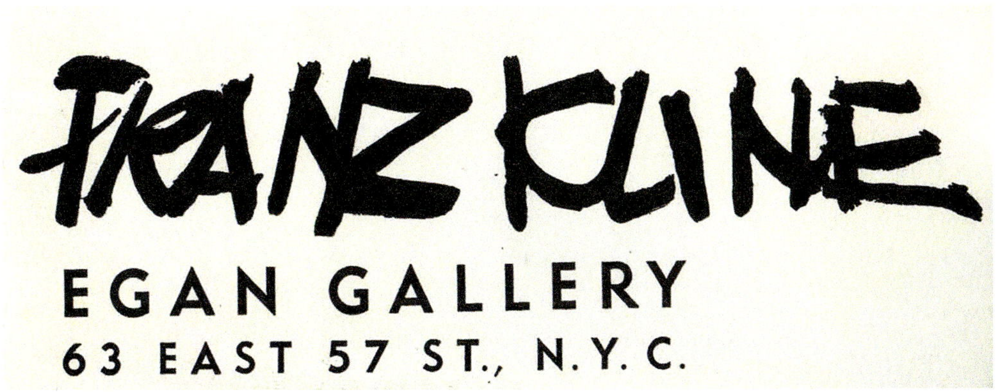

Announcement for Kline's first solo show at the Egan Gallery, New York, 1950. (*Paolo Pelosini*)

knowing, it had to do with giving ... when you've finished giving, the look surprises you as well as everyone else."[73]

When Kline painted *Mahoning* (the title image of Chapter 5) in 1956, did he somehow journey away from his Greenwich Village studio to the Mahoning Valley of his youth? Could the anxiety of trying to get home before his stepfather, or the rush of young love, be found among the strokes and gestures of his brush? What was his subconscious providing when he chose *Mahoning* as its title? Or had he chosen it at random simply because he liked the sound?

Harry Gaugh allows for a compromise. "*Mahoning* does not pleasantly embody locale and season but carves out rigorous territory all its own," he wrote. "Kline's 'site abstractions' find natural counterparts in eastern Pennsylvania, particularly the coal country, with its seasonal and geologic severity, but they reach beyond landscape into unmapped places of tumult and catharsis. *Mahoning* comes as close to ancient Thebes as to Mauch Chunk Mountain in the dead of winter."[74]

All that is known for sure is that *Mahoning*, painted on a canvas 7-foot square, was also good enough to be shrunken down to the size of a postage stamp when the U.S. Postal Service selected it for a series called "Four Centuries of American Art." On the faces of Franz's old friends waiting in line at the Lehighton Post Office on the morning in 1998 when the stamp was first sold, one can only imagine the delight as they emerged from the Post Office to drive or walk along the stamp's namesake street.

Fifty years before the stamp, when Kline's mother could no longer take care of Elizabeth, Franz had her recommitted to Central Islip. Her second hospitalization lasted fourteen years. Claire Mosser remembered a visit from Franz during this time. "He came alone and sketched our child Diane at our house in Bethlehem," he said. "Elizabeth was at the hospital and not communicating, and he was very upset about it."[75]

Fielding Dawson described his mentor's appearance then:

> His face unshaven was drawn and hollow, his lips were severely pulled down, and his eyes angled down so heavily he had an almost Oriental, introspective and tragic expression. I said gently, "Franz." He looked down into his hands, and there was a snapshot. I stood beside him and he showed it to me. A handsome woman with round glasses strode in front of parked cars in the 1930s. Her expression was straightforward and dramatic, yet quite shy. His wife Elizabeth. He slowly put the photo in his wallet in his pocket. He murmured an affection. He looked at the bar.[76]

10

Lehighton: Legionnaires Commission a Mural of Kline's Hometown

I suppose Lehighton is the same little Dutch settlement wrapped up in a cloud of coal dirt—however I miss it with all my friends.

Franz Kline
Letter to Lavona Edgar, October 1931

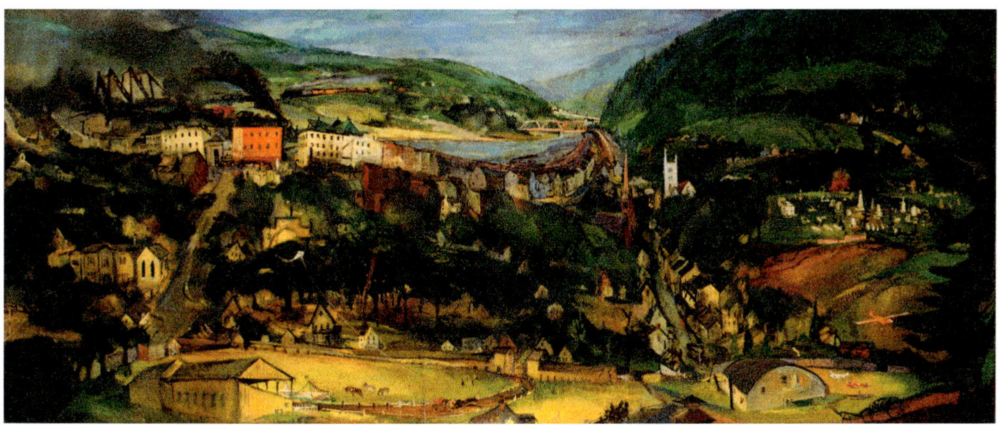

Lehighton mural, 1945, the Allentown Art Museum of the Lehigh Valley. (*Joshua Finsel/Lehighton Legion Post #314 © 2018 Franz Kline Estate/Artists Rights Society (ARS), New York*)

Franz occasionally brought friends from New York home to visit Lehighton. Whether they came to see the setting of Kline's stories, or just to take a break from the city, the guests almost always ended up at Anne's kitchen table with a steaming pot of tea. On one trip, Kline brought Peter Martin, owner of City Lights in San Francisco. Martin's partner in bookselling and publishing was Lawrence Ferlinghetti, the man who wrote that "poetry is the shadow cast by our streetlight imaginations." The activist poet had likely been a topic of conversation that evening, as Franz and Peter stayed up sipping English tea—bolstered with other spiritous drinks—long into the night. Rapt, Louise listened to them from upstairs through a vent in the floor:

> Franz was telling Peter about our area and I heard him say, "You know, they renamed it Jim Thorpe." Franz loved the Indian name Mauch Chunk and thought it went with the town's architecture and surrounding mountains. He said, "It's like it was always Mauch Chunk, a marvelous sounding name. It has so much history behind it. This whole area is filled with history; our step-father told us everything as children, about the *Leni Lenapian* Indian tribes, the Gnadenhütten massacre, our graveyard where the martyred Moravians are buried in a common grave."
>
> And then Franz lowered his voice and said very seriously, "My brother Jacques is the poet of the family, and my brother Fred, he's so serious and such a perfectionist that it breaks your heart, and then you've got my sister Louise" ... and then the oil burner kicked on, and I never found out what he said about me, but to this day I've wondered.[1]

Franz had likely taken Martin to the American Legion that weekend to have lunch and a beer or two in the room where he painted a mural of the town years earlier, in 1945. Chef Agnes Seltzer was known to make the chicken salad especially for him.

Kline painted the mural the year after he won the Wallace-Truman prize for the second time, so his name had been freshly splashed across the newspapers when members of the

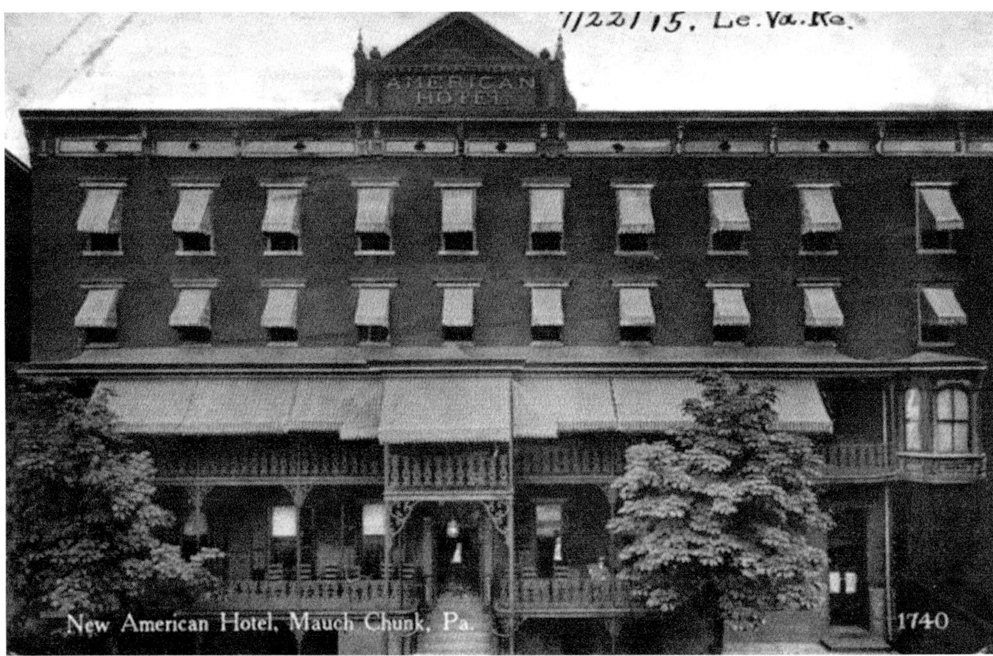

The American Hotel, *c.* 1915, Mauch Chunk, PA, a fine example of the town's Victorian architecture. Renamed The Inn at Jim Thorpe, this historic building witnessed Carbon County's gilded years when the coal and railroad industries thrived.

Shoemaker/Haydt Post No. 314 offered him the commission. The mural was to be the finishing touch of their new banquet room, painted on the wall behind the 47-foot bar.

"With Adolf Hitler defeated," historian Ronald Rabenold explained, "the legion expanded with a cavernous banquet hall in the style of the open-beamed ceilings of Europe."[2]

After one member suggested a mirror to finish off the area behind the new bar, Commander Frank Bayer shook his head and asked, "Don't you think that a painting of the area would be better, maybe a mural by a local artist?" The fact that Bayer owned a paint store may have had something to do with his idea. In any case, Kline was one of the first names suggested.

There was the news of Kline's recent accolades in New York, but it's also likely that some of the Legionnaires remembered Kline's "illustrated lecture" in the high school auditorium after his return from England.[3] Others may have recalled his talk on "The Art of Picture Making" at the Municipal building.[4] His "oil paintings, etchings, pen & ink illustrations, wash drawings, sketches, and portraits" had all been on display.[5] Those who had been Kline's classmates undoubtedly had their own stories to tell. Bayer's paint store had once awarded young Franz a watercolor set for winning a contest back in Miss Stauffer's art class.

Resolved to hire Kline, a small group of Legionnaires boarded a train for New York on a cold day in November. The men arrived at his studio, and Kline welcomed them in. He later took them on a tour of the many bars he decorated. Impressed by the experience, the Lehightonians offered Kline $600.[6] Franz held his breath. Mistaking his silence for consideration, one Legion member asked, if it was not enough for him, could he think of anyone else? Kline could think of only one man, "an elderly sign-painter," he said, provoking a few laughs. He continued: "The old man's hands shake uncontrollably." Kline was play-acting now. "But once he lined up his hands to the canvas, he could draw a line as straight as it needed to be. Art could always cure him, even if only for a few seconds at a time."[7] Followed by something to the effect of, "Six hundred will do." Smiling and shaking Kline's hand in turn, the veterans lined up to leave. They gave him two weeks to finish it.

Working in Lehighton for such a stretch required some adjustment. Elizabeth did not usually travel well, but she had stayed at her mother-in-law's house enough by then to be comfortable. Franz was hopeful the money would grant his wife more peace of mind, so he set out in earnest, excited to be back around old friends like Stanley Harleman.

A few pieces related to Stanley in Kline's *catalogue raisonné* include *Harleman*, a bold abstract from 1960, and a rare sculptural piece of Stanley's profile in plaster, *circa* 1930. This unique piece is a complete departure from Kline's early work and has until this book remained mostly unknown. Even less known was Stanley's role in helping Kline gain the perspective necessary to paint the 14-foot behemoth behind the Legion bar. To be clear, Stanley never picked up a brush, he simply lifted the artist up into the air in his plane. As Kline painted, he was back in Stump's propeller plane, soaring over the bowl of tree-covered mountains, smiling and sketching wildly as his old friend cut circles through the sky.

Below the plane was the American Legion itself, housed within a large Victorian home donated by the widow of James Blakeslee, Henrietta, as a memorial to her husband's service in the Spanish-American War. With new waves of veterans joining the post after World War II, members voted to expand. A banquet room was built onto the back of the

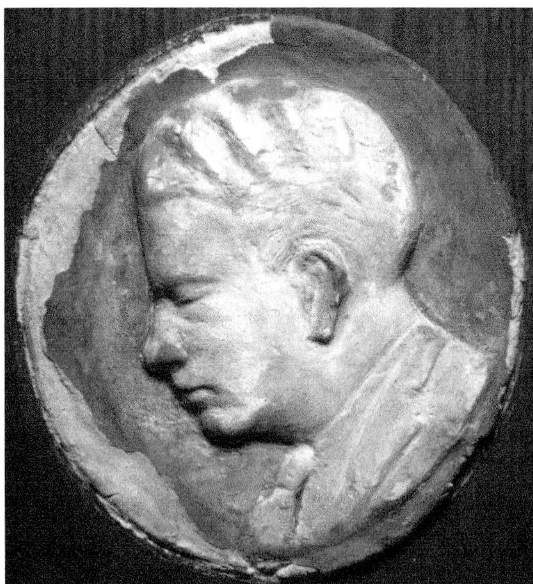

Stanley Harleman, sculpture, *c.* 1930. Kline's unique sculptural tribute to his friend. (*Mrs. Stanley Harleman and family © 2018 Franz Kline Estate/Artists Rights Society (ARS), New York*)

house. Inside the addition was a long bar made of dark wood that curved out from the western wall.

There is a myth among Lehightonians that Kline glued the huge canvas on the wall behind the bar with beer-paste. Another legend has him ceremoniously sealing off the finished work with a spray of beer. However, when you ask the people who were actually in the room, neither one was true. Frank Bayer, Jr., son of the late Commander, confirmed that his father hired his own paint store employees to hang the canvas, and that they used wallpaper glue.[8] Beer, Bayer said, was only ever used for social lubrication.

In addition to the aerial views of his memory, Kline likely took in the panoramic perspective from the Orioles Club, perched on the side of the northwest mountain facing town. Multiple sources say that Franz made sketches while looking down from there, where, like his mural, one could see all the way to the Lehigh Gap on a clear day. Using the mountain gap as a reference in the background, Kline began to paint the sweeping folds of the foothills all rolling in together on the flat wall. The artist's view approached town from the northwest, back in a time when the valley was still mostly forest and farms.

The Legion Commander's daughter, Elizabeth "Honey" Bayer, remembered watching Kline balance on the narrow ledge of the back bar as he painted. "He stood so close," she said, "and the way he used those gestures, it was fascinating."[9]

Today in the early twenty-first century, the mural of Lehighton takes on a fairy-tale quality. It's as if it belonged to a simpler and quieter era. "Emotion recollected in tranquility," Louise said, quoting Wordsworth.[10] In the foreground are the fairgrounds. Children fly kites on the field behind Kline's house, back where he once hung screaming from a tree until his crooked arm straightened. "There's the loft of the barn where our family watched the Fourth of July fireworks," Louise pointed out.[11] Four major churches are visible, including the All Saints Episcopal where Anne walked seven blocks each day to pray.[12] The goalpost where Franz kicked footballs is in the lower left, aside the school and Miss Roedel's brick boarding house.

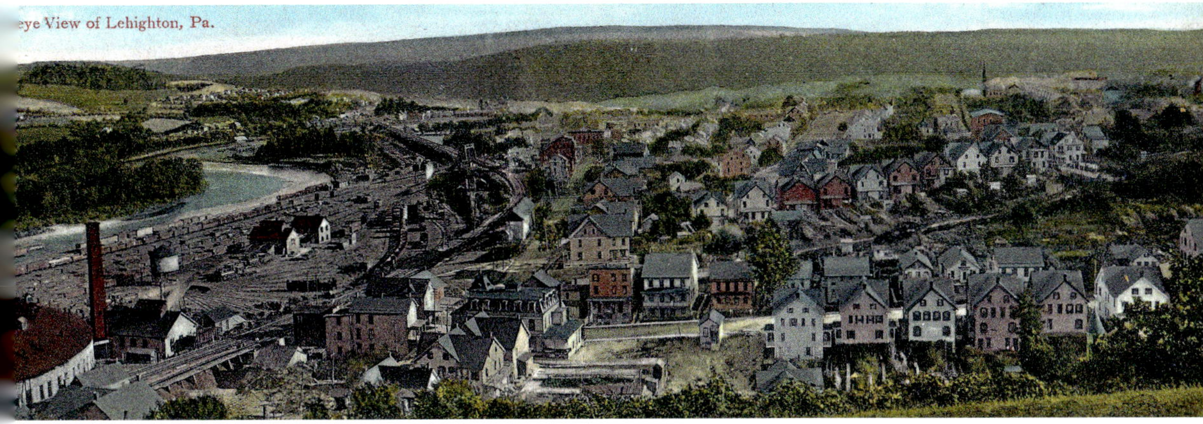

Bird's Eye View of Lehighton, 1920. A panoramic postcard of Kline's hometown shows the Lehigh River, Packerton Yards, and Lehigh Valley Railroad roundhouse, lower left. (*Ron Rabenold*)

There is a statue of Revolutionary War Colonel Jacob Weiss in the lower park behind the bandshell where musicians performed in the open air. The "wild and lovely" grove of trees "full of tea berries and forget-me-nots" contained Louise's path home from school.[13]

The mural is more populated than what it appears at first glance. If you are like the authors of this book, a poster-sized print of it can hang in your home for years before you notice the two railroad workers to the right of the large plume of dark smoke. Shifting one's attention to the right, at the base of the mountains is a cemetery on the site of the Gnadenhütten massacre. Kline's memorial to the area's first white settlers, the Moravian Brethren, rises like a phoenix above the hallowed ground. There, at the foot of the Blue Mountains, where the Six Iroquois Nations traded wampum. The Lehigh River swells blue from the center. Framed in green, obelisks commemorating the fallen sit among a smattering of graves.

In a few subtle ways Kline's mural is more than a painting. It is a confession, a richly-colored ode to home. Secrets lie among the brushstrokes. Two in particular remained hidden for over forty years until 1986. The first was discovered by author Rebecca Finsel right before she was about to be interviewed for a cable television show called *Coffee Break*:

> The host and I were standing around, waiting for the cameraman to perfect his lighting. It was the first time I had ever been so close to the mural after the protective glass was taken down. The cameraman situated us in the center of the painting, so he could get a balanced shot. Knowing about where Kline's white house would have been based on its position of the gates of the fairgrounds—which just happens to be right in the center-foreground—I began to let my eyes wander upward when I spotted a heart. Painted gray-black on black and adeptly camouflaged, the heart rose up out of the bridge of the house. Moments later we were on the air announcing the discovery.
>
> I waited until my next visit to Louise Kline before I asked her about the heart. She said that she had never known about it before. I handed her a photograph of the detail, and her face brightened into a huge smile. It was almost as if her brother had spoken to her from beyond.

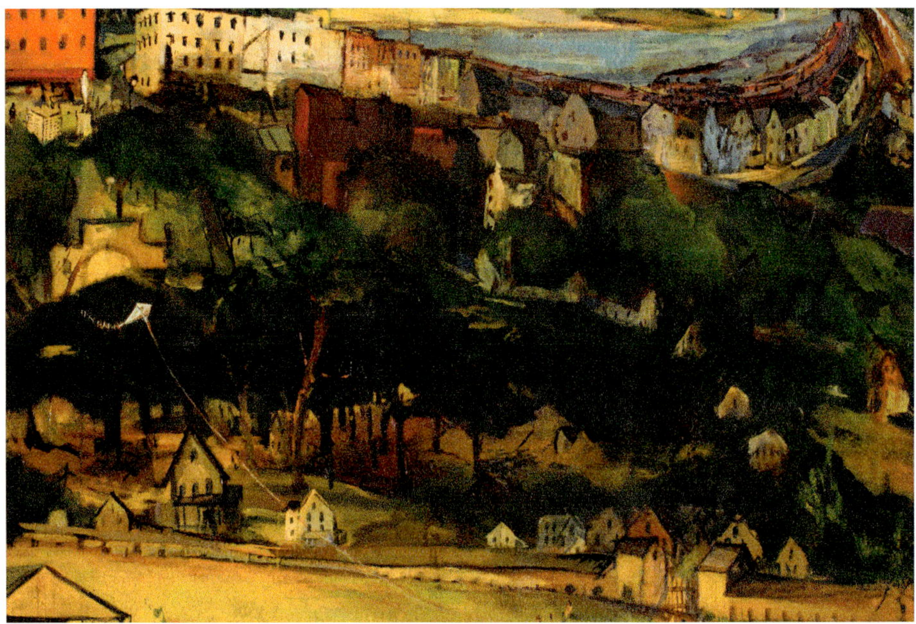

Detail, *Lehighton mural*, 1945. The community grove and the blue swell of the Lehigh River. (*Joshua Finsel/Lehighton Legion Post #314 © 2018 Franz Kline Estate/Artists Rights Society (ARS), New York*)

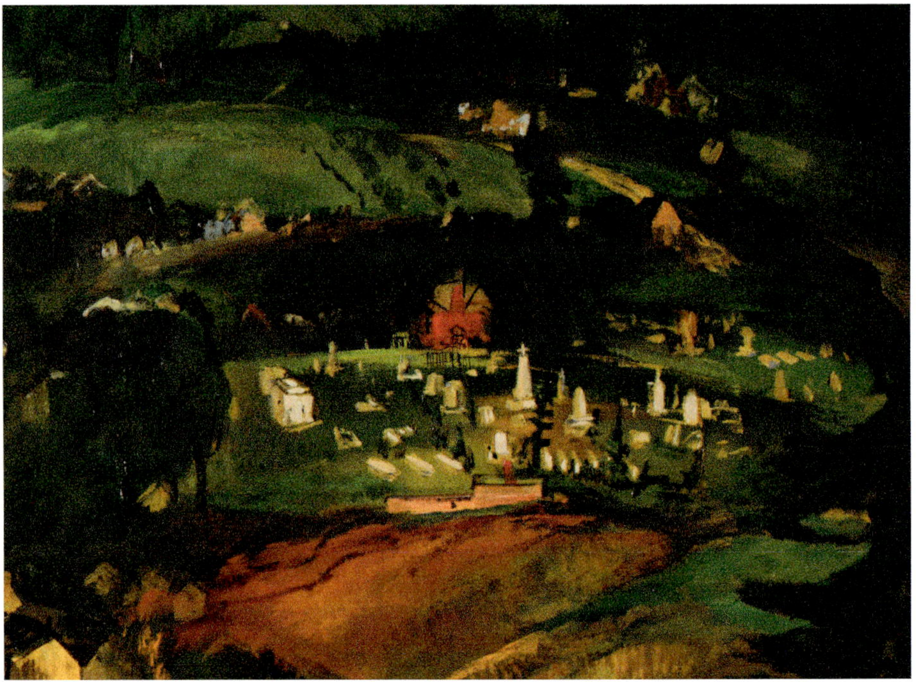

Detail, *Lehighton mural*, 1945. The Gnadenhütten/Lehighton Cemetery, the site of the early Moravian settlement and massacre. (*Joshua Finsel/Lehighton Legion Post #314 © 2018 Franz Kline Estate/Artists Rights Society (ARS), New York*)

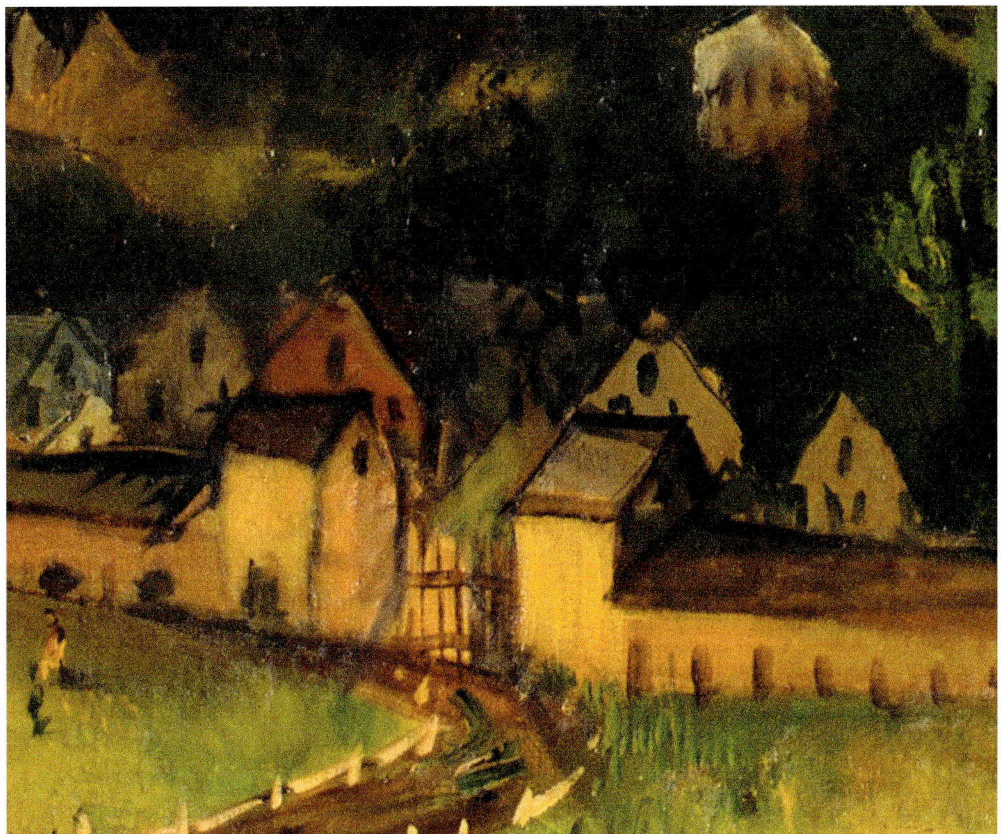

Detail, *Lehighton mural*, 1945. Kline's boyhood home in Lehighton has a heart painted over the ridge of the roof that remained undiscovered for over forty years. (*Joshua Finsel/Lehighton Legion Post #314 © 2018 Franz Kline Estate/Artists Rights Society (ARS), New York*)

A second secret was discovered when Rebecca returned a few years later with her oldest son, Joshua, to take photos of the mural for this book. After setting up an elaborate system of lights, Joshua noticed something interesting, what appeared to be a backwards "K" in the same color tone as the heart. Had Kline meant to sign his name, but settled on the symbol of love? Then Joshua pointed out two short nubs pointing south off the "K." We thought it might be a stretch to call it a signature at first until we noticed how it imitates Kline's signature on another painting, *Untitled-Locomotive*, created at about roughly the same time, *c.* 1945-47. Prior to Joshua's hunch, the mural had been thought unsigned.

Three trains billowing black smoke figure prominently in the background hauling anthracite coal. Snaking tracks link the machinery, traffic, and other trappings of their boundary-expanding force. Two of Kline's favorite steam engines, *Diamond* (1960) and *Chief* (1950), one of the Lehigh Valley's bigger locomotives, are honored in later works. *Chief* depicts an immense, bull-like force ploughing across a white space of equal power. Kline named other paintings with titles evocative of trains including *C & O* (1958), *Light Mechanic* (1960), *Caboose* (1961), *Riverbed* (1961), and likely others.

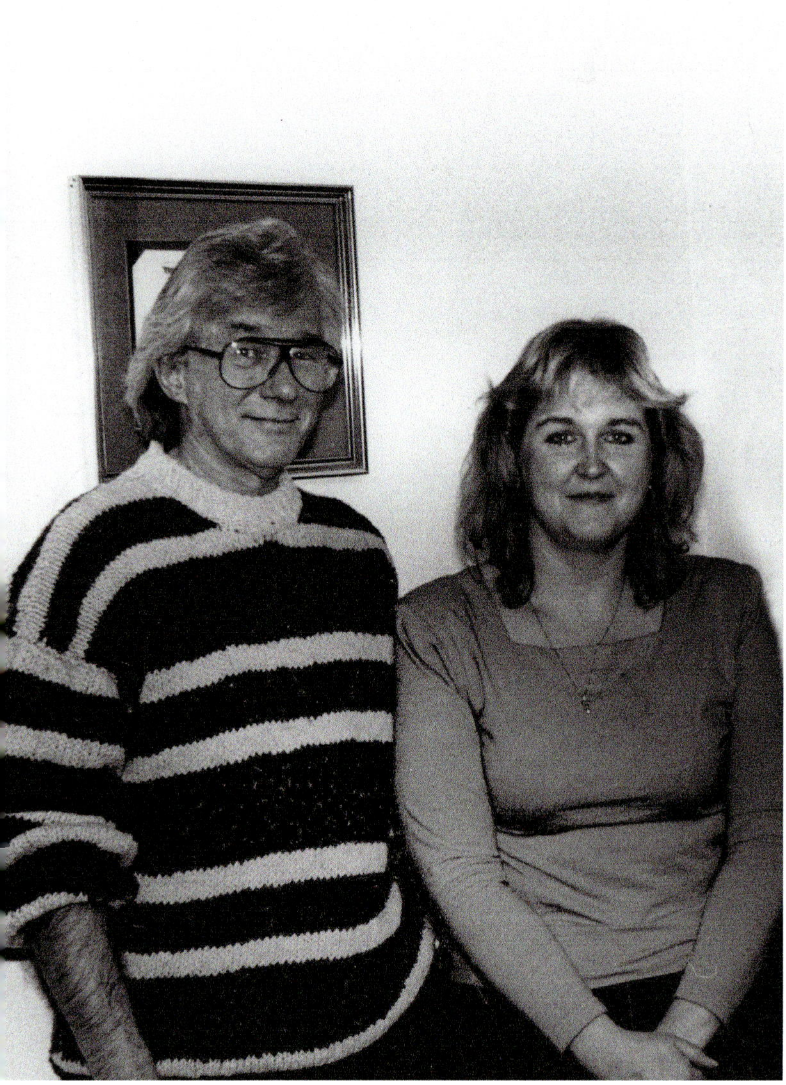

Left: Artist Edward Meneeley (left) with author Rebecca Rabenold-Finsel, founding members of the Franz Kline Society in Lehighton, *c.* 1989.

Below: Detail, *Lehighton mural*, 1945, depicting three trains. Among other things, trains conjure feelings of restlessness and longing. (*Joshua Finsel/ Lehighton Legion Post #314 © 2018 Franz Kline Estate/Artists Rights Society (ARS), New York*)

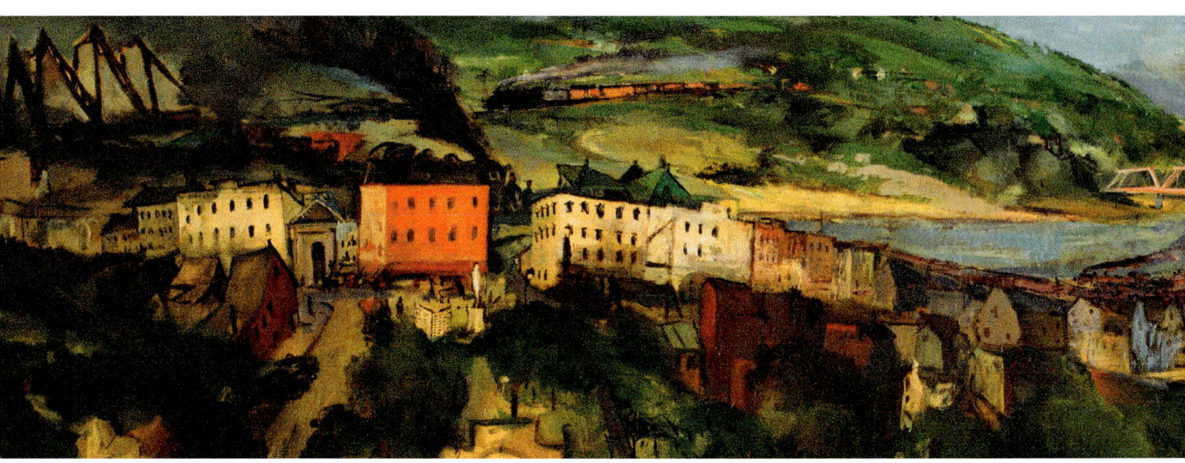

A dedication ceremony was held on Thursday, December 27, 1945, two days after Christmas. The crowd was standing room only. Organ music announced that they were about to get down to business. Franz and Elizabeth arrived. Everyone was asked to stand for the pledge. The Lehighton Band played "The Star-Spangled Banner"—"O say can you see..." The contractor presented the keys to Incoming Commander Schwartz. The chaplain prayed. The Orpheus Male Chorus sang. Three area burgesses gave greetings.

The new room was 40 × 90 feet with a large stone fireplace at the far end behind the stage. There was also a modern kitchen, office, and cloakroom constructed. On the floor below was a spacious, utilitarian basement. During the day, light streamed in on either side of the mural. A large double doorway led to an expansive porch with "a splendid view of the Lower Mahoning Valley."[14]

Kline's painting drew some criticism over drinks later that night. "His friends teased him about it not being painted to scale," Louise said.[15] "These men were used to looking at maps for moving troops. 'Of course not,' Franz said, 'but how about the local squad this year?' 'But Franz,' another friend said, 'Loren Bisbing's house isn't really right next door to your house, right?'"

"To be right," Kline later said, "is the most terrific personal state that nobody is interested in."[16]

After joking off his friends' comments, Franz rejoined his table. Louise and her husband, Jim Kelly, had come. Loretta and Charles Gernerd sat beside them with their daughter, Patsy, who remembered admiring something about Elizabeth that night. "She was sociable," Patsy said, "at least until the ceremony was over, yet during the entire two weeks that Franz painted it, Elizabeth seldom left the bedroom; not even for meals."[17]

Honey Bayer remembered seeing Franz and Elizabeth together that night:

> Franz was a very personable person when he'd come home from Greenwich Village. His hand was always out to shake someone's else's. The word got out when he was in town. This was a major work, and he was very fond of Lehighton. I saw Franz and his wife at the Legion dedication that December and they were huddled together, clinging to one another, as if they were going through something terrible.[18]

Once featured in the PBS series *Strokes of Genius*, the mural has been compared to *The Lackawanna Valley* by George Inness. In 2016, the Allentown Art Museum purchased the Legion's mural. According to Ron Rabenold, "As a result of the steep decline in living WWII veterans, the Lehighton members knew they couldn't provide the museum quality, climate-control the work needed" and it was "already showing steady signs of degradation."[19]

When first proposed, the sale raised several questions throughout the community, including: how the heck did they expect to remove it from the wall? It had hung there for sixty years by 2016, and the colors had become muted and dark. When entering from across the room, one could only make out a few random splashes of color. Many people in the community didn't even know the masterpiece existed, including artist Brad Kunkle, an area native.

"Kline's mural of our town was in a members-only club to which my parents did not belong," Kunkle wrote. "Maybe that's why I don't recall truly discovering Kline until he was exposed to me in college Art History 101. I would learn to understand that this man...in my art history book...went to the same high school as me!?! In that crucial time as a student...wondering what I was going to "be," it felt as if Kline's spirit was encouraging me to paint, telling me that country boys from Lehighton—the sons of farmers and teachers and coal miners and mechanics—could grow up to be ARTISTS."

Finally, on November 3, 2016, workers from the Luca Bonetti art conservation team began to roll the mural off the wall. The first step was to cover the entire face with a protective layer of Japanese tissue paper. The team then began to loosen the edges enough to work small amounts of water behind the canvas to release the glue. A nylon border was later added to the back of the canvas, so it could be stretched on a wooden frame for display. Then came the painstaking task of scraping away plaster and glue off the back.[20] Before installation at the Allentown Museum, the mural was fully restored.

The last time Kline sat sipping beer beneath his homage to the town was during his thirtieth-year class reunion on a Sunday in September 1961, eight months before he died. The $3.50 tickets covered "Pennsylvania Dutch style" entrées: pork and sauerkraut, mashed potatoes, and corn. His reservation was for two people but he arrived alone. On the reply addressed to Carl Langkamer, he wrote: "Best Wishes Carl.[21] Anxious to see everybody—Franz." He arrived late. He had been having a hard time getting his gray Thunderbird out of second gear.

Best Wishes Carl.
Anxious to see
everybody—
Franz.

LEHIGHTON AMERICAN LEGION
CLASS OF 1931 — 30th ANNIVERSARY REUNION
Sunday, September 3, 1961 6:00 P. M.
Turkey and Ham Supper $3.50 per person

☑ I will attend the Class of '31 Reunion.
☐ I will not attend the Class of '31 Reunion.
I will be accompanied by: Husband ____; Wife____; Guest ✓
or Guests____.
I am enclosing $ 7.00 to cover 2 reservations.
Deadline for Reservations August 30, 1961
Name Franz Kline
Address 242 W. 14 St. City Nyc

Mr. Carl L. Langkamer
123. South. Seventh St
Lehighton, Penna

Reservation sent to Carl Langkamer from Franz Kline for his thirtieth-class reunion in 1961. (*Mr. and Mrs. Carl Langkamer*)

11
Requiem

[Kline] is the action painter par excellence. He did not wish to be "in" his painting, as Pollock did, but to create the event of his passage, at whatever intersection of space and time, through the world.

Frank O'Hara
"Franz Kline"

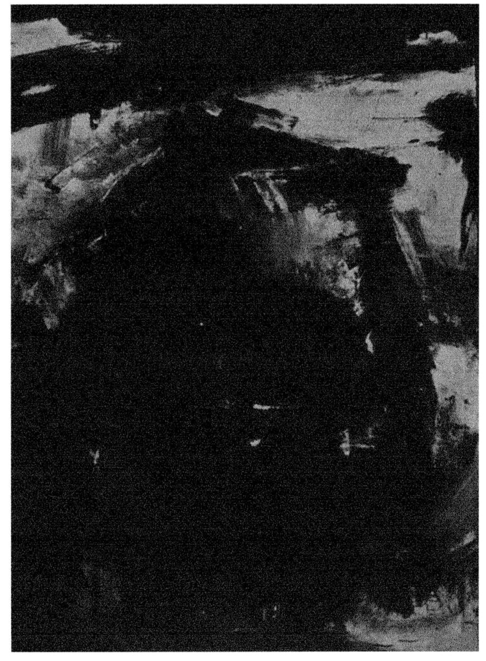

Requiem, 1958. (*Private Collection © 2018 Franz Kline Estate/Artists Rights Society (ARS), New York*)

The second time Kline's wife, Elizabeth, was institutionalized, she remained at Central Islip for fourteen years. During that time, Franz had other significant relationships. The first was with Nancy Ward, twin sister to Willem de Kooning's second wife, Joan. The second, and longest lasting, was with Elisabeth Ross Zogbaum, ex-wife of artist Wilfred Zogbaum. Friends called her Betsy.

Franz met Betsy at a party in East Hampton in the summer of 1950, about four years after his wife was committed. Betsy was commuting to New York and needed able-bodied men to help her move a few things. De Kooning volunteered. "He was a marvelous man,"

Betsy Zogbaum said, "and later Bill and Franz came over to the house for cocktails. Franz's wit and storytelling made him the center of attention."[1]

Betsy Zogbaum and Franz lived together for a few months, but as they began to share more of their lives, they decided to maintain certain boundaries. "We had separate apartments because I had a child to raise and was up at 7 a.m., while Franz liked the night life," Zogbaum said. "He came to stay when he wanted peace and quiet. When he was bored, he went to the studio to paint, but mostly to the Cedar Bar."[2]

According to Irving Sandler, Franz "held court at the Cedar Street Tavern almost every night after ten."[3] There, Kline "could play the dandy or the clown, act like Ted Lewis, Wallace Beery, or Mae West, talk about rugs, vintage cars, Gericault's horse, baseball, and Baron Gros. He loved jazz and Wagner. He was a confirmed New Yorker but had roots that he never forgot in the gritty coal country of eastern Pennsylvania.... He could juggle life until it came up fun."[4]

By the late 1950s, Kline was in the prime of his career. As his celebrity status intensified, it became harder to get him alone for a conversation because there was always someone else hovering around him. Louise felt the crunch: "As Elaine De Kooning once told me, 'The trouble was that everyone wanted a part of him.'"[5] There was even a story going around the Village about a young painter with a passing resemblance to Franz. One night, his lookalike picked up a girl at the Cedar and went back to her place for a night of creaking bed springs. The next morning, as his doppelgänger got out of bed, the girl asked, "How do you like your eggs, Franz?"[6]

Kline was a legend in his own time. Louise believed that her brother's fame made him appreciate his family even more. He began to look forward to visits from his mother and stepfather. Ambrose also loved New York, especially all of the people-watching. "Franz used to say, 'You know what Father wants to see when he comes to the Village? All the odd people,'" Louise said. "Father had eccentricities to rival Mother's own. He enjoyed traveling and didn't need to be entertained, a quality Franz admired about Ambrose."[7] On one visit to see Franz in Provincetown in 1959, Ambrose preferred to fly from LaGuardia just so he could sit and watch everything at the airport for a while before taking off. Franz was supposed to meet his family at the Provincetown airport when they landed, but he was late and his mother "just about died."[8] Franz arrived after a short while, but, before allowing his parents time to settle in, he insisted on showing them the hedges interlaced with roses in the garden. "Franz was showing mother around," Louise said, "all the while admonishing her, 'Don't ask Betsy so many questions.'[9] His studio in the back was the perfect place because when he got tired of entertaining, he could just go up for a nap and lock himself in."

Betsy bought tickets for the family to see a play by Eugene O'Neill at the Provincetown Theater. During the day, Louise said, "Franz took us to antique shops along the beach. He bought a hat and a compote with Emily Dickinson's name on it."[10] The following night was a party at Hans Hofmann's house.

One of the "myths" about Franz that bothered Louise were stories about her brother studying under Hofmann. While the artists knew each other, and both were selected to represent the United States at the Venice Biennale in 1960, Louise insisted that Hans never taught Franz in any official capacity. "Hans was deaf in one ear," Louise said, "and

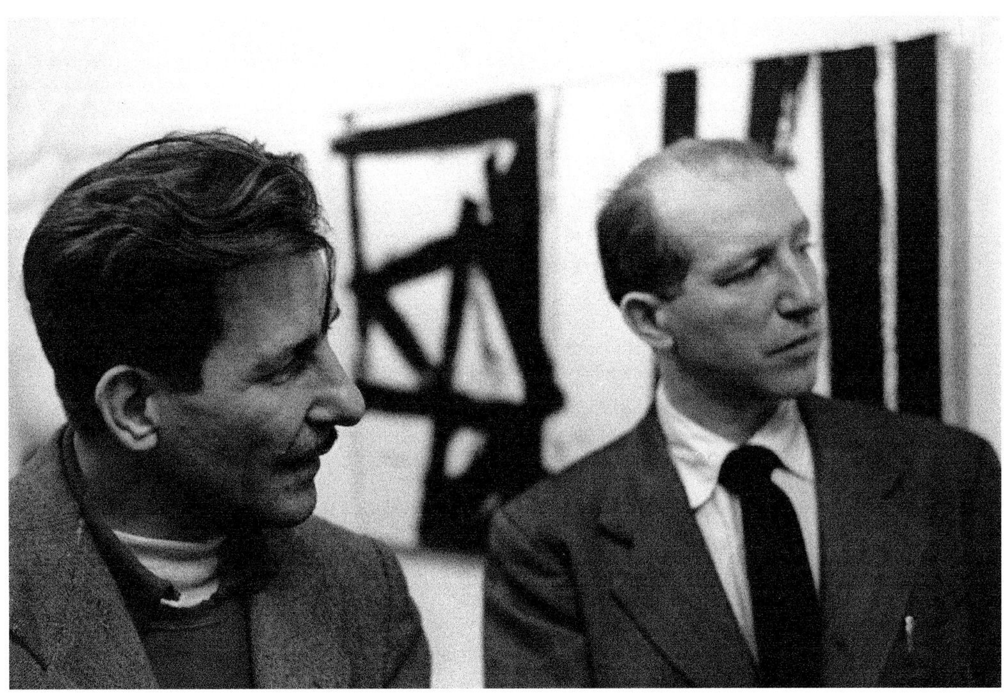

Above: Franz Kline and Jack Tworkov, *c.* 1954, friends and fellow teachers at Black Mountain College. (*Photographer unknown. Courtesy Estate of Jack Tworkov, New York*)

Right: *Provincetown Theater*, 1947. (*A. E. Bayer Estate © 2018 Franz Kline Estate/ Artists Rights Society (ARS), New York*)

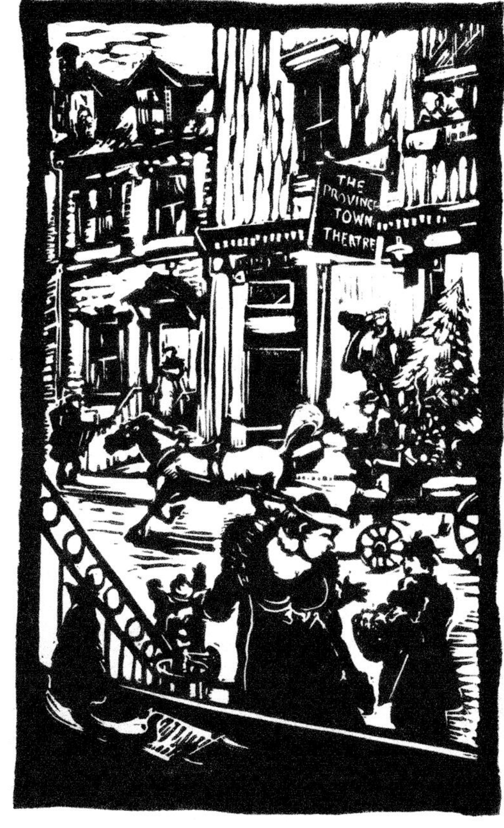

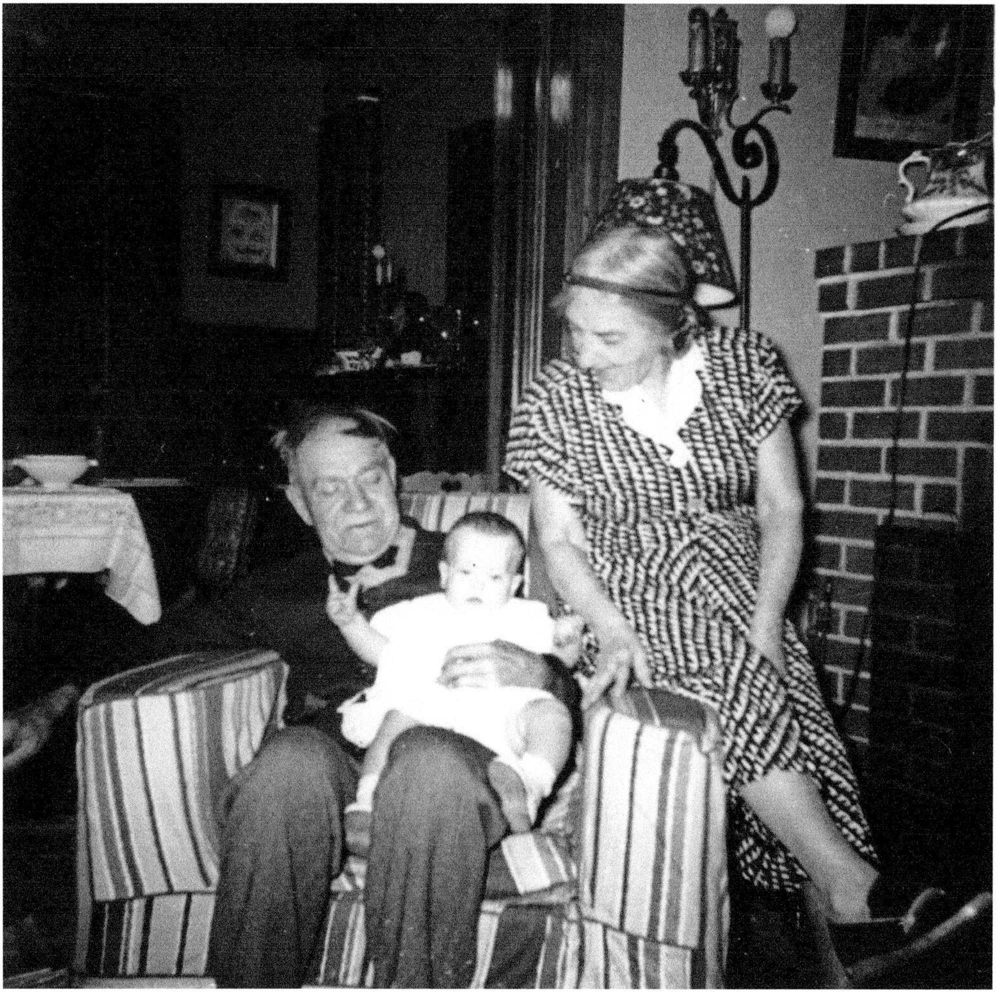

Ambrose and Anne in 1939 in their Lehighton home. (*Kim Graver Steinberger and family*)

mother sat and talked into his bad ear until 3 a.m. at his party. Hans just sat there the whole time, shaking his head, and agreeing with every word. When mother found out later that the man could not even hear her, she was livid. But Ambrose knew, and he couldn't wait to tease her about it."[11]

Despite Anne and Ambrose's marriage of necessity, they ultimately developed a strong bond with a deep underlying love. Except for one short separation in 1939, they remained together until the end. During their brief time apart in 1939, Anne returned to South 9th Street after a couple of weeks of living with Louise and her newlywed husband near Penn State University. Life without Ambrose was not as Anne envisioned it. She missed Maybert's daughter, Janny, who stayed in Lehighton with her grandfather. Sensing that her mother ought to return to Lehighton, Louise asked Wilbur Warner, the Lehighton postmaster, to scout out the Snyder house as a way to "test the waters." Warner's mail carrier gave this report:

> I watched for your package to the baby (Janny) and interviewed the carrier when he returned. It was delivered to Mr. Snyder, who was working in the yard at the time. As for your yard, it has undergone some changes. The hedge has been cut down very hard and the group of trees and shrubbery in the corner (which I always admired so much) have disappeared.[12]

Ambrose delivered on his promise to "rip her mess out." When Anne came back, her shrubbery might have been gone, but she was home to stay. She and Ambrose did not argue about who would outlive the other as much after that, though Ambrose would ultimately prevail, if only by a year or so—but that is skipping ahead. At the time of their visit to Provincetown, news of Franz's success had spread across the nation in magazines like *Life*, *Cosmopolitan*, and many others. *Avanti!*, a newspaper in Rome, called Kline the "Elvis Presley in Art." In *Horizon* magazine appeared an article about artists living in Provincetown which described Kline's lifestyle there:

> Franz Kline says he likes Provincetown because it is both quiet and jazzy.... Kline insures his quiet by living on a back street and keeping his telephone number unlisted; but as an artist in the very front rank of the abstract expressionists, he is hardly an anonymous figure, and knowing tourists have no trouble spotting him as he drives around town in his Jaguar.... Behind his rambling home is a large boat-builder's barn that he has converted into a studio. Here he has ample room to paint the huge, slashing canvases for which he is internationally famous.[13]

On one trip home later that year, Kline decided to drive his Thunderbird through the Pocono Mountains and stop at antique shops on the way to the Great Lehighton Fair. His parents' neighbor, William Sheckler, made extra money parking cars on his vacant lot across the street, and remembered this encounter:

> Franz pulled up in his Thunderbird and asked, "Can I park in your lot? It's safer than on the street with the fair going on." I knew that Franz was concerned about his car getting bumped or scratched, so I pointed him in the direction of one of the safer parking spots in the back. After I gave him the go ahead, he drove up the street a bit and around the back into the lot and smashed right into a post. I felt bad for him, but he didn't get upset; he just sort of got out, looked things over and shrugged. Then he went to the fair. That was Franz![14]

The degree of fame he experienced late in his career was far different from the celebrity-status he had experienced earlier on in life, and it came with much higher stakes. Louise recalled a high pressure opening at the Sidney Janis Gallery:

> That night his work was all modern black-and white-paintings, mother, Ambrose and I were waiting for him at the gallery. Finally, Franz arrived and he was taking my mother here and there, and she went over to Sidney Janis. "Well really," she said, "What happened to Franz? He always painted like Gainsborough and Rembrandt and all the

> great painters." And [Janis] said, "Well, my dear, in years to come, people are going to paint like Franz Kline."[15]

After the Sidney Janis show, Franz gave his mother two paintings, *The Horse*, which was painted at his Third Street studio, and *The Doves*, done El Greco style in green and black.[16] Kline's notoriety as an artist become so intense that, according to artist Ed Meneeley, Franz secretly took on a second studio on 13th Street. It adjoined the one he leased four years earlier at 242 W. 14th Street. Meneeley said that you could access the hidden space via the fire escape. Incognito there, he could paint in peace and have a place to store his work away from the prying eyes of dealers or the friends he brought back for drinks after last call. Pete Hamill described one such encounter with Kline:

> "It's closing time, isn't it?" he said one night, gazing around the almost empty Cedar. And then he led a few of us up to Fourteenth Street for a nightcap at this studio. I'd never been in a real painter's studio before. That dark loft was clearly a place of work. I could see rolls of canvas, buckets of paint, large house painters' brushes, cans of turpentine, baking pans caked with paint. The floor looked like a Pollock. There were small painted drawings scattered around, some of them on the floor, proof that Franz knew what he was going to paint when he approached the canvas.[17]

As Kline became more famous, his relationship with his family was a welcome relief from all the superficial glitz. Franz remained humble about his wealth and notoriety, remarking, "Most of my life, I've had no money and managed to get along. Right now I sell a few pictures. Nothing changes. I don't count on it lasting."[18]

Although to the public it may have seemed like Kline became successful overnight, his status as a leading artist and the high prices for his paintings were the culmination of decades of grueling work and sacrifice. Noted Pennsylvania folk artist Sterling Strausser, in correspondence to the author, shared this insight into the pressure accompanying Kline's fame: "When Franz had achieved some fame, he told Louise Nevelson, a good friend, that he was frightened to death whenever he stood facing a blank canvas. That puzzled me at first. I didn't realize the strain of being at the peak and not wanting to fall off."[19]

Kline's presence now became sought after by prominent people from all walks of life, including politicians like Nelson Rockefeller and Hollywood actors like Hedy Lamarr. Lamarr wrote a letter to Kline in 1959 which read: "When I first saw one of your paintings, done about 1950, I had to sit down because it did something to me."[20]

During the last years of his life, Kline produced some of his most magnificent works, including: *New Year's Wall Night 1960* and *Delaware Gap*. He was also making strides back to adding more color.

Franz and Betsy Zogbaum later toured Europe together. In a postcard to Jack Tworkov, *c.* 1960, Kline wrote: "We've come down from Paris to Venice and motored through the towns of the artists to Florence, then to Sienna & Rome.... The countryside, the cathedrals, and the people. What an exciting trip."[21] Franz was treated "like a royal guest of both the Italian and Japanese governments. They paid all of his expenses and gave him a limo."[22]

With increased acclaim came more glamorous invitations, including one handwritten from Jacqueline Kennedy for Franz to dine at the White House the night the French Minister of Culture, Andre Malraux, announced he was allowing the *Mona Lisa* to travel to America.

"I worked carefully on the guest list," Kennedy said, "wanting to include artists admired abroad, not only the traditional, established ones." She found them. Mark Rothko and Franz Kline, noted Abstract Expressionists, along with "painter of the people" Andrew Wyeth. [23] The rest of the seating chart revealed a *who's who* of cultural importance, including Charles Lindbergh, Geraldine Page, Irwin Shaw, Leonard Bernstein, George Balanchine, Thornton Wilder, Robert Penn Warren, Isaac Stern, Saul Bellow, Elia Kazan, Paddy Chayefsky, Lee Strasberg, Tennessee Williams, Arthur Miller, and Robert Lowell. Kline's invitation confirmed his place among other historical greats, but his seat ultimately remained empty, for his health was failing fast.

In May 1962, a letter came from Yale University offering him the Chair of the Art Department, but he never received it. Following Kline's extended trip abroad with Betsy Zogbaum, he became noticeably ill. His doctor sent him to Johns Hopkins in Baltimore, Maryland, for tests in April 1961, and he was diagnosed with a rheumatic heart.

Kline later tried to continue work as usual, but by February 1962, he suffered a heart attack and had to be rushed to St. Clare's Hospital. Once released, he moved in with Betsy Zogbaum and was put on a strict diet, but he stopped painting and never fully regained his health. Louise first sensed something was wrong on New Year's Eve. "Someone said they had been with him earlier in the evening and that he could hardly make the steps. He always called Mother on New Year's Eve and this time it got very late and he still didn't call. Mother sat up waiting. I finally put her to bed and then he called. He sounded like he had bronchitis or a really bad cold and was dying on his feet."[24]

By March, Franz was still not getting better. His family was not aware of the seriousness of his condition, by his request, until Betsy Zogbaum called Kline's brother, Jacques, who later broke the news to his family.

Franz spent the last months of his life in Betsy's townhouse with oxygen tubes in his nose under the care of a private nurse. Rumors circulated that Kline suffered from lead poisoning from his favorite pencils, manufactured near Leningrad. Louise immediately traveled to New York the same day Jacques related to her the gravity of the situation. She recalled the walk up to see him:

> The apartment had green velvet steps, with a French provincial sitting room, and then more steps. It was hot and the doors were open. It was in the wholesale district. Mark Rothko was there. Cigarette smoke filled the air. Mary Grant, a friend of Betsy's was the first person I saw, and she told me I couldn't see him. I nearly died. Mary said, "We called Elizabeth, his wife, but we are afraid to meet her when she comes." I told her that they shouldn't be afraid of Elizabeth, while just as well assuring them that she wouldn't come. Then I said, "Well, I've come a long way." There was an older woman there, a practical nurse. I said, "I'm Franz's sister." She said, "Just go in." He didn't know I was coming. I walked in and he was sitting on a chaise lounge, his hair so black

like mother's and those big deep-set eyes. He said, "Oh, hello Louise." I thought, *Franz, you should be in the hospital*, but I didn't want to scare him.

I took one look at him and I thought I'd collapse. "I didn't know you were sick," I said. "Jimmy Mazatelli was coming to see his brother in Brooklyn and, like Robert Frost, I thought why should I give my life to earn a living when I could come see you. I think I'll stay."

He looked at me and smiled. Then he introduced me to the nurse as his "little sister." And I said, "Your little sister has a couple of grey hairs in the front." And then he turned to the nurse and he said, "We're a loving brother and sister." And I wanted to melt in tears, but I was the only person from our family there, so I had to fight it. Then Betsy came in and asked me to have a seat. "You can't talk to him too long," she said. When she went out, we talked again. Then she came back in and said, "Bernard Reis is here and Lee Eastman," and Franz said, "Oh dear." I later asked Franz, "Who does he think he is?" Franz said that he "controls the purse strings." When Betsy went down to talk to them, I could see the distress on Franz's face. They were putting pressure on him for more paintings, he said. I stayed with Franz awhile, and the same little fellow who slept on the floor by Franz's bed came in with groceries, including food, beer, and cigarettes, but he forgot the milk and the nurse scolded him. And Franz lay there dying. He had this little automatic thing with tubes in his nose with oxygen and I thought, "Oh, God, Franz, you should be in a hospital."

And I thought, nobody was taking care of him. He was dying, and nobody was doing anything! I was hardly there before Sidney Janis, Bernard Reis, and Lee Eastman came up. I was distressed, so Mark Rothko took me for a walk. He told me that out of all the family of artists, Franz was the most lovable and least changed by success.

When I came back, the three men were outside. Reis said he was having a doctor sent so Franz could be admitted into a hospital. I told him that Franz should have been in the hospital already, and he said, "This is the big city Louise, you know how slowly things work."

I was so upset I went for another walk. Rothko said he was very fond of our mother, and we spent a while discussing the effects that Franz's death would have on her. I told Rothko that even though Franz was sick, I was sure Bernard Reis was pressuring him to produce. That night Jimmy and I sat outside in the car until Dr. Theodore Edlich, one of Franz's first patrons, arrived. Edlich said he would transfer his files to the new doctor at the hospital. He said, "Tomorrow when the ambulance comes, make sure they have the oxygen turned on. I wanted to stay there at Betsy's with Franz that night, but they told me they had made arrangements for me to stay at the Beekman Towers. I didn't want to stay there so I went with Jimmy to stay at his brother's house in Brooklyn.

I slept with my clothes on because I thought they could call at any moment and say Franz had died. He had given me a key to his townhouse shortly after he purchased it, but I wanted to wait until he was safely admitted into the hospital before I went there. The next day, when the ambulance came, I sat with him. Dr. Edlich told me to make sure the oxygen was on and to keep him calm. I went to the ambulance and saw Betsy. I could tell she didn't want Franz to go, and I felt so bad for her. They brought him down on a stretcher and the oxygen was in his nose and his black eyes were trying to smile and I thought, *Oh, Franz if only I can get you there. I can't be mother, but I'll get you there.* Betsy had to run across the street and get somebody to take the door off the hinges, so they could get his stretcher out. I rode with him in the ambulance. "What will you tell mother?" he asked. I choked up. I thought we would never get there. We were weaving in and out of traffic. They immediately put him in a private room with an oxygen tent, and Franz said, "It's so good not to have to breathe the smell of rubber."

Then the surgeon came into the room and said, "I see you are from Lehighton."

I said, "Yes, but we were born on West River Street in Wilkes-Barre."

"Did you know the Marcy's?" he asked.

They had lived next door to us, although they were older, and knew mother. The doctor said he knew them. Then, quietly, he said to me on the side that Franz could die while we were talking, that Franz had one of the largest hearts he had ever seen and that he should have been in the hospital a long time ago. I looked at Franz and said, "You know your doctor knows people that know our family," and that made him calmer.

The doctor left and came back shortly. He said to Franz, "You haven't slept in years, have you? I want you to just sit back and just make believe you're a vegetable." And when the doctor left again, Franz looked at me, felt the plastic around him, and—there was that humor again—he said, "I feel like I'm in the A & P. Imagine being something as uninteresting as a vegetable."

Then the darling little blonde nurse came in. She offered him puréed apricots or rhubarb sauce. I knew what he'd take because he loved rhubarb sauce. Mother used to make that. The nurse said she was on another case but that she could be a part-time private nurse for him until he found one. That relieved him. After she left, there was not much conversation, just a sense of relief to have gotten him there.

The next day I made arrangements to get my scheduling straightened out at Elizabethtown, the university where I taught and to inform Mother's doctor that she could collapse at any moment. I told Franz I was going to call Jacques to come while I was gone, and he said, "Louise don't talk so loud."

Jacques came while I was away. When he got to the hospital, he asked Betsy to give him the keys to the 14th Street studio so he and his wife could stay there until I got back on Monday. After I came back, I was with Franz every day, even though Bernard Reis tried to dismiss me. He appeared every morning and tried to dictate when I should visit and when I should go. There was also the same little fellow who came to the hospital and wanted to sleep on the floor by Franz's bed.

Even though we tried to keep Franz alive, the end came a lot more quickly than I could have imagined. When I could sense it was near, I called Fred. Our brother brought some young girl with him, to help him make sure he could get across the streets because, with his poor eyesight, he couldn't tell whether the lights were green or red. When Fred saw Franz, he dissolved into tears.

I had been just talking to mother on the phone down the hall, and then to Elizabeth, before going back in his room. I looked at Franz and he seemed so uncomfortable. I reached inside the tent and said, "Here, I'll boost you a little." I had just put my arms underneath him when he said, "Hold me tight." And then he died.[25]

Kline died on May 13, 1962, two days after the White House dinner he was invited to attend. Even his closest friends were not aware of his escalating physical problems. His decline was said to have been caused by the childhood heart ailment exacerbated by a lifetime of heavy drinking, smoking, and sleep deprivation. Betsy encouraged him to change his lifestyle, and for a while he stopped smoking and drinking. "I was surprised how his temperament was still sunny," she said, "but then he felt a little bit better and just started up with it again."[26]

Along with his "rheumatic heart," Kline had been battling melancholy for years. Like many men of his day, he worked hard to keep his vulnerabilities hidden. Robert Motherwell was one of a few people who Franz connected with on a deeper level. After Kline's passing, Motherwell described Franz as "funny, and shrewd, filled with comradely affection even tenderness, which covered something much deeper and blacker that we all respected."[27]

During the last week of his life, family members lodged in Kline's 14th Street studio while visiting the hospital. Between traveling and being ill, Franz had not been to the studio much over the past year. He had given Louise keys when he purchased the property, and as soon as she opened the door she said it had changed considerably.

> The day after Franz died Bernard Reis drove me all over New York to select a coffin. It wasn't until after that when I finally took Elizabeth to Bernard Reis's office. I told Reis that Elizabeth had never seen Franz's studio, and that I wanted to take her there. I had a suitcase and other things down there too I needed to get. Reis said he would see if he could get us a taxi. Before we left his office, in front of everyone, Reis said to Elizabeth, "I understand that Franz has always paid for your apartment." She said, "Yes." He said, "He came to see you every week?" "Yes, that's right," she said. "And he gave you so much for living and so much for your psychiatrist?" And he said, "Now that he is dead, you are going to have to do with a lot less than that." I was appalled. I thought, "She's his wife and still needs care. Franz would want her to have it. What's he trying to do?" Then we took a taxi with Reis, and Elizabeth went inside Franz's studio. Franz wasn't that careful about filing and organizing his things, yet now everything seemed to be packed up. Things in every room were being readied for storage. They had all these paintings, and we asked if we could have one, but Reis denied us. The table was loaded with paintings, mounted and ready to go. They must have been working there all morning. I asked Lee Eastman about the will and he said he didn't draw it up, Reis did. He said that they did it in a hurry because Franz was rushing to go to the Venice Biennale.
>
> I asked Reis if we could each pick a painting, a small one or two. There was a turquoise one I liked because Franz had told me he painted it the same shade as a dress I bought in New York. He said he loved that color and was putting it in a painting. Reis said it would depend. But we never got anything, even our father's tie-pin that mother had given Franz was gone. As I talked to Reis, Fred was looking at one of Franz's books about Japanese silk prints. Reis told him to put it back, that it was a very expensive book. I could see Fred's eyes flash. "What gives you the right?" he asked. "It's all in legal hands now," Reis said.

"We're his family," I said. "We have never asked for anything. When Franz was alive, I could have had anything I wanted. I remember once in his studio he was playing 'Gigi' on the stereo and I said I loved it and he said, 'Take the record home with you.' If I mentioned liking anything, he would make me take it." But Reis didn't respond. We aren't the kind of family that would usurp another's possessions, but I took two Phil May drawings for sentimental reasons, and then I went into the kitchen for the coin silver spoons he bought in Provincetown. I once told Franz that I admired them, and he told me to take them, but I knew they were special. He had bought them for Elizabeth when she was in the hospital. And I thought, "I'm going to take that little folder, and put it in my pocketbook." I also took his clock and pill box, thinking that I'd give something to everyone in the family.

I started to cry. Fred wanted to carry my top coat, but it had all of Franz's things I took underneath. Fred said, "Please stop crying." And I stopped him from coming near me. "Don't take my coat," I said, "it has Franz's things in it, you might let them fall." We were so disenchanted and upset, and then Elizabeth said, "There's our little yellow chair from our first apartment."

I gave Elizabeth the condolence letter from Adlai Stevenson. There were so many lovely notes with gorgeous floral arrangements, but someone took them all from the night table drawer at the hospital where the nurse put them aside for me. Someone also took his lovely foreign watch from the hospital, and his blue housecoat from Italy. Elizabeth was the prime beneficiary and eventually got her choice of his personal belongings. She chose the silk sofas and cocktail tables. She was also given a few drawings. She wanted the painting *White Door* but was denied.[28]

Kline's New York funeral was held at St. Bartholomew's on Park Avenue. De Kooning and Rothko wept on each other's shoulders.[29] In his eulogy, Motherwell later wrote:

> No one can feel the death of Franz Kline without a wrench. We have lost part of the modern art world.... It is not only someone born in a foreign land, like Gorky, who feels alienated from the world around us. Franz struck me as deeply alienated in some ways—and consequently craving affection on a broad scale. But he was not alienated from the act of painting: thus, his work's startling and moving verve, though in the background of its immediate feeling, there was always its anxious overtones. Franz projected as a person the sense of a man who was trying to save his own soul through his gift, and that he wanted to share this possible miraculous event with you. But he could not take care of himself! (It would have meant another existence). Those few of us who know of his true condition—not from him but from his doctors—watched in helpless dismay the chances he took. But if he could have taken care of himself, he would not have been that enchanter we all knew, as Franz Kline, generous and heedless.[30]

The next day, Franz's body traveled to Lehighton for a viewing at the Garrett Funeral Home. Grace Ahner, Kline's childhood friend, was the first to arrive. Franz wore a pair of black slacks with a white shirt and black shoes. The local newspapers described his friends paying their last respects "to the boy they had known so well, to the artist they barely understood."

Franz had three services in all. The last took place in Wilkes-Barre, after which he was buried on the family plot overlooking the Susquehanna River in Hollenback Cemetery. His mother, remaining in a state of shock, did not attend any of the three. "During the funeral I had to put Mother to bed," Louise said.[31] "She never got over Franz's death. She couldn't get up on her feet, the shock was too much." Two years later in 1964, Anne died at the age of seventy-eight. Ambrose followed about a year later.

In death, Franz reunited with his father forty-five years after Anthony Carlton's tragic end. He is now joined by his other family, including Louise. The rhododendrons from their old estate on West River Street were still in place when Franz was buried in 1962, but they have since been chopped down. Kline's grave is marked by a flat, red granite headstone for two, but the block reserved for his wife's name remains vacant.

After Elizabeth Kline was released from Central Islip for the second time in 1960, Franz found her an apartment near the hospital and continued to take care of her expenses. At one point, he consulted a lawyer about divorce, but decided against it. He visited her weekly, took her out for dinners, bought her a baby grand piano, and paid for her lessons. Elizabeth later told Louise that inside the asylum they made her scrub the floors and that she felt like she had been kept there too long.

"Elizabeth asked to be buried with Franz," Louise said, "and I agreed, but she later changed her mind. Her lawyer said she preferred to be buried at St. Elizabeth's. After Franz's death, Elizabeth became reclusive and then finally cut off all communications. She wrote to say that she would no longer be going out in public because she would not have people pointing and staring at her as Franz Kline's widow. In her last letter, she said that Bernard Reis was making her take another sanity test to receive her inheritance, and that she refused to take it because she had been discharged from the hospital.[32]

After her husband's death, Elizabeth wrote a letter to the editor of *ArtNews*: "Sir: In reference to your magnificent article on the subject of my husband, the late Franz Kline [Nov. '62].... I wish to comment on certain statements." Elizabeth goes on to correct certain points about her husband's life—the correct years of his stay in London, the true identity of Mars, the correct spelling of Sadler's Wells, etc.—along with these insightful lines: "Mrs. deKooning remarks that 'any extension of [his work's] visual actuality ... into biography would appear to be falsifications.' Yet the subtitle of the article is 'Painter of his own life.' This later fact is true, and far more so than anyone has yet realized."

With a remarkable degree of intellectualism, Elizabeth directly refutes those who would deny that her husband's "biography" had anything to do with his work's "visual actuality," as if he had somehow removed his life out of his life's work. Here is how she closed the record:

> [De Kooning] has painted a portrait-in-words which brilliantly portrays the "gay Cavalier" of gregarious occasions. Franz Kline was actually a many-faceted personality, a composite of contradictions. This is manifest in the incredible contrasts, technically and spiritually, between his early and later works. —Elizabeth V. Kline, Central Islip, NY.[33]

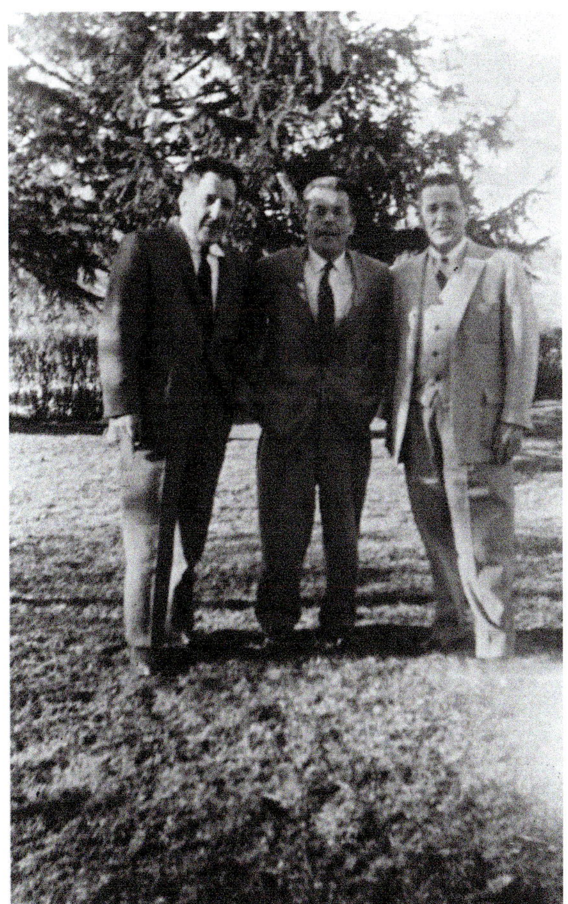

Above left: Franz and his brothers, Frederick (center) and Jacques, in Lehighton, *c.* 1958. (*Harold Rabenold*)

Above right: Untitled homage by Dan Finsel, 2014. (*Daniel Finsel*)

Kline's career was filled with awards and accolades, including credit among his colleagues for changing the scope of art history itself. But it was a simple message from a friend—one tied to a bouquet of yellow tulips next to his hospital bed—that spoke the loudest to Louise. The note from Motherwell read: "To Franz, You always did have the biggest heart."[34]

12 Collected Letters and Additional Works

To view the early scrawlings of a master artist like Kline is an educational and inspirational experience. To view early artworks that have never been widely seen is akin to seeing a great buried treasure suddenly unearthed.

Professor Howie Weiss, Maryland Institute, College of Art
Personal correspondence

1. Franz Kline to Alvirda K. Arner Ginder, December 20, 1928
2. Franz Kline to Alvirda K. Arner Ginder, December 21, 1928
3. Franz Kline to Lavona Edgar, October, 1931
4. Franz Kline to Ralph Beisel, December 4, 1933
5. Franz Kline to Ralph Beisel, November 9, 1935
6. Franz Kline to Frederick Ryan, August 10, 1936
7. Franz Kline to Frederick and Beatrice Ryan, January 21, 1940
8. Franz Kline to Frederick and Beatrice Ryan, April 24, 1940
9. Franz Kline to Frederick and Beatrice Ryan, June 2, 1940
10. Franz Kline to Frederick and Beatrice Ryan, June 23, 1940
11. Franz Kline to Frederick and Beatrice Ryan, July 1, 1940
12. Franz Kline to Frederick and Beatrice Ryan, July 4, 1940
13. Franz Kline to Frederick and Beatrice Ryan, July 11, 1940
14. Franz Kline to Frederick and Beatrice Ryan, August 14, 1940
15. Franz Kline to Frederick and Beatrice Ryan, August __, 1940
16. Jack Tworkov to Franz Kline, January 24, 1950
17. Franz Kline to Jack Tworkov, July 28, 1952
18. Franz Kline to Frederick Ryan, May 16, 1958
19. Franz Kline to Frederick Ryan, Sunday, December 16, 1958

Letters were more than a way for Kline to stay in contact with friends and family. Often, the simple act of pen on paper, the gestural movement of the hand, helped soothe him to sleep. A blank page was a stage to play with a new pen or artistic signature. While a student in Boston, Kline wrote letters just before bed as a way of unwinding, many written in an elaborate hand. Whether penning a witty card or a heart-to-heart note, Kline's tone, even when clowning around, remained sincere, and his letters reveal his deep well of empathy for others and a rare glimpse into some of the artist's most intimate thoughts. Additional letters are found in Chapters 5 and 6. Please note: all spelling irregularities are true to the original letters. Enjoy.

1. Franz Kline to Alvirda K. Arner Ginder, December 20, 1928

Dear Virdy,

I don't know why you think you've caused any bad feelings. Gee! I hope you don't think "Dot" Lush could come between us. All you've said of her is true. It puzzles me trying to think how you found it all out. Gosh! Every girl I ever talk or write to talks of this "Dot" Lush. It seems so queer because I can truthfully say I say nothing to her but "Hello" and that only occurs once in a while. Gee! She doesn't stand a chance with you.

I now want to thank you for your kind congratulations, but please express it by glancing in my direction during auditorium periods at least once in awhile. Gosh! I sit there looking at you and you never even notice me. Well, I'm glad I can now say you have your book-ends at last. But please, don't insist on paying me. Because the only thing I will accept is a night with you like the one on Wes Kriedler's porch swing. If that isn't asking too much of you! I'll let you answer this question in your next note. Please don't think you're asking too much of me to make you a cigarette stand. I would give you mine, but I've found so many improvements on it and I find it too small. Yours will be larger and more neat in appearance. Before closing I wish to ask you to answer this note today—Thursday 20th.

With Love, Franz

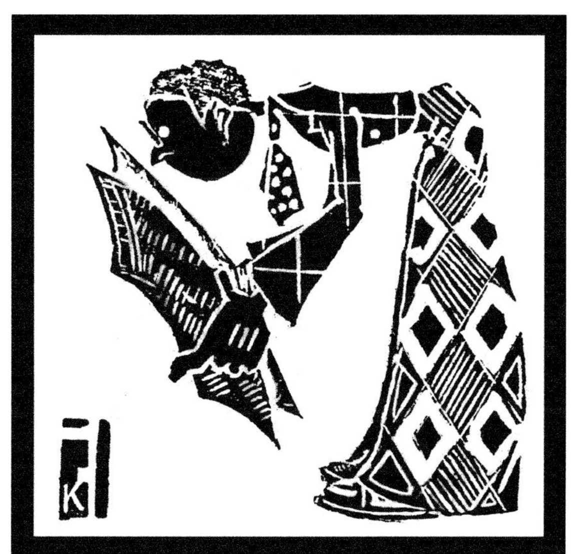

Leni Habit, 1931, *The Leni Lenapian* linoleum block print features bell-bottom trousers, flared sleeves, and polka dot tie. Large hands hold a newspaper while eyeglasses teeter on his nose. Note the backwards "F" in the initials. (*© 2018 Franz Kline Estate/Artists Rights Society (ARS), New York*)

2. Franz Kline to Alvirda K. Arner Ginder, December 21, 1928

My dear Virdy,

I suppose this will be my last note to you with 1928 as a heading. But please don't you wait until next year to answer.

So you thought I saw you this morning in the auditorium. Well I did! But I was disappointed, for I thought I was going to get a better view of you on the stage and you never appeared. So I had to be content with sudden glimpses of you, as I gazed down the front row. Don't you worry about my getting sore eyes 'cause gee, kid your worth blinking at.

Gosh, Virdy I'm sorry you thought I intended to visit you at your home! Cause Gee! kid I know my mother wouldn't allow it any more than I think my mother would. But someday something will turn up when we can be together. I hope it will be soon. How about you? Gee! I wonder if all girls are like you? I don't believe it. It beats me how enthusiastic you become over a set of bookends. Gosh! Virdy who wouldn't enjoy making anything for you.

Now I'm going to ask of you a favor. Will you give me one of your pictures? Just, tell Louise you are going to give me one instead of her. And if she wants to see it she can ask me, I'll let her look at it once in a while. In case I don't get a chance to talk with you before the 25th, I want to

wish you a Very Merry Christmas.

Thursday even

Franz

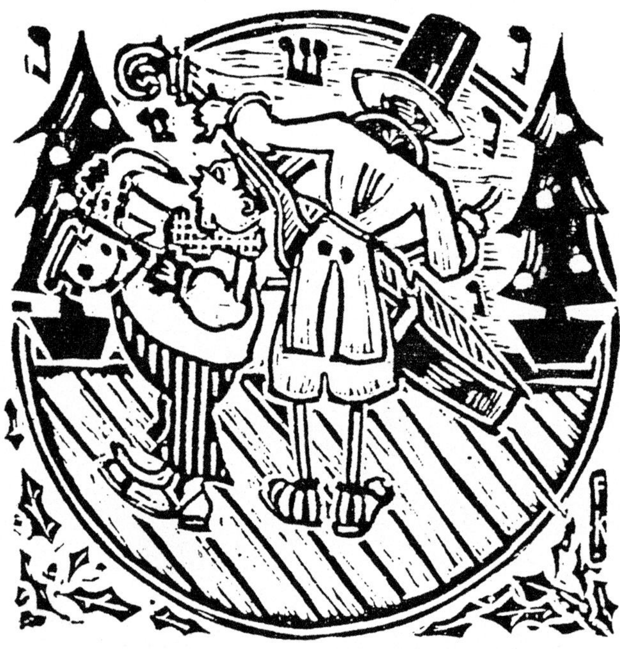

Christmas Eve, December 23, 1930, *The Leni Lenapian*. (*Alvirda K. Arner Ginder © 2018 Franz Kline Estate/ Artists Rights Society (ARS), New York*)

3. Franz Kline to Lavona Edgar, October, 1931

37 Evans Road
Brookline, Massachusetts
Dear Lavona,

No doubt you've many times wondered if I'd keep my promise to you—I have, at last, and here's my letter. Hasn't the time passed quickly, it seems but a few nites ago that I bid you goodnite at the door I so often visited.

Well, Lavona, how's chemistry coming along—ah! I just knew you'd love it. And tell me isn't it grand and glorious to be a senior?

Well it's only half as enjoyable as being a freshman again! I suppose Edith has kept you up to date with my doings and goings—so there is no use of going over them again. In brief words—I am as happy and ambitious as ever, met loads of interesting as well as attractive new friends of both sexes, my artwork is all I pictured it to you, and being in "Big Boston" is great. There's so much doing, so much to do and see. I suppose Lehighton is the same little Dutch settlement wrapped up in a cloud of coal dirt—however I miss it with all my friends.

A letter from Milly Held tells me the strong Lehighton football squad is a bit crippled. Lavona, what's wrong with the team, will they never win a game. Gee, every Saturday I wish I was with them going to school on Sat morning I run—side step & kick, dreaming I'm still a member of the LHS eleven. Up here I don't even hear how they make out until a week later. The only school scores I hear are Harvard, B.U., Yale and Army. Shimmer keeps me in touch with Lafayette now and then. They are all interesting to me, but not half what Lehighton high's activities are. Someday you too will experience the same feeling.

Lavona! You remember my telling you how interesting and amusing you'd find Mr. Niehoff in Senior History—Well one of my Art Profs is just Callie's type. A big brother rather than a teacher! The other nite he had me down at his fraternity KVO—I met a bunch of fine fellows—students of BU. The evening ended up in an elaborate banquet. The Sunday before he invited me over to his studio—gee! It's great, paintings, sketches, statues, relics in ancient art—well everything! He even lent me a costume for our Hallow'een dance at the Studio this fri nite. Miss Roedel tells me that the "red Hot Senior Dance ensemble" is trying to persuade Mr. David to allow dances in the high school building. I hope they succeed. It may mean a Halloween dance for you also.

And now for the part in which I know you'll find interesting—I have a roommate—He's from Maine—tonite we bought a Drip-o-lite coffee percolator so we laugh at each other while eating doughnuts and drinking coffee—our mid-nite luncheon. He with me is supposedly an art student, but half the time we don't know whether we're budding artists or blooming fools but we're happy and get along fine together. Some nites we even go on dates together. The "Sargent School" of Ed. [education] seems to be quite an interesting study. You can imagine it is—Miss Obert is an alumnus. Well, Lavona, I've just come in and on into the nite I am keeping my promise. Jerry my mate is fast asleep—yeah he even snores once in a while and me, well my eyes are blinkin with every tick of my alarm clock.

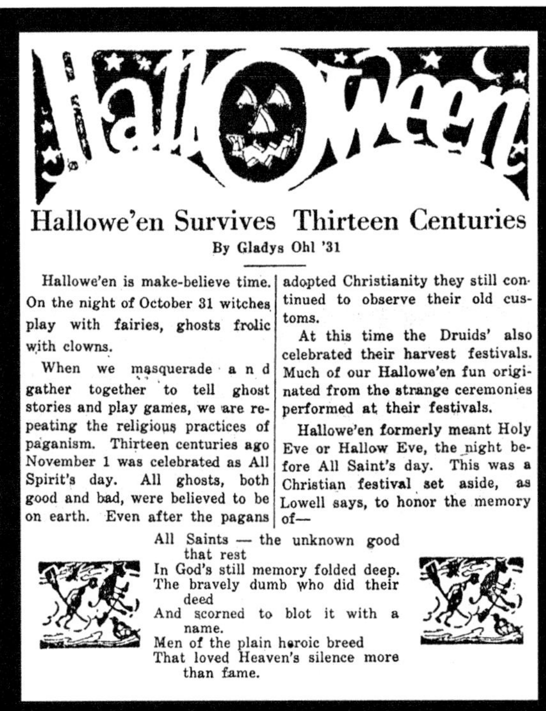

Hallowe'en Survives Thirteen Centuries

By Gladys Ohl '31

Hallowe'en is make-believe time. On the night of October 31 witches play with fairies, ghosts frolic with clowns.

When we masquerade and gather together to tell ghost stories and play games, we are repeating the religious practices of paganism. Thirteen centuries ago November 1 was celebrated as All Spirit's day. All ghosts, both good and bad, were believed to be on earth. Even after the pagans adopted Christianity they still continued to observe their old customs.

At this time the Druids' also celebrated their harvest festivals. Much of our Hallowe'en fun originated from the strange ceremonies performed at their festivals.

Hallowe'en formerly meant Holy Eve or Hallow Eve, the night before All Saint's day. This was a Christian festival set aside, as Lowell says, to honor the memory of—

All Saints — the unknown good that rest
In God's still memory folded deep.
The bravely dumb who did their deed
And scorned to blot it with a name.
Men of the plain heroic breed
That loved Heaven's silence more than fame.

Halloween, 1931, *The Leni Lenapian*, linoleum block print. "At Halloween, Franz and Fred would dress like pirates or hobos or something awful like that," quote by Louise Kline-Kelly. (*© 2018 Franz Kline Estate/Artists Rights Society (ARS), New York*)

Before closing let me ask you to write an answer as long as this letter. Soon. Give my regards to all my friends and yours—See ya at Christmas time!

Good-by, Franz

—Tell your Dad I'm still keep'in training for the Park Ponies Football team!

4. Franz Kline to Ralph Beisel, December 4, 1933

Mon. Eve

Dear Chick,

I intended to answer your letter before the holidays, but it just seems I didn't get to it. I spent Thanksgiving at a girl's home in Haverille, Mass. She goes to school here with me and rooms here at 114 Hemenway—so you see Chicken things are doing.

Well, Chick here's the dope. Werdell, my roommate I told you so much about didn't get his machine yet. So I'll be going home by railroad pass. My folks are sending me one. I wish I could have been arranged that we go home together but I'm glad that you will have a lift as far as New Jersey. I suppose you'll go the rest of the way by truck. Anyhow, Chicken I'll see you in town. I'm not sure when my vacation begins. I suppose I'll be taking off a little early so I can make my regular stop off in Easton.

It's great to hear you are getting along so well in your studies that's what counts Ralph—even 'Josie Obert' would tell you that. I suppose football will come next year much to your pleasure.

It was awfully nice of our Pal Snyder to send you my address that's one thing he did that pleases me. By the way Chick three Saturdays ago when West Point played Harvard Butch Ginder spent the day and evening up to 12 bells with me. He looked the nuts in his uniform; say's they work him pretty hard and that classes are stiff as hell! We had two dames hanging on us, went to a show etc.

Wasn't the Army-Notre Dame a surprise—How is Maine in the art of boot'n the pig skin? Big men? And how do chances look for you?

School down here is still quite the nutz I'm fairing fairly well. The social life's better 'n ever chicken, I'm sure you would enjoy it. Do you have much time for anything but studies up your way? We'll discuss that all at Xmas time "Chicken". I suppose you're quite anxious to visit the old burg. I am myself, still we'll both be glad to leave again. I don't know much about the town; I haven't heard anything from any of the guys. I suppose the weather is quite [ ] up there in them there hills. We had a young blizzard today.

Well, Chicken it's soon time to hit the blankets. Write me before you depart for home and I'll answer more hastily this time.

Good Luck Chicken. I'll see you in town. I'm awaiting all the dope from Maine U. and I have a little to give you to chick. So long Beisel.

Your Pal, Franz

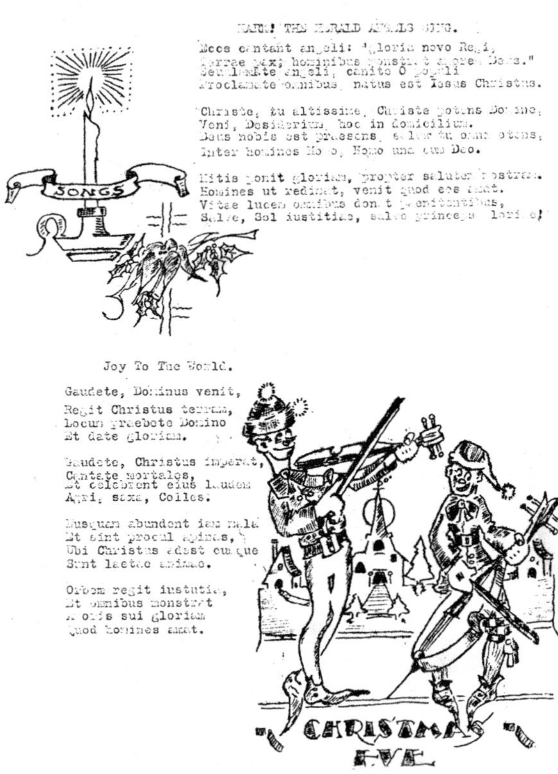

Christmas Program, 1928, Lehighton High School. (*Mildred Held © 2018 Franz Kline Estate/Artists Rights Society (ARS), New York*)

5. Franz Kline to Ralph Beisel, November 9, 1935

29 Belsize Crescent
London, Eng. NWS
Dear Ralph:

I am sorry to hear of the sadness which has come into your life in the event of your father's death. May I extend my sympathies. I know he was liked and will be missed by many.

I trust you shall be able to carry on with your studies and wish you the best luck with them and your football career at Maine.

London is swell, I'm wild about all this picturesque quaintness. School with Mr. Spurrier though quite different—from my Boston studies is ideal.

I know you are faring well chicken both in classes and on the gridiron, wish I could see you in action.

Best of luck and again my deepest sympathies.

Your friend and classmate, Franz Kline.

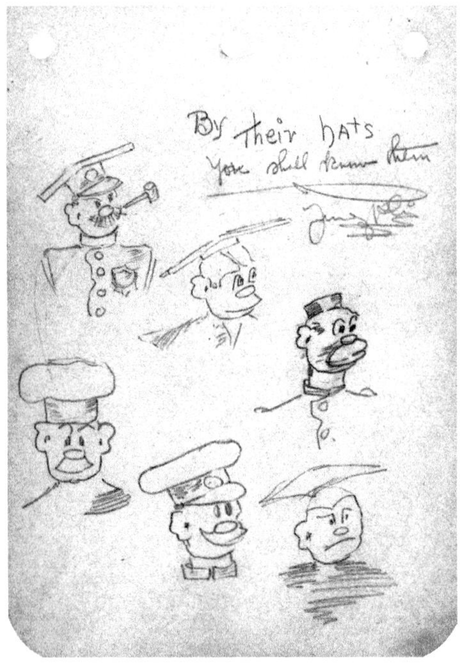

By Their Hats You Shall Know Them, 1930. (*William Bittner © 2018 Franz Kline Estate/ Artists Rights Society (ARS), New York*)

6. Franz Kline to Frederick Ryan, August 10, 1936

121 Westbourne Grove
London W2

Dear Freddie; Here it is the end of the school year and I am just getting round to answering your letter. Forgive me if you can Fred! Several times I started to write you; then thinking the subject matter wasn't interesting enough I gave it up. Well at least I certainly have allotted myself time enough to gather some items by now—haven't I? I've thought, talked of you and anticipated writing you since the time of your letter so you have by no means Fred, been forgotten. I've often wished you were here and that we could have some of our old discussions again together. I guess we both have some different and interesting ideas now.

Well Freddie its no use going on "on how much I like London" you can imagine it all. From every standpoint it's great. Subject matter of all types and the home and working grounds of all our illustrative masters. Whistler, Abbey, May, etc. And if Sargent Whistler and Abbey liked enough to work here I certainly would be a Jerry Milliken if I wouldn't.

Well let's start with the present and work back to the past.

Last week an old school teacher of mine spent the week in London and then flew on to Paris. I took it upon myself to show her what I knew of London from the Abbey & St. Pauls to the museums and May's originals. Anyhow she bought three original pencil studies of Sir Henry Irving for £5 and gave them to me. Beautiful studies they are valued at £20. So I have still to get over the excitement and enjoyment of it all. One of them is reproduced in James Thorpes Book on Phil May. By now I have ten books on him some first editions so you see I still have old Phil in the blood.

Next. four of my studies have been selected by the "Artist" publication to be reproduced in its' pages in an article on Future Artists. I think 15 were chosen, and four of them were mine. I haven't yet found out when they will be published but shall let you know.

I don't suppose you know Spurrier's work very well Fred although he has had quite a few illustrations published in America. He himself as well as his work are very strange and difficult to discuss. Very different from Crosman and Durkee and the usual American illustrator although he formerly was a friend of Cyrus Cuneo and influenced by him. Spurrier is without doubt London's or Englands most popular and best illustrator and a very vercital [*sic.*] man indeed. He exhibited in the Royal Academy this year. Does poster work and book illustration. The Victoria and Albert Museum have a collection of his studies illustrations and water colours. So he carries some weight. I should say the nearest American illustrator to his view, and style in the method of work is Wallace Morgan. The photograph and drawing from [?] doesn't interest him in the least so he wasn't very impressed with my collection of Crosman's work. another very similar approach and outlook is found in Dame Laura Knight. He handles humorous subjects as well so naturally I became very interested in his ideas and methods of building an illustration. Sketchbook, the model and invention are the forms of reference he uses. So as a result I have rafts of sketches from the streets etc. and a gang of incomplete illustrations etc.

The technical side of the thing and so called flare seem of very little interest to him and in his drawings you see just about as much as Morgan, Wartman or some of the Esquire men display. Hence I am trying to let good drawing predominate the otherwise technical "smartness" my work seemed to have. And is it tough! Spurriers' masters consist of first Rembrandt, the French School, and Keene of Punch fame. In books he has written he claims Charles Keene a master of all time. and Rembrandt the master of all time! Another paragraph read the American illustrator was worth study and interest only when he was trying to be either funny or sarcastic, most of them being too sentimental.

Anyhow Fred it would be interesting the next time you see Crosman to get his views on Spurriers' work and outlook. By the way how's the school coming? I mean yours. I trust you are doing alright. Send me the news on your activities, Fred. Martha told me quite a bit when she first came over, sounds interesting.

I can see you now at the drawing desk with the crow cwill [*sic.*] pen. Stick to it Fred. I'm doing the same. Forgive the scribble but this is a pen I picked up today for 5/ to draw with on the streets. An ordinary fountain pen, shall I give you a sample of its scratches. Here they are. [At the top of this page are pen sketches of three female heads and examples of cross-hatching]. Not bad for $1.25 is it Fred?

Oh by the way Fred, I saw three original Abbey drawings. They are at the Victoria-Albert museum beautiful pen drawings. One from Old Songs and She Stoops to Conquer. The figures are about the size of this page. That is, the length of one figure. I've had out originals of just about every pen draughtsman I could get and studied them. Keene, May, Daumier, Foran etc.

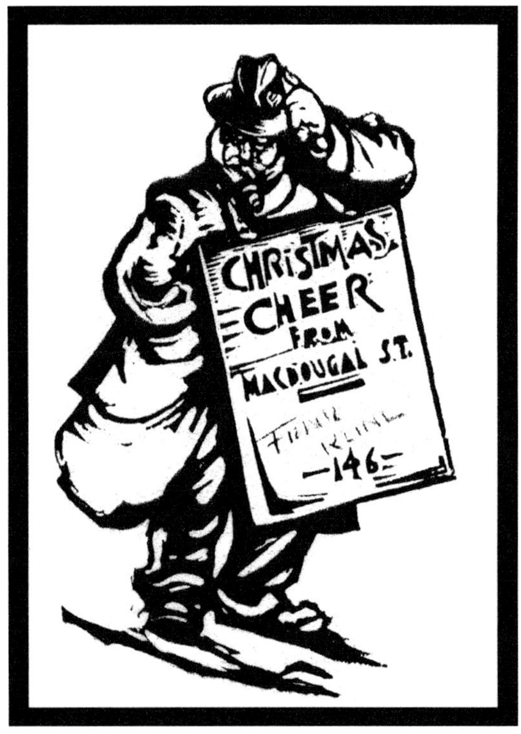

Christmas Cheer from MacDougal Street, 1946. (*A. E. Bayer Estate © 2018 Franz Kline Estate/Artists Rights Society (ARS), New York*)

Well Freddie, the wee hours are hear again and I must hit the hay. Wish you were here or I were there, we could have a nickel hamburger and a coffee. Write me soon and give me all the news on the remenants [*sic.*] of the old Art League and Back Bay in general.

Give my regards to Mr. Crosman Argue and Durkee if you see them.

Best wishes to your family. How's Olive coming along in the dentist profession?

Regards from Martha who sits propped up in bed eating candy and reading. For her there's no place like U.S.A. until she gets there!

Forgive the long delay Fred I'll be more punctual from now on. Good luck and many strong lines.

From your Sincere Pal, Franz

7. Franz Kline to Frederick and Beatrice Ryan, January 21, 1940

71 W 3rd St.
N.Y.C.

Dear Freddie & Bea:

It was great to hear from you again—We knew there must have been something brewing up thar' on the hill—So now it's a home it sounds wonderful—and your descriptive facilities with the pen, Fred are adept both with the figure and the word—makes my new studio here—just round the corner from MacDougal Street sound like a fortune teller's tent—and I'm mad about the possibilities of it. You've just got to come down and see it.

Fred I just can't tell you how we felt to hear of Jim's end. We knew nothing about it—it's hardly believable—the little I knew Jim makes me appreciate how you feel—and had I never met him—from your letter alone I'd know him—and know your sadness. He must always have been—and then to read your paragraphs, Freddie I'm proud to know one knows the real things and can express them in your way and to Jim—having met him only a few times as I did—my feeling was the same as yours at the ending of the first paragraph—the death of your old friend Jim McGarrigal.

Forgive the short note Fred & Bea we're both here trying to fix up a top floor with everything the old masters would have loved—cheap rent, lots of room, light, and silence after MacDougal St. Will write you and perhaps take a bus to Boston one week-end soon. I'm happy that everything is going well. I liked your letter head Bea—now do use more of them on our new address.

Elizabeth has been ill with the flu and I know you appreciate what this moving by hand can be.

So till soon again all the best of luck to you all. We're glad your all well and spirits and hopes are high.

Yours,
Elizabeth and Franz

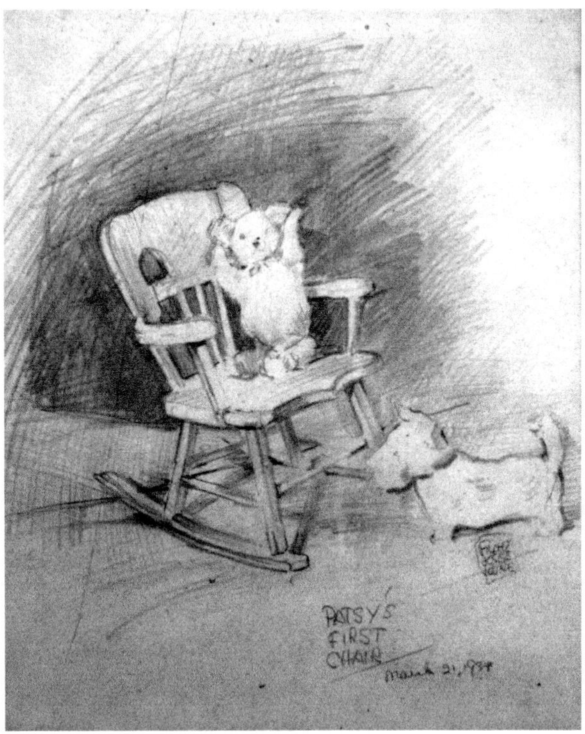

Patsy's First Chair, 1944. Drawing of Patsy Gernerd's rocking chair, with Teddy Bear and stuffed toy Scotty dog. Kline was in Lehighton on break from the Boston Art Students League. (*Patsy Gernerd Aldrich and family © 2018 Franz Kline Estate/Artists Rights Society (ARS), New York*)

8. Franz Kline to Frederick and Beatrice Ryan, April 24, 1940

71 W. 3rd St.
New York City

Dear Freddie & Bea:

I can't tell you how happy we were to receive your letter. Everything sounds swell—you can add us to the long line of the enveous! And your kind invitation—well it's welcomed by us both. Now here's the set up down here—the same slow up after Christmas descended here and things have been really bad! With the exception of a set of three miniatures, the sale of a few etchings and a few framing jobs—there just hasn't been any business to talk about. However I have used my time painting and I have a collection of small oils—which I intend to sell during the out door show—due soon! We would like to just pack up things and leave for your country estate but it will take a little preparation on our part. Paying up a few bills—and arranging a sub let to a couple, friends of ours. So if you don't mind Fred. This will take a few weeks and we should then be ready to shove off! Elizabeth hasn't been really well since the beginning of the new year. However now she feels fit and with some decent weather she'll be fit again. She's had several cases of flue and colds—and I'm sure that getting out of New York for the summer would be the best things—for us both in fact! Your home and property sound marvelous—I can imagine how happy and enthusiastic you both are—and we'd just love to give you every assistance possible in making it what you desire.

Fred—I remember that swell tool box and tools your father gave you and I think I share the same love of putting them to use. I have a collection of tools too which I shall bring along. For the past several months we've had the same sort of lark as you—only on a much smaller scale—The studio now is quite grand—I think its the most picturesque in the vicinity—and just how we ever got on MacDougel St. I don't know. Limited resources made it impossible to do all I wanted to with it—however it's a real studio in any condition. Now that summer is here the up keep is much less without that heating problem—and so—even if we didn't wish to sub let it we could keep it going in our absence—and if we should wish to remain in New England with you—well—loads of our friends would just love this place. Besides I've really got a collection of heavy bulky belongings and here they're safe—the etching press etc.!!

So in the near future Fred—we'll be making preparations—and collecting some cash I hope! and just as soon as we can—we'll write you our intentions on leaving. In the mean time do let us know what we should bring—or send ahead of us—oh! by the way—Elizabeth wants me to ask you—can we bring our pussy cat. You remember her Bea. If there is any reason why we shouldn't, do let us know and we'll understand.

Little Jimmy looks lovely—and I'm sure you are glad to have him running around in the country. I'm anxious to see him and the proud Pa Pa and Ma Ma—now promise me you won't put ideas into Elizabeths' head.

Your neighbors sound swell—and looking forward to sessions such as we used to have is alone worth dropping everything down here—that is if there were anything to drop!—And if your interested Fred—there's a friend of mine down here—with a wonderful collection of Crosman's work—He has work covering every stage of his career. I'll see if I can't get it for you—at least I'll borrow it. Being rather a tight commercial minded chap he talks of selling all the time. so the hope that I could obtain it, cause he doesn't value it other than the possibility of its sale value is rather scarce. Jack Patterson stopped in the other day—He's still in the acting business—busy rehearsing. I never see Helen Pitts. I looked her up several times—but she moved and goodness knows where to ! The other day I met a professional dancer from Boston. Perhaps you've heard of him Edaurd Du Buron [Edouard Du Boron]. He seemed to know all the old Bostonians [of] our tales—Danny Brewster, Major [Ernest L. Major]—Chase Dexter—Hazelton and the Vesper George crew. We had quite a discussion.

And now in closing—back to the most intended subject—seeing you again. Let us know what we should bring—house hold linen—towels sheets etc—and we've a silex coffee percolator. As far as clothes go—well all I've got is old ones—and I've put Elizabeth in a real Bohemian garb—slacks and sweaters. We're now in the process of brushing the wardrobe up for spring—though the weather seems to ignore that fact that spring should come next.

Elizabeth sends her regards and thanks Bea for her little note anxiously looking forward to seeing the New England part of the world! She's an awfully good mender of socks and things Bea and should be able to take a lot of stitches off your hands.

Looking forward to seeing you both—thanking you again and wishing you all three! the best of luck till the bus pulls in.

Yours, Your Pal Franz

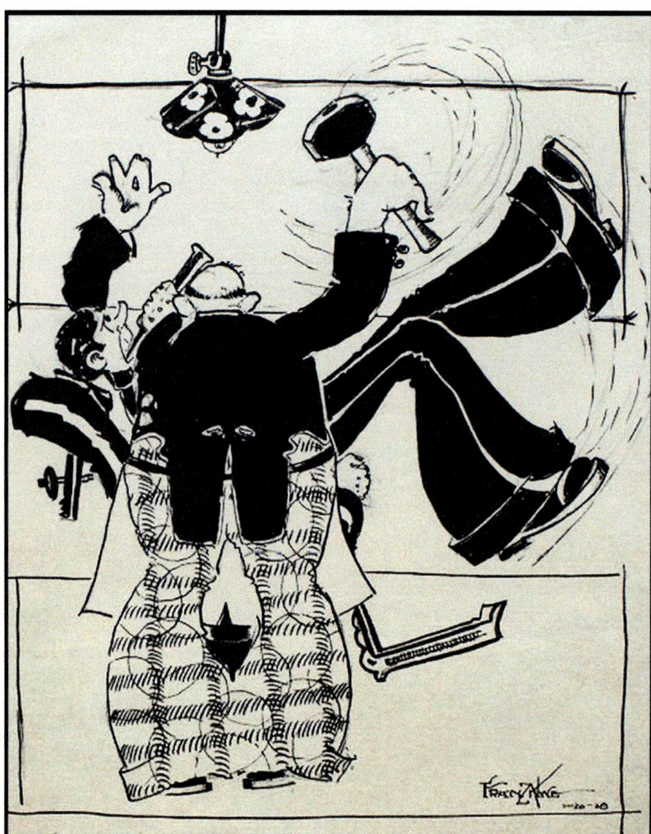

Untitled, Dentist, c. 1934. (*Gordon Ripkey © 2018 Franz Kline Estate/Artists Rights Society (ARS), New York*)

9. Franz Kline to Frederick and Beatrice Ryan, June 2, 1940

71 W. 3rd St.
New York City

Dear Freddy & Bea:

I'm sorry not to have kept in touch with you. for the past two weeks I've really been busy with this out door art show. Financially it wasn't anything near worth while. I sold an oil—$15 a $2 pen sketch and have several orders which goodness knows may never arrive - All the sales were very bad—However I did get the first prize award—in black and white—a pen sketch—which will hang in the Whitney Modern Museum for the coming week and then join a traveling show to important eastern cities. The show ran for two weeks due to bad weather—which has now turned to hot as hell!

For Four days last week I had a job at Radio City—painting spots and airplanes for the Science in Industry Exhibit at the World's Fair—this netted me $25. which helped straighten out several bills. So Fred I feel sure that very shortly now we can get ready to close up shop for the summer. Elizabeth feels much better she's been very active with me for the past few weeks and we feel anxious about getting prepared to leave hot New York.

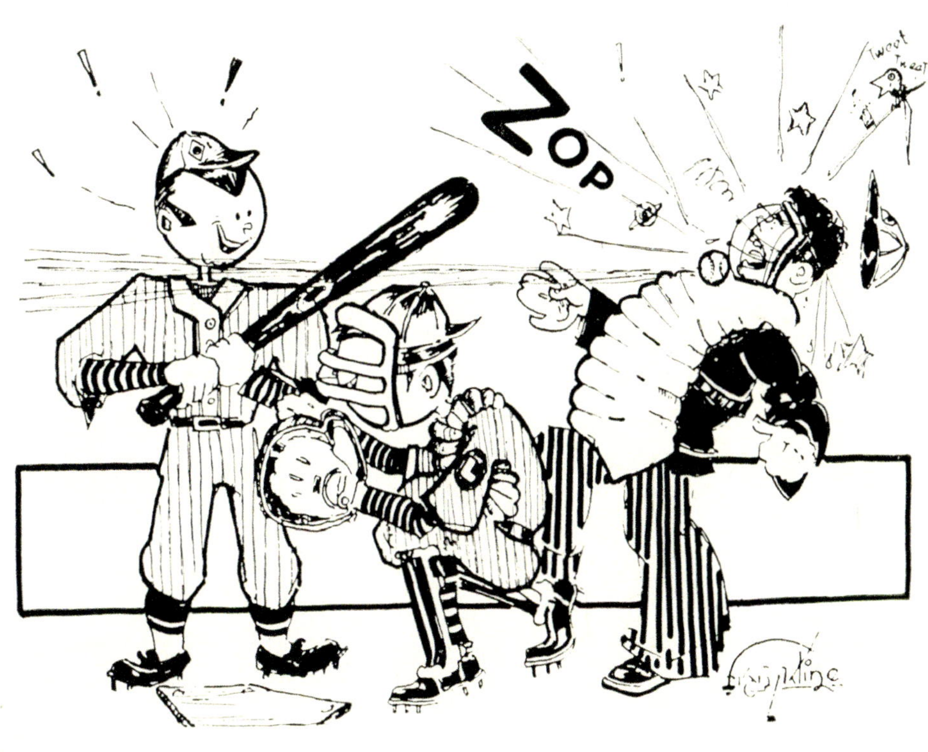

Baseball, 1931 *Gachtin Bambil*. Yearbook cartoon. The gestural qualities in this cartoon have an almost animated quality of movement. (© *2018 Franz Kline Estate/Artists Rights Society (ARS), New York*)

Fred I hope this delay is not inconveniencing you both. You see it was all these hanging debts which had to be paid. Then besides there is the sadness of a friend of mine here—I think Bea met him—[Theodore] Van Cina a 75 year old Dutch painter I've known him for over a year now—He's dying in the Bellevue Hospital penniless with outstanding debts and canvases here and there with deposits of a few dollars on each. So I am rounding up his possessions and trying to cancel off his debts with sales of his work. Poor old chap—you'd love him Fred—Last evening we had dinner with Jack Patterson who lives but 5 blocks from us—he's still the same joke teller—He's acting here in N.Y.

Well Fred how are things shaping up—now don't do all the work before we get there.

Do write us and shortly if every things ok. we'll let you know when we can leave—

Best wishes to you all,
Elizabeth & Franz

10. Franz Kline to Frederick and Beatrice Ryan, June 23, 1940

71 W. 3rd St.
New York City

Dear Freddy & Bea:

I'm sorry to have been so tardy in reply to your letter. These last few days have been busy ones since I thought it would be the means of closing shop and actually accepting your kind invitation that we look forward to as the days pass. I've been working on those Dutch water colours—and am still waiting for payment from the dealer—If & when it comes totaling about $30 we'll be able to give the land lady half and pack off. I'm afraid the horrible condition of Europe and war scare here seems to keep these buying people from actually buying anything except absolute necessities. Then to add to it I didn't yet get the prize money from the Washington Square Ass. This should amount to another $20 or so—These with a few other orders & pot boilers have just ceased—hence we haven't come up.

We received your check Fred—Thanks—we'll only use it if necessary—as a last resort. I had the land lady cash it for us just in case it becomes necessary to make use of it as transport.

You see Fred it is necessary to pay up a few bills and at least a months rent in advance before we can go and be assured that our things are safe. If these few things do come through everything will be ok. So we hope each week that they will and perhaps this week will be the one—There are a few things as prospects again—Bar Decoration—a portrait and the sale of another picture—but hell you just can't seem to depend on anything down here. I hope things with you aren't so bad. And I am sorry to not be able to be helping you—for damn it I just love to get out of this city and be up there with you. Every one else seems to be getting away—every one except my artist friends—and they seem to be in just the same straights as we are.

Jack Patterson left for Vermont last week—and we attended the farewell party—with plenty of jokes & stories as usual—Crosman Durkee & the league—the main subject.

Several friends sent me birth announcements, artists—say I feel out of the running—and we just can't enter it with business as it is. Oh! the cat may substitute for we had a mate for her 2 weeks ago—we don't think it took!

We've both been well—though Elizabeth is worried for her family in London—we're certainly living in the age of change; seems every day brings sadder news for the future of France & England. Both you and Elizabeth knew France—Paris—gosh just what can't happen these days.

How's little Jimmy? and the business of reconditioning the homestead? Fred we'll get there just as soon as we possibly can—so please do forgive all this wasted time which could be so much more happily spent and more beneficial to your plans. How does the war affect your business—I suppose a little both ways.

By the way my friend Van Cina, the Dutch painter who almost passed on—is improving nicely he's out of bed—and if he steadily strengthens should leave the Bellevue in 2 weeks time. He's 75 you know—and what energy and love of life.

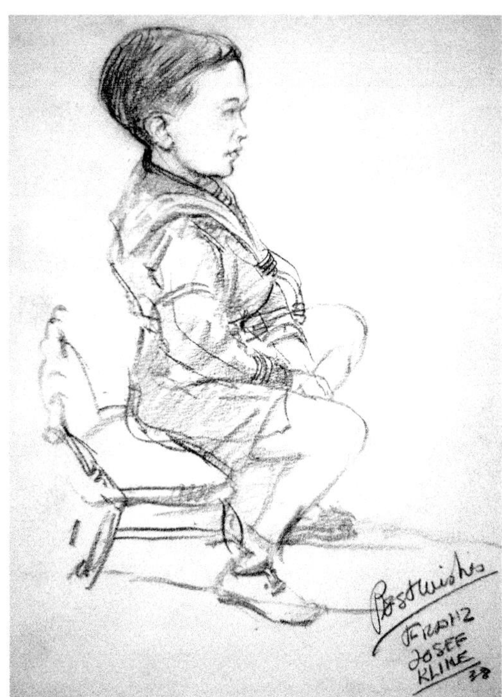

Henry Bisbing, 1938, son of Kline's close friend Loren Bisbing. (*Mr. and Mrs. Henry Bisbing © 2018 Franz Kline Estate/Artists Rights Society (ARS), New York*)

We hope you are both well and that this scribble of mine can soon be replaced with words—that the summer doesn't waste away before we can leave, and that these much discussed pot boilers do their duty to make everything come to a boiling point.

Best wishes from

Elizabeth who's busy trying to get the washing done—boiling tea kettles.

Yours always, Franz

11. Franz Kline to Frederick and Beatrice Ryan, July 1, 1940

71 W 3rd St.

Dear Freddie & Bea:

again there has been a slight delay in reply, but this time I've had better news—I received the first prize money—$15. and the June rent has been payed—together with the fact that I sold six $2 water colors of the west—paying half the grocery bill with a few necessary purchases and a supply of food.

To-day I went to Long Island inquiring about the Holland + Belgium water colors. They haven't gone yet but I will find out during this week what is to be their chances and if by Friday they haven't sold I will take them to Wannamakers and try and make a cash sale. They should bring $30 or $35 at a very reasonable sale price.

I have also distributed several oils and pen sketches at galleries here in the village. Regarding the studio I have packed the things together—greeced the press—and put all the loose articles away. A few gifts such as a lovely can[e] chair and an eight foot high book case were given to us in exchange for a portrait study by a couple leaving for south america. All these make the studio more livable especially for Elizabeth.

Fred I want to thank you for the suggestion of helping to settle our bill question. It's kind of you and an offer we really don't want you to actually have to carry through—for things can't [be] easy for you either we know.

Anyhow these are the plans so far—because I am mind full of the lapse of time and your need for physical help with your work. You see the living problem has been hell here during the winter—mainly because we have had to heat all our own hot water—in a tea kettle!!! on an electric stove with the electric bill to pay each month—nearing the 10 dollar mark at times. Hence Elizabeth has been the one to suffer mainly—lack of baths etc.—discomfort and ill health being a result for her.

So we have decided—a hot water heater is the first essential and once that is obtained she can carry on and I will leave in advance to get up to you—then she can get on with her things here—have rest and early hours and the convenience of finishing all the work inconvenience has caused.

So if I can soon collect this money on the pictures and a few other jobs—I'll install the hot water heater—leave Elizabeth some cash and take the next bus for Hopkinton this I'm sure will please Elizabeth, who being very English, still likes time to prepare as the English always do (especially these hectic days) and it will save time by going up in advance!

A friend of mine has recently installed a heater in his bath room so I will have help with experience and within a day or two after the purchase everything should be set and usable. Regarding the expense it will be a question of a second hand purchase such as my tub was and the installation cost will be omitted—a big help!

So Fred—you can expect me at least just as soon as finances allow I'll let you know by mail or wire.

If it is a question of your not being able to await this probable loss of days then the only way will be for me to inform you of the expense as to most reasonable; not that I want you to! and I'll take the time to install it and leave.

How does this sound to you? You see Fred—my usual manner would be to just drop everything but you understand Elizabeth's plight and those with the damn slowers in being able to turn over money wastes so much time.

I'll tell you all in full when I get there. Forgive the delay again. I hope I'm not inconveniencing you too much. I'm glad to hear work is picking up and I hope I can work out a way to get there soon to help.

Best wishes to Jimmy your friends and to you Freddy & Bea

Love from Elizabeth (washing up as usual)

Yours, Franz

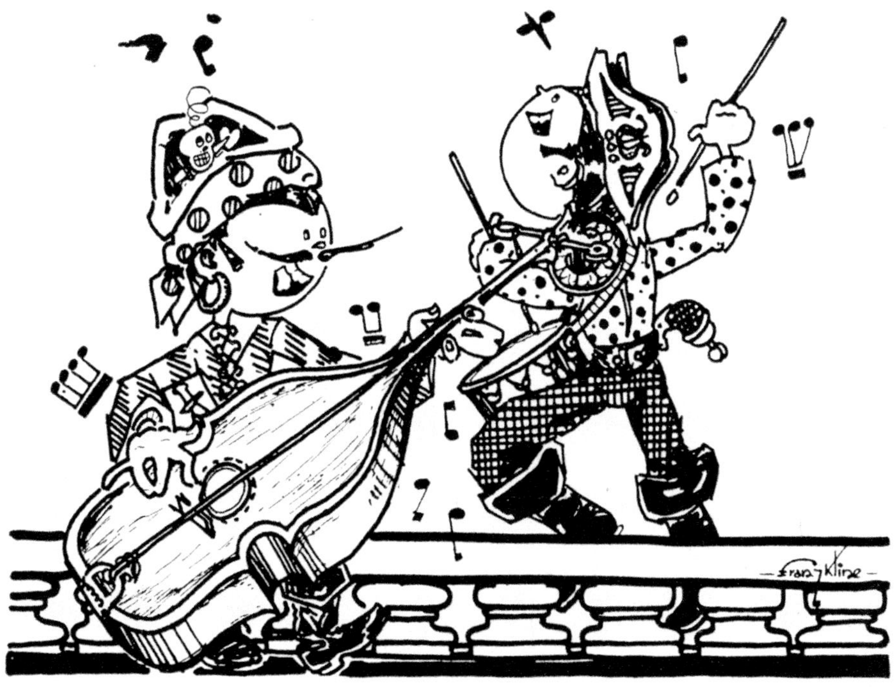

Music, 1931, *Gachtin Bambil*. (© 2018 Franz Kline Estate/Artists Rights Society (ARS), New York)

12. Franz Kline to Frederick and Beatrice Ryan, July 4, 1940

71 W 3rd St N.Y.C.

12/30 pm

Dear Freddie & Bea:

I received your urgent letter this morning—and I certainly understand the entire situation and now I can give you a definite plan.

If you can answer this immediately by special mail we can get the reply on Saturday, I trust.

Out of a clear sky, the night before last—our land lord—who leased our place—told us he intended to move—I was worried about our quarters at first—but since have fixed things up—because incidentally a friend of mine was looking for a place and he is to take this one left vacant by our landlord leaving the situation. For us the same only different and both likable neighbors.

At the same time a friend of mine stopped in from the west coast—a sketch artist who formerly lived here in the village. I told him of our difficulties and your situation—so the three of us Elizabeth included worked out this plan—

If you can Freddie—just send us down $10 by Saturday or Sunday—then this friend of mine—John Erin—whom you will no doubt remember meeting—can take off immediately by bus and within in a few days I can follow.

Because of the present plan—namely Elizabeth's staying on here for a few weeks—and John's substituting with my coming up in a few days—John has worked with me—and I'm sure you will find he has a definite feeling for the doll work. He's a swell fellow who will understand everything you wish to carry out. He can then explain better our situation to you while I do a few necessary things here within the days lapsing before I come up—you needn't make any special arrangements for him—he's used to making do with anything as we our and he will be of assistance to you I'm sure—I will then ensure a few things here for Elizabeth's comfort & a few improvements—do a few jobs for a few dollars—and be up with you during the week. John will explain fully all the details.

You see Freddie we're not doing this to delay or substitute me. For John is very understanding as I know you are and unless I thought he would be of aid at this time I wouldn't suggest this move. Regarding later on and Elizabeths arrival well John's position will be just as it is now and anything or anyway you'll wish to arrange it. He can return here or he can stay and help if need be—so you won't be embarrassed by the feeling that you are obliged to keep him on if you don't wish to.

So regarding the money you send me it can be subtracted later on as I appreciate and John understands.

And when you meet John you'll know the understanding I am trying to impart so hurriedly. You'll find him no trouble with attitude exactly like mine—and a mature in tune with ours—

Mean time I'll tackle these few difficulties here, Elizabeth will feel better and everything should work out helping your problems.

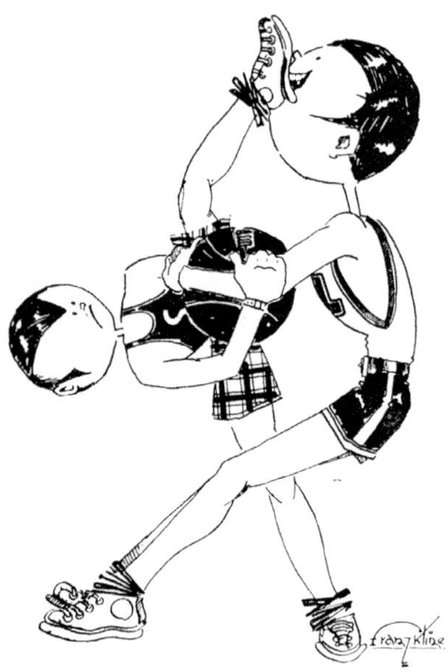

Basketball, *The Leni Lenapian*, December 9, 1930 and *Gachtin Bambil*, 1931. (*© 2018 Franz Kline Estate/Artists Rights Society (ARS), New York*)

Elizabeth thanks you for your considering letter your kind suggestions and thoughts for her contentment. We send you Bea & Jimmy all our best wishes—Hoping to see you soon this time definitely and trust my plan Freddie for I think it will work out excellently for us all,

Yours your friend and Pal, Franz

13. Franz Kline to Frederick and Beatrice Ryan, July 11, 1940

71 W. 3rd Street N.Y.C.
Dear Freddy and Bea,

I'm sorry not to have acknowledged your reply to my letter earlier in the week—but in trying to get things ready for my departure—we all have been most occupied and I've accomplished many mundane things. The studio is indeed in a more livable condition and now I feel Elizabeth can be comfortable in my absence.

John understands your situation and I'm sorry to have misinterpreted your letter—however I know you appreciate why and now that I can get away everything should be ok.

My friend has settled in—subletting for my former land lord. The light and gas have been changed—in our name and now Elizabeth can have the convenience of hot water and baths—enabling her to get back to normal in readiness to join us. Sooah! Fred I will leave this weekend probably not till Sunday but by the beginning of the week I'll be there. Elizabeth will stay on here and John will probably use the studio in my absence

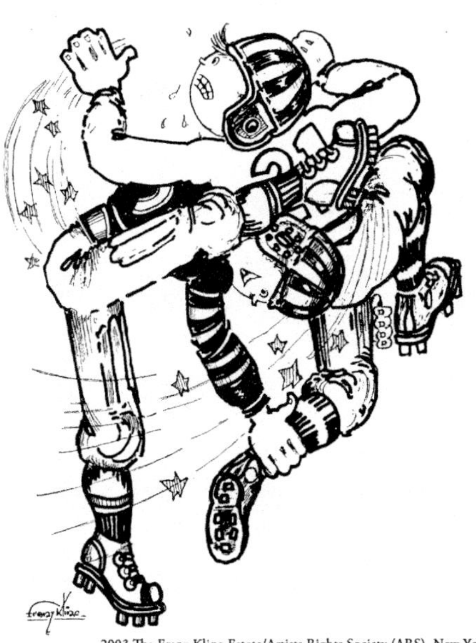

Football, 1931, *Gachtin Bambil*. (© 2018 Franz Kline Estate/Artists Rights Society (ARS), New York)

as a hang out and company for Elizabeth—I've developed an ingrown sist—on my left cheek which I've had lanced today—I must go to the hospital again Sat am but it's nothing serious.

Again Fred there's lots of things I could talk and write about but the main thing is I'm anxious to get up with you. I hope Bea Jimmy and the girls are well. That the work hasn't been getting you down and that I haven't caused too much in difficulties adding to your worries.

I've got all the direction so I'll be alright and I do feel happier at helping this end a bit before leaving.

Best wishes from Elizabeth and John and I'll see you soon

Yours Franz, your friend

14. Franz Kline to Frederick and Beatrice Ryan, August 14, 1940

71 West 3rd St.
New York City
Dear Fred & Bea:

I'd hoped to hear from you and write you a proper letter, but I suppose you've been working day + night—as I have been forced to do—due to the fact that the anticipated decorating job hasn't begun as yet and the ever present living rate that never seems to be defeated.

I know you must be terribly disappointed in my unsuccessful attempt to get that job over with to be free to help with your plans. Yet I know you will understand the impossibility of my letting things mount up down here and the need for me to be the earning capacity for my meager home-stead.

Fortunately there were the usual few small jobs which enabled me to catch up on some of the outstanding expenses—and the decorating job is still to be had when these would be night club owners complete the ground work. In the mean time the smaller regular in a way jobs must do the trick.

I hope you received the sketch book Bea—and the stumps—will get the pens to you in a day or so. I don't suppose there is any hope of your turning a hand to any other work than the dolls Gee, I certainly feel a disappointment to you for—I do realize your anxiousness to get the roof completed and the painting started. I do still hope to be able to arrange to get back up soon.

Bea that mad chap Grilli showed up and I've work out another illustration for him—poor chap he makes little money and so he'll pay it off little by little.

Elizabeth is well—tho' very worried over the present scenes in England. She sends her best wishes to you all—I've described every foot of your beautiful property to her—drawn floor plans etc.—even the crooked walls Charlotte!!

This is awful writing paper I know—you'd think I was sending this air mail to war torn Europe.

Oh by the way Fred I seemed to have lost my tobacco pouch—I think I must have dropped it on the bus enroute—but I hope against hope that I left it on your table—no!? I guess it's gone!

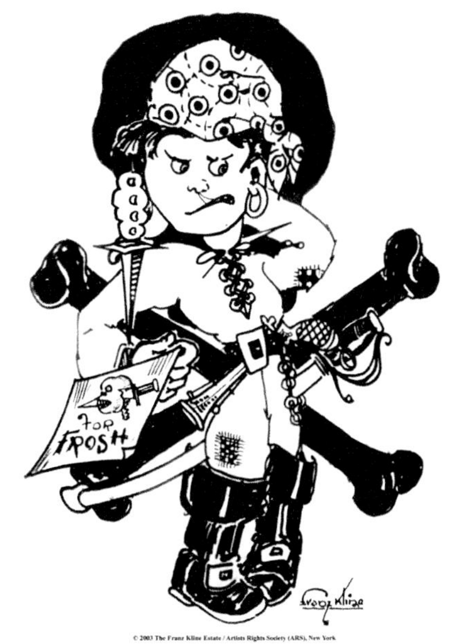

Sophomores, 1931, *Gachtin Bambil*. Kline's drawing skills were outstanding early on and he spent years in life classes learning to draw. His influences and idols were illustrators who are practically unknown to art students now. (© *2018 Franz Kline Estate/Artists Rights Society (ARS), New York*)

Then there are a few other items I always leave behind—a hair brush—a small belt of canvas for my shorts—and I hope—! my water colour box. !!!

I know the other thing, paper portfolio etc intentionally left.

I wonder if you could gather them together for me—send them C.O.D.—if it's not too much trouble!

Regarding the chair + frames don't bother cause I can get them later—when I come again I hope—Let me know how much the chap wants to put the seat in the chair and I'll send you the cash.

Nothing new or interesting goes on down here accept the war news. I've been painting but selling nothing.

John Erin has come back from the north again—and the hot water flows from the tap!

Best wishes to you all,

Yours, Franz

Again—Forgive this parchment!.

15. Franz Kline to Frederick and Beatrice Ryan, August, 1940

71 West 3rd St.

New York City

Dear Freddy Bea & Charlotte:

This is my third attempt at trying to formulate a coherent letter to you all. Seems as tho' the sun is acting as a magnate drawing my roof garden studio closer to the heated circle—92 degrees today However I have taken two baths drank a few bottles of Pepsi Cola some ice tea, and a pint of milk—so now I seem more capable of actually completing a letter.

I arrived in New York at 7:15 am after a much more comfortable trip that the one enroute to Framingham and after a short nap Sunday morning woke to this terrific heat; your present doll studio is mild compared to this.

The refrigerator is still part of the studio atmosphere so my telegram certainly must have done the trick. Of course Elizabeth had to hear of all our accomplishments the home, little Jimmy
and my description of your colorful bit of New England. She laughed to hear of the auction sale.
You being a Bit Faar back from the Rhoad—etc.

John Erin took off for Atlantic City yesterday - I suppose he hopes for that sketch artists paradise! Things here are just as I left them—business rather slow and the typical bad taste of the Italian [ ] from every nite club—makes me miss the quiet of little Hopkinton even tho' things do die at 11 pm.

Regarding the decorating job—Fred—things have changed their progress a bit—for the better financially, but regarding the time element—not as I had hoped.

First of all the beginning of the job will not start for 4 or 5 days and then it will be a daily wage affair—this of course affects the time margin—for the sooner one completes the work the less he is payed. However there is the possibility that this can be changed to what I had formerly described to you and in any case it will amount to $75 or $80 which of course is nothing to be sneezed upon. Regarding your work on hand and the definite need of help I know this will be disappointing news. Still I will do all with in my power to speed the activity and get the thing over with—for in any case it's hardly the type of job that one would worry over—artistically. They of course will give us a down payment which should help our expenses for necessities here. Meantime my rent becomes due on Thursday and I must scrape around to see if I can manage a few smaller jobs—today I began a lettering job on a contractor's truck which will pay in the usual poor way—$4. Then Grilli the mad man should appear tomorrow for another illustration.

The hope of selling those Dutch water colors looks rather bad since the Major put his tongue in the matter—but this is the usual situation as the rent becomes due. Now don't feel as tho' you must stretch your capital to aid me hurriedly I'll manage some how—and I know your position well.

I hope you received favorable news on the reproduction of the smaller doll set for Schwarz and that my complicated set up down here will not cause you to lose too much time in production. I'll try to straiten up affairs down here just as soon as I can and there is always hope that a few decently paid commissions will appear—if we don't melt away in the mean time.

I'll get those stumps for you also Bea's newsprint paper and any other needed art material—ink, paint brushes, etc. let me know. I won't forget the pens either!

I'm seeing Cap [ ], the fellow I'm to work with on the job—tomorrow so if any more time saving arrangements can be pushed across I'll see that they are negotiated.

Mean-time keep the buffer going—and I hope the weather will turn cooler for you all. Best wishes to everyone—I'll look up the photo of you and Durkee and other things that might interest you—Perhaps a Picasso for Charlotte!! or a straight wall?

Elizabeth includes a note for Bea and her best wishes with mine to you all.

Yours, Franz

16. Jack Tworkov to Franz Kline, January 24, 1950

Dear Franz—Nothing is so encouraging to an artist than the friendly attitude of his dealer—and for that I am very grateful to you. Many thanks. I had not too much hope for sales so I am not too disappointed. I am sorry for you though. Lawrence Heller was in New York and he said he had a friend whom he'll try to sell something. Tell him I wrote to you about it, and if he hasn't been in this will give you an excuse for calling him up.

I found the "Star" review very enjoyable. You can't quarrel with anybody who finds your paintings dull. You've simply failed with that person, there is no answer. But Jane Watson Crane makes a statement in the clipping you sent me (the clipping is not complete and I don't know whether it applies to my pictures or not although I suspect that it does) which can be answered. I refer to, and I quote: Is there not behind all the verbiage a lurking fear that the modernism which is now over 40 years old is beginning to gel into an academism of its own? End quote. To use her own phrase I suspect that she would find it highly desirable if modern painting did indeed settle into an academism with which she is familiar and understands. Question this lady and you'll see that the only "modern" painting towards which she has any tolerance is regurgitating Matisse, Braque, Picasso, Klee, etc. Precisely the painters who refused to settle into academism, who refused to work with what has been well digested, she suspects, fears, and therefore dislikes.

Her phrase, "laying his experiments before the public" lacks any kind of originality. It was said by Ruskin of Whistler, and by every critic of lesser stature of every modern painter from the impressionists to the present day. Critics like Jane Watson Crane always succumb to the accepted, and keep the door shut to the newcomer. Witness Devree in last Sunday Times: he speaks of Juan Gris' abstracts as "well founded in Representation drawing." Holy Mackerel. How much further can you bow down before dead art when it's become accepted. Try to imagine what Devree would have said of cubism when it first appeared.

But why bore you with all this. I imagine you are well familiar with all this. Please don't think I'm defending myself. I'm thinking of the whole group of American Artists who are trying to stand on their own feet—not because we are nationalistic, or we are in competition with European artists, but because our own environment doesn't encourage us to develop further the elegance of Braque, or the wistful whimsical introspection of Klee (to mention just two of the masters whose followers in this country most impressed that part of the art public with advanced sensibilities)

The artists I like best are the ones who have stopped playing the esthete—people who do not live other artists' biographies.

Dear Franz whatever the outcome of this show I shall always be gratefully yours Jack Tworkov.

17. Franz Kline to Jack Tworkov, Monday, July 28, 1952

Black Mountain College
Black Mountain, North Carolina

Dear Jack,

I'm sure you are wondering about the arrival of your work and materials. Rob Rosenburg is going to Virginia tomorrow to pick up Twombly—and promises—to get your things off—next day—he has been running errands and arranging for his passport etc. so I guess he hasn't had time to get your things off.

I'm quite settled here in the studio, the dog Tommy follows me everywhere. I had the first class Friday at 4 pm and one this morning at 10:30—and am gradually getting used to the hot periods of the day and trying to work evenings—and mornings.

I hope your trip was enjoyable—tho I wish you could have stayed on longer. Everyone liked you being here so much and your work with them. Cage and Cunningham—arrived safely.

Best wishes to Welly—and the children.

I'll write you soon again.

Sincerely yours, Franz

18. Franz Kline to Frederick Ryan, May 16, 1958

New York City
242 W 14 St.

Dear Freddie:

I've been meaning all this time to answer your letter I so enjoyed hearing from you and meeting your son.

Since then I moved and with an exhibition in back of my head for months I've been kinda' beside my-self. [Kline is referring to an exhibition held from May 19 to June 14, 1958 at the Sidney Janis Gallery.]

How-ever everything is up at the gallery and the "show" starts on Monday—
I'm sending off an announcement, or poster which I think is a little large!

I finally have a decent studio here on 14th Street large and light. Hope you and Bea get down to N.Y. and just drop me a note a day or so ahead. It was nice to hear of your activities and think of days in Boston. I'm glad your back at painting and showing good luck with everything Fred regards to Bea and the family and I do hope to see you soon.

Sincerely your old friend, Franz

19. Franz Kline Letter to Frederick and Beatrice Ryan, Sunday, December 16, 1958

242 W. 14 St. NYC

Dear Fred & Bea.

Enjoyed your letter so much Fred. I remember Olive Doris and your mother. Gainsboro Str. Dancing with Olive with you and I in the company of Martha Kinney! The old Frause Restr. The Mug Store those cross hatch crow-quill pens—Abbey & Crosman.

Your stories of Ernest L. Major. I tell them over and over again Fred.

It seems so odd to be that abstract expressionist refered to—of course I've been here now for the past 20 years—Here in the Village all that time wondering what painting is—wanting to paint—Influenced like we all are by other painters and friends like us who follow the muse—

I think of you Fred, Boston, your drawing and paintings; Bea those dolls—and seeing Jimmy! remembering painting him when he was crawling on the floor with a copper jug & then to see him and hear him say I'm the son of Freddy Ryan.

Anyhow its not bad to be an old painter!!

I do hope you can come to the city—and maybe before then I'll see you in Providense. I may drive up to the cape during the Holidays with a friend—If I do I'll let you know. a card or i'll phone—

Thanks for the news article I know Bill McGee

Do say hello for me to your sisters and your mother. and Merry Xmas to Bea and the children.

Franz

Franz was only 48 years old when he wrote the above letter to Frederick Ryan referring to himself as an old painter. Although not aged, "he had become an idol and mentor to the young would-be abstract artists in Greenwich Village who treated him like a patriarch." That summer Franz visited the Ryan family on his way to Cape Cod. "I only have one recollection of meeting Kline. It was in my father's studio in Providence, Rhode Island in 1959. Franz was driving up from NYC to Provincetown with a friend, the writer, Fielding Dawson. I was only twelve at the time, so I don't remember much. I do remember much talk about how Kline was doing his huge abstracts with "tongue-in-cheek" as well as denying any connection with Oriental calligraphy, or that he got the idea from using an overhead projector. I believe that Kline either really was painting with tongue-in-cheek, because he was tired of being poor, or just couldn't bring himself to admit to my father, a classically trained artist whom Kline knew held abstract art in contempt, that he took his art, and himself seriously. I remember my father showing Franz a box full of letters from Franz and Franz being surprised my dad had kept them all those years. Before leaving Franz sat for a quick portrait for my Dad during that visit. We all went out in the driveway to admire Franz's new Thunderbird. If I remember correctly it was black. Franz said it looked like an airplane. Ryan asked his friend about his "extreme changeover from his small and delicate line works to his huge and brutal abstracts." "He said simply," according to Ryan "I guess one can't help being influenced by the painters around one. Although both of us would have scoffed at the idea at the time, that visit proved to be our last meeting before his untimely death."

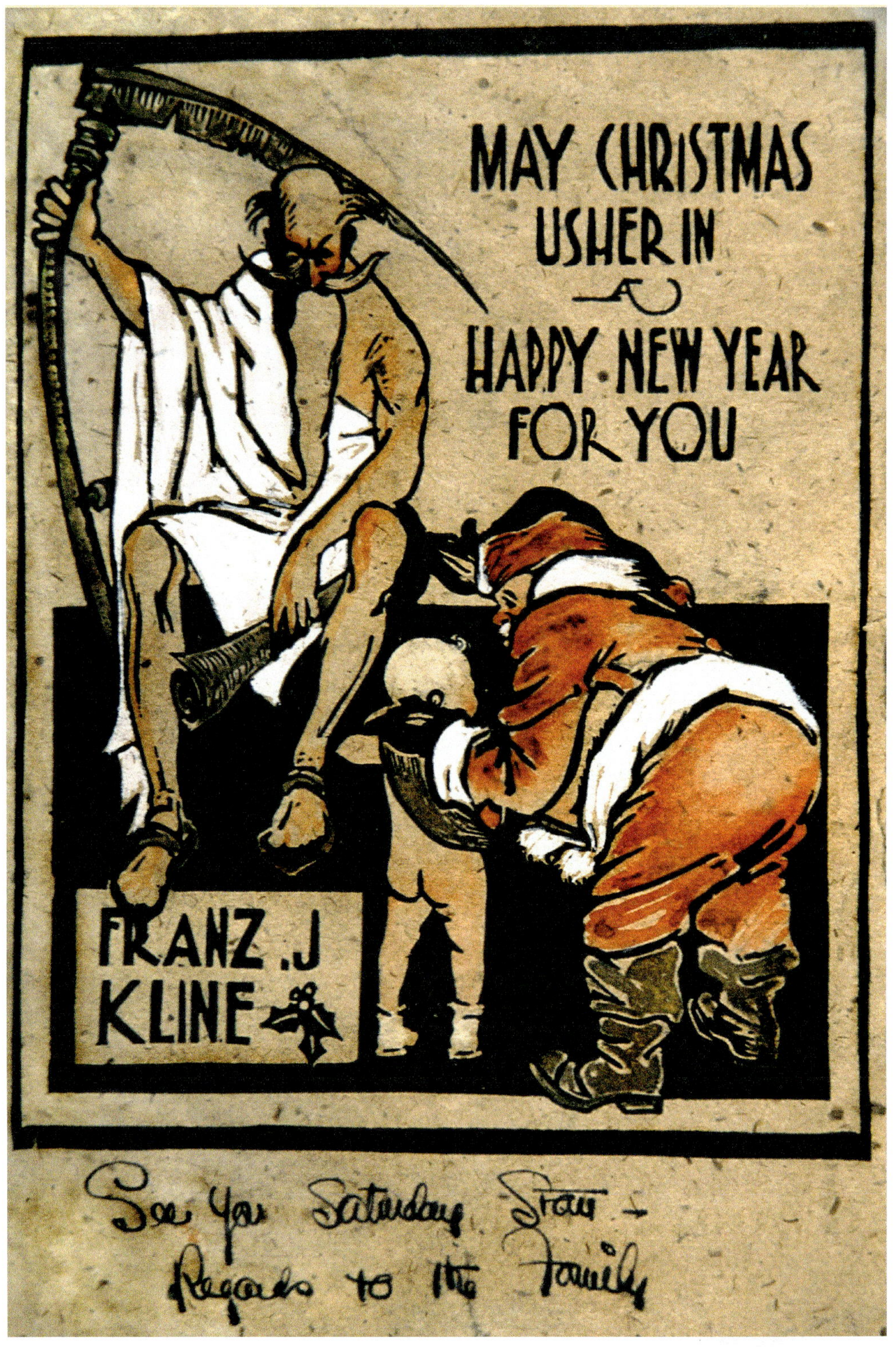

May Christmas Usher in a Happy New Year for You, 1938. (*Mrs. Stanley Harleman and family © 2018 Franz Kline Estate/Artists Rights Society (ARS), New York*)

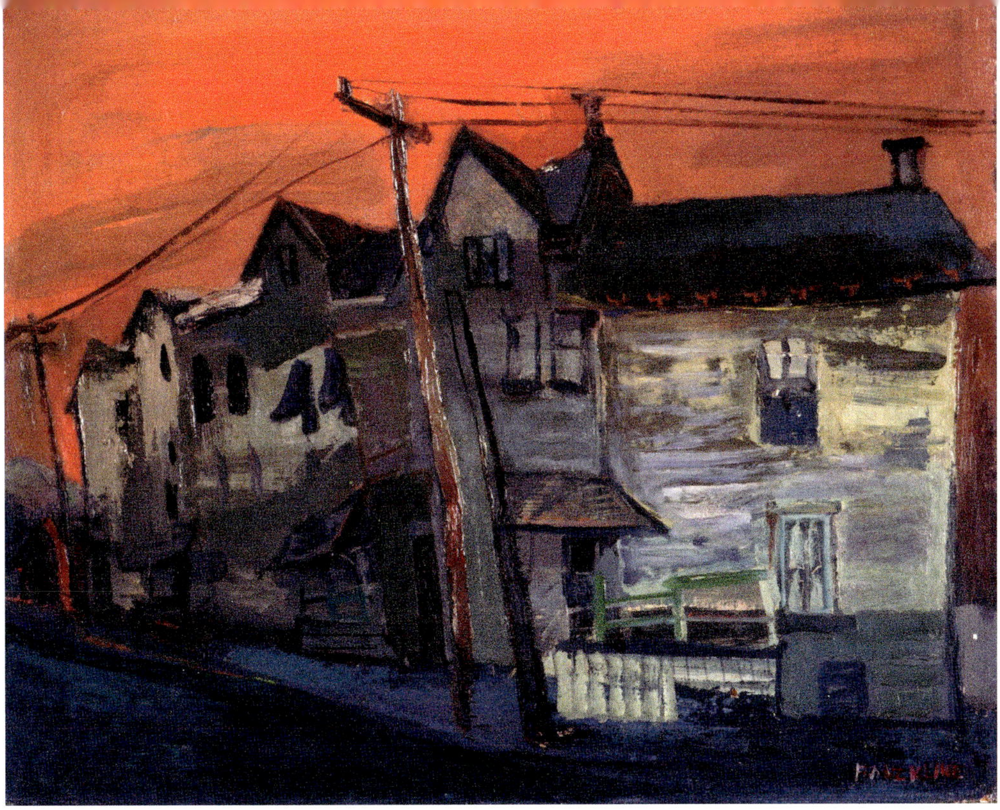

Above: Pennsylvania Street Scene (Pennsylvania Mining Town), 1947. (*Private Collection © 2018 Franz Kline Estate/Artists Rights Society (ARS), New York*)

Below: Untitled Christmas Card, 1940. A crescent moon hangs over a structure reminiscent of Lehighton High School. (*Paolo Pelosini © 2018 Franz Kline Estate/Artists Rights Society (ARS), New York*)

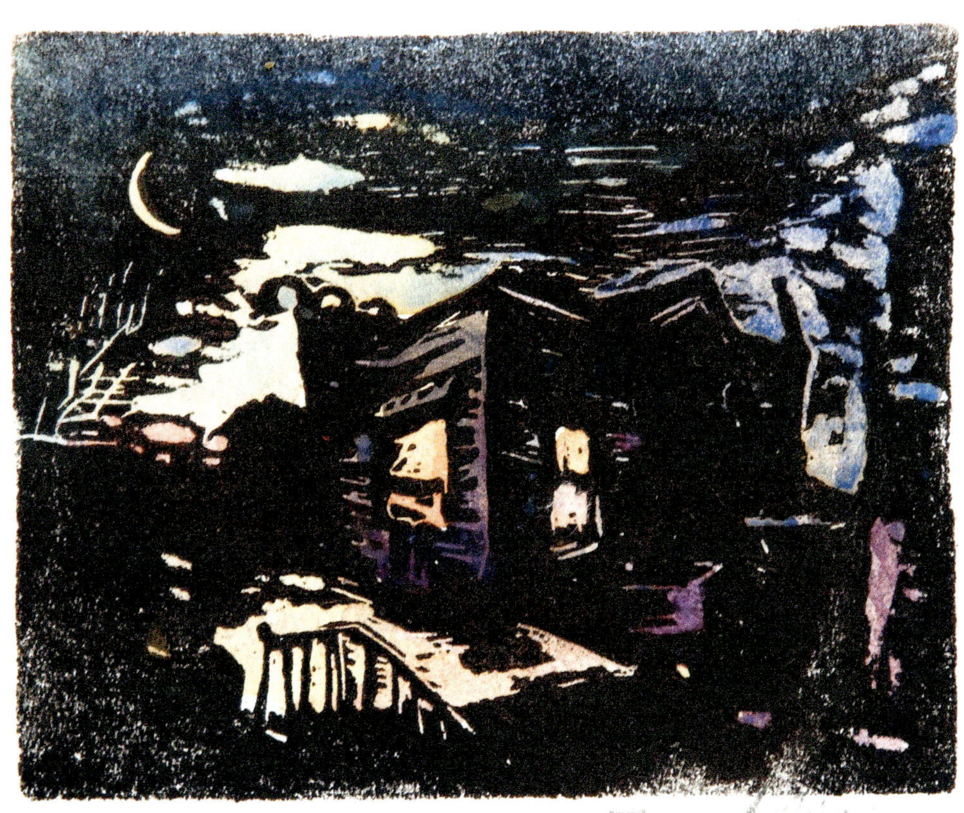

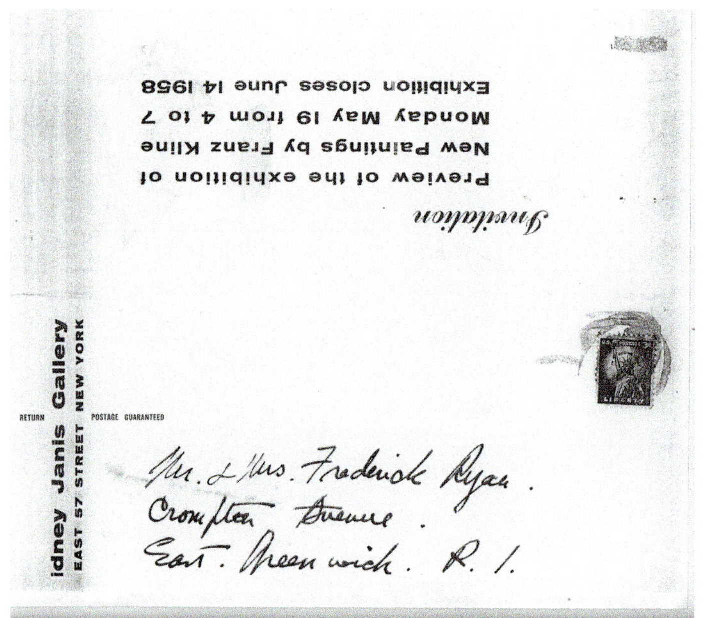

Invitation from Franz to Frederick Ryan and his wife for the Sidney Janis show in New York, May 19, 1958–June 14, 1958. (*Frederick Ryan Jr.*)

The Leni Lenapian

LITERARY SUPPLEMENT

VOLUME IV — LEHIGHTON HIGH SCHOOL, FEBRUARY 3, 1931 — NUMBER 10

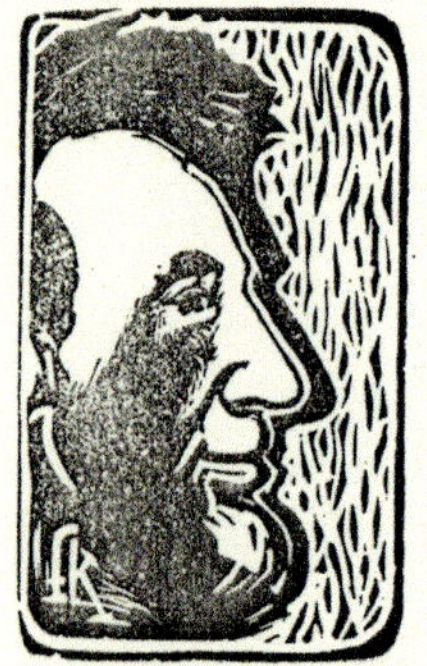

LINCOLN

Just a common man? Then the greatest yet,
The world has ever known.
The greatest man! The people's man!
They claim him for their own.
No fame is his? He holds the hearts
Of all who love his name.
His deeds, for those he loved and served,
Have won eternal fame.
He, slavery's holding bonds destroyed,
And nation's hope repaired.
He gave his great advice to help,
When all the states despaired.
At Gettysburg, the wondering crowd!
His heart with passion beat.
He won them all! The people then,
Knelt down at Lincoln's feet.

TAM O'SHANTER

("With apologies to Burns")

Gay Tam O'Shanter had a wife
Who tried, he vowed, to run his life;
But on a luckless market day
Our Tam resolved to have his way.
And so he parked his flivver wheezy
For hours before a Scotch speakeasy;
He had some Scotch—then had some more,
And so the day to evening wore.
Poor reckless Tam did cry aloud,
"I'll pay for drinks for all the crowd!"
And after that, he drank some gin.
Then, tho't he, "Dankin' is a sin."
"Here," cried the host, "Do have some rye!"
Then being Scotch, he had to try;
He'd drunk so much that he was floored,
They bore him out to his auld Ford.
Weel seated in his dear Liz,
(A better car did ne'er fiz)
Our Tam drove on thru dub and mire,
Despizing wind, and rain, and fire.
Whiles glow'rin' round wi' prudent care
Lest some state trooper should find him there;
An' soon he entered the haunted woods,
Where once unwary traveler'd stood
Before he had been whisked away,
Ne'r to be seen e'en to this day.
Up in this wood Tam saw a shack,
And curious, steered good Lizzie back;
Tam's eyes were very dim and poor—
He could not see beyond the door.
But Lizzie stalled, right sare astonished
Till, by hand and heel admonished,
She ventured forward to the light,
And wow! Tam saw an unco sight.
It was so strange it near upsot him,
A gang of witches danced 'Black Bottom.'
A banjo and a ukelele

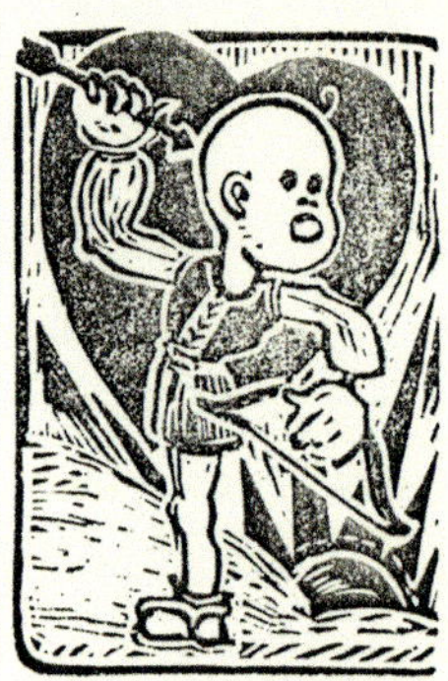

BOBBY'S VALENTINE

(The nite before)

Where'd all my Chris'mus money go?
That's somep'n I'd like to know.
There used to be so much of it,
And now I haven't got a bit.

I've got to send a Valentine;
I ought to have at least a dime,
For pretty ones are awful dear,
And plain ones too, cost lots, I fear.

I wish an idea'd come to me,
This darn old snow is all I see.
Snow ain't—Oh wait—Oh say I know—
I'll make my Valentine from snow.

My teacher says I'm good in Art,
And I'll do this with all my heart;
I'll steal right up to Nancy's house,
And do my job just like a mouse.

This cupid here, that arrow there.

Front page of *The Leni Lenapian*, February 3, 1931 with Kline's *Lincoln* linoleum block print and *Bobby's Valentine*. (*© 2018 Franz Kline Estate/Artists Rights Society (ARS), New York*)

The Leni Lenapian

OF LEHIGHTON HIGH SCHOOL

Vol. IV No. 12 | LEHIGHTON, PA. TUESDAY MARCH 3, 1931 | 5c a copy

Maroon Must Shake 'Slate' Jinx Tonite

LAST GAME TUESDAY

Lehighton broke the Slatington jinx last year by beating them for the first time in years in Lehighton. Tho' Slatington came thru 41-16 in the first game earlier in the season, there is no reason why the Maroon should not be able to break the old jinx in the slate town tonight. The girls are expected to repeat their previous 41-21 victory.

When the Lehighton teams stack up against Catasauqua at the latter's place on Friday evening in the last league contest of the season it will be a toss-up for the laurels. The league standing of both groups of teams may be dependent on the results, which previously were 29-23 against the boys and 22-20 for the girls. This is the last girls' game of the season.

The final attraction of the season will be a home attraction next Tuesday when Lansford returns the varsity and junior varsity games. The Lansford games were in the red previously 27-21 and 20-18 respectively, but the home court should avail the boys the necessary points for a victorious finish.

LENAPIAN RECEIVES 1931 P. S. P. A. RATING

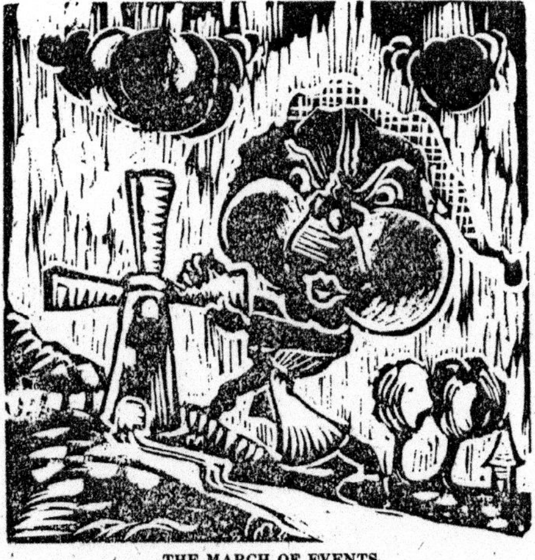

THE MARCH OF EVENTS

JUNIORS ANNOUNCE CAST FOR CLASS PLAY

After two sessions of try-outs, Miss Roedell, the coach, has chosen the cast for the annual junior play, which will be presented on Friday, March 27.

The artists for "At the Sign of the Pewter Jug" are as follows: Suzanne Shuler, Dorothy Swoyer;

THREE ALUMNI PERFORM WITH TEMPLE GLEE CLUB

Last Friday afternoon the Temple glee club entertained the combined junior and senior high schools. Three former Lehighton boys belong to the organization: Edwin McCormick, manager; Wilmer Held, tenor; and Nathan Heiligman, xylophone solist. The

Hansel and Gretel Operetta Friday

FIRST WARD PRODUCTION

Friday evening, the pupils of first ward will render a musical operétta, "Hansel and Gretel" in the high school auditorium. The admission for the play is thirty-five cents and the profits will be used to purchase necessities such as books and magazines for the first ward school.

Hansel and Gretel are put to work to pick berries in the forest. Instead, they play and sing. At night, tired, the sandman puts them to sleep. Angels guard them from harm while they sleep. The next morning, the dew man awakens them. Hungry, they eat cookies from the witch's cookie house. She seizes them, but some time later, Gretel tricks her and the children escape. The children's mother and father and the children are happily reunited.

The cast is composed entirely of juveniles. The cookies, the sandman, the dew man and the angels are impersonated by the children. The characters are as follows: Mother, Marjorie Butz; Father, Paul Dougher; Hansel, David Wehr; Gretel, Jean Keiper; Cookie witch, Jean Swartz; Sandman, Carmine Hill; Dew man, Harlan Roth.

GYM TEAM TRAINING

Above: Front page of *The Leni Lenapian*, March 3, 1931 with Kline's *The March of Events*. (*© 2018 Franz Kline Estate/Artists Rights Society (ARS), New York*)

Right: Just Two Bits, *The Leni Lenapian*, April 14, 1931 by Franz Kline. (*© 2018 Franz Kline Estate/ Artists Rights Society (ARS), New York*)

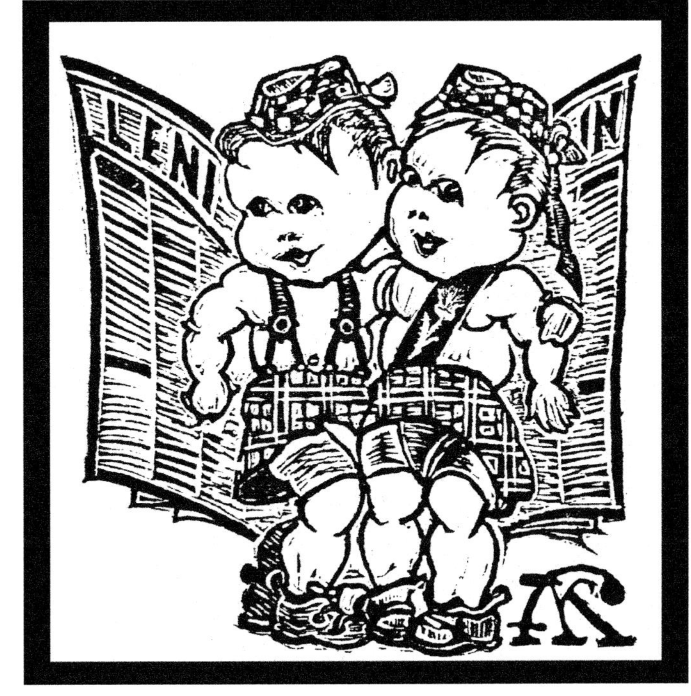

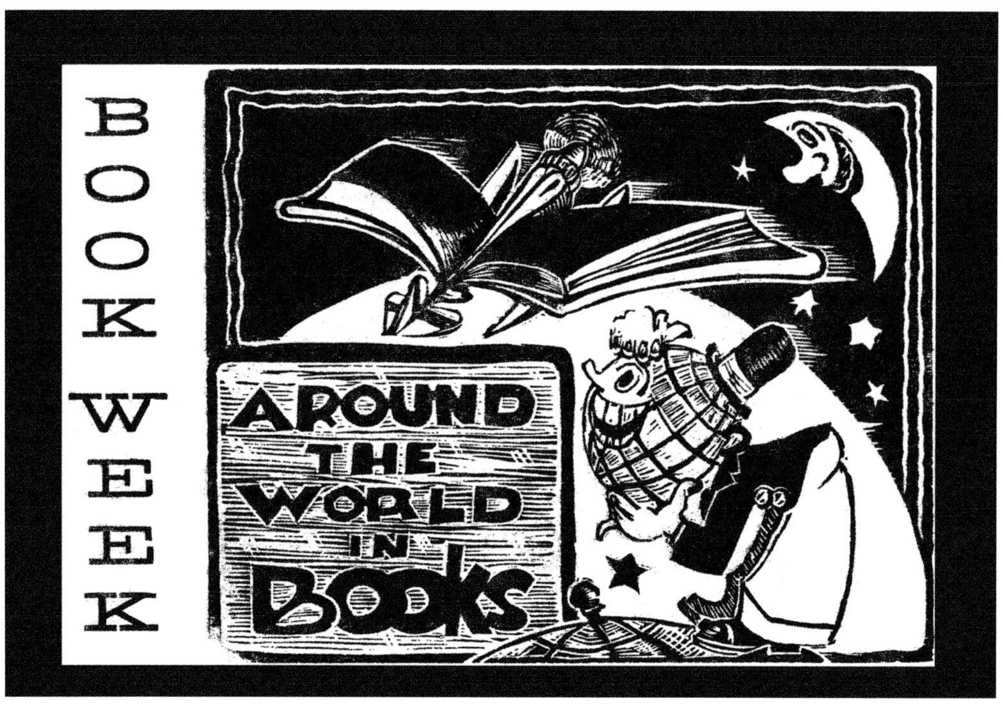

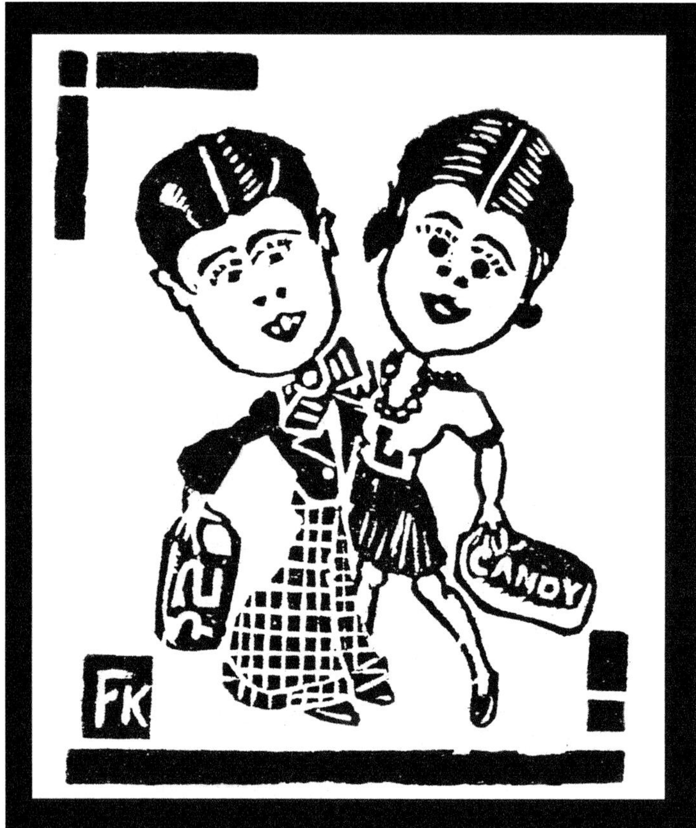

Above: Around the World in Books, The Leni Lenapian, linoleum block print, November 10, 1931. (*© 2018 Franz Kline Estate/Artists Rights Society (ARS), New York*)

Left: Prize! Prize! Prize!, The Leni Lenapian, linoleum block print, November 5, 1929, during Kline's senior year. (*© 2018 Franz Kline Estate/Artists Rights Society (ARS), New York*)

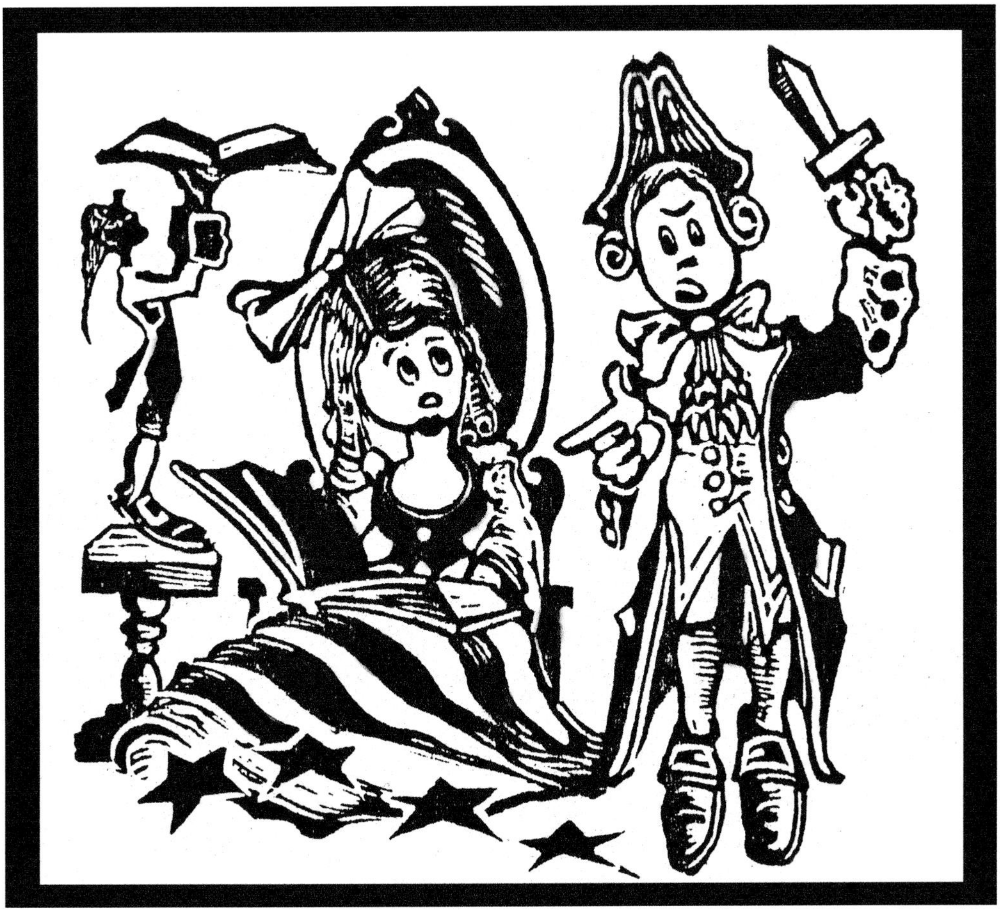

Above: Books for Young America, The Leni Lenapian, November 8, 1932, after Kline returned from England and was living in New York.

Right: Growing Up With Books, The Leni Lenapian, November 7, 1933. Linoleum cut while a student at the Boston Art Students League. The Grim Reaper with the Book of Life, a sickle, an hourglass, a baby on a stack of books, and a graduate with diploma in hand. (*Grace Rhodes © 2018 Franz Kline Estate/ Artists Rights Society (ARS), New York*)

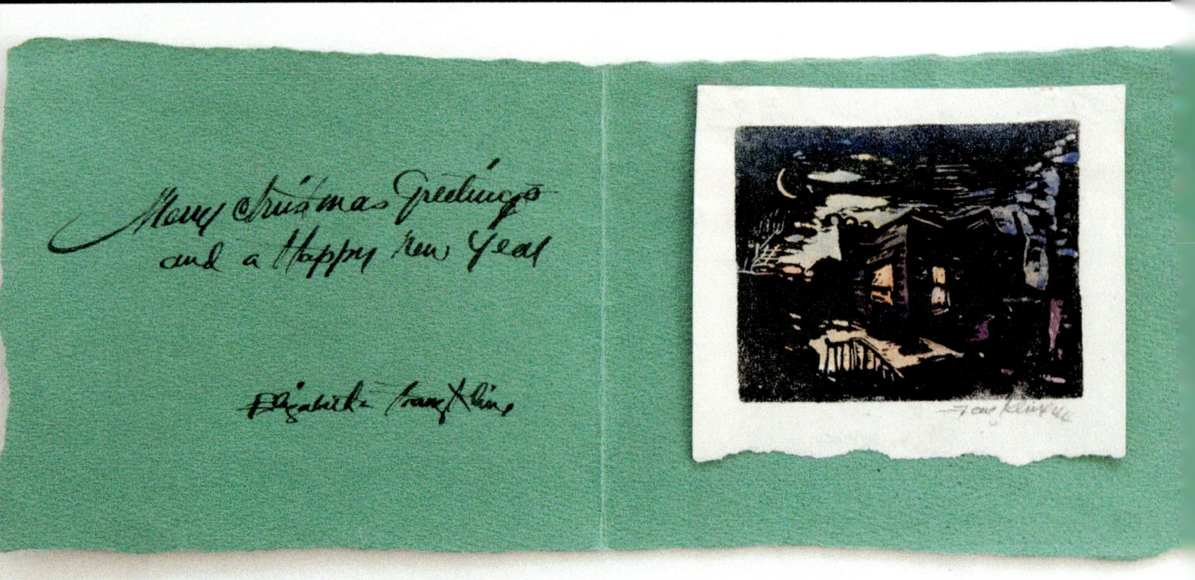

Untitled Christmas card signed by Elizabeth and Franz Kline in 1944. (*Paolo Pelosini © 2018 Franz Kline Estate/Artists Rights Society (ARS), New York*)

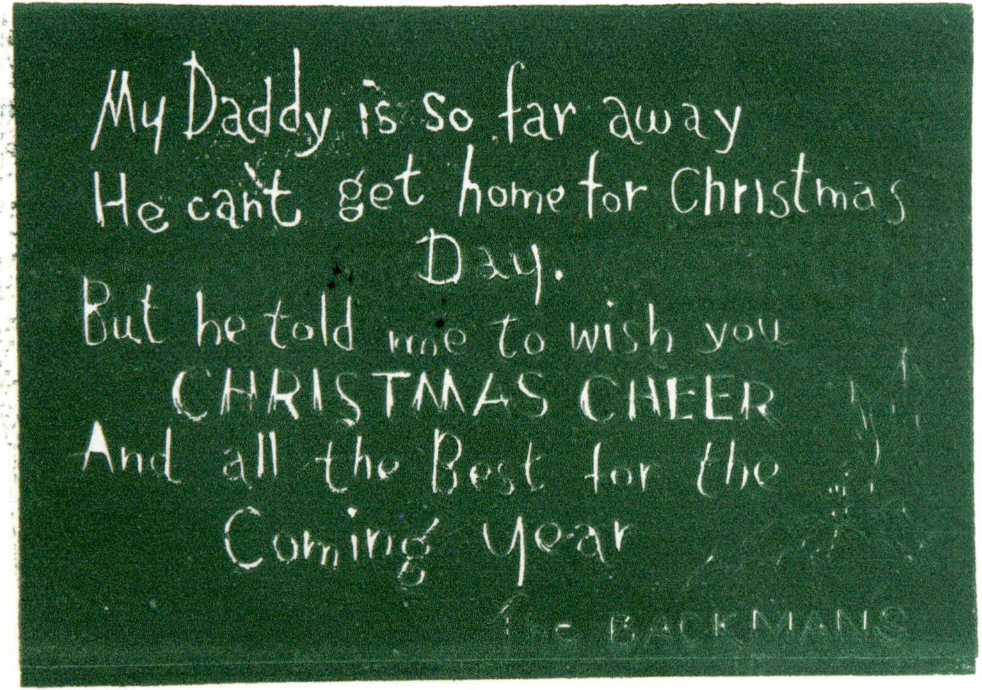

Etched inscription by Franz Kline commissioned by the Backman Family as part of a Christmas card designed by Kline. (*Paolo Pelosini © 2018 Franz Kline Estate/Artists Rights Society (ARS), New York*)

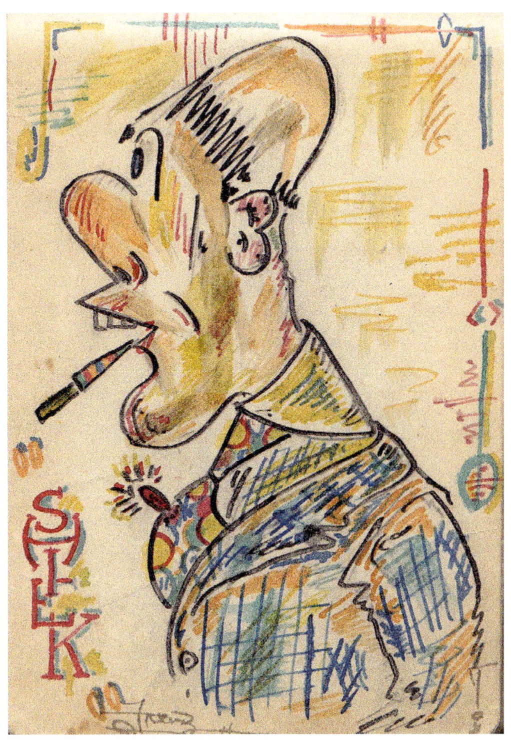

Right: Sheik, colorful clown-like figure in colored ink over pencil drawn in the autograph book of a high school friend. (*© 2018 Franz Kline Estate/Artists Rights Society (ARS), New York*)

Below: Untitled, Tea Time, attributed to Franz Kline, *c.* 1940. Provenance can be traced, from a box marked "Kline" that belonged to Frederick Ryan and his wife, Beatrice, along with a collection of letters from Franz Kline. The Ryan family had a long association with Franz and had received gifts of other paintings, including a London sketchbook. (*Frederick Ryan, Jr.*)

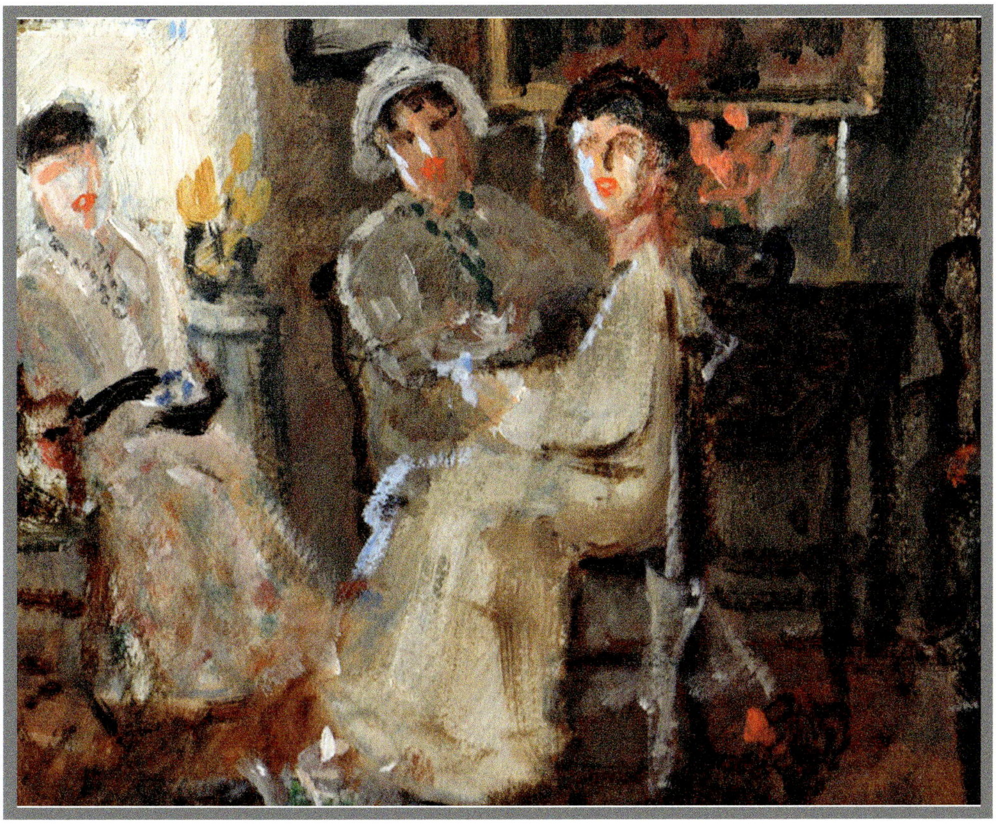

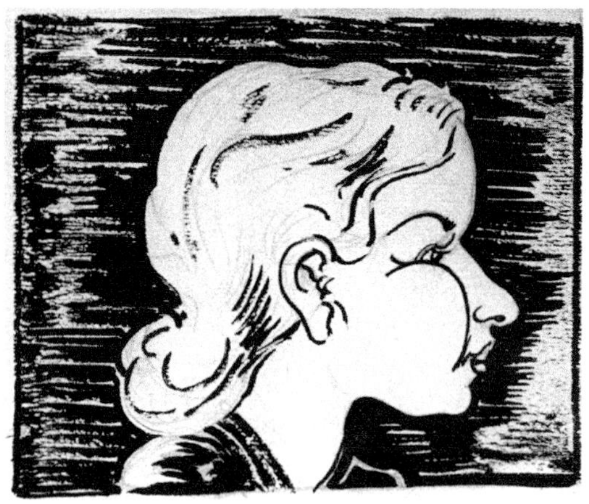

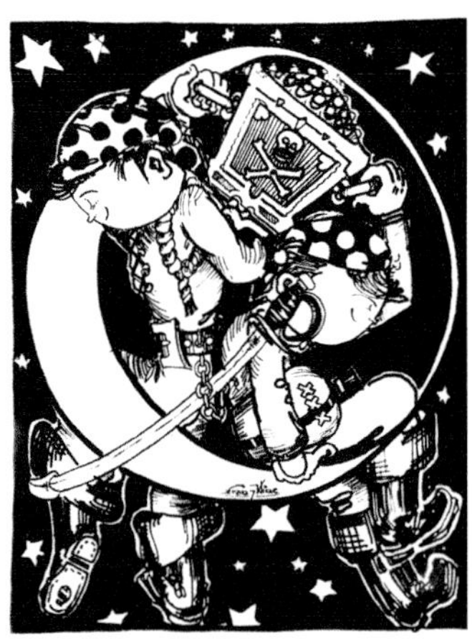

Above left: Louise Kline-Kelly, 1933 ink and pencil. "After Franz drew my portrait, I heard him in the other room, saying, 'I've got it, I've got it.' It was my nose that he got. My mother said, 'If you think that looks like your beautiful sister...'" (*Dr. Louise Kline-Kelly © 2018 Franz Kline Estate/ Artists Rights Society (ARS), New York*)

Above right: Crescent Moon, 1931. *Gachtin Bambil.* (*Patsy Gernerd Aldrich and family © 2018 Franz Kline Estate/Artists Rights Society (ARS), New York*)

Below left: Seniors, 1931, *Gachtin Bambil.* Kline's senior class outing was held at Mountain Lake House, an old Pocono resort. In an old rustic bungalow, dinner was served at 7 p.m. with Franz Kline as toastmaster. (*Patsy Gernerd Aldrich and family © 2018 Franz Kline Estate/Artists Rights Society (ARS), New York*)

Below right: Junior High, 1931, *Gachtin Bambil.* Kline's artistic talents were in great demand in high school, yet he rarely turned anyone down. (*Patsy Gernerd Aldrich and family © 2018 Franz Kline Estate/Artists Rights Society (ARS), New York*)

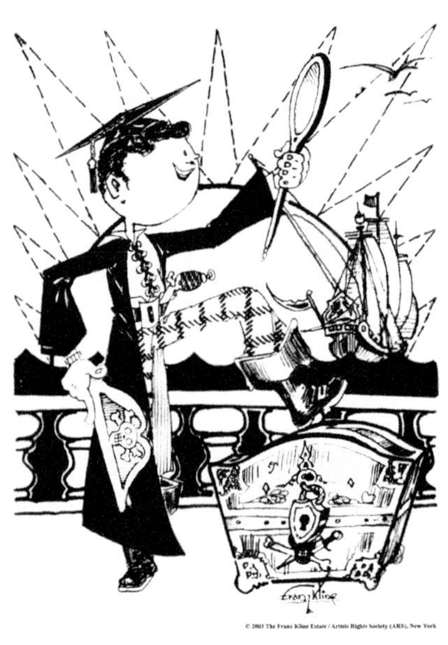

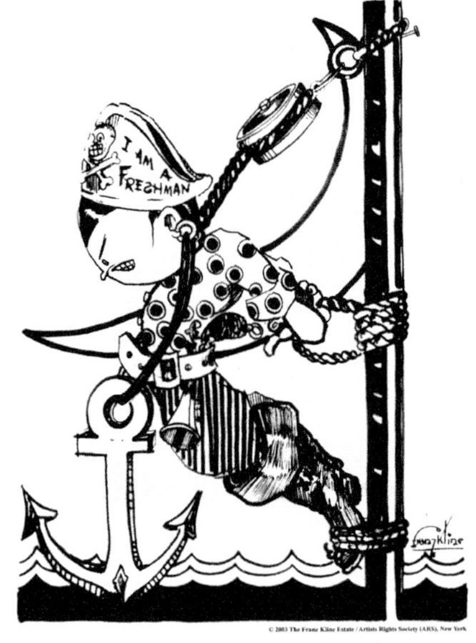

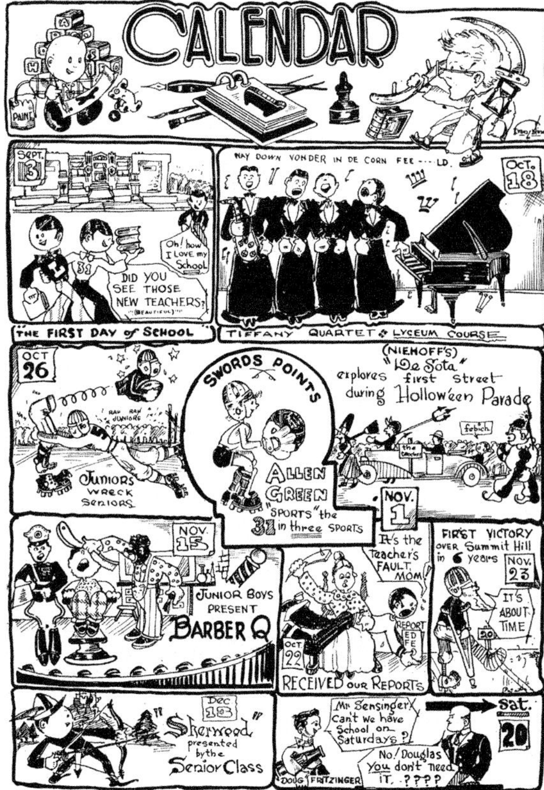

Calendar, Gachtin Bambil, 1931. Kline's comics in his yearbooks are exceptional. Each little chamber encapsulates some aspect of the school year, resplendent with the artist's personal charm. Basketball players wear WWI helmets, Stanley Harleman rules the Junior Candy Stand, and more. (*© 2018 Franz Kline Estate/Artists Rights Society (ARS), New York*)

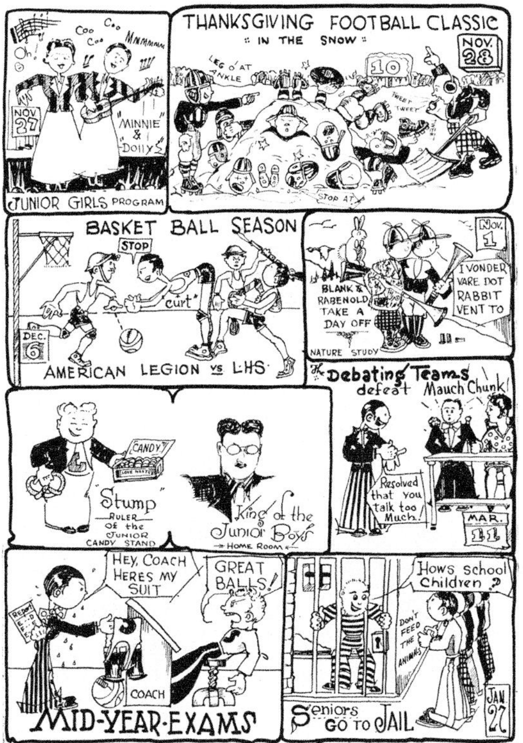

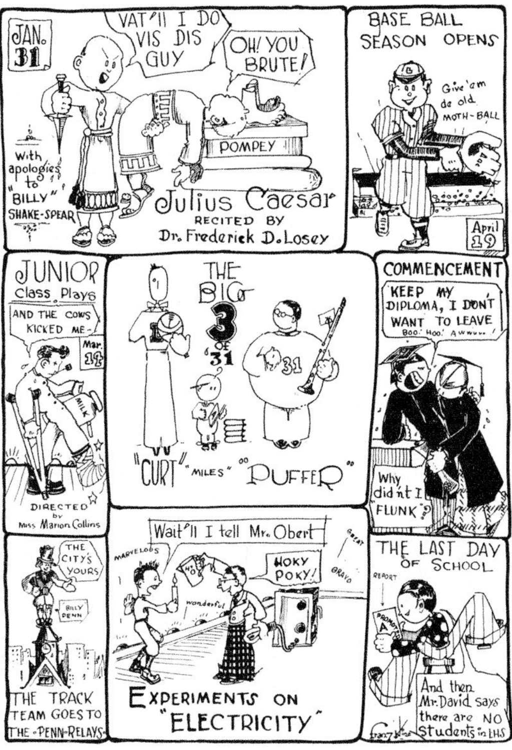

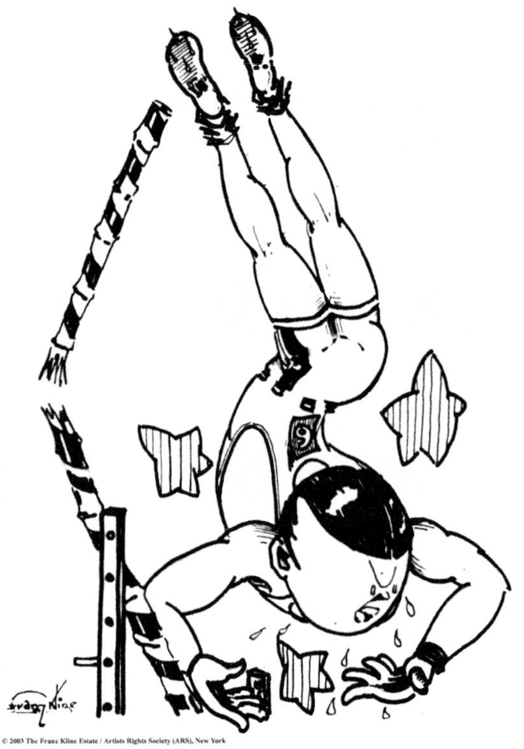

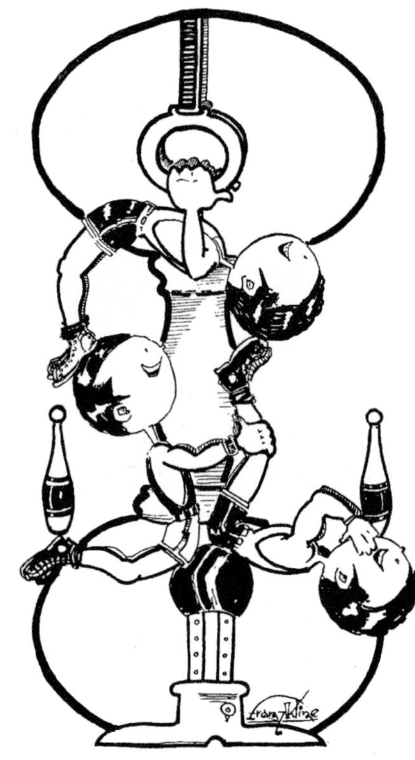

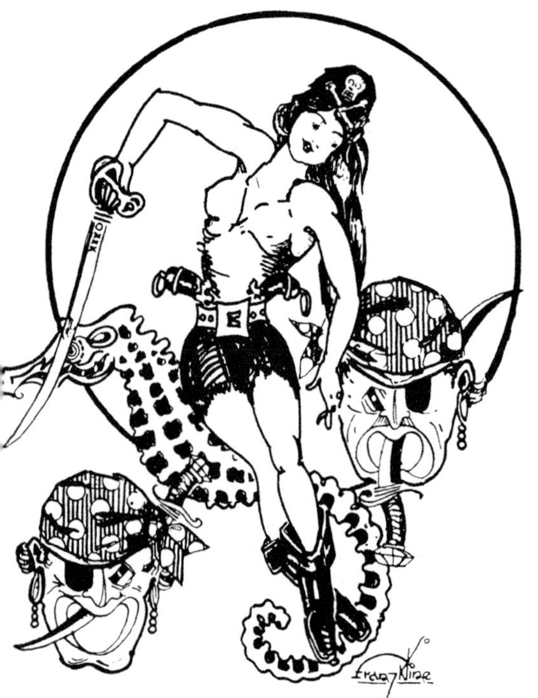

Above left: Track, *Gachtin Bambil*, 1931. (*© 2018 Franz Kline Estate/Artists Rights Society (ARS), New York*)

Above right: Gymnastics, *Gachtin Bambil*, 1931. Kline once said, "People have come from the tradition of looking at drawings, they look at the lines; until you go to art school and then the drawing teacher tells you to look at the white spaces in it." (*© 2018 Franz Kline Estate/Artists Rights Society (ARS), New York*)

Left: Dramatics, *Gachtin Bambil*, 1931. In high school, Kline's muse was a mystery. In Boston, she was a slim, long-legged art student named Martha Kinney who quickly became his constant date and favorite model. From that point on, her proportions and characteristics dominated all his drawings. (*© 2018 Franz Kline Estate/Artists Rights Society (ARS), New York*)

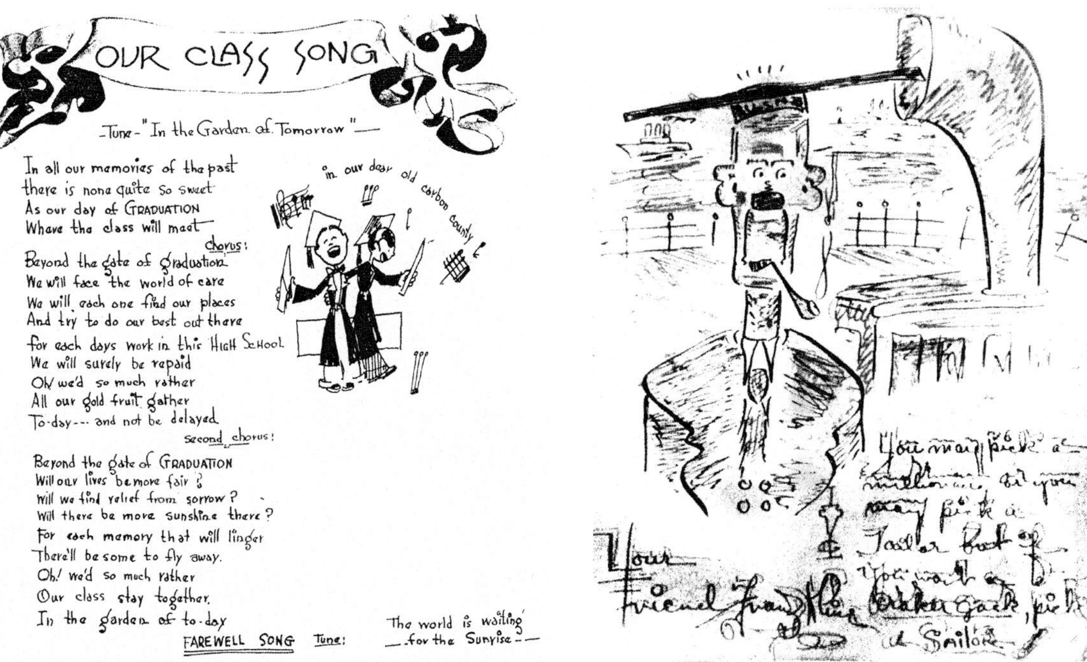

Above left: *Our Class Song*, 1931. "In the Garden of Tomorrow … where the class will meet." Franz Kline illustrated this Graduation Memories book with a farewell song to his high school friend Alvirda Arner. (*Alvirda K. Arner Ginder © 2018 Franz Kline Estate/Artists Rights Society (ARS), New York*)

Above right: Untitled Military Sketch, c. 1928. (*Florence Harleman Kresge © 2018 Franz Kline Estate/Artists Rights Society (ARS), New York*)

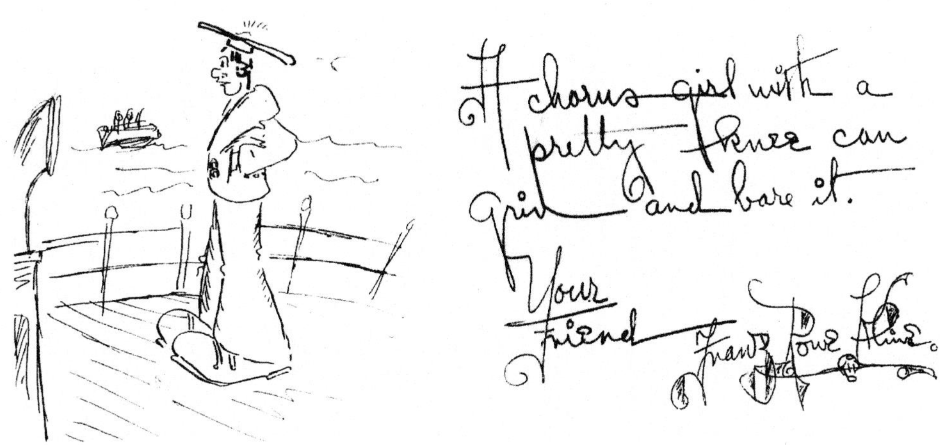

Untitled Military Sketch, c. 1928. "If you want a cracker jack, pick a sailor." One of Kline's favorite U.S. Navy "flat hats and quirky verse." (*© 2018 Franz Kline Estate/Artists Rights Society (ARS), New York*)

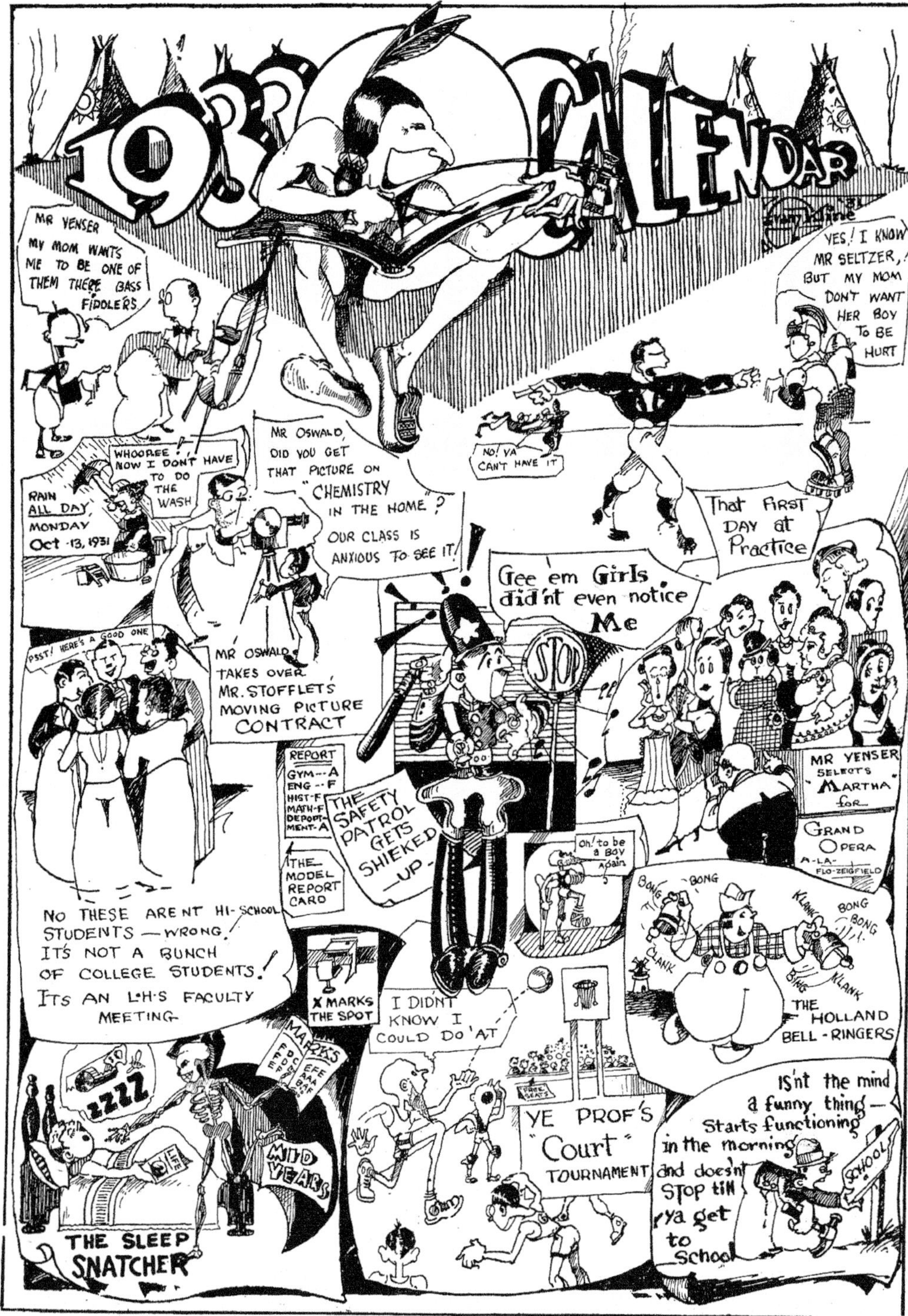

Gachtin Bambil, 1933 calendar, features humorous vignettes about teachers, poking fun at the baseball team and more. (*© 2018 Franz Kline Estate/Artists Rights Society (ARS), New York*)

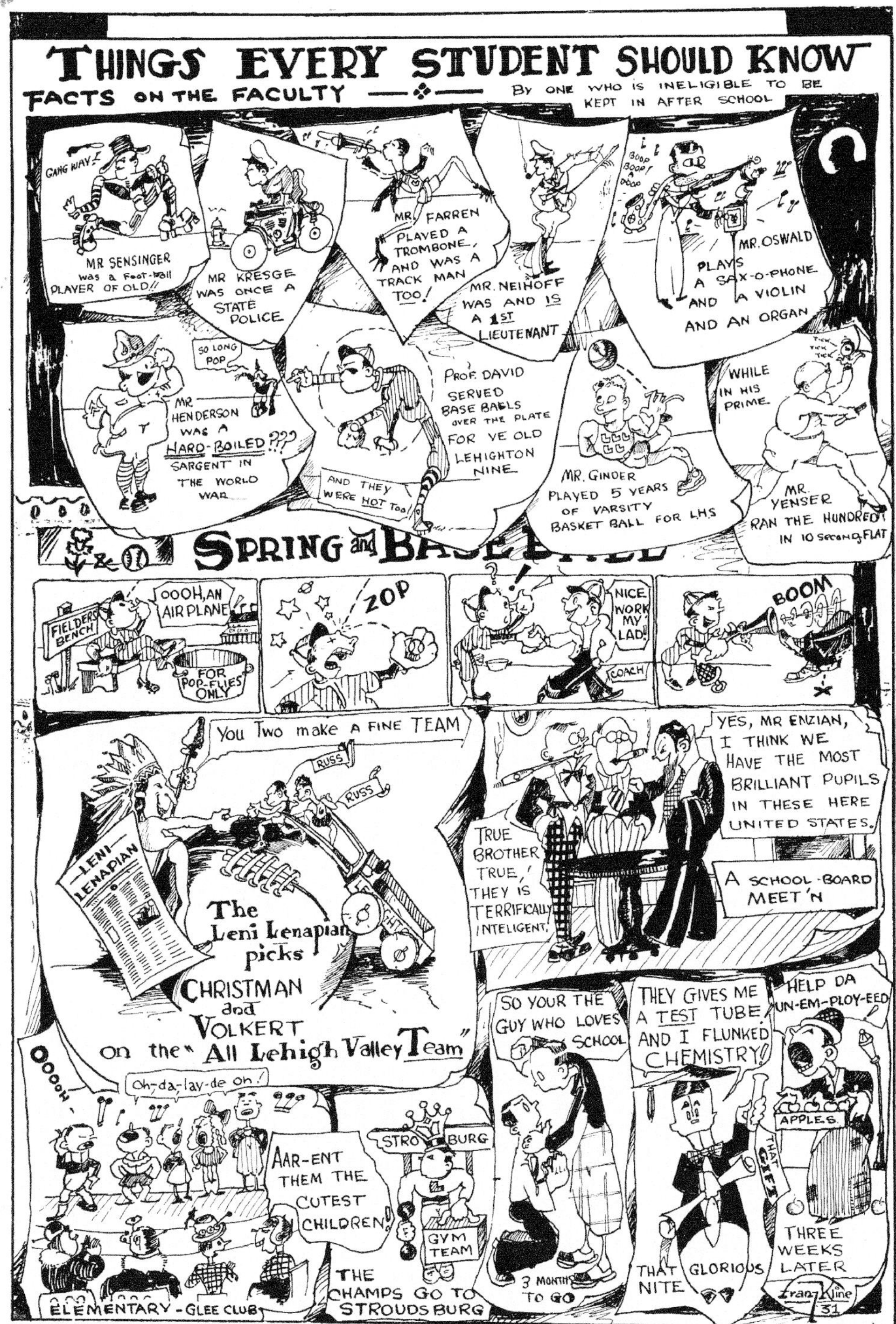

Gachtin Bambil, 1933 calendar, Page 2. (*© 2018 Franz Kline Estate/Artists Rights Society (ARS), New York*)

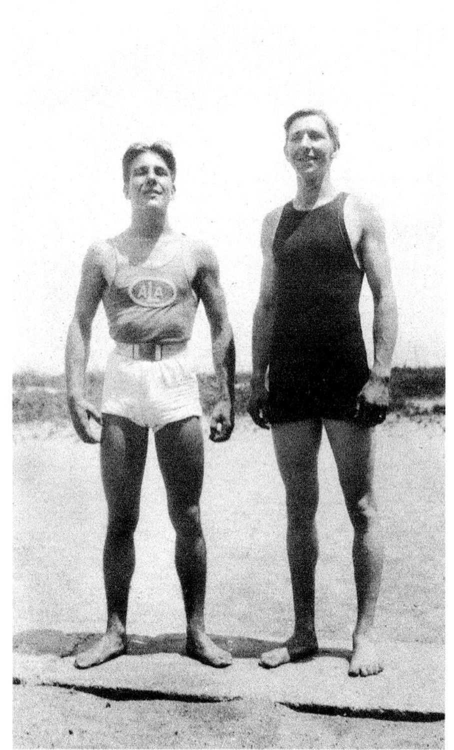

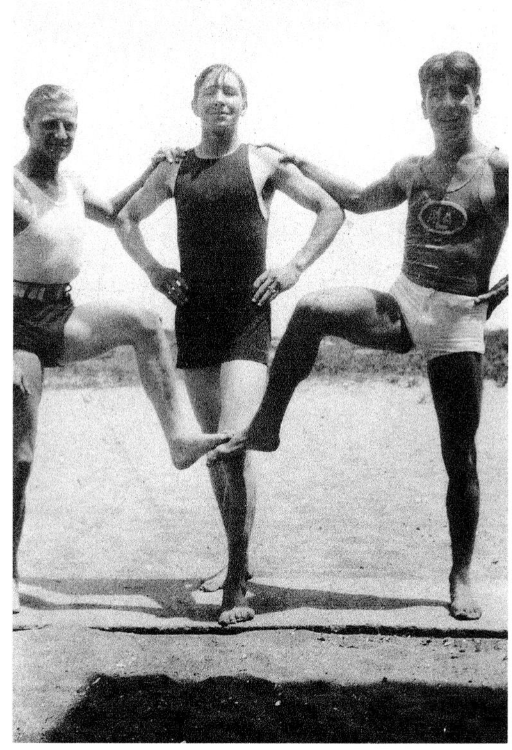

Above left: Henry Bretney and Franz Kline, *c.* 1928, at Citizens Military Training Camp. (*Henry Bretney*)

Above right: Kline with Bretney and Harry Febich, *c.* 1928, at Citizens Military Training Camp. (*Henry Bretney*)

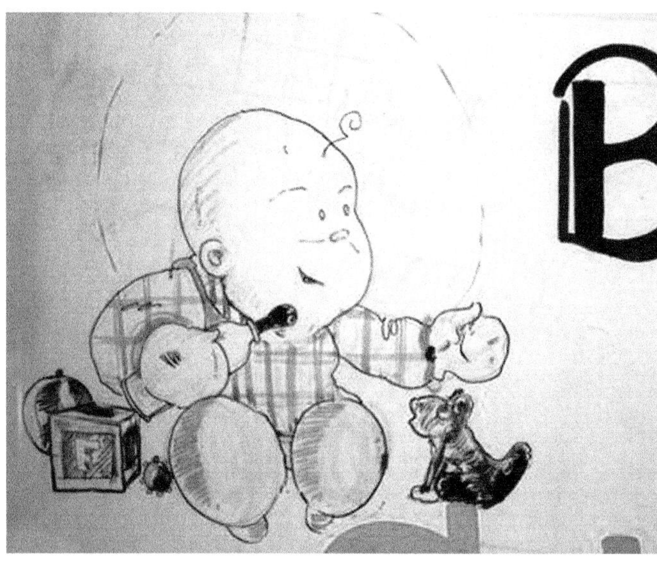

Fairyland Farms (Baby), 1929, detail of baby used in Fairyland Farms Ad. (*Winona Diehl Rifenbary © 2018 Franz Kline Estate/ Artists Rights Society (ARS), New York*)

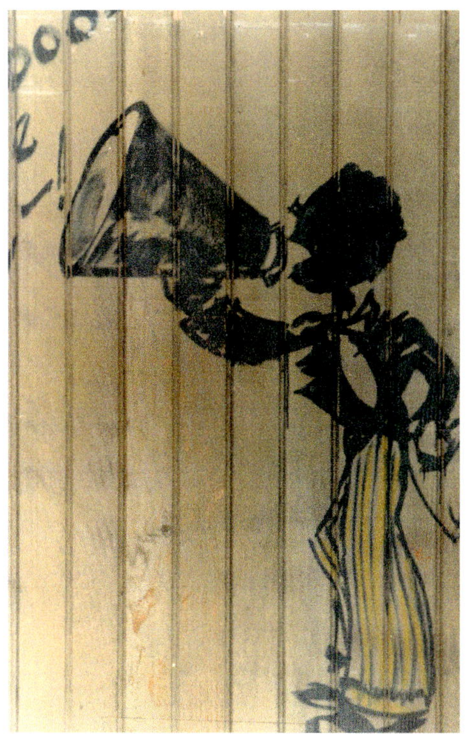

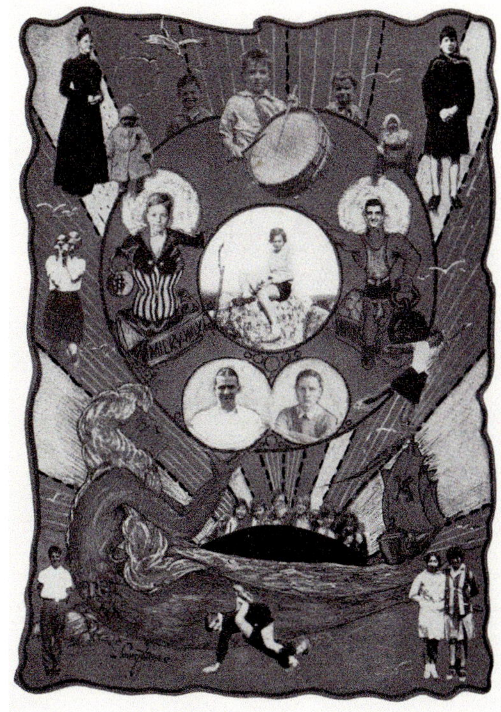

Above left: Jazz Mural musician with megaphone, 1933. (*Larry and Charlene Graver © 2018 Franz Kline Estate/Artists Rights Society (ARS), New York*)

Above right: Untitled, Photo Collage by Franz Kline, *Gachtin Bambil*, 1931. (*© 2018 Franz Kline Estate/Artists Rights Society (ARS), New York*)

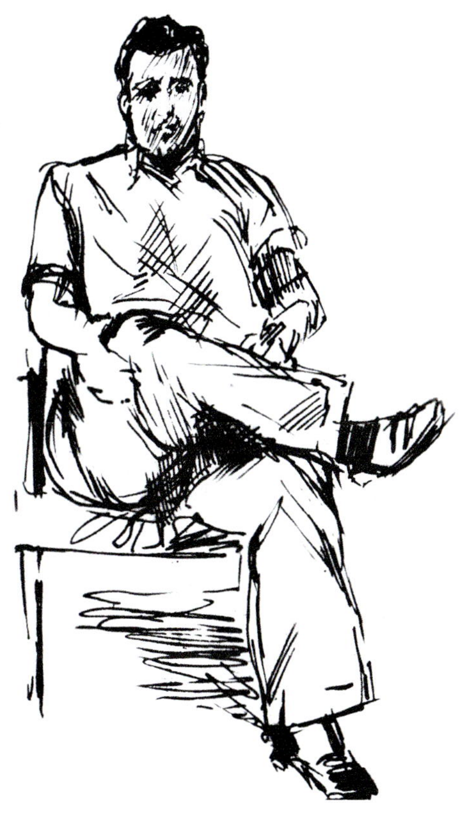

Right: Charles Gernerd, *c.* 1942, ink on paper. School teacher Gernerd was a close friend of Franz, who resided with wife Loretta and daughter Patsy in the Snyder's second floor apartment. (*Patsy Gernerd Aldrich and family © 2018 Franz Kline Estate/Artists Rights Society (ARS), New York*)

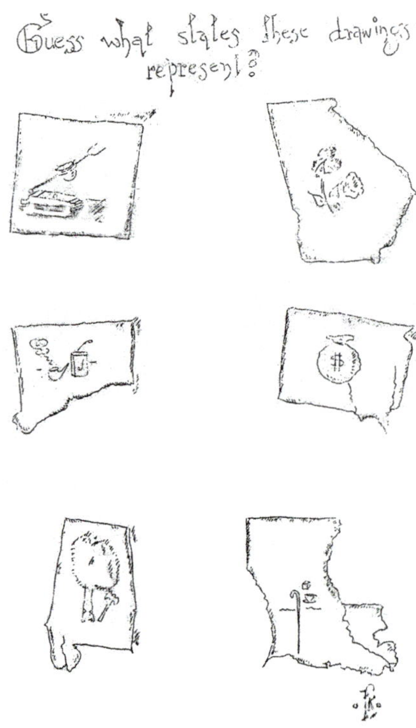

Left: Guess What States, 1926, *Junior Whispers*, one of the earliest examples of Franz Kline's drawing styles. (*Kathryn Oppold and Robert Warner 2018 © 2018 Franz Kline Estate/Artists Rights Society (ARS), New York*)

Below: Pennsylvania Landscape. (*Private Collection © 2018 Franz Kline Estate/ Artists Rights Society (ARS), New York*)

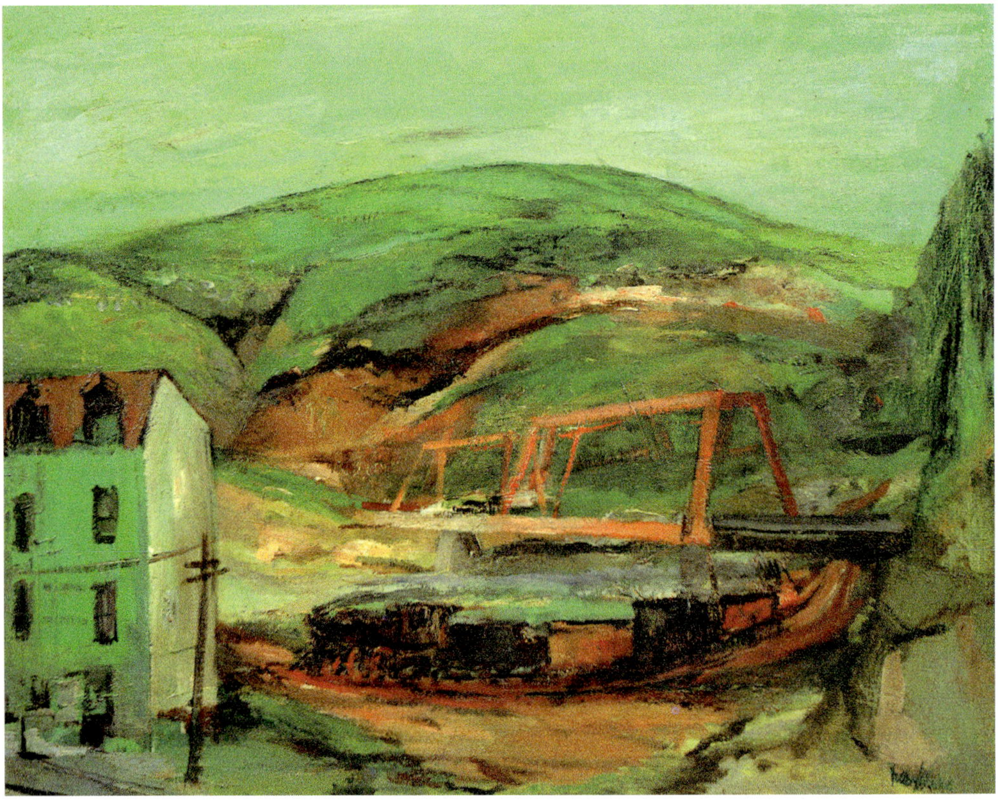

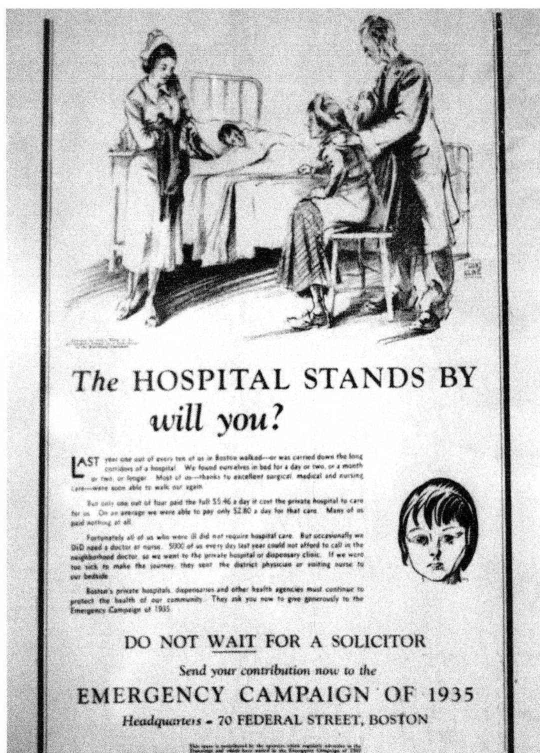

Emergency Campaign Poster of 1935. Kline's winning poster was featured numerous times in the *Boston Globe* to advertise the annual charity in Boston. (*Dr. Louise Kline-Kelly © 2018 Franz Kline Estate/Artists Rights Society (ARS), New York*)

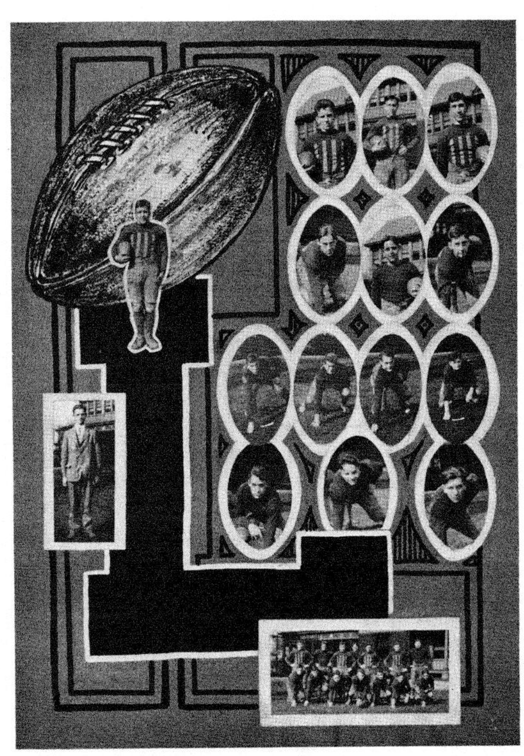

Football Collage, Gachtin Bambil, 1931. Kline's photo is nearest to the football. (*© 2018 Franz Kline Estate/Artists Rights Society (ARS), New York*)

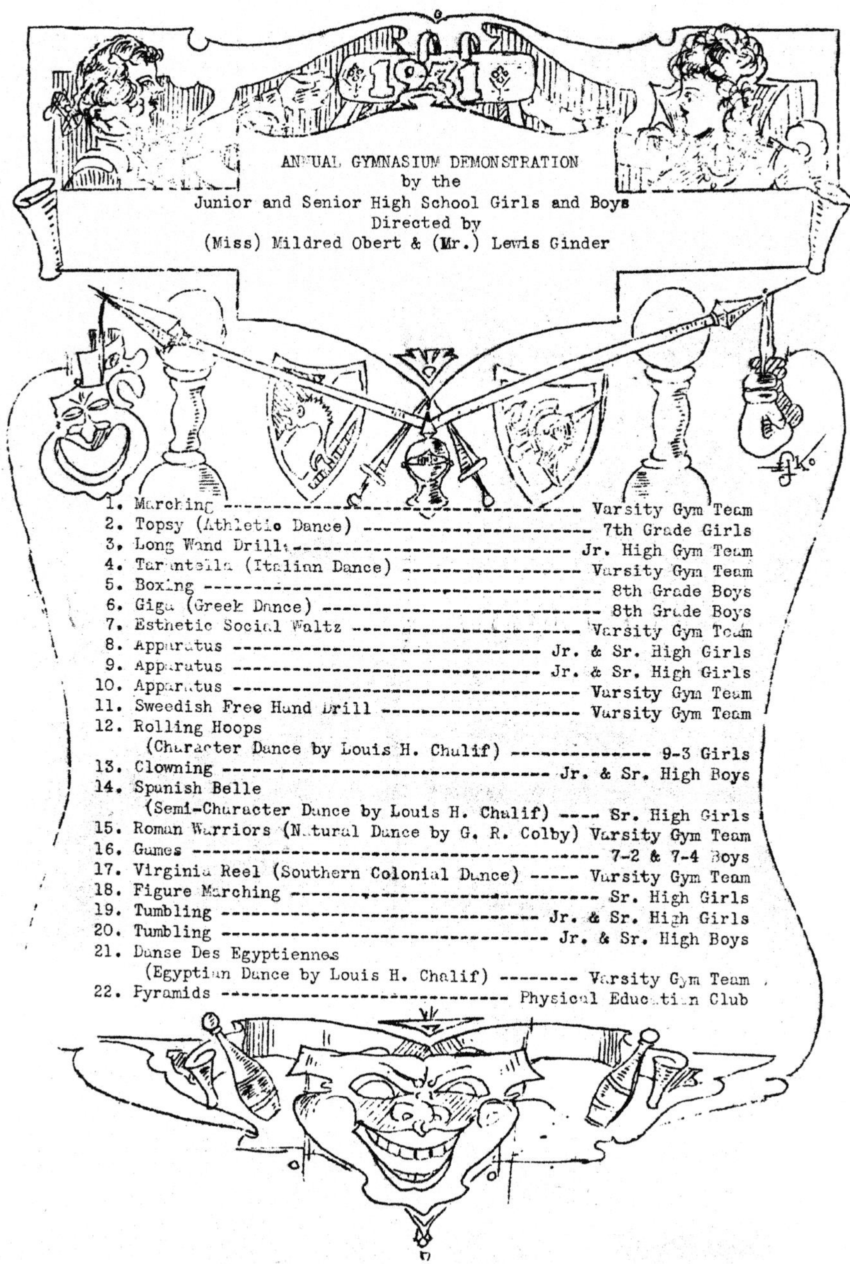
1931

ANNUAL GYMNASIUM DEMONSTRATION
by the
Junior and Senior High School Girls and Boys
Directed by
(Miss) Mildred Obert & (Mr.) Lewis Ginder

1. Marching ---------- Varsity Gym Team
2. Topsy (Athletic Dance) ---------- 7th Grade Girls
3. Long Wand Drill ---------- Jr. High Gym Team
4. Tarantella (Italian Dance) ---------- Varsity Gym Team
5. Boxing ---------- 8th Grade Boys
6. Giga (Greek Dance) ---------- 8th Grade Boys
7. Esthetic Social Waltz ---------- Varsity Gym Team
8. Apparatus ---------- Jr. & Sr. High Girls
9. Apparatus ---------- Jr. & Sr. High Girls
10. Apparatus ---------- Varsity Gym Team
11. Sweedish Free Hand Drill ---------- Varsity Gym Team
12. Rolling Hoops
    (Character Dance by Louis H. Chalif) ---------- 9-3 Girls
13. Clowning ---------- Jr. & Sr. High Boys
14. Spanish Belle
    (Semi-Character Dance by Louis H. Chalif) ---- Sr. High Girls
15. Roman Warriors (Natural Dance by G. R. Colby) Varsity Gym Team
16. Games ---------- 7-2 & 7-4 Boys
17. Virginia Reel (Southern Colonial Dance) ----- Varsity Gym Team
18. Figure Marching ---------- Sr. High Girls
19. Tumbling ---------- Jr. & Sr. High Girls
20. Tumbling ---------- Jr. & Sr. High Boys
21. Danse Des Egyptiennes
    (Egyptian Dance by Louis H. Chalif) -------- Varsity Gym Team
22. Pyramids ---------- Physical Education Club

Gymnastics Demonstration Program, 1931, commissioned by physical education teachers Mildred Obert and Lewis Ginder. (*Mildred Held © 2018 Franz Kline Estate/Artists Rights Society (ARS), New York*)

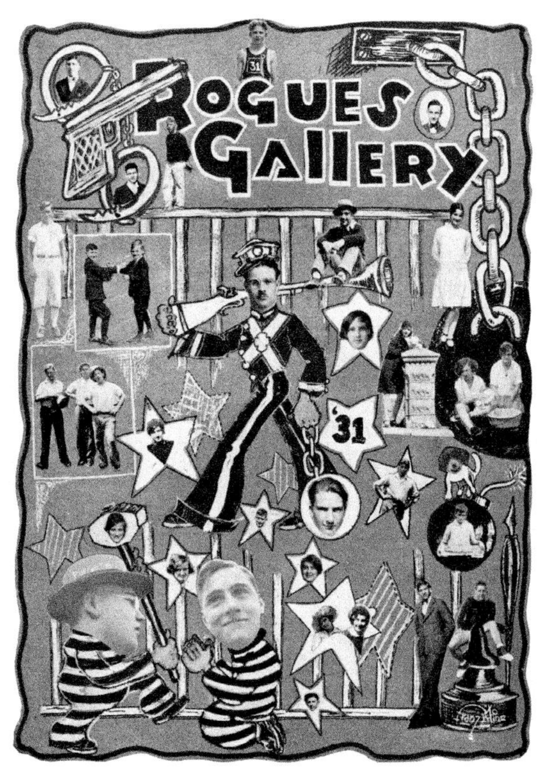

Right: Rogues Gallery collage, *Gachtin Bambil*, 1931. Kline's law and order theme uses photos of classmates and teacher, Carl Niehoff, as the enforcer. In a letter from Boston University, Kline explained his admiration for Niehoff: "One of my Art Profs is just Callie's type. A big brother rather than a teacher!" (© *2018 Franz Kline Estate/Artists Rights Society (ARS), New York*)

Below: Junior Whispers staff photo, Junior High School newspaper, Kline is in the center of the back row 1928. (*Kathryne Oppold and Robert Wagner*)

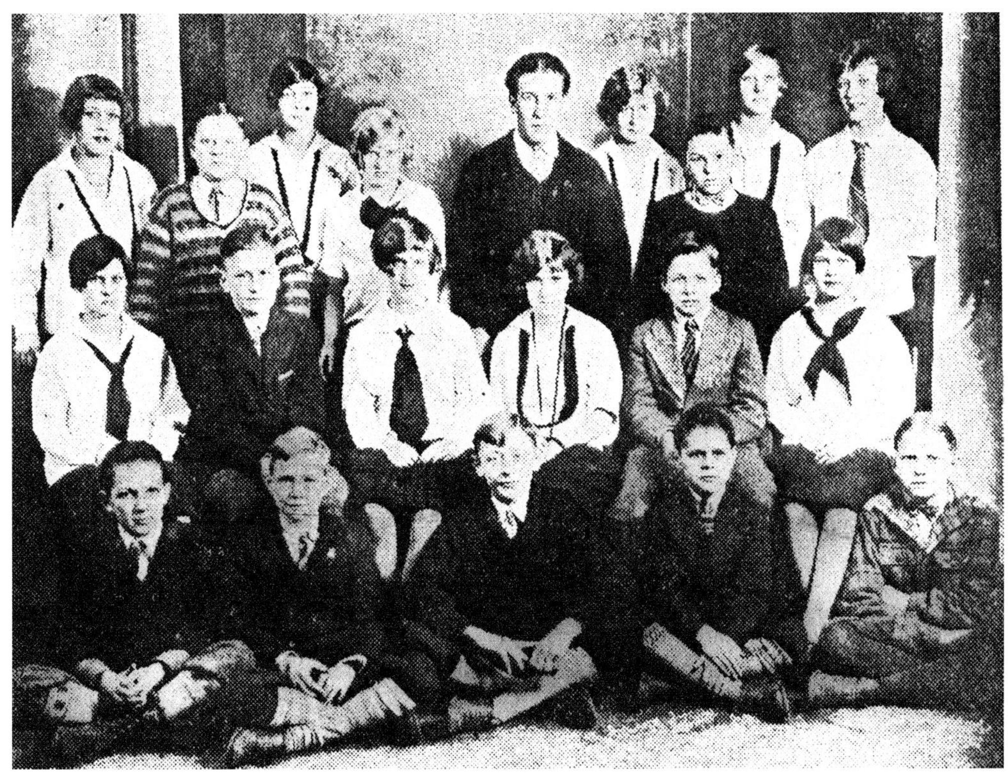

37 Evans Road
Brookline
Boston, Mass.

Dear Lavona,

No doubt you've many times wondered if I'd keep my promise to you — I have, at last, and here's my letter.

Has not the time passed quickly. It seems but a few nites ago that I bid you Good-nite at the door I so often visited.

Well! Lavona, how's Chemistry coming along — ah! I just knew you'd love it! and tell me is it grand and glorious to be a Senior?

2.

Well it's only half as enjoyable as being a Freshman again. I suppose Edith has kept you up to date with my doings & goings — so there is no use of going over that again. In brief words — I am as happy and ambitious as ever, met loads of "interesting as well as attractive new friends of both sex, my art work is all I pictured it to you as being, and "Big Bo is great. There's so much doing, so mu to do and see. I suppose Lehighton is the same little dutch settlement wrapped up in a cloud of coal dirt — how-ever I mi it with all my friends.

A letter from "Milly" Hel

Letter from Kline to Lavona Edgar, 1931. Kline writes "I've just come in and into the night I am keeping my promise. Jerry my mate is fast asleep. AND me, well my eyes are blinking with every tick of the alarm clock. Write an answer as long as this letter." (*Lavona Ronemus © 2018 Franz Kline Estate/Artists Rights Society (ARS), New York*)

3.

[te]lls me the strong Lehighton foot ball squad is a bit crippled. Lavona, [wh]at's wrong with the team, will they [n]ever win a game. Gee! every Saturday I [w]ish I was with them, going to school [o]n Sat morning I run, - side step & kick, dreaming [I]'m still a member of the LHS eleven. - Up here [I] don't even hear how they make out until [a] week later. The only school scores I hear [ar]e Harvard, B.U., Yale and Army. [S]kimmer keeps me in touch with Lafayette now & then. [T]hey're all interesting but to me, not half [w]hat Lehighton High's activities are. Someday you too will experience the

same feeling.

Lavona! - You remember my telling you how interesting and amusing you'd find Mr. Nickoff in Senior History - Well one of my Art profs. is just calling type. A big brother rather than a teacher! The other nite he had me down at his fraternity K∇Φ - I met a bunch of fine fellows - students of B.U. The evening ended up in an elaborate banquet. - The Sunday before he invited me over to his studio - Gee: it's great, paintings, sketches, statues, relics in ancient art - well everything! He even lent me a costume for our Hallow'een dance at the Studio - [illegible]

5.

Miss Roedel tells me the "Red Hot Senior dance ensemble" is trying to persuade Mr David to allow dances in the High School Bldg. - I hope they succeed - It may mean a Hallowe'en Dance for you also!

And now for the part in which I know you'll find interest - [illegible] Dave - room mate - He's from Maine - tonite we bought a Drip-O-lite coffee percolator so we laugh at each other while eating dough nuts & drinking coffee - our mid-nite luncheon. He with me is a supposedly Art student, half the time we dont know whether we're Budding Artists - or Blooming Fools - but we're happy and

got along fine together. Some nites we even go on dates together. - The "Sargent School" of Physical Ed. seems to be quite an interesting study. You can imagine it is - Miss Obert is an alumnus!

Well Lavona I've just come in - and on in - to the nite I am keeping my promise! "Jerry" my mate is fast asleep - yeah he even snores once in a while; and me - well my eyes are blinking with every tick of my alarm clock.

Before closing let me ask you to write an answer as long as this letter. Soon!!!

Give my regards to all my friends and yours -

See you a Christmas time!

Goo-by!

Franz

Tell your Dad - I'm still keep'n training for the TRACK Posies - Football team!

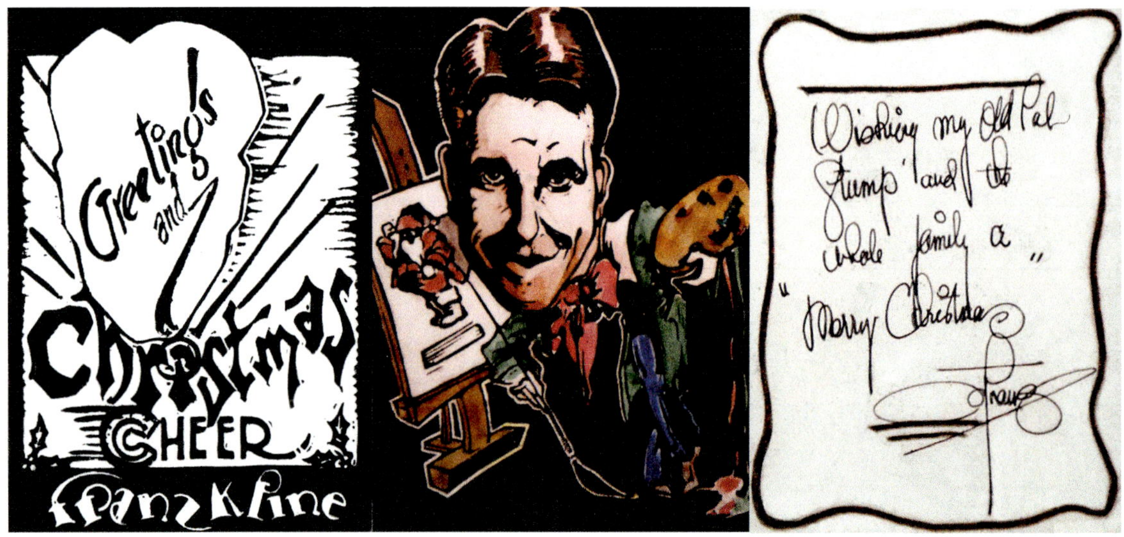

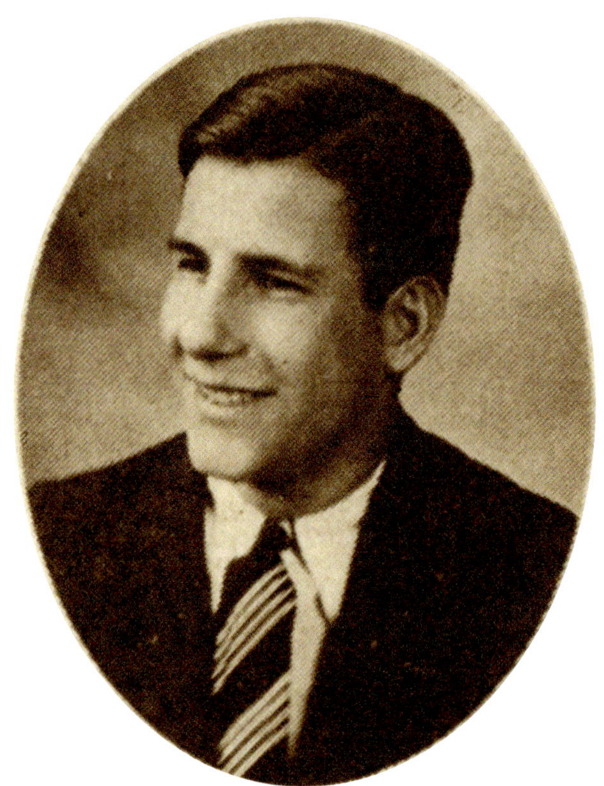

Above: Boston University Christmas Card, complete view, 1931. (*Mrs. Stanley Harleman and family © 2018 Franz Kline Estate/Artists Rights Society (ARS), New York*)

Left: Franz Kline, *Gachtin Bambil*, 1931, Junior Class Yearbook Photo.

Appendix

Frederick Ryan, Sr., "Franz Kline as I Knew Him," Unpublished Essay, 1960

"Franz Kline as I Knew Him"

We first met in Boston in the autumn of 1932. Franz had been attending classes at an art department of Boston University which had been discontinued by that institution as a depression economy measure, and two of the instructors, a Canadian named Arthur Argue, and a Mr. Frank Durkee had decided to carry on by establishing a school of their own. Frank Durkee, a "superb figure draughtsman," had been trained by the celebrated George Bridgman of the New York Art Students' League, who had produced the series of anatomy and figure drawing books that used to be the art student's bible. I might add for whatever interest it may hold for Canadian readers that Bridgman, the drawing teacher of Norman Rockwell, Dean Cornwell and many other "name" illustrators and painters was a Canadian born in Ontario in 1863, I was recently informed by his son who has presented me with a collection of his father's original drawings.

Durkee wanted to pattern his school after the New York Art Students' League and named it the "Boston Art Students' League" starting with a nucleus of his pupils from Boston University who wished to continue under his instruction and Franz Kline was one of this group. The new school was located in the large semi-basement of Boston's Fenway Studio Building on Ipswich Street. Mr. Argue an Art Education major, became registrar and general manager of the enterprise, and Mr. Durkee chief instructor.

A passion to master the secrets of fine figure drawing governed the school like a religion and several distinguished figure draughtsman, impressed by our zeal, devoted their services as part time instructors, among them John H. Crosman, a famous pen and ink illustrator of the day who had a studio upstairs, and the mural painter Richard Andrew, who had been a pupil in France of Jean-Paul Laurens and Gerome.

This was the background against which Franz Kline and I first studied together. He was twenty-two years old; he had been born in Wilkes-Barre, Pennsylvania, of a Pennsylvania German father and an English-born mother. He was short in stature and muscular in build with a breezy devil-may-care manner and a rollicking sense of humor. I was a bit older, twenty five, had been born in Charlottetown, P.A. I had studied several years at the

Mass. College of Art, then at The École des Beaux-Arts in Paris. I had returned to Boston in the depression, and as the market for art was practically nil decided to spend as much time as I could in further study.

Every morning from nine until twelve we drew the figure in charcoal from a nude model working in the same pose all morning, and sometimes for several mornings in succession; and each afternoon we worked from one until four in twenty-minute sketches from the model, using pencils of various kinds, the pose being changed for each sketch. Completely absorbed in our drawing we worked in a silence broken only the low voice of the instructor giving a criticism and the occasional sighs and groans of baffled or discouraged students. Franz drew with a great deal of facility and slickness if not always with accuracy. One day I heard Mr. Durkee tell him: "You have an awful lot of facility, but if you don't look out it's going to ruin you!" Franz's goal in those days was to draw easily a "smart" type of female figure that would make him a successful and money-making illustrator. His taste in male subjects ran more to character studies, including figures created out of his head resembling Dickens characters and the actor W. C. Fields. These types appeared over and over again on his sketchpad and on scrap paper.

We soon became chums and spent our time together in our out-of-school hours, going to museums and exhibitions and visiting second hand book stores in search of art books and finely illustrated volumes, as well as old issues of the *Studio* magazine.

Mr. Crosman was willing to teach any of us pen-and-ink technique and Franz and I, proving to be the only members of the group willing to tackle that difficult medium, took him up on it. He lent us out-of-print volumes of drawings by Edwin Austin Abbey to copy, as well as his own originals to study, and we rummaged through Public Library files to find old prints of the highly imaginative new drawings of Joseph Clement Coll. (In New York some ten years later, Franz succeeded in buying the original of one of these Coll drawings and made me a gift of it which I still treasure.) We lived within a few doors of one another, and spent our evenings either at his place or mine burning a great deal of midnight oil struggling over new drawings which we would later show to Mr. Crosman for his criticism. Frequently we sketched each other. (Like most illustrators, Crosman had photographic shots made of his models in the attitudes and lighting he needed, which he by no means copied, but used merely for desirable information in completing his previously worked and compositions for illustrations in national magazines.) On various occasions, Franz and I posed for Mr. Crosman and rather recognizable likenesses of us appeared from time to time as fictional characters in such publications as the *Ladies' Home Journal*, *Collier's*, and *McCall's*. We thought this a real lark and felt ourselves to be participants in at least some capacity in the field of national magazine illustration.

We worked hard and earnestly, but our life was not all work and no play. The school had occasional dances and parties, and I was able to introduce Franz to a slim, pretty and long-legged girl art student I knew (Martha Kinney Baker) who quickly became his constant date and favorite model over a period of years. From that point on, her proportions and characteristics dominated all his drawings of [women at that time... text illegible]. In due time, she reciprocated by introducing me to the equally stunning and talented young lady artist whom I married.

Meanwhile, we continued our grind of study together for a total of figure drawing and pen technique. We had experimented with various kinds of pens and gained considerable facility in the medium. The smaller the drawing the better Franz like it. The pearly tones achieved by E. A. Abbey, who virtually painted with a pen, were a joy and an inspiration to him. On a brief trip to New York he met the pen illustrator John Richard Flanagan, and came back to regale me with whatever hints of handling the medium he could glean from him. Then he discovered in a book picked up in a second hand store the work of the English pen draughtsman Phil May and that became his lifelong passion. Later in England, he acquired Phil May books and prints at every opportunity.

My own real interest was oil painting and fine art. I had exhibited a portrait in the Paris Salon while in France, and had been influenced by personal acquaintance with Jacques Emile Blanche pupil and protégé of Monet, Degas, and Renoir the friends of his parents. But the Great Depression was on and commercial art might prove one's salvation, and line drawing was cheaper to reproduce than other mediums, the discipline it provided could always prove an asset in painting in the future and Franz and I genuinely liked the medium for its own sake. Later I had occasion to use it in some illustration work, and Franz applied his knowledge of it to the field of etching.

Occasionally, during this depression period, we received commercial art assignments to do for small sums. On one occasion, Franz obtained a commission to do gold leaf lettering on a doctor's office window and asked me to help him do it. I had never handled gold leaf and then discovered that he hadn't either, but had accepted the job anyway. The pay was to be the grand total of $15.00, out of which Franz had to supply the gold leaf and other materials.

With fantastically adroit clumsiness we bluffed our way through it, putting on a performance that would have done credit to the Marx Brothers, thankful in our hearts that the window was about five stories above Boston Common, where nobody could detect our bungling incompetence. If our patron is still living he is the only doctor in Boston who can boast a genuine Franz Kline on his office window. He was a plastic surgeon and during our labors entertained us with an account of being approached a short time before by a tough looking character acting as spokesman for a "friend" who wished his face "changed so that he could not be recognized." The doctor felt convinced that the "friend" was the notorious gangster John Dillinger who was in hiding somewhere at that time and he had turned down the request.

Throughout this ludicrous caper Franz had put on an air of confidence and knowing what he was doing that was a masterpiece of showmanship. He was a natural born raconteur and dearly loved telling funny anecdotes or hearing them told with an appropriate mimicry of voice and gestures. Generations of art students, including myself had attended painting classes of dear old Ernest Le Major at the Mass. College of Art and we all had a fund of funny stories of Mr. Major's theatrics which were added for emphasis while he instilled in us reverence for the old masters and his idol "Jimmy" Whistler, these stories were a particular delight to Franz whose sense of humor was irrepressible.

After we had spent three years of intensive diligent study at the Boston Art Students League, it was permanently closed, as Mr. Durkee who had been gassed in World War I was too ill to continue it. Our group disbanded, and a new phase of experience began for Franz—he went to London for further study at The Heatherley School of Fine Art. In London, his taste for subtle and refined line drawings did not wane, but if anything was intensified. This is proven by one of his letters to me from London one of which was dated August 10, 1936 which I quote in part:

> Well Freddie its no use going on how much I like London. You can imagine it all. From every stand point it's great. Subject matter of all types and the home and working grounds of all our illustrator masters, Whistler, Abbey, May etc. And if Sargeant, Whistler and Abbey liked it enough to work here I certainly would be a chump if I couldn't.
>
> Last week an old school teacher of mine spent the week in London and then flew on to Paris. I took it upon myself to show her what I knew of London From the Abbey and St. Paul's to the museums and May's original. Anyhow she bought three original pencil studies of Sir Henry Irving for £5 and gave them to me. Beautiful studies they are valued at £20 so I have still to get over the excitement and enjoyment of it all. One of them is reproduced in James Thorpe's book on Phil May. By now I have ten books on him, some first editions, so you see I still have old Phil in the blood.
>
> Next, four of my studies have been selected the *Artist* publication to be reproduced in...

I still have a bundle of his letters including those sent me from London, which he describes his study of original pen drawings by E. A. Abbey, Keene of *Punch*, Phil May, Daumier, and Forain. He collected Phil May books whenever he could obtain them until he had ten of them, according to these letters, and one of his former school teachers from Pennsylvania on a trip to Europe bought him as a gift three original pencil drawings by Phil May as a gesture of thanks for his guiding her in London.

He loved London and its atmosphere and constantly carried a sketch book making countless pen sketches of street scenes, street characters, horses and carts, and so forth as well as figure groups in pubs and music halls and interiors of his studio quarters. One of these sketch books is in my possession, received from him as a gift after his return to America. Sometimes his London letters were decorated with little pen drawings and various strokes and scribbles to demonstrate to me the results of a particular pen he had just bought. He recounts that four of his studies were selected for publication by the *Artist* publication to be reproduced in an article on Future Artists.

This particular letter ends "Wish you were here or I were there. We could have a nickle hamburger and a coffee." And is signed "Good luck and many strong lines."

Our next meeting was in 1940 when Franz spent the summer with my wife and me at a picturesque old farmhouse we had bought in the New England village of Hopkinton, Mass. We drew and painted together and one hot afternoon when our year-old son, Jimmy, was clad only in a diaper and was playing with a small copper kettle I used for a still-life prop, Franz dashed off a small oil sketch of him, back view, kettle in hand. I have been told that this oil sketch is now a prized possession in a Long Island private collection but purchased only after Franz made his name as an abstract expressionist, as in 1940 he could hardly sell his work at all. Upon his return to America, he had settled in Greenwich Village with the English girl he had married. He had bought an etching press and did numerous works in that medium always on a tiny scale. I have several of them, received as gifts at Christmas time. He did some oil painting of a representational sort and some linoleum block prints. Occasionally he sold works but for giveaway prices and life was hard and discouraging for him. In spite of his past intense interest in illustration, he somehow did not seem to fit into the New York illustration field at all. He was always essentially a sketcher never seeming to correct or finish anything to the standard that success as an illustrator in New York demanded or would have required. Also the fine line type of illustrations of the past in which he had steeped himself was no longer in demand and new and different full color techniques and mediums reigned supreme.

In our summer together in the country, we not only drew and painted and attended country auctions picking up old picture frames for trifling sums, but we had many long discussions on art.

Surprising as it may seem, in view of his later world fame as an abstractionist, his contempt for abstract art was at that time bitter and undisguised and on one occasion he said "In order to be a success in art today one has to do something so utterly absurd that nobody can ignore it." Whether or not his later huge, overpowering black and white abstracts produced with a housepainter's brush, were done with tongue-in-cheek to pull the legs of the pseudo-intellectual critics the reader will have to judge for himself. Commentators on Franz's abstract works have read things into them that he himself never intended. When *Life* magazine reproduced one of his big abstracts with a photo of the steelwork of a bridge on the opposite page and a statement that the pattern of the bridge had inspired the painting, Franz told my wife, Bea, and son, Jimmy, that very same week while the *Life* issue was still current that he had never even thought of the bridge when he did the painting, and such an idea was purely an invention on the part of *Life*'s writer. Other writers have said he was inspired by oriental calligraphy, but he denied that too.

In a 1958 letter, after I had mailed him a news clipping about himself from a New England paper, he wrote: "It seems so odd to be that Abstract Expressionist referred to. Of course I've been here now for the past twenty years. Here in the Village all that time wondering what painting is—wanting to paint influenced like we all are by other painters and friends like us who follow the muse."

On a trip to New York with my son, Jimmy, now grown up, had called on Franz, who had not seen him since his babyhood, so the letter continues: "I think of you Fred—Boston—your drawing and painting—Bea and seeing Jimmy! Remembering painting him when he was crawling on the floor with a copper jug and then to see him and hear him say, 'I'm the son of Freddy Ryan.' Anyhow, it's not bad to be an old painter!"

He was then only forty-eight, but as the idol and mentor of all the young would-be abstract expressionists in Greenwich Village he seemed to them a patriarch. The following summer, he visited us again in New England. More of his own generation was his friend Willem de Kooning, to whom he introduced my son, Jimmy, in New York.

The following summer, he visited me again in New England (it was our last meeting before his death) and he agreed to sit for a portrait. I questioned him regarding his extreme changeover from his small and delicate line works to his huge and brutal abstracts, he said simply, "I guess one can't help being influenced by the painters around one." Although both of us would have scoffed at the idea at the time, that visit proved to be our last meeting before his untimely death at the age of only fifty-two.

Endnotes

Chapter 1

1. Rosenberg, C. M., *Child Labor in America: A History* (Jefferson, NC: McFarland, 2013), p. 96.
2. Dr. Louise Kline-Kelly, interview with RRF, State College, PA, February 23, 1987.
3. "Barnam & Bailey's Circus," *Harrisburg Telegraph* (Harrisburg, PA), April 15, 1915, p. 9.
4. Gaugh, H. F., *Franz Kline* (New York: Abbeville Press, 1985), p. 68.
5. Florence Harleman Kresge, interview with RRF, Lehighton, PA, April 29, 1986
6. Edward Meneeley, interview with Joel Finsel, December 22, 2006.
7. Dr. Louise Kline-Kelly, interview with RRF, State College, PA, February 23, 1987.
8. *Ibid.*
9. "Buys Back Old Home, Then Kills Himself," *Lebanon Daily News* (Lebanon, PA), Wednesday, August 22, 1917, p. 6.
10. Dr. Louise Kline-Kelly, interview with RRF, State College, PA, February 23, 1987.
11. *Ibid.*
12. Dr. Daniel Davies to RRF interview, March 3, 1997.
13. Dr. Louise Kline-Kelly, interview with RRF, State College, PA, April 8, 1986.
14. Dr. Louise Kline-Kelly, interview with RRF, State College, PA, February 23, 1987.
15. "Echoes of the Week," *The Wilkes-Barre Sunday Independent* (Wilkes-Barre, PA), August 26, 1917, p. 18.
16. Dr. Louise Kline-Kelly, interview with RRF, State College, PA, April 8, 1986.
17. *Ibid.*
18. Girard College Application, Number 10503, Admitted March 21, 1919. Girard College Archives, Philadelphia, PA.
19. Dr. Louise Kline-Kelly, interview with RRF, State College, PA, February 23, 1987.
20. Dr. Louise Kline-Kelly, interview with RRF, State College, PA, April 8, 1986.
21. *Ibid.*

Chapter 2

1. Simpson, S., *Biography of Stephen Girard* (Philadelphia, PA: R. L. Bonsai, 1832), pp. 56–57.
2. Ingram, H. A., *The Life and Character of Stephen Girard* (Philadelphia, PA: E. Stanley Hart, 1884), p. 77.
3. *Ibid.*
4. *Ibid.*

5. *The Will of the Late Stephen Girard Esq. Procured from the Office for the Probate of Wills with a Short Biography of His Life* (Philadelphia, PA: Thomas Desilver, 1847), p. 17.
6. Arey, H., *The Girard College and Its Founder* (Philadelphia, PA: C. Sherman, 1854), p. 55.
7. *The Will of the Late Stephen Girard Esq. Procured from the Office for the Probate of Wills with a Short Biography of His Life* (Philadelphia, PA: Thomas Desilver, 1847), p. 20.
8. *Ibid.*
9. Robert H. Scheirer to RRF, personal letter, March 11, 1986.
10. Robert H. Scheirer to RRF, personal letter, August 5, 1986.
11. *Ibid.*
12. *The Starry Cross* (Philadelphia, PA), vol. 32, no. 1 (January 1923).
13. Robert H. Scheirer to RRF, personal letter, March 11, 1986.
14. *Ibid.*
15. Dr. Louise Kline-Kelly, interview with RRF, State College, PA, April 8, 1986.
16. *Ibid.*
17. Robert H. Scheirer to RRF, personal letter, March 11, 1986.
18. Dr. Louise Kline-Kelly, interview with RRF, State College, PA, April 8, 1986.

Chapter 3

1. "Stakulsky Being Sued in Sensational Case," *Pittston Gazette* (Pittston, PA), May 4, 1917, p. 1.
2. "Alleges Assault with Telephone," *The Wilkes Barre-Record* (Wilkes-Barre, PA), Oct. 4, 1921, p. 3.
3. Ms. Katharine Brown to Mrs. Anne Kline, April 1918. Author's archive.
4. Rosdahl, C. B., and Kowalski, M. T., *Textbook of Basic Nursing* (Philadelphia, PA: Lippincott, 2008), p. 3.
5. McDonald, L., *Collected Works of Florence Nightingale* (Waterloo, Ontario: Wilfrid Laurier University, 2009), p. 751.
6. Rosdahl, C. B., and Kowalski, M. T., *Textbook of Basic Nursing* (Philadelphia, PA: Lippincott, 2008), p. 3.
7. *Ibid.*
8. Anne R. Kline, notebook, St. Luke's Hospital Training School for Nurses, Nov. 5, 1919. Author's archive.
9. Mrs. Ira Snyder interview with RRF, Lehighton, Pennsylvania, December 12, 1989.
10. Dr. Daniel Davies interview with RRF, February 12, 1986.
11. Grace Mosser Ahner interview with RRF, August 19, 1986.
12. Dr. Daniel Davies to RRF, telephone interview, February 12, 1990.
13. Grace Mosser Ahner interview with RRF, August 19, 1986.
14. Dr. Louise Kline-Kelly interview with RRF, State College, PA, April 8, 1986.
15. Reichel, W., (ed.), *Memorials of the Moravian Church*, vol. I (Philadelphia, PA: J.B. Lippincott, 1870), p. 17.
16. Kolin, A., *Political Economy of Labor Repression in the United States* (Lanham, MD: Lexington Books, 2017), p. 142.
17. "Injunction Hearing," *The Daily Times* (Mauch Chunk, PA), Friday, August 11, 1922, p. 1.
18. *Ibid.*
19. *Ibid.*
20. "Strikebreaker Pelted With Rotten Eggs," *The Morning Call* (Allentown, PA), Thursday, July 27, 1922, p. 1.
21. "Big Parade in Lehighton," *The Daily Times* (Mauch Chunk, PA), Saturday, August 5, 1922, p. 1.
22. *Ibid.*
23. "Injunction Hearing," *The Daily Times* (Mauch Chunk, PA), Friday, August 11, 1922, p. 1.

24. "Strikebreaker Pelted With Rotten Eggs," *The Morning Call* (Allentown, PA), Thursday, July 27, 1922, p. 1.
25. "Injunction Hearing," *The Daily Times* (Mauch Chunk, PA), Friday, August 11, 1922, p. 1.
26. *Ibid.*
27. *Ibid.*
28. *Ibid.*
29. "Ed. M'Ginley Shot By Capt. David Johnson," *The Daily Times* (Mauch Chunk, PA), Tuesday, October 3, 1922, p. 1.
30. "Ex-Railroad Guard Suicides," *The Daily Times* (Mauch Chunk, PA), Saturday, September 16, 1922, p. 1.
31. Elisabeth Ross Zogbaum, telephone interview with RRF, January 4, 1987.
32. "Another Man Held For Dynamiting L.V. Dam At Beaver Run," *The Morning Call* (Allentown, PA), Tuesday, December 19, 1922, p. 1.
33. Mr. Harold Rabenold interview with RRF, June 6, 1986.
34. Dr. Daniel Davies to RRF, telephone interview, February 12, 1990.
35. Grace Mosser Ahner interview with RRF, August 19, 1986
36. Patsy Gernerd Aldrich interview with RRF, August 16, 1995.
37. Dr. Louise Kline-Kelly interview with RRF, State College, PA, April 8, 1986.
38. "An Innovator Who Painted Pennsylvania," *The Philadelphia Inquirer* (PA), Sunday, June 22, 1986, p. 13K.

Chapter 4

1. Simpson, S., *Biography of Stephen Girard With His Will Affixed* (Philadelphia, PA: Thomas Bonsal), 1832, appendix p. 20.
2. Herrick, C. A., *The History of Girard College* (Philadelphia, PA: Girard College), p. 358.
3. Sand, R., and Laurent, E., "Franz Josef Kline," *Girard College: A Living History* (New York, NY: Oakley Publishing, 2009), pp. 51–52.
4. Franz Kline's Discharge Report, No. 323, July 1, 1925, Girard College Archives, Philadelphia, PA.
5. Dr. Louise Kline-Kelly interview with RRF, State College, Pennsylvania, April 8, 1986.
6. Claire Mosser interview with RRF, Lehighton, Pennsylvania, June 10, 1986.
7. "Art View," *The New York Times*, January 19, 1986.
8. Sue Hahn personal letter to RRF, May 9, 1986.
9. Dr. Louise Kline-Kelly interview with RRF, State College, Pennsylvania, April 8, 1986.
10. Spangenberg, Rev. A., *The Life of Nicholas Lewis Count Zinzendorf* (London, England: Holdsworth), 1838, p. 157.
11. de Schweinitz, P., and Rice, W. H., "Gnadenhuetten on the Mahoning. Historical and Commemorative. 1746–1755," *Transactions of the Moravian Historical Society*, vol. 7, no. 5 (1906), p. 380, www.jstor.org/stable/41179636.
12. Henning, D. C., "Penn's Walking Purchase," *Tales of the Blue Mountains*, *Historical Society of Schuylkill County*, vol. III, (1911), p. 224.
13. *United States, Congressional Record: Proceedings and Debates of the Fifty-Eight Congress, Second Session* (Washington, DC: GPO, 1873), p. 3620.
14. Dr. Louise Kline Kelly interview with RRF, State College, PA, March 16, 1986.
15. Grace Mosser Ahner interview with RRF, Lehighton, Pennsylvania, August 19, 1986.
16. Dr. Louise Kline-Kelly interview with RRF, State College, Pennsylvania, April 8, 1986.
17. Samuel D. Wehr, "Boyhood in Lehighton," *The Times News* (Lehighton, PA), 1978.
18. Dr. Louise Kline-Kelly interview with RRF, State College, Pennsylvania, April 8, 1986.
19. Elisabeth Ross Zogbaum, telephone interview with RRF, January 4, 1987.
20. Mr. Harold Rabenold interview with RRF, June 6, 1986.
21. *The Leni Lenapian*, May 25, 1929.

22. Franz Kline to Dr. Witherbee, January 2, 1929, Records of Girard College.

Chapter 5

1. Franz Kline, Mahoning, 1956, Holdings Description, Whitney Museum of American Art, New York, collection.whitney.org/object/1997.
2. Ohio Federal Writers' Project, Warren and Trumbull County (1938), 13; Daniel G. Brinton, *The Lenape and their Legends* (Philadelphia, PA: D. G. Brinton Publisher, 1885), p. 249.
3. Bright, W., *Native American Placenames of the United States* (Norman, OK: University of Oklahoma Press, 2007), p. 62.
4. Dr. Robert Mattison to RRF, email, September 5, 2007.
5. Elisabeth Ross Zogbaum, telephone interview with RRF, January 4, 1987.
6. Alvirda K. Arner Ginder interview with RRF, Lehighton, Pennsylvania, August 10, 1986.
7. Joe Strohl to RRF, Lehighton, PA, July 10, 1986.
8. Alvirda K. Arner Ginder, interview with RRF, Lehighton, Pennsylvania, August 10, 1986.
9. Dr. Louise Kline-Kelly interview with RRF, State College, Pennsylvania, March 16, 1986.
10. Mildred Held, interview with RRF, Lehighton, Pennsylvania, June 7, 1984.
11. Alvirda K. Arner Ginder interview with RRF, Lehighton, Pennsylvania, August 10, 1986.
12. "Franz Kline Elected Football Captain for 1929 Season: 16 Letter Men Eligible to Vote," *The Leni Lenapian* (Lehighton, PA), April 1929, p. 3.
13. "Guess Who," *The Leni Lenapian* (Lehighton, PA), September 9, 1930, p. 2.
14. "Monroe Students Organize Forces For Camp Papers," *Daily Press* (Newport News, VA), Wednesday, July 9, 1930, p. 7.
15. Mr. Henry Bretney interview with RRF, Lehighton, Pennsylvania, July 17, 1986.
16. Carl Langkamer interview with RRF, Lehighton, Pennsylvania, April 4, 1986.
17. Dr. Louise Kline-Kelly interview with RRF, State College, Pennsylvania, March 16, 1986.
18. Roedel, M., "The Artist," *Third and Last* (New York, NY: Vantage Press, 1979), pp. 23–24.
19. Kline, F., "Calendar," *The Gachtin Bambil* (Lehighton, PA), 1931, pp. 126–127.
20. "Alumni Finally," *The Leni Lenapian* (Lehighton, PA), December 18, 1929.
21. Rettod, L., "Do You Know That," *The Leni Lenapian* (Lehighton, PA), September 9, 1930, p. 3.
22. "Here and There," *The Leni Lenapian* (Lehighton, PA), October 28, 1930, p. 3.
23. "What Others Think," *The Leni Lenapian* (Lehighton, PA), April 14, 1931.
24. Orenstein, R. H., "Jake Arner At The Heart Of Carbon Aviation History," *The Morning Call* (Allentown, PA), July 2, 1987.
25. Roedel, M., "First Flight," *Third and Last* (New York, NY: Vantage Press), pp. 9–10.
26. Elisabeth Ross Zogbaum, telephone interview with RRF, September 19, 1987.
27. Mr. Harold Rabenold interview with RRF, June 6, 1986.

Chapter 6

1. Edith Smith, interview with RRF, June 29, 1986.
2. *Ibid.*
3. Grace Ahner, interview with RRF, August 19, 1986.
4. Roedel, M., "Soliloquy of a Leading Lady," *Scraps* (New York, NY: Vantage Press, 1976), p. 8.
5. Ruth Ritter Baum, telephone interview with RRF, March 3, 1986.
6. Roedel, M., "The Artist," *Third and Last* (New York, NY: Vantage Press, 1979), p. 24.
7. *Ibid.*, p. 23.
8. Ralph Beisel, interview, Lehighton, Pennsylvania, June 11, 1986.
9. Lavona Edgar Ronemus, interview, Lehighton, Pennsylvania, June 11, 1986.

10. Elisabeth Ross Zogbaum, telephone interview with RRF, January 4, 1987.
11. Harold Frendt, interview with RRF, June 6, 1986.
12. Melvin Moyer, interview, Lehighton, Pennsylvania, February 28, 1987.
13. *Ibid.*
14. Davies, D., "Franz Kline: Odd Man Out," unpublished correspondence, February 24, 1994.
15. Daniel Davies to Rebecca Finsel, personal letter, March 3, 1997.
16. *The Leni Lenapian* (Lehighton, PA), September, 1931.
17. *Ibid.*
18. *The Leni Lenapian* (Lehighton, PA), January 30, 1932.
19. Strapp, W. F., *Portrait of the Art World: A Century of Artnews Photographs* (New Haven, CT: Yale University Press, 2002), p. 42.

Chapter 7

1. Florence Harleman Kresge interview with RRF, Lehighton, PA, April 29, 1986. The bond resonated three decades later when Kline sent the following message to Florence in 1958:

   > Dear Mr. and Mrs. Kresge—Mother wrote me today of Mrs. Harleman's passing. I want to send my sympathies to her boys—whom I've always remembered as my friends, remembering the little house they built for her, the sadness of Mr. Harleman's death; and her warmth to me as Stan's school-mate. My deepest sympathy to you all.

2. Rabenold, L., "The Spider," *The Leni Lenapian* (Lehighton, PA), March 29, 1932.
3. "B. U. School of Art to Be Discontinued—Lack of Endowment Is Blamed," *The Boston Globe* (Boston, MA), May 18, 1932.
4. Ryan, F., "Franz Kline As I Knew Him," unpublished essay, *circa* 1960. See appendix.
5. *Ibid.*
6. *Ibid.*
7. *Ibid.*
8. *Ibid.*
9. *Ibid.* Ten years later, in 1942, Franz bought an original J.C. Coll in New York and gave it to Ryan as a gift.
10. *Ibid.*
11. *Ibid.*
12. *Ibid.*
13. "Palace Club Cafe Opens Tonight at Palmerton," *The Morning Call* (Allentown, PA), Wednesday, Nov. 29, 1933, p. 15.
14. Ryan, F., "Franz Kline As I Knew Him," unpublished essay, *circa* 1960. See appendix.
15. *Ibid.*
16. *Ibid.*
17. *Ibid.*
18. *Ibid.*
19. *Ibid.*
20. Patsy Gernerd Aldrich interview with RRF, August 16, 1995. Franz was invited to meet J. R. Flanagan at Maplehurst in Stroudsburg through Patsy's father Charles in the summer of 1931. Afterwards, Kline's desire to follow Flanagan's footsteps intensified.
21. Ryan, F., "Franz Kline As I Knew Him," unpublished essay, *circa* 1960. See appendix.
22. *Ibid.*
23. *Ibid.*
24. *Ibid.*
25. *Ibid.*
26. *Ibid.*
27. *Ibid.*

28. *Ibid.*

Chapter 8

1. "Lehighton-Sails to Study Art in London," *The Morning Call* (Allentown, PA), October 7, 1935, p. 17.
2. Dr. Louise Kline-Kelly, interview with RRF, State College, PA, April 8, 1986.
3. "Phil May 1864–1903," Tate Modern, www.tate.org.uk/art/artists/phil-may-1600; Philip W. May, en.wikipedia.org/wiki/Phil_May_(caricaturist).
4. Gaugh, H. F., *Franz Kline* (New York, NY: Abbeville Press, 1985), p. 176.
5. Ryan, F., "Franz Kline As I Knew Him," unpublished essay, *circa* 1960. See appendix.
6. *Ibid.*; Franz Kline to Frederick Ryan, January 21, 1940. See appendix.
7. Franz Kline to Frederick Ryan, personal letter, January 21, 1940.
8. Gaugh, H. F., *Franz Kline* (New York, NY: Abbeville Press, 1985), p. 176.
9. Franz Kline to Frederick Ryan, personal letter, January 21, 1940.
10. Gaugh, H. F., *Franz Kline* (New York, NY: Abbeville Press, 1985), p. 176.
11. Martha Kinney to Frederick Ryan, postcard, 1936.
12. Franz Kline to Frederick Ryan, personal letter, January 21, 1940.
13. Gaugh, H. F., *Franz Kline* (New York, NY: Abbeville Press, 1985), p. 176.
14. Franz Kline to Ralph Beisel, personal letter, November 9, 1936.
15. *Benezit Dictionary of British Graphic Artists and Illustrators*, vol. 1 (New York, NY: Oxford University Press, 2012), p. 409.
16. "From a Window in Fleet Street," *The Ottawa Journal* (Ontario, Canada), Friday, June 25, p. 8.
17. Franz Kline to Frederick Ryan, personal letter, January 21, 1940.
18. Gaugh, H. F., *Franz Kline* (New York, NY: Abbeville Press, 1985), p. 176.
19. Roedel, M., "The Artist," *Third and Last* (New York, NY: Vantage Press, 1979), p. 24.
20. *Ibid.*
21. *Ibid.*
22. *Ibid.*
23. Balfour, P., *The Daily Sketch* (London, England), August 1937.
24. Elisabeth Ross Zogbaum, telephone interview with RRF, January 4, 1987.
25. List of United States Citizens for the Immigration Authorities, S. S. Manhattan, 11 February 1938.
26. Roedel, M., "The Artist," *Third and Last* (New York, NY: Vantage Press, 1979), pp. 24–25.
27. *Ibid.*
28. *Ibid.*
29. Roedel, M., "The Artist," *Third and Last* (New York, NY: Vantage Press, 1979), pp. 25–26.
30. Claire Mosser, interview with RRF, Bethlehem, Pennsylvania, January 7, 1986.
31. Roedel, M., "The Artist," Third and Last (Vantage Press: New York, 1979), pp. 25–26.

Chapter 9

1. *Mauch Chunk Times News* (Lehighton, PA), Monday, December 6, 1938, which reads: "George Metzler was appointed substitute teacher in the English Department of Lehighton High School … in place of Miss Mathilda Roedel who resigned last night because of ill health."
2. Roedel, M., "The Bencher," *Scraps* (New York, NY: Vantage Press, 1976), p. 13.
3. Dr. Louise Kelly Kline, interview with RRF, May 24, 1986.
4. *Ibid.*
5. Patsy Gernerd Aldrich, interview with RRF, August 16, 1995.

6. O'Hara, F., "Franz Kline Talking," *Evergreen Review* (Autumn, 1958), p. 62; Albers, P., *Joan Mitchell: Lady Painter* (New York, NY: Knopf, 2011), p. 148.
7. Evelyn Toynton, *Jackson Pollock* (New Haven, CT: Yale University Press, 2012), pp. 61–62.
8. Franz Kline to Frederick Ryan, personal letter, July 1, 1940, authors' collection. See Chapter 12.
9. Kline, E., "Letter to the Editor," *ArtNews*, 61 (January 1963), p. 6.
10. Claire Mosser, interview with RRF, Bethlehem, PA, January 7, 1986.
11. Henry Bretney, interview with RRF, Lehighton, PA, July 17, 1986.
12. Mrs. Melba Harleman, interview with RRF, Lehighton, PA, August 7, 1986.
13. Lavona Edgar Ronemus, interview with RRF, Lehighton, PA, June 11, 1986.
14. Franz Kline to Frederick Ryan, Sr., April 24, 1940.
15. Sandler, I., *A Sweeper Up After Artists* (London, England: Thames and Hudson, 2003), p. 21.
16. Roedel, M., "The Artist," *Third and Last* (New York, NY: Vantage Press, 1979), p. 26.
17. "290 Artists Open Outdoor Display," *The New York Times* (New York, NY) Saturday, June 3, 1939, p. 26.
18. *Ibid.*
19. *Ibid.*
20. Franz Kline to Frederick Ryan, personal letter, June 2, 1940.
21. Franz Kline to Frederick Ryan, personal letter, April 24, 1940.
22. Franz Kline to Frederick Ryan, personal letter, June 23, 1940.
23. Franz Kline to Frederick Ryan, personal letter, July 11, 1940. Franz struck up a friendship with Charlotte Benoit, Beatrice Ryan's twenty-four-year-old sister who worked in the doll factory. Frederick Ryan, Jr., spoke to his Aunt Charlotte about Franz during their last visit together:

    > Despite Charlotte being totally blind at the time of our meeting, she lit up with delight talking about Franz. Charlotte was very fond of Franz. Charlotte told me in 2005 how she and Franz would sit on the porch, late in the evening and would talk till all hours, and as a habit, Franz would always eat, late at night, before bed. Charlotte also told me that at the end of his stay, he would proclaim 'my off is all' apparently meaning that his vacation is finished, which is an expression we in New England had never heard of.

24. Ryan, F., "Franz Kline As I Knew Him," unpublished essay, *circa* 1960. See appendix.
25. Sandler, I., *A Sweeper Up After Artists* (London, England: Thames and Hudson, 2003), p. 24. Sandler goes on to talk about how the Cedar's "anonymity … served a purpose." And how the place seemed like "the right place for artists who refused to accept fixed categories" because the Cedar Street Tavern "couldn't even get its name right," as it was not located on Cedar Street at all and took its name from the sign of a defunct establishment.
26. Claire Mosser, interview with RRF, Bethlehem, PA, January 7, 1986.
27. *Ibid.*
28. *The Evening Sun* (Hanover, PA), Saturday, June 30, 1945, p. 4, www.newspapers.com/image/81534031.
29. Gruen, J., *The Party's Over Now* (New York, NY: Pushcart Press, 1967), p. 233.
30. Smith, G. W., and Naifeh, S., *Jackson Pollock: An American Saga* (New York, NY: Clarkson N. Potter, 1995), p. 12.
31. Dawson, F., *An Emotional Memoir of Franz Kline* (New York, NY, Pantheon, 1967), pp. 78–83, 85.
32. Dr. Robert Mattison, from Martin Gladu's "The Titles of Franz Kline's Works: a Taxonomy," www.scribd.com/document/206034870.
33. de Kooning, E., "Franz Kline: Painter of His Own Life," *ArtNews* (November, 1962), p. 65.
34. Cernuschi, C., "Franz Kline's Probst I: A Cognitive Approach to Gestural Abstraction," *Journal of the Museum of Fine Arts*, Boston, vol. 6 (1994), p. 76.
35. Dawson, F., *An Emotional Memoir of Franz Kline* (New York, NY: Pantheon, 1967), p. 84.
36. Gruen, J., *The Party's Over Now* (New York, NY: Viking, 1972), p. 219.

37. Motherwell, R., "Homage to Franz Kline," *Franz Kline The Color Abstractions* (The Phillips Collection: Washington, D.C., 1979), p. 43.
38. Hamill, P., *Piecework: Writings on Men and Women, Fools and Heroes, Lost Cities, Vanished Calamities, and How the Weather Was* (New York, NY: Little, Brown, 2009), p. 301.
39. O'Hara, F., "Franz Kline," *Art Chronicles 1954–1966* (New York, NY: George Braziller, 1975), p. 40; Sandler, I., *A Sweeper Up After Artists* (London, England: Thames and Hudson, 2003), p. 57. Sandler described Kline as "the most amiable of the older abstract-expressionists" who "would talk with anyone" and was the "most accessible of his peers."
40. Sandler, I., *A Sweeper Up After Artists* (London: Thames and Hudson, 2003), p. 57. Sandler described Kline as "the most amiable of the older abstract expressionists" who "would talk with anyone" and was the "most accessible of his peers."
41. Edward Halter Meneeley, interview with JF, Lehighton, PA, December 5, 2004.
42. Sandler, I., *A Sweeper Up After Artists* (London, England: Thames and Hudson, 2003), p. 57.
43. Kuh, K., *The Artist's Voice* (New York, NY: Harper & Row, 1962), pp. 148–9.
44. Gaugh, H. F., *The Vital Gesture: Franz Kline* (New York, NY: Abbeville Press, 1994), p. 56.
45. Dr. Louise Kline-Kelly, interview with RRF, State College, PA, April 8, 1986. The location of the painting's scene in The Morning Call, February 26, 1943, specifies "a section north of Palmerton."
46. *Ibid.*
47. Jewell, E. A., "END-OF-THE-SEASON MELANGE," *The New York Times* (New York, NY), June 6, 1943.
48. Gaugh, H. F., *The Vital Gesture: Franz Kline* (New York, NY: Abbeville Press, 1994), pp. 38, 176.
49. Toynton, J., *Jackson Pollock* (New Haven, CT: Yale University Press, 2012), pp. 61–62; Kees, W., "Art," *The Nation* (January 7, 1950).
50. "Kline Wins Prize With 'Lehigh River' Picture," *The Wilkes-Barre Record* (PA), Saturday, April 29, 1944, p. 3.
51. Dr. Louise Kline-Kelly, interview with RRF, State College, Pennsylvania, April 8, 1986.
52. *Ibid*
53. Ken Lobien, interview with RRF, Lehighton, PA, June 3, 1986.
54. Grace Rhoads, interview with RRF, Lehighton, PA, June 1, 1989.
55. Elisabeth Ross Zogbaum, telephone interview with RRF, September 19, 1987.
56. Dr. Louise Kline-Kelly, interview with RRF, State College, PA, April 8, 1986.
57. *Ibid.*
58. Claire Mosser, interview with RRF, Bethlehem, PA, January 7, 1986.
59. Dr. Louise Kline-Kelly, interview with RRF, May 22, 1986.
60. *Ibid.*
61. Patsy Gernerd Aldrich, interview with RRF, Allentown, PA, August 16, 1995.
62. Gaugh, H. F., *Franz Kline* (New York, NY: Abbeville Press, 1985), pp. 79–81.
63. Karen Warshal to Rebecca Finsel, personal letter, 1986.
64. *Ibid.*; Karen Warshal, "A Critical Analysis of Abstract Expressionism through the Work of Franz Kline," Master's Thesis, Tufts University, 1986.
65. de Kooning, E., "Two Americans in Action: Franz Kline/Mark Rothko," *ArtNews Annual*, No. 27, Part II (November 1957), p. 179; Sandler, I., "Franz Kline The Industrial Sublime," in *Franz Kline Coal and Steel*, by Robert S. Mattison (Allentown Art Museum of the Lehigh Valley, 2012), p. 104.
66. Hawley-Dolan, A., and Winner, E., "Seeing the Mind Behind the Art," *Psychological Science*, vol. 22, No. 4 (April 2011), p. 435.
67. Sandler, I., *A Sweeper Up After Artists* (London, England: Thames and Hudson, 2003), p. 10.
68. *Ibid.*

69. Gaugh, H. F., *Franz Kline* (New York, NY: Abbeville Press, 1985), p. 178.
70. Mattison, R. S., *Franz Kline Coal and Steel* (Allentown Art Museum of the Lehigh Valley, 2012), p. 79.
71. "Famed Abstractionist Artist Franz Kline Dies at 52," *The Morning Call* (Allentown, PA), Tuesday, May 15, 1962, p. 5.
72. Franz Kline, interviewed by David Sylvester, in Ross, C., (ed.), *Abstract Expressionism: Creators and Critics* (NY: Abrams, 1990), p. 93.
73. O'Hara, F., "Franz Kline Talking," *Evergreen Review* (Autumn 1958), p. 64.
74. Gaugh, H. F., *Franz Kline* (New York, NY: Abbeville Press, 1985), pp. 120–122.
75. Claire Mosser, interview with RRF, Bethlehem, PA, January 7, 1986.
76. Dawson, F., *An Emotional Memoir of Franz Kline* (New York, NY: Random House, 1967), p. 75.

Chapter 10

1. Dr. Louise Kline Kelly, interview with RRF, State College, Pennsylvania, March 16, 1986.
2. Rabenold, R., "Franz Kline: A Study in Conflict," Sunday, February 12, 2017, blogspot.com/2017/02/kline.html.
3. *The Morning Call* (Allentown, PA), Friday, March 4, 1938, p. 39.
4. "Artist Speaks To Woman's Club," *The Morning Call* (Allentown, PA), Thursday, March 10, 1938, p. 24.
5. *Ibid.*
6. Elizabeth Honey Bayer, interview with RRF, Lehighton, PA, June 6, 1986.
7. Elisabeth Ross Zogbaum, telephone interview with RRF, September 19, 1987.
8. Frank Bayer, Jr., interview with RRF, Lehighton, PA, February 6, 2008.
9. Elizabeth Honey Bayer, interview with RRF, Lehighton, PA, June 6, 1986.
10. Dr. Louise Kline Kelly, interview with RRF, State College, PA, March 16, 1986.
11. *Ibid.*
12. Gladys Rabenold to RRF, personal letter, Lehighton, PA, March 2, 1986.
13. Dr. Louise Kline Kelly, interview with RRF, State College, PA, March 16, 1986.
14. *Dedication Ceremony Program*, Shoemaker-Haydt Legion Post #314, Lehighton, PA., December 27, 1945.
15. Dr. Louise Kline Kelly, interview with RRF, State College, PA, March 16, 1986.
16. O'Hara, F., *Franz Kline* (1960), p. 52.
17. Patsy Gernerd Aldrich, interview with RRF, Allentown, PA, August 16, 1995.
18. Elizabeth Bayer, interview with RRF, Lehighton, PA, June 6, 1986.
19. Rabenold, R., "Franz Kline: A Study in Conflict," Sunday, February 12, 2017; blogspot.com/2017/02/kline.html.-
20. *Ibid.*
21. Franz Kline to Carl Langkamer, personal note, June 29, 1961.

Chapter 11

1. Elisabeth Ross Zogbaum, telephone interview with RRF, January 4, 1987.
2. *Ibid.*
3. Sandler, I., *A Sweeper Up After Artists* (London, England: Thames & Hudson, 2004), p. 57.
4. *Ibid.*
5. Dr. Louise Kline-Kelly, interview with RRF, March 16, 1986.
6. Wetzteon, R., *Republic of Dreams: Greenwich Village: The American Bohemia, 1910–1960* (New York, NY: Simon and Schuster, 2007), p. 564.
7. Dr. Louise Kline-Kelly interview with RRF, State College, PA, April 8, 1986.
8. *Ibid.*

9. *Ibid.*
10. *Ibid.*
11. *Ibid.*
12. Wilbur G. Warner letter to Dr. Louise Kline-Kelly, June 13, 1939.
13. "Franz Kline," *Horizon*, vol. 13 (July 1961), p. 18.
14. William Scheckler, interview with RRF, Lehighton, PA, April 13, 1985.
15. Salisbury, S., "An Innovator Who Painted Pennsylvania," *The Philadelphia Inquirer*, Sunday, June 22, 1986, p. 1-K,
16. Dr. Louise Kline-Kelly, telephone interview with RRF, May 22, 1986.
17. Hamill, P., *Piecework: Writings on Men and Women, Fools and Heroes, Lost Cities, Vanished Calamities, and How the Weather Was* (New York, NY: Little, Brown, 2009), p. 304.
18. Rodman, S., *Conversations with Artists* (New York, NY: 1957) p. 69.
19. Sterling Strausser, interview with RRF, July 12, 1985.
20. Hedy Lamarr to Franz Kline, July 19, 1959, www.starsandletters.blogspot.com/2014/10/hedy-lamarrs-art-choice.html.
21. Franz Kline and Elisabeth Ross Zogbaum, postcard to Mr. and Mrs. Jack Tworkov c. 1960 Courtesy Estate of Jack Tworkov, New York.
22. Claire Mosser interview with RRF, Lehighton, PA, January 7, 1986.
23. Davis, M. L., *Mona Lisa in Camelot* (Portland, OR: RHYW, 2010), p. 56.
24. Dr. Louise Kline Kelly, interview with RRF, State College, PA, March 16, 1986.
25. *Ibid.*
26. Elisabeth Ross Zogbaum, telephone interview with RRF, January 4, 1987.
27. *The Writings of Robert Motherwell* (Berkeley, CA: University of California Press, 2007), p. 212.
28. Dr. Louise Kline Kelly, interview with RRF, State College, PA, March 16, 1986.
29. Roedel, M., "The Artist," *Third and Last* (New York, NY: Vantage Press, 1979), p. 26.
30. Motherwell, R., "Homage to Franz Kline," *Franz Kline The Color Abstractions* (The Phillips Collection: Washington, D.C., 1979), p. 43.
31. Dr. Louise Kline Kelly, interview with RRF, State College, PA, March 16, 1986.
32. *Ibid.*
33. Kline, E., "Letter to the Editor," *ArtNews*, vol. 61 (January 1963), p. 6.
34. Dr. Louise Kline Kelly, interview with RRF, State College, PA, March 16, 1986.

Bibliography

"290 Artists Open Outdoor Display," *The New York Times*, p. 26 (New York, NY: June 3, 1939)

Albers, P., *Joan Mitchell: Lady Painter* (New York, NY: Knopf, 2011)

"An Innovator Who Painted Pennsylvania," *The Philadelphia Inquirer*, p. 1-K (Philadelphia, PA: June 22, 1986)

"Another Man Held For Dynamiting L.V. Dam At Beaver Run," *The Morning Call*, p. 1 (Allentown, PA: December 19, 1944)

"Art View: Franz Kline—A Legacy in Black and White," *The New York Times*, p. 2029, (New York, NY: 1986)

"Artist Speaks to Woman's Club," *The Morning Call*, p. 24 (Allentown, PA: March 10, 1938)

Ashton, D., *The New York School: A Cultural Reckoning* (New York, NY: Penguin, 1980)

"B.U. School of Art to Be Discontinued—Lack of Endowment Is Blamed," *The Boston Globe* (Boston, MA: May 18, 1932)

Balfour, P., "Mr. Gossip," *The Daily Sketch* (London, UK: August 1937)

Belgrad, D., *The Culture of Spontaneity: Improvisation and the Arts in Postwar America* (Chicago: University of Chicago Press, 1999)

Berkson, B., "Kline's True Colors," *Art in America* (New York, NY: Art in America, 1986)

Berkson, B., Seidell, D., Foster S. C., and Friedman, B. H., *Franz Kline: Art and the Structure of Identity* (Barcelona, Spain: Fundació Antoni Tápies, 1994)

Brenson, M., "Review/Art; The Show at the Armory: Dealers' Days in the Sun," *The New York Times*, p. 29 (New York, NY: February 23, 1990, Late Edition)

Bright, W., *Native American Placenames of the United States*, p. 62 (Norman, OK: University of Oklahoma Press, 2007)

Brinton, D. G., *The Lenape and their Legends with the Complete Text and Symbols of the Walam Glum*, A New Translation (Philadelphia, PA: D. G. Brinton Publisher, 1885)

Butler, C., *Postmodernism* (New York, NY: Oxford University Press, 2002)

"Buys Back Old Home, Then Kills Himself," *Lebanon Daily News*, p. 6 (Lebanon, PA: August 22, 1917)

Cernuschi, C., "Franz Kline's Probst I: A Cognitive Approach to Gestural Abstraction," *Journal of the Museum of Fine Arts*, vol. 6, p. 76 (Boston, MA: 1994)

"City Lights Bookstore 50th Anniversary: The Birth of Cool: 1953–1960," *San Francisco Chronicle*, p. 3 (San Francisco, CA: June 8, 2003)

Davis, M. L., *Mona Lisa in Camelot*, p. 56 (Portland, OR: RHYW, 2010)

Dawson, F., *An Emotional Memoir of Franz Kline* (New York, NY: Pantheon, 1967)

De Kooning, E., "Franz Kline: Painter of His Own Life," *ArtNews*, vol. 61 (New York, NY: ArtNews, November 1962)

De Kooning, E., "Two Americans in Action: Franz Kline/Mark Rothko," *ArtNews Annual*, vol. 27, p. 96 (New York, NY: 1958)

De Kooning, E., *Franz Kline Memorial Exhibition* (Washington, DC: Washington Gallery of Modern Art, 1962)

De Schweinitz, P., and Rice, W. H., "Gnadenhuetten on the Mahoning. Historical and Commemorative. 1746—1755," *Transactions of the Moravian Historical Society*, vol. 7, no. 5, p. 380 (Bethlehem, PA: Moravian Historical Society, 1906)

Ebbert, L., and Ripkey, G., *Lehighton* (Charleston, SC: Arcadia, 2013)

"Echoes of the Week," *The Wilkes Barre Sunday Independent*, p. 18 (Wilkes Barre, PA: August 26, 1917)

"Ed. M'Ginley Shot By Capt. David Johnson," *The Daily Times*, p. 1 (Mauch Chunk, PA: October 3, 1922)

"Famed Abstractionist Artist Franz Kline Dies at 52," *The Morning Call*, p. 5 (Allentown, PA: May 15, 1962)

Feldman, M., *Give My Regards to Eighth Street* (Cambridge, MA: Exact Change, 2000)

Finsel, R., *Carbon County* (Charleston, SC: Arcadia, 2004)

Frankenthaler at Eighty: Six Decades (New York, NY: Knoedler, 2008)

"Franz Kline Elected Football Captain for 1929 Season: 16 Letter Men Eligible to Vote," *The Leni Lenapian*, p. 3 (Lehighton, PA: April 1929)

Franz Kline Memorial Exhibition (Washington, DC: Washington Gallery of Modern Art, 1962)

"Franz Kline," *Horizon*, vol. 13, p. 18 (Rockville, MD: July 1961)

Franz Kline: The Color Abstractions (Washington, D.C.: The Phillips Collection, 1979)

Franz Kline's Discharge Report, no. 323, July 1, 1925, Girard College Archives, Philadelphia, PA.

Freund, A. B., "The Art World's Secret Vault," *Town & Country* (New York, NY: March 2010)

Friedman, B.H., *Jackson Pollock: Energy Made Visible* (New York, NY: McGraw Hill, 1972)

"From a Window in Fleet Street," *The Ottawa Journal*, p. 8 (Ontario, Canada: June 25, 1937)

Gaugh, H. F., "Franz Kline: The Man and the Myth," *ArtNews* (New York, NY: December 1985)

Gaugh, H. F., *The Vital Gesture: Franz Kline* (New York, NY: Abbeville Press, 1985)

Gladu, M., "The Titles of Franz Kline's Works: a Taxonomy," www.scribd.com/document/206034870

Goodnough, R., "Kline Paints a Picture," *ArtNews* (New York, NY: December 1952)

Gordon, J., *Franz Kline 1910–1962* (New York, NY: Whitney Museum, 1969)

Gruen, J., *The Party's Over Now* (New York, NY: Pushcart Press, 1972)

Hamill, P., *Piecework: Writings on Men and Women, Fools and Heroes, Lost Cities, Vanished Calamities, and How the Weather Was* (New York, NY: Little, Brown, 2009)

Hawley-Dolan, A. and Winner, E., "Seeing the Mind Behind the Art," *Psychological Science*, vol. 22, no. 4, p. 435 (Thousand Oaks, CA: April 2011)

Hellstein, V., "Abstract Expressionism's Counterculture: The Club, the Cold War, and the New Sensibility," (New York, NY: New Perspectives on Abstract Expressionism: A Young Scholar's Panel, Museum of Modern Art, 2011)

Henning, D. C., "Penn's Walking Purchase," *Tales of the Blue Mountains*, vol. III, p. 224 (Historical Society of Schuylkill County, 1911)

History of the Lehigh Valley Region: A Comprehensive Plan Research Report (November 1963)

Holmes, C., "This Is the Beat Generation," *The New York Times Magazine* (New York, NY: November 16, 1952)

Hughes, R., "Art: Energy in Black and White," *Time* (New York, NY: February 10, 1986)

Hughes, R., "Art: The Man Who Painted Impact," *Time* (New York, NY: January 23, 1995)

Ingram, H. A., *The Life and Character of Stephen Girard* (Philadelphia, PA: E. Stanley Hart, 1884)

"Injunction Hearing," *The Daily Times*, p. 1 (Mauch Chunk, PA: August 11, 1922)

"Jacqueline Kennedy Entertains: The Art of the White House Dinner April 12, 2007–April 3, 2008," John F. Kennedy Presidential Library and Museum, www.jfklibrary.org, (Boston, MA: April 3, 2008)

Jewell, E. A., "End-of-the-Season Melange," *New York Times* (New York, NY: June 6, 1943)

Johnson, R., "A Microscopic/Telescopic Collage of The Empire Finals at Verona," Jacket 38, (Balmain, NSW: 2009)

Kees, W., "Art," *The Nation*, p. 19 (New York, NY: January 7, 1950)

Kerouac, J., *Book of Blues* (New York, NY: Penguin Poets, 1995)

"Kline Wins Prize with 'Lehigh River' Picture," *The Wilkes-Barre Record*, p. 3 (Wilkes Barre PA: April 29, 1944)
Kline, E., "Letter to the Editor," *ArtNews*, vol. 61 p. 6 (New York, NY: January 1963)
Knox, S., "Abstract Art is Going to Europe to Represent American Culture," *The New York Times* (New York, NY: March 11, 1958)
Kokkinen, E., and MIT Committee on the Visual Arts, *Drawings by Five Abstract Expressionist Painters: Arshile Gorky, Willem de Kooning, Jackson Pollock, Franz Kline, Philip Guston: An Exhibition* (Cambridge, MA: MIT Hayden Gallery, 1975)
Kuh, K., *The Artists Voice: Talks with Seventeen Artists* (New York, NY: Harper and Row, 1962)
"Lehighton-Sails to Study Art in London," *The Morning Call*, p. 17 (Allentown, PA: October 7, 1935)
Lucie-Smith, E., *Lives of the Great Twentieth-Century Artists* (New York, NY: Rizzoli, 1977)
Mattison, R., *Franz Kline Coal and Steel* (Allentown, PA: Allentown Art Museum, 2012)
McCafferty, M., *Native American Placenames of the United States*, p. 152 (Urbana, IL: University of Illinois Press, 2008)
Metzger, R., *Franz Kline The Jazz Murals* (Lewisburg, PA: Center Gallery of Bucknell University, 1989)
Mitchell, F., Franz Kline, *The Early Works as Signals* (Binghamton, NY: University Art Gallery, 1977)
"Monroe Students Organize Forces For Camp Papers," *The Daily Press*, p. 7 (Newport News, VA: July 9, 1930)
Motherwell, R. "Homage to Franz Kline," *Franz Kline: The Color Abstractions*, Phillips Collection (Washington, D.C.: 1979)
Motherwell, R., *The Writings of Robert Motherwell* (Berkeley, CA: University of California Press, 2007
"New Cocktail Lounge at El Chico, New York's Famed Spanish Night Club," *The Evening Sun*, p. 4 (Hanover, PA: June 30, 1945)
O'Hara, F., "Franz Kline Talking," *Evergreen Review*, vol. 2, no. 6 (New York, NY: Autumn, 1958)
O'Hara, F., *Art Chronicles: 1954–1966* (New York, NY: George Braziller, 1975)
Orenstein, R. H., "Jake Arner At The Heart Of Carbon Aviation History," *The Morning Call* (Allentown PA: July 2, 1987)
"Palace Club Cafe Opens Tonight at Palmerton," *The Morning Call*, p. 15 (Allentown, PA: November 29, 1933)
Perl, J., "Strokes of Genius," *Vogue* (New York, NY: May 1994)
"Phil May 1864–1903," Tate Modern, www.tate.org.uk/art/artists/phil-may-1600.
Phillips, L. and Berger, M., *Beat Culture and the New America 1950–1965* (New York, NY; Whitney Museum of American Art, 1995)
Rabenold, L., "The Spider—Franz Kline and Claire Mosser of Days Gone By," *The Leni Lenapian* (Lehighton, PA: March 29, 1932)
Rabenold, R., "Franz Kline: A Study in Conflict," (Lehighton PA: 2017) www.culturedcarboncounty.blogspot.com/2017/02/kline.html.
Rapaport, B. and Stayton, K., *Vital Forms: American Art and Design in the Atomic Age, 1940–1960* (New York, NY: Abrams, 2001)
"Razzle Dazzle," *Benezit Dictionary of British Graphic Artists and Illustrators*, vol. 1, p. 409 (Oxford University Press, 2012)
Reichel, W., *Memorials of the Moravian Church*, vol. I, p. 17 (Philadelphia, PA: J.B. Lippincott, 1870)
Rodman, S., "An Important Abstractionist," *Cosmopolitan*, p. 69 (New York, NY: February 1959)
Roedel, M., "Soliloquy of a Leading Lady," *Scraps* (New York, NY: Vantage Press, 1976)
Roedel, M., "The Artist," *Third and Last* (New York, NY: Vantage Press, 1979)
Rosenberg, C. M., *Child Labor in America: A History*, p. 96 (Jefferson, NC: McFarland, 2013)
Ross, C., "Franz Kline, Interviewed by David Sylvester," *Abstract Expressionism: Creators and Critics* (New York, NY: Abrams, 1990)

Ryan, F., "Franz Kline As I Knew Him," see appendix of this book.

Salisbury, S., "An Innovator Who Painted Pennsylvania," *The Philadelphia Inquirer*, p. 1K (Philadelphia, PA: June 22, 1986)

Sand, R. and Laurent, E., "Franz Josef Kline," *Girard College: A Living History*, pp. 51–52 (New York, NY: Oakley Publishing, 2009)

Sandler, I., "Franz Kline: The Industrial Sublime," *Franz Kline Coal and Steel*, by Robert S. Mattison, p. 104 (Allentown, PA: Allentown Art Museum, 2012)

Sandler, I., *A Sweeper Up After Artists*, pp. 58–59 (London, UK: Thames & Hudson, 2004)

Sandler, I., *The New York School*, p. 33 (New York, NY: Harper & Row, 1978)

Schweitzer, R., *Franz Kline: Early Works on Paper* (Scranton, PA: Everhart Museum, October, 1986)

Seidell, D. A., "Art Criticism as Narrative Strategy: Clement Greenberg's Critical Encounter with Franz Kline," *Journal of Modern Literature*, 26-3/4 (Bloomington, IN: Spring, 2004)

"Senior Class History," *Gachtin Bambil* (Lehighton, PA: 1932)

Smith, G. and Naifeh, S., *Jackson Pollock: An American Saga* (New York, NY: Clarkson N. Potter, 1995)

Smithsonian National Portrait Gallery, "Franz Kline 1910–1962—Portrait of the World—A Century of ArtNews Photographs," *ArtNews* (New York, NY: Accessed June 1, 2010, www.spg.si.edu/artnews/kline.html)

Spangenberg, Rev. A., *The Life of Nicholas Lewis Count Zinzendorf* (London, UK: Holdsworth, 1838)

[St.] John of the Cross, *Dark Night of the Soul* (Boston, MA: Wyatt North, 2012)

Stallabrass, J., *Contemporary Art* (New York, NY: Oxford University Press, 2004)

Stein, G., *Lectures in America* (Boston, M.A.: Beacon, 1935)

Stevens, C., *Brian Wall* (London, England: Momentum, 2006)

Strapp, W. *Portrait of the Art World: A Century of ArtNews Photographs*, p. 42 (New Haven, CT: Yale University Press, 2002)

Sylvester, D., *An Interview with Artists* (New Haven, CT: Yale University Press, 2002)

"The Art of Picture Making at the Municipal Building, Artist Speaks To Woman's Club," *The Morning Call*, p. 24 (Allentown, PA: 1938)

"The Lettermen of the Lehigh Valley Interscholastic League Banquet" *The Leni Lenapian* (Lehighton, PA: May 25, 1929)

The Will of the Late Stephen Girard Esq., ... with a Short Biography of His Life (Philadelphia, PA: Thomas Desilver, 1847)

Todd, S., "Lehighton Art to be Sold in New York," *The Morning Call* (Allentown, PA: February 2, 1992)

Todd, S., "Lehighton Murals Unsold at Auction," *The Morning Call* (Allentown, PA: March 4, 1992)

Toynton, J., *Jackson Pollock* (New Haven, CT: Yale University Press, 2012)

Tuchman, M., *New York School—The First Generation—Paintings of the 1940s and 1950s* (Los Angeles, CA: Los Angeles County Museum of Art, 1965)

Updike, J., *Still Looking: Essays on American Art* (New York, NY: Knopf, 2005)

Warshal, K., "A Critical Analysis of Abstract Expressionism through the Work of Franz Kline," Master's Thesis (Boston, MA: Tufts University, 1986)

Watkin, W., *In the Process of Poetry: The New York School and the Avant-garde* (Lewisburg, PA: Bucknell University Press, 2001)

Wehr, S. "Boyhood in Lehighton," *The Times News* (Lehighton, PA: 1978)

Wetzteon, R., *Republic of Dreams: Greenwich Village: The American Bohemia, 1910–1960* (New York, NY: Simon and Schuster, 2007)

Whitney Museum of American Art, "The New Decade: 35 American Painters and Sculptors" (New York, NY: Whitney Museum of American Art, 1955)

Index